P9-DBO-544

15-
JT

The Ultimate Guide to Obtaining a Divorce

The No-Fault Divorce Toolkit

The Ultimate Guide to Obtaining a Divorce

The No-Fault Divorce Toolkit

DANIEL SITARZ, ATTORNEY-AT-LAW

Nova Publishing Company
Small Business and Consumer Legal Books
Carbondale Illinois

© 2009 Daniel Sitarz

All rights reserved. This publication may not be reproduced in whole or in part by any means without prior written consent. Editorial assistance by Janet Harris Sitarz, Melanie Bray, and Caitlin King. Manufactured in the United States.

ISBN: 978-1-892949-35-6   Book/CD   ($39.95)

Sitarz, Dan, 1948-
The no-fault divorce toolkit / Daniel Sitarz. -- 1st ed. -- Carbondale, Ill. : Nova Pub. Co., c2009.
p. ; cm. + CD-ROM (4 3/4 in.) (Legal toolkit series)
At head of title: The ultimate guide to obtaining a divorce. CD contains forms, and includes Adobe Acrobat reader software. Includes index.

1. No-fault divorce--United States--Popular works. 2. No-fault divorce--United States--States--Popular works. 3. No-fault divorce--United States--Forms. 4. Divorce--Law and legislation--United States--Popular works. 5. Divorce--Law and legislation--United States--States--Popular works. 6. Divorce--United States--Forms. I. Title. II. Title: Ultimate guide to obtaining a divorce. III. Series.

KF535.Z9 .S576 2009   346.7301/66--dc22 0901

Nova Publishing Company is dedicated to providing up-to-date and accurate legal information to the public. All Nova publications are periodically revised to contain the latest available legal information.

1st Edition; 1st Printing   March, 2009

This publication is designed to provide accurate and authoritative information in regard to the subject matter covered. It is sold with the understanding that the publisher and author are not engaged in rendering legal, accounting, or other professional services. If legal advice or other expert assistance is required, the services of a competent professional person should be sought.
—From a Declaration of Principles jointly adopted by a Committee of the American Bar Association and a Committee of Publishers

DISCLAIMER

Because of possible unanticipated changes in governing statutes and case law relating to the application of any information contained in this book, the author, publisher, and any and all persons or entities involved in any way in the preparation, publication, sale, or distribution of this book disclaim all responsibility for the legal effects or consequences of any document prepared or action taken in reliance upon information contained in this book. No representations, either express or implied, are made or given regarding the legal consequences of the use of any information contained in this book. Purchasers and persons intending to use this book for the preparation of any legal documents are advised to check specifically on the current applicable laws in any jurisdiction in which they intend the documents to be effective.

Nova Publishing Green Business Policies

Nova Publishing Company takes seriously the impact of book publishing on the Earth and its resources. Nova Publishing Company is committed to protecting the environment and to the responsible use of natural resources. As a book publisher, with paper as a core part of our business, we are very concerned about the future of the world's remaining endangered forests and the environmental impacts of paper production. We are committed to implementing policies that will support the preservation of endangered forests globally and to advancing 'best practices' within the book and paper industries. Nova Publishing Company is committed to preserving ancient forests and natural resources. Our company's policy is to print all of our books on 100% recycled paper, with 100% post-consumer waste content, de-inked in a chlorine-free process. In addition, all Nova Publishing Company books are printed using soy-based inks. As a result of these environmental policies, Nova Publishing Company has saved hundreds of thousands of gallons of water, hundreds of thousands of kilowatts of electricity, thousand of pounds of pollution and carbon dioxide, and thousands of trees that would otherwise have been used in the traditional manner of publishing its books. Nova Publishing Company is very proud to be one of the first members of the Green Press Initiative, a nonprofit program dedicated to supporting publishers in their efforts to reduce their use of fiber obtained from endangered forests. (see:www.greenpressinitiative.org). Nova Publishing Company is also proud to be an initial signatory on the Book Industry Treatise on Responsible Paper Use. In addition, Nova Publishing Company uses all compact fluorescent lighting; recycles all office paper products, aluminum and plastic beverage containers, and printer cartridges; uses 100% post-consumer fiber, process-chlorine-free, acid-free paper for 95% of in-house paper use; and, when possible, uses electronic equipment that is EPA Energy Star-certified. Nova's freight shipments are coordinated to minimize energy use whenever possible. Finally, all carbon emissions from Nova Publishing Company office energy use are offset by the purchase of wind-energy credits that are used to subsidize the building of wind turbines on the Rosebud Sioux Reservation in South Dakota (see www.nativeenergy.com). We strongly encourage other publishers and all partners in publishing supply chains to adopt similar policies.

Nova Publishing Company
Small Business and Consumer Legal Books and Software
1103 West College St.
Carbondale, IL 62901
Editorial: (800) 748-1175
www.novapublishing.com

Distributed by:
National Book Network
4501 Forbes Blvd., Suite 200
Lanham, MD 20706
Orders: (800) 462-6420
free shipping on internet orders

Table of Contents

Introduction to the No-Fault Divorce Toolkit

Divorce has become a fact of life in today's society. Approximately one-half of all marriages entered into this year will eventually end in divorce. Each year over two million people get divorced and the custody of over one million children is decided. The legal cost of divorce in America is well over $1 billion dollars every year.

More damaging, however, are the emotional and psychological costs of divorce. This emotional damage is directly increased as the hostility of a divorce escalates. Unfortunately, although some form of no-fault divorce is now the law in every state, the American legal system tends to cause, rather than prevent, antagonism in divorce. The U.S. legal system is an adversary system. It is designed to breed and thrive on conflict. Such a system as applied to divorce may have made sense long ago when divorce was not favored in society. However, in today's society, where divorce is fully accepted, the legal system as it is applied by most lawyers tends to add to the pain of divorce.

In many situations, the simple addition of two lawyers to the problems encountered by a couple considering divorce will merely intensify any conflict. The reason for this is rooted in the way that most lawyers approach divorce. They want to "win" a divorce and they convince their clients that "winning" is important. By doing this, the lawyers set up an enormously costly game of legal chess with the spouses and any children of a marriage as pawns in the game.

The legal maneuvering generally begins with the lawyer preparing a list of demands highly favorable to his or her own client. The client is urged to ask for everything: the house, the car, custody of the children, huge amounts of alimony and child support, the household possessions … , etc. This is explained to the client as a necessary step in the negotiations process. Of course, the other spouse will be outraged when confronted with such a list of demands and will immediately seek out a mercenary lawyer to draw up a list of equally outrageous counter-demands. Thus, the battle lines will have been drawn. The attempt to amicably dissolve a marriage and get on with one's life will have escalated into an economic and psychological war which will cause enormous suffering and long-term misery for the participants.

The only "winners" in a divorce that has turned into a battle will be the lawyers. The longer the divorce goes on and the more complicated and antagonistic that it gets, the more money the lawyers will make. There have actually been cases in which a divorcing couple's home has been sold as a result of the divorce and *all* of the proceeds of the sale have been used to pay the couple's legal fees in getting the divorce. In other words, if the battle rages long enough, it may be the lawyers who will get the house, the car, the jewelry … , and so on.

There is an alternative to turning a divorce into a war waged by competing lawyers. This alternative is not for everyone, but it can be used by many people who simply wish to end a marriage as easily and as fairly as possible. The alternative to a divorce war is a divorce or legal separation by agreement. It is obtained by the spouses sitting down and peacefully discussing how they wish to divide their property and bills and how they wish to arrange for the care of their children. It can very often be done in a civilized and amicable manner. The couple's agreements are then put in writing in the form of a *Marital Settlement Agreement*, which is a binding contract through which a couple can legally agree to settle all of the issues surrounding their separation and possible subsequent divorce. This agreement can be the basis of a legal separation or it can be used for the ensuing divorce, which can also be routinely handled without the use of an expensive lawyer.

This book will provide all of the information necessary to obtain a divorce by agreement. Chapter 1 of this book provides a general overview of the laws relating to divorce and how the legal process works in a divorce. It also discusses the impact of the switch to a national no-fault divorce system and explains how to use this book. Chapter 2 goes over some of the basic preliminary considerations to divorce: Where can we obtain the divorce? What are the grounds for divorce? What steps must be taken to obtain the divorce? The next six chapters deal with the actual preparation and signing of a Marital Settlement Agreement. For each important topic (property division, alimony, child custody and visitation, and child support), legal guidelines, questionnaires, worksheets, and sample clauses are provided. The final four chapters deal with using the Agreement to obtain a no-fault divorce in any state. Guidelines, questionnaires, and sample forms are provided, as well as instructions for court testimony and appearances. The Appendix contains a detailed compilation of the laws relating to divorce in all 50 states and Washington D.C.

Instructions for Using Forms-on-CD

Quick Start Installation:
1. Insert the enclosed CD in your computer's CD drive.
2. The installation program will start automatically. Follow the on-screen dialog and make the appropriate choices.
3. If the CD installation does not start automatically, click on START, then RUN, then BROWSE and select your CD drive and then the file "Install.exe". Finally, click OK to run the installation program.

Installation Instructions for MAC:
1. Insert the enclosed CD in your CD drive and click on it.
2. Copy the folder "Divorce Forms for MACs" to your hard drive.

All of the forms which are included in this book have been provided on the Forms-on-CD for your use if you have access to a computer. If you have completed the Forms-on-CD installation program, all of the forms will have been copied to your computer's hard drive. By default, these files are installed in the C:\Divorce Toolkit\ Forms folder which is created by the installation program. (Note for MAC users: see instructions above). Opening the Forms folder will provide you with access to folders for each of the topics corresponding to chapters in the book. Within each chapter, the forms are provided in two separate formats:

Text forms which may be opened, prepared, and printed from within your own word processing program (such as Microsoft Word®, or WordPerfect®). The text forms all have the file extension: .txt. These forms are located in the TEXT FORMS folders supplied for each chapter's forms. You may wish to use the forms in this format if you will be making changes to text of the forms. To access these forms, please see page 12.

PDF forms which may be filled in on your computer screen and printed out on any printer. This particular format provides the most widely-used cross-platform format for accessing computer files. Files in this format may be opened as images on your computer and printed out on any printer. The files in Adobe PDF format all have the file extension: .pdf. Although this format provides the easiest method for completing the forms, the forms in this format can not be altered (other than to fill in the information required on the blanks provided). To access the PDF forms, please see below. If you wish to alter the language in any of the forms, you will need to access the forms in their text-only versions. To access these PDF forms, please see 11.

To Access Adobe PDF Forms

1. You must have already installed the Adobe Acrobat Reader® program to your computer's hard drive. This program is installed automatically by the installation program. (MAC users will need to install this program via www.adobe.com).

2. On your computer's desktop, you will find a shortcut icon labeled "Acrobat Reader®" Using your mouse, left double click on this icon. This will open the Acrobat Reader® program. When the Acrobat Reader® program is opened for the first time, you will need to accept the Licensing Agreement from Adobe in order to use this program. Click "Accept" when given the option to accept or decline the Agreement.

3. Once the Acrobat Reader® program is open on your computer, click on FILE (in the upper left-hand corner of the upper taskbar). Then click on OPEN in the drop down menu. Depending on which version of Windows or other operating system you are using, a box will open which will allow you to access files on your computer's hard drive. The files for Divorce Toolkit are located on your computer's "C" drive, under the folder "Divorce Toolkit." In this folder, you will find a subfolder "Forms." (Note: if you installed the forms folder on a different drive, access the forms on that particular drive).

4. If you desire to work with one of the forms, you should then left double-click your mouse on the sub-folder: "Forms." This will open two folders: one for text forms and one for PDF forms. Left double click your mouse on the PDF forms folder and a list of the PDF forms for that topic should appear. Left double click your mouse on the form of your choice. This will open the appropriate form within the Adobe Acrobat Reader® program.

To Fill in Forms in the Adobe Acrobat Reader® Program

1. Once you have opened the appropriate form in the Acrobat Reader® program, filling in the form is a simple process. A 'hand tool' icon will be your cursor in the Acrobat Reader® program. Move the 'hand tool' cursor to the first blank space that will need to be completed on the form. A vertical line or "I-beam" should appear at the beginning of the first space on a form that you will need to fill in. You may then begin to type the necessary information in the space provided. When you have filled in the first blank space, hit the TAB key on your keyboard. This will move the 'hand' cursor to the next space which must be filled in. Please note that some of the spaces in the forms must be completed by hand, specifically the signature, witness, and notary blanks.

2. Move through the form, completing each required space, and hitting TAB to move to the next space to be filled in. (Please note: hitting TAB after the last fill-in will return you to the first page of the form.)

For information on what is required for each blank on the forms, please read the instructions in this book. When you have completed all of the fill-ins, you may print out the form on your computer's printe and you may save the completed form. If you wish to save the completed form, you should rename the form so that your hard drive will retain an unaltered version of the form.

To Access and Complete the Text Forms

For your convenience, all of the forms in this book are also provided as text-only forms which may be altered and saved. To open and use any of the text forms:

1. First, open your preferred word processing program. Then click on FILE (in the upper left-hand corner of the upper taskbar). Then click on OPEN in the drop down menu. Depending on which version of Windows or other operating system you are using, a box will open which will allow you to access files on your computer's hard drive. The files for Divorce Toolkit are located on your computer's "C" drive, under the folder "Divorce Toolkit." In this folder, you will find a sub-folder: "Forms."

2. If you desire to work with one of the forms, you should then left double-click your mouse on the sub-folder: "Forms." A list of form topics (corresponding to the chapters in the book) will appear and you should then left double-click your mouse on the topic of your choice. This will open two folders: one for text forms and one for PDF forms. Left double click your mouse on the text forms folder and a list of the text forms for that topic should appear. Left double click your mouse on the form of your choice. This will open the appropriate form within your word processing program.

3. You may now fill in the necessary information while the text-only file is open in your word processing program. You may need to adjust margins and/or line endings of the form to fit your particular word processing program. Note that there is an asterisk (*) in every location in these forms where information will need to be included. Replace each asterisk with the necessary information. When the form is complete, you may print out the completed form and/or you may save the completed form. If you wish to save the completed form, you should rename the form so that your hard drive will retain an unaltered version of the form.

Technical Support

Nova Publishing will provide technical support for installing the provided software. Please also note that Nova Publishing Company cannot provide legal advice regarding the effect or use of the forms on this software. For questions about installing the Forms-on-CD, you may call Nova Technical Support at 1-800-748-1175.

In addition, Nova cannot provide technical support for the use of the Adobe Acrobat Reader®. For any questions relating to Adobe Acrobat Reader®, please access Adobe Technical Support at www.adobe.com/support/main.html or you may search for assistance in the HELP area of Adobe Acrobat Reader® (located in approximately the center of the top line of the program's desktop).

List of Forms-on-CD

(Forms are formatted as PDF or text files, or both, as noted.)

Preliminary Questionnaire (PDF file only)
Document Checklist (PDF file only)
Property Questionnaire (PDF file only)
Property Division Worksheet (PDF file only)
Financial Statement (PDF file only)
Alimony Questionnaire (PDF file only)
Child Custody Questionnaire (PDF file only)
Custody and Visitation Worksheet (PDF file only)
Child Support Worksheet (PDF file only)
Child Support Guidelines (PDF file only)
Marital Settlement Agreement (PDF and text file)
    Alimony Clauses (text files)
    Child Custody Clauses (text files)
    Child Support Clauses (text files)
Extra Page Form (PDF file only)
Petition or Complaint (PDF and text file)
Appearance, Consent and Waiver (PDF and text file)
Declaration Under Uniform Child Custody Jurisdiction Act (PDF and text file)
Final Judgement or Decree (PDF and text file)
Testimony Worksheet (PDF and text file)
State-Specific Divorce Forms (PDF files only) Note: These forms are included in the folder named "State-Specific Forms" that will be added to your hard drive upon installation.

Chapter 1

Understanding Divorce Law

There has been a sweeping revolution in divorce law in the United States during the past 35 years, and it is still under way. The changes brought about by this revolution have fundamentally altered the framework of how a divorce is obtained and how divorce affects spouses and children. These dramatic legal changes are, as yet, relatively unknown to the general public and are still not fully understood even by the lawyers and judges who administer the new laws. In order to begin the process of your divorce or separation with realistic expectations, it is very important to understand the new framework of divorce law.

Divorce in the United States is governed by individual state law. Each state has its own particular laws to deal with all aspects of the divorce process, from residency requirements, to child custody, to the division of property. Until 1970, divorce was universally viewed as a social ill, to be avoided and discouraged by the laws of society. Courts in all 50 states granted divorces only on the basis of some marital fault: adultery, abandonment, physical abuse, mental cruelty, or some other form of misconduct. There was a winner (the innocent spouse) and a loser (the guilty spouse). The fruits of divorce were passed out according to the fault of the spouses. If a husband was adulterous or at

Toolkit Tip!

To use this book successfully, you will need to review your own state's divorce laws as detailed in the Appendix.

fault in some other way, the wife was often awarded generous alimony, a larger portion of the marital property, custody of the couple's children, and ample child support. Alternatively, if the wife was found to be at fault, she was often denied alimony, given far less or even none of the couple's property, and could be prevented from having custody of her children. The innocent spouse was rewarded for having been faithful to the vows of marriage and the guilty spouse was punished for his or her marital misconduct.

This traditional system of divorce began to change in 1970. In that year, California passed the first no-fault divorce laws in the U.S. Since then, the sweeping changes brought about by no-fault divorce have spread across the country, concluding when South Dakota became the final state to embrace no-fault divorce. No-fault divorce is now the law in all 50 of the United States and Washington D.C.

What is No-fault Divorce?

No-fault divorce is exactly what it sounds like. There is no "fault" involved in the grounds for divorce. Neither spouse must prove that the other spouse has been guilty of misconduct. In fact, any misconduct is essentially irrelevant to obtaining the divorce. Adultery and other forms of marital misconduct are generally no longer penalized by the law of divorce. (In some states, however, misconduct may still have an effect on custody and alimony awards, but these states are gradually changing to systems in which misconduct plays no role at all in any of the divorce proceedings. Also, some states continue to retain some of the original fault-based grounds for divorce along with a no-fault method of divorce.)

> ☀️**Toolkit Tip!**
>
> Many states still retain "fault-based" types of divorce. Please see the Appendix for information relating to your specific state laws.

The initial reasoning behind the change to no-fault divorce was to attempt to lessen the antagonism and pain of divorce. No longer would detectives need to be hired to prove adultery; no longer would a couple's "dirty laundry" need to be aired in public; no longer would a battle be waged regarding who was at fault in the marriage. A marriage could be terminated simply because the spouses no longer felt that the marriage could survive.

To some extent, no-fault divorce has succeeded. Divorce has been changed from a moral action in which a guilty spouse is punished and an innocent spouse is rewarded to essentially an economic action. The focus has changed from proving fault in a marriage to deciding the practical matters of dividing the couple's property and providing for child custody and childcare. Although there have been recent attempts to revoke some states' no-fault divorce laws, to date, none of these attempts have been successful. The public still believes strongly that no-fault divorce is not a cause of marital breakdown, but instead, is a valuable method for peacefully ending marriages that have become unsuccessful.

Along with these changes in the grounds for divorce, other equally important changes in divorce law have occurred. In many cases, divorce may now be obtained unilaterally, without the agreement of the other spouse. There is no realistic method left to prevent a divorce if one of the spouses is determined to go through with a divorce. Consent of the other spouse is no longer necessary in a majority of states. The rules regarding how a couple's property is divided, how alimony is determined, and how child custody and child support are awarded have all also been radically altered in the past three and a half decades.

The Division of Marital Property

Toolkit Tip!

Dividing your marital property in a fair and just manner is often the most difficult part of the divorce process.

In the area of property, the new divorce laws have brought about radical changes. Traditionally, in all but the few community-property states, the division of a couple's property upon divorce was a simple matter. The spouse whose name was on the title to the property was the owner of the property. In most cases, this was the husband. If the wife had no property of her own, she was given a share of the husband's property. Generally, however, she was awarded no more than one-third of the property. If jointly-owned property was divided, it was often done on the basis of who contributed the most money to its purchase. Again, the husband usually took the lion's share. The wife was given no credit for her non-monetary contributions to the marriage or to the purchase of property. Her homemaking and child-rearing efforts counted for nothing in the traditional method of property division. A wife's own career sacrifices to put her husband through school, in order that he might better the living standards of the family, were also not taken into consideration.

Those simple and highly discriminatory rules have been universally overturned in every state. The property acquired during a marriage is now considered owned in equal or equitable shares by both spouses, regardless of whose name is on the title. In many states, spouses are specifically given credit for homemaking duties and an effort is made to provide some level of compensation for the sacrifices of a spouse who aids another in achieving a degree in higher education. The division of property is now based on a view that marriage is essentially an equal partnership, rather than on a determination of who contributed the most actual cash to the marriage. Chapter 3 contains a comprehensive explanation of property division and related matters.

Alimony and Maintenance

Prior to the recent changes in the law, many wives were considered to be eligible for and even entitled to continued support by their ex-husbands after the marriage, often for the rest of their lives or until their subsequent remarriage. This support was provided to the wives by alimony payments.

This portion of the divorce laws has also been the subject of dramatic change. Alimony is no longer the province of the wife alone. It is now available to either spouse. A well-off wife may now be required to provide support for an indigent ex-husband. Alimony is no longer even called alimony in many jurisdictions; it is now referred to as "maintenance" or "spousal support." No longer is alimony regarded as an absolute right; no longer is alimony generally awarded on a permanent basis.

Awards of maintenance are now generally viewed as temporary in nature, designed to allow the ex-spouse adequate time to become self-sufficient; either through education, career training, or work. Awards of maintenance are now primarily based on the needs of the spouse and are not awarded for "innocence" from misconduct. Maintenance and spousal support will be dealt with in detail in Chapter 4.

⚡ Warning!

If you have been married for over 10 years and have not been employed for much of that period, you should seek the advice of a competent attorney.

Child Custody

☼ Toolkit Tip!

Child custody issues are often difficult for many parents. Courts always attempt to make custody decisions based on the "best interests" of the child in question.

In the past, the law assumed that mothers were best suited to care for minor children. When a family was broken by divorce, there was a strong legal presumption that the mother, and only the mother, was to get custody. Traditionally, the only way a father could get custody was to prove that the mother was totally "unfit" to care for the child. This was a very difficult legal hurdle, given that the laws and the courts highly favored the mother having custody of any children. It required the father who desired custody to dredge up as much negative information as possible about the mother and present it in open court in as damaging a method as possible. This method of determining custody also tended to make the children pawns in the divorce negotiation, much to the detriment of the children.

This presumption in favor of the mother being granted custody of minor children is no longer the law in any state. Both parents are now presumed to be equally qualified to be granted custody, unless there is strong evidence to the contrary. The gender of the parent is irrelevant. Sole custody by one parent is also no longer considered the only proper method for child care after divorce. Most states have adopted rules allowing and even encouraging joint custody by both natural parents.

In practice, however, mothers continue to retain custody in the vast majority of the cases. Physical custody of minor children is still awarded to mothers in some 90 percent of all custody cases. This is simply a reflection of the fact that mothers in the U.S. are still overwhelmingly the primary caregivers to children. Increasingly, however, divorced fathers have been allowed more voice in the major decisions affecting the child through the alternative of "joint" custody.

A further major change in divorce laws as they relate to children is the adoption by all states of the Uniform Child Custody Jurisdiction Act. This act attempts to deal with the problem of child-snatching and parents taking children across state borders in an attempt to avoid adverse custody decisions. The details of custody and jurisdiction in custody cases will be explained in greater detail in Chapter 5.

Child Support

One of the continuing tragedies of divorce is the failure of many children of divorce to receive adequate child support. In over 50 percent of all child support situations, the required payments are either paid late or not at all. Even in those cases where the payments are made on time, many of the child support awards are totally inadequate to provide satisfactory care for the children. Dramatic changes in the laws relating to child support have been enacted in the last decade in an effort to correct this situation.

⚡ Warning!

Federal law now provides states with many powerful tools for ensuring that child support payments are kept up-to-date.

Mandated by recent federal legislation, comprehensive new guidelines for determining the level of support required have recently been adopted in individual states. These detailed rules provide specific procedures and criteria for assuring that each child receives adequate support from both parents upon divorce.

In an effort to institute a national system to enforce the collection of delinquent child support payments, the Uniform Reciprocal Enforcement of Support Act has been adopted by all states. Numerous strict laws have also been passed in many states to aid in the collection of overdue support payments. In addition, the federal government has enacted other tough national legislation in an attempt to solve this problem. The laws relating to child support are covered in Chapter 6.

Divorce in General

These major changes in all phases of divorce law have begun to incorporate the equally important changes that have taken place in society in general during the past 35 years. Economics has replaced morality as the overriding concern in many aspects of American society. Women are gradually being treated more equally and fairly under the law. They are no longer considered as the subordinate spouse in a marriage. In awarding child custody, maintenance, and property, both spouses are on a more equal footing under the new divorce laws. These changes have been very rapid and dramatic. They have, in fact, often outpaced the ability of the legal system to cope with them. Judges and lawyers have had a somewhat difficult time putting these new laws into practice where there is no precedent to deal with potential problems that may arise. The change to no-fault divorce has made the area of divorce law the only area of law in which the traditional win/lose context of the legal system does not seem to apply. Lawyers and judges are both trained and experienced in a system of law which has antagonistic and adversarial competition as its basis, and thus are often ill-suited to effectively deal with the no-fault basis of the new divorce laws.

The change to no-fault divorce has somewhat reduced the potential for conflict in divorce by removing the need to prove that one of the spouses is guilty of some form of marital misconduct. However, there is still considerable room for difficulty in the decisions regarding child custody and support and in the division of property.

✐ Definition:

Uncontested Divorce:
A divorce in which the opposing spouse takes no legal part in contesting any of the issues of the divorce.

Just because a divorce is obtained on a no-fault basis does not mean that it is an uncontested divorce. A true *uncontested divorce* is one in which the opposing spouse takes no legal part in contesting any of the decisions made regarding property, custody, maintenance, or child support. There is no necessity for an actual trial regarding aspects of a divorce in an uncontested divorce, although there is generally still a court hearing held to determine compliance with basic legal requirements. In an uncontested divorce, the opposing spouse may take no part at all, can be entirely absent from the state, or may file legal documents agreeing not to contest any terms of the divorce. An uncontested divorce in which only one spouse makes the decisions on the legal matters (usually an uncontested default divorce) is not generally the most effective manner to obtain a divorce which is fair and just to both spouses. Uncontested divorces may be obtained, however, on the basis of an agreement between the spouses, as explained in the next section.

In a *contested divorce*, the spouses are both involved in a legal battle over some or all of these aspects of divorce. A contested divorce can be brought on no-fault grounds, yet include a bitter dispute over child custody, alimony, or property. Despite the advances made in overcoming some of the trauma of divorce by the switch to a no-fault system, contested divorces still provide an arena for lengthy and bitter hostilities.

20

Divorce by Agreement

The alternative to both the uncontested default divorce (in which one spouse does not participate in the decision-making) and the contested divorce is the *divorce by agreement*. In this type of divorce, fault is not a factor. In a divorce by agreement, both spouses play a part in all of the decisions affecting the couple and any children that they may have. In this type of divorce or separation, fairness is the key. For this type of divorce to succeed, the agreement between the spouses must be as fair and as just as is possible under the circumstances. This type of divorce is not only accepted but is actually encouraged in virtually all states. In a modern divorce setting, a marital settlement agreement is an indispensable alternative to the traditional hostility of ending a marriage.

> **☼ Toolkit Tip!**
>
> The focus of this book is to assist you in obtaining a no-fault divorce by agreement with your spouse on the major issues involved in your divorce.

There are many important benefits to obtaining a divorce by agreement. Perhaps the most important benefit is that there is far less chance that the divorce will escalate into a hostile battle. When revenge and animosity are not factors, there is a greater opportunity that the divorce settlement will accurately reflect what the spouses really desire to obtain from the divorce. If the decisions regarding the care and custody of any children are reached through rational and mature discussions, there is a greater chance that the decisions reached will be abided by without future hostility. A further benefit of a divorce settlement that is made without the assistance of attorneys is the avoidance of major legal expenses in connection with a divorce.

Divorce by agreement is the focus of this book. How to approach each of the relevant areas that require agreement will be explained in the following chapters. The actual preparation of a legally-binding marital settlement agreement will also be detailed in the following chapters. Finally, the steps necessary to obtain a no-fault divorce which incorporates the terms of the Marital Settlement Agreement will be shown.

For a divorce by agreement to be successful, both spouses must participate openly and honestly in discussing the matters to be resolved. Both spouses must be willing to compromise on major decisions and work to reach a satisfactory agreement. Both spouses must be a part of the process of preparing a settlement agreement. It may often be very difficult to calmly discuss the issues to be covered in a divorce settlement with a spouse one no longer cares to be married to. However, the valuable benefits of a divorce by agreement are only available to those spouses who can still rationally confer on the matters to be decided.

> **֊Ỳ֊Toolkit Tip!**
>
> As you go through the information in this book, you will need to check with the details of your own state's divorce laws in the Appendix.

The instructions and information that follow are designed to facilitate an amicable settlement of all of the matters which arise in the normal course of a divorce. The standards that are applied and the guidelines that are provided are based on the general modern trends of no-fault divorce laws in the United States. However, although individual state laws have moved much closer to a common ground in the area of divorce in recent years, there are still important differences in the laws of each state. For this purpose, a comprehensive Appendix has been provided at the end of this book that outlines in detail the specific individual characteristics of each state's laws relating to alimony, property division, child custody, and child support. Throughout this book, there will often be references to this Appendix to check on the specifics of particular state laws. The introductory notes in the Appendix should be read first for an explanation of what information is presented and how to put that information to practical use.

Can You Do Your Own Divorce?

The simple answer to this question is YES. Every person has the right to represent him or herself in court without the use of an attorney. This is a well-established legal principle. The basic minimal qualifications to handle your own divorce are simply the ability to read and write basic English and understand this book. However, there are certain situations in which it is not advisable to attempt to obtain a divorce without the aid of a competent attorney. The following checklist will outline those situations. If the answers to all of the questions are YES, then this book may be confidently used to prepare a marital settlement agreement.

Yes No

❑ ❑ Have you and your spouse essentially agreed that you both wish to end your marriage and go your separate ways in peace?

❑ ❑ Do you feel that you and your spouse can cooperate enough to come to some form of fair agreement regarding the division of all of your property and bills?

❑ ❑ If you have children, do you feel certain that you and your spouse can reach a fair and reasonable agreement regarding child custody, visitation, and child support?

❑ ❑ Are you able to firmly state your wishes to your spouse and not be intimidated by him or her and has your marriage been totally free of spouse or child abuse?

❑ ❑ Are you or your spouse NOT in active military service?

❑ ❑ Have no previous legal proceedings been instituted for divorce, legal separation, child custody, or domestic violence between you and your spouse?

❑ ❑ If you have been married for over five years, are you presently employed or capable of supporting yourself?

> **⚡ Warning!**
>
> If you answer ANY of these questions with a NO, you should seek the advice of an attorney. The information in this book will still assist you in understanding your divorce, but you may need legal representation to safely proceed with your divorce.

If *any* of the answers to the previous questions are NO, then it is highly advisable to seek the aid of an attorney. Competent low-cost legal aid is often available from local Legal Aid Society offices or from local legal clinics. Law schools in your area may have programs that can provide free or low-cost help with simple legal matters. State Bar Associations often have low-cost legal referral services also.

> ## ⚡ Warning!
>
> If at any time during your divorce discussions, if your spouse files any legal papers regarding a divorce outside the context of your discussion, you should immediately seek the advice of an attorney.

If during the process of attempting to prepare a marital settlement agreement, you or your spouse become hostile to the point of being unable to rationally discuss the terms of a settlement, it is advisable to seek an attorney or mediator for assistance. In addition, if at any time during the process of attempting to obtain a divorce you become overwhelmed by the complications involved or become confused regarding your rights, it is advisable to seek the assistance of an attorney. Very importantly, if at any time your spouse files any legal papers for a divorce outside the context of your settlement discussions or if your spouse retains an attorney, you *must* seek legal help immediately.

The focus of the recent changes in the divorce laws is to lessen the chances for animosity to develop between the divorcing spouses. To this end, the lawyers and judges who make up the legal system should and generally do attempt to be helpful to those who wish to represent themselves in court. However, in some counties in the United States, there may continue to be very strong resistance to allowing self-help divorces. Local judges, attorneys, and even court clerks may make the legal process much more difficult than necessary in an effort to discourage self-help law. Unfortunately, if unusually strong hostility is encountered when dealing with the local legal system on a self-help basis, there may be no realistic alternative other than obtaining a lawyer. You should be able to find an attorney who will use the materials that you have already prepared. This will still be far more economical than having a lawyer do all of the work involved.

Even if you decide that it is advisable to use an attorney, the information in this book will be useful. First, it will provide you with practical legal advice regarding the issues involved in a divorce or separation. This will allow you to cope, on an informed and intelligent basis, with the decisions that you face . The discussion of the various divorce matters and the information contained in the Appendix relating to your individual state laws will provide you with an understanding of the relevant points of law that will make it much easier to talk with and understand your lawyer. In addition, the various checklists and questionnaires will enable you to complete much of the preliminary work involved in any divorce prior to seeking an attorney. If you do eventually decide to hire an attorney, the more information that you have gathered yourself in advance will mean that your attorney will not have to spend time on such preliminary matters and will be able to prepare the necessary papers much faster. This, of course, should mean that your eventual legal fees will be less. Do not, in any event, feel discouraged if you come to the conclusion that the aid of an attorney is necessary. Separation and divorce are major emotional and economic events and should be approached with sufficient information and assistance to allow you to feel as comfortable and at ease as is possible under the circumstances.

How to Use This Book

The information that follows is set out in a step-by-step fashion. However, it is intended that the entire book be read first by both spouses before attempting to reach any final decisions on the relevant issues. This will allow you and your spouse to gain an equal understanding of all of the matters and to fully appreciate how the decisions involved in a divorce are interrelated.

> **Toolkit Tip!**
> Both spouses should read this entire book so that each understands the details of the issues that will be discussed.

Once the entire book has been read by both you and your spouse, you will be ready to confer on each issue and reach a workable decision. On each of the main areas covered (property division, alimony, child custody, and child support), there is a questionnaire provided for you to assemble the necessary information and focus on the issues. After each questionnaire, there follows a discussion of the law and a set of general guidelines in order to assist you in the decision-making process. After each discussion, several alternate paragraphs outlining the various choices available are provided for inclusion in your marital settlement agreement. Once you have reached an agreement on each of the relevant points, a paragraph should be chosen that clearly states your decision.

When all of the decisions have been made and all of the appropriate paragraphs have been chosen, you will be instructed on how to assemble the individual pages into a final agreement. You will then be instructed on how to sign and have the document notarized. Your settlement agreement will be a valid legal contract and will allow you and your spouse to separate legally and live under the specific terms of the agreement prior to your divorce being finalized.

If you and your spouse are still able to work together to some extent, the steps necessary to obtain a divorce are not that difficult to follow. You will probably find that preparing your settlement agreement is far less difficult than filling out an income tax return. Understanding and controlling the phases of your own divorce will also allow you to begin the process of accepting your divorce and moving forward with your life in a positive way.

> **☼ Toolkit Tip!**
>
> The standards that are used in this book are based on the standards that are used by judges in divorce courts across the U.S.

As you are working on your settlement agreement, remember that although the standards that are provided in this book are generalized to some extent, they are the basis for the decisions that are made in every divorce nationwide. As you negotiate with your spouse using the guidelines presented in this book, you will be following a general framework of what you could expect if you wind up in court. If your discussions with your spouse fail and your divorce becomes contested, these basic guidelines are still what will be used by a judge to make the important decisions in your case. In that case, however, expensive lawyers will be required, hostilities will likely erupt, and your divorce will become more and more unpleasant. You will still get a divorce, but it will cost you more money and more pain. It is much better to try to resolve your differences and reach a fair agreement without enlisting attorneys.

Mediation

If after an honest attempt to come to an agreement, you and your spouse are still unable to reach an accord, there are other methods of dispute resolution available before you seek legal help. The use of a neutral third person can often make the difference in negotiating a settlement. The third person can be a member of the clergy, a marriage or family counselor, or a professional mediator. Some states have counseling or conciliation services available for just this purpose. The use of these services is generally free and available to any who request it. Look in the yellow pages in your area, ask the clerk of your local court, or check with your local social services agencies for a referral to such counseling.

Divorce mediation is a process in which the spouses consult with a trained professional and discuss their disagreements until an understanding is reached. A professional mediator does not make the decisions. Rather, he or she is trained in conflict resolution and in methods of coaching disagreeing spouses to work out their own agreements. Submitting disputed issues to mediation is a commitment to work cooperatively.

The use of an independent mediator or counseling service should be viewed as a positive step. Often, the use of mediation services will provide all of the additional help that is needed for a couple to reach a satisfactory agreement. Mediation is an alternative method to resolve your differences on a cooperative basis. All of the issues involved in your divorce can be the subject of successful mediation: property division, child custody and visitation, child support, and alimony. Mediation can often enable a couple to reach agreement without resorting to the adversarial legal process.

> **☼ Toolkit Tip!**
>
> If you are unable to come to an agreement with your spouse, before you consult an attorney, you may wish to use the services of a professional mediator.

Most likely, you and your spouse will be able to reach agreement on many of the issues that you will confront in your divorce process. In some cases, however, there may be bitter disagreement over a single problem or issue. Such disagreement may often lead to a breakdown of the entire process of negotiation. If you and your spouse run into such difficulty as you go through the process of reaching an amicable marital settlement, you should reread this section. Rather than discard all of the efforts that you have made in reaching agreement on the other points in your divorce, consider the use of mediation or counseling services to enable you to get past your particular sticking point. You and your spouse will tell the mediator what it is you want to achieve. Mediation is not a marriage counseling service designed to get the two of you back together. It will be an attempt to aid you in peacefully and rationally resolving your disagreements regarding the terms of your separation and divorce.

There are many organizations that may be able to provide you with information in obtaining professional mediation services. The Academy of Family Mediators (5 Militia Drive, Lexington MA 02421; phone: 781-674-2663; email: afmoffice@mediators.org; and website: www.mediationadr.net) is a national family mediation association and provides information regarding regional mediation services.

☼Toolkit Tip!

Check with your state bar association or with the court clerk in the county in which you live to see if there are any mediation services provided in your area.

Many states also provide professional mediation for divorce and family law situations. State Bar Associations generally maintain lists of qualified mediators in the area of divorce and family law.

Mediation is a voluntary process and you and your spouse may choose to withdraw from mediation at any time. Mediators are not judges and have no power to force decisions on you or your spouse. Unlike a legal court proceeding, the sessions will be private and informal and will allow both you and your spouse to calmly discuss your situation and focus your disagreements. Mediators are professionally trained in the process of resolving disputes and will attempt to provide you with experienced guidance in your discussions.

General Note Regarding Terminology

In recent years, many states have changed the terminology that applies to divorce law. Divorce may now be called dissolution of marriage; alimony may be referred to as spousal support or maintenance; child custody may be known as primary parental responsibility and a parent with custody may be referred to as a managing conservator. There may be other unfamiliar legal terms used to describe common ideas. Throughout this book, the common general usage terms will be used: divorce, alimony, child custody, child support, and visitation. However, the listing in the Appendix for each state's specific laws will use the official state language for each term. In addition, most states have laws in effect which state that either terminology may be used: the familiar words or the new legal terms.

Chapter 2

Preliminary Matters

The first and most important preliminary matter that you and your spouse must both confront is: Do you really want a divorce? No guidelines, questionnaires, or checklists are provided in this book for answering this basic question. However, you are urged to think very seriously about the answer to this question as you read through this entire book. Until your divorce is actually finalized by a court of law, you can attempt at any time to reconcile your differences with your spouse and continue with your marriage. None of the steps that you will take until your divorce is final are necessarily irreversible. Divorce is a very big step in your life and should not be taken lightly.

☆ Toolkit Tip!

The most important question that you must ask yourself is:

Do you really want a divorce?

For many people, separation is the first step in the divorce process. You and your spouse may decide to separate under the terms of a separation agreement or you may wish to seek an actual legal separation from a court. A legal court-ordered separation is slightly different than a separation by agreement. Legal court-ordered separations are not provided for in all states. However, a marital separation by mutual agreement is recognized and honored in every state. Check the Appendix for the law in your state. In a legal court-ordered separation, there is actually a court order that specifies that the couple is separated. This court order may set out all of the terms of the separation, or the court order may simply validate all of the terms that the couple have already agreed to in a separation agreement. Neither a legal court-ordered separation nor a separation agreement will legally end the marriage. Only a divorce can do that.

There are some distinct benefits to a separation prior to divorce. First, the period of separation from your spouse begins to prepare you for the emotional impact of divorce. In a separation, you may enter into an agreement covering all of the issues that arise during the course of an actual divorce, and it is much easier to mutually change the terms of this agreement prior to an actual divorce. In some ways, a separation may act as a trial divorce. You can always get back together with your spouse, if you both desire. In addition, some couples who do not wish to divorce decide to live separately for religious or moral reasons.

> **♀̇ Toolkit Tip!**
>
> A marital settlement agreement will be the basis for your eventual divorce. With it you and your spouse will make all of the major decisions relating to your divorce.

The marital settlement agreement that you prepare using this book may be used in the same manner as a separation agreement. It will cover all of the same concerns as a separation agreement. Your marital settlement agreement addresses the issue of separation and may be used if you desire to enter into a legal court-ordered separation. Your state's listing in the Appendix briefly explains the law regarding legal court-ordered separations in your state.

In this chapter, you will begin the process of making the decisions necessary to prepare a marital settlement agreement. This agreement will cover all of the terms of your eventual divorce. Included in your agreement will be all of the decisions that you and your spouse make regarding how your property and bills are divided, whether either of you should get alimony, and, if you have any children, who will have custody of them and how their support will be provided. This agreement, when signed by you and your spouse, will become a valid legal contract that will be enforceable in a court of law if either you or your spouse violate its terms. In addition, the agreement that you prepare will be used in your actual divorce proceedings. Judges will not generally change any of the terms in a marital settlement agreement, unless they feel that the terms are obviously unfair, were obtained by force or threats, or are not in the best interests of any children.

On the next few pages you will fill out a questionnaire that covers basic personal information and details the history of your marriage. By filling in this questionnaire and the ones in the next four chapters, you will be able to have all of the necessary and relevant information in front of you for preparing your agreement. Following the questionnaire, there is a list of important documents that should be assembled and kept on hand for use during the process of your divorce. There will then be a discussion of some of the preliminary matters that must be understood.

The method set out in this book for preparing a marital settlement agreement is essentially identical to the method used by the vast majority of lawyers who handle divorces. Upon visiting a lawyer for a divorce, you would be asked to fill out an extensive questionnaire covering all of the aspects that might arise in the course of your divorce proceeding. The lawyer would then determine what you want to achieve in your divorce; what property you wish to retain, which parent you wish to have custody, and whether child support or alimony is desired. Your lawyer and your spouse's lawyer would then attempt to negotiate the various issues, and if possible, put them in the form of a marital settlement. The lawyers would use legal texts that contain clauses very similar to the ones that follow to prepare your agreement. The only difference is that the language in the agreement that most lawyers would prepare would be unintelligible to most people.

> **☼ Toolkit Tip!**
>
> The techniques used in this book for developing a marital settlement agreement are the same as used by most lawyers.

You and your spouse, however, are the two people who know the most about your current relationship. You both are the two most qualified people to understand what each wants out of the marriage. If you can both cooperate enough to agree to the terms of your marital settlement agreement, your subsequent divorce should be achieved with far less difficulty and expense than if you use the services of lawyers. If you can't agree to the terms of your agreement without lawyers, it is not likely that you will be able to agree once you both have hired lawyers. If you can't come to an agreement, even with the assistance of lawyers, a judge who knows very little about you and your spouse will make the important decisions that you were unable to make.

With these points in mind, try to make an honest and mature effort to reach an agreement with your spouse that will be fair and workable for both of you. An agreement that is one-sided,

> **:Ö: Toolkit Tip!**
>
> If you do not feel that you and your spouse can reach a fair agreement, you should consult an attorney.

unfair, or made in haste just to get it over with is worse than no agreement at all. To use this book correctly will take some time. It is time that you would normally be paying for a lawyer to complete the same tasks. In effect, you and your spouse will be saving two times a lawyer's normal hourly fees (about $150.00 per hour x two) for every hour that you both spend doing the work yourselves. In addition, the time that you spend achieving an agreement that is fair to both of you will be repaid many times over in the ease with which you will both make the transition from married to single life.

Preliminary Questionnaire

Wife's full name: _____

Wife's former or maiden name: _____

Does wife desire to use her former name? _____

Wife's social security number: _____

Wife's date of birth: _____

Wife's present address:

Wife's future address (if known):

Date future address is valid: _____

Wife's present phone number: _____

Wife's present occupation: _____

Wife's present place of employment:

Wife's general health:

Was wife previously married? _____
   If YES, how was marriage terminated (divorce, death, etc.)?

Husband's full name: _____

Husband's social security number: _____

Husband's date of birth: _____

Husband's present address:

Husband's future address (if known):

Date future address is valid: _____

Husband's present phone number: _____

Husband's present occupation: _____

Husband's present place of employment:

Was husband previously married?_____
   If YES, how was marriage terminated (divorce, death, etc.)?

Full address(es) where husband and wife have lived during the past 12 months:

Date of marriage: _____
Place of marriage:

 Are you and your spouse separated?   _____
   If YES, on what date did you separate? _____
Have you previously separated at any time? _____
   If YES, on what dates and for how long?

Names and birthdates of any children of this marriage (born or adopted):

Document Checklist

The following is a listing of various documents that may be necessary during your divorce. The list is as comprehensive as possible and many of the documents may not apply to your individual situation. If you have the documents listed in your possession, assemble them into one place and make a note of that fact on this list. If your spouse has the documents, request that he or she do the same. If you know that the document exists, but do not have access to it, make a note to that effect on this list.

- ❏ Wife's Birth Certificate:
- ❏ Husband's Birth Certificate:
- ❏ Immigration and Naturalization Documents:
- ❏ Marriage License:
- ❏ Birth Certificates of any Children:
- ❏ Any Written Agreements between Wife and Husband:
- ❏ Social Security Cards:
- ❏ Documents relating to any prior marriage:
- ❏ All documents relating to income, expenses, and property:
    - ❏ Federal, state, and local income tax returns:
    - ❏ Payroll stubs and W-2 Forms:
    - ❏ Records regarding any other income:
    - ❏ Records regarding monthly living expenses:
    - ❏ Pension and retirement plan policies and records:
    - ❏ Stock option and profit-sharing plans and records:
    - ❏ Personal financial statements:
    - ❏ Business tax returns:
    - ❏ Business financial statements:
    - ❏ Deeds to any real estate:
    - ❏ Mortgages or deeds of trust for any real estate:
    - ❏ Copies of any leases:
    - ❏ Checking account statements:
    - ❏ Savings account statements and passbooks:
    - ❏ Certificates of Deposit:
    - ❏ Stock certificates and bonds:

- ❏ Securities stockbroker account statements:
- ❏ Titles to cars, boats, motorcycles, etc.:
- ❏ Any outstanding loan documents:
- ❏ Credit card records:
- ❏ Records of any other debts:
- ❏ Life insurance policies:
- ❏ Health insurance policies:
- ❏ Auto insurance policies:
- ❏ Homeowner's insurance policy:
- ❏ Other insurance policies:
- ❏ Inventory of contents of safety deposit boxes:
- ❏ Appraisals of any property:
- ❏ Records of any gifts or inheritances:

After you have filled in this first questionnaire and assembled the necessary documents, you are ready to begin the process of preparing your marital settlement agreement and obtaining your divorce. Based on what you have put on your questionnaire, you must make certain preliminary decisions. First, you must decide in which state and county (or parish) you will be allowed to file for your divorce. Following that decision, you must determine what the specific grounds for your divorce will be.

Where Can You File for Your Divorce?

Before you begin to prepare your actual divorce papers, you need to know exactly where you will be filing for your divorce. Three legal considerations enter into this decision. The first is residency. All states have some type of residency requirement regarding filing for divorce. You may only file for your divorce in the state in which you or your spouse reside. Residency is also referred to in some states as domicile. Both terms refer to the place where you permanently live; the place where you return to after any temporary absence. In general, you must have been a resident of the state in which you wish to file for divorce for some length of time in order for the court to hear your case.

> **☼ Toolkit Tip!**
>
> You will need to consult your own state's residency requirements in the Appendix to determine where you will be able to file for your divorce.

Each state has differing residency requirements and these are shown in the Appendix. Some states require that you be a resident for 1 year in the state before you will be allowed to file for divorce. A few states merely require that you actually be a bona-fide resident; there is no time limit specified. In general, you will be allowed to file for divorce in the state in which you were married if you have lived there since marriage or in the state in which you currently reside if you have met the residency requirements as shown in the Appendix. It is not a good idea to move about frequently when you are contemplating divorce, as this may delay your ability to file for divorce in the state and county that you wish.

The other two considerations for determining where to file are technical legal ones: jurisdiction and venue. Jurisdiction refers

☼ Toolkit Tip!

You will also need to consult your own state's venue requirements in the Appendix to determine which county (or parish) you will be able to file for your divorce.

to the authority of the court to make binding orders regarding the subject matter of the case (in this instance, divorce) and regarding the people involved in the case. In some states, residency is a jurisdictional requirement. In others, it is not. Notification of the opposing party in a lawsuit also generally provides the court with jurisdiction over the person. Jurisdictional considerations are also important in determining which actual court within the state is the proper one for divorce proceedings. Venue refers to the legal selection of which county (or parish) should be the actual site of the trial. Both venue and jurisdiction decisions are based on the actual statutes in your particular state. Some states may require the divorce proceedings to be instituted in the county where the spouse the divorce is filed against lives. Other states may require that the lawsuit be in the county where the spouse filing for divorce lives. Still other states may allow the divorce action in any county where either spouse resides. Check with the Appendix to determine the rules in effect in your state.

It is recommended that, until your divorce is completed, you and your spouse remain in the same state. It will also make compliance with these technical legal requirements easier if you both remain in the same county. Of course, that may not always be possible. If you and your spouse have lived in the same county and the same state for one year, you can be assured that it is in that state and county that you will be allowed to file for your divorce. If you have moved around frequently or if you have separated and live in different states, it may be somewhat more difficult to determine which state and county is proper. Some states will allow a spouse in a divorce suit to waive any venue or jurisdiction difficulties. Other states take the position that a person can not waive such legal formalities. If you can not easily determine which state and county to properly file for your divorce by using the Appendix in this book, you will need to consult a lawyer on this decision. You should still be able to prepare and file your own divorce papers once you have ascertained where exactly they should be filed.

The state which you choose for filing for your divorce should be the state whose Appendix you refer to for the rest of this book. The county which you have determined is correct will be the county in which you file your actual divorce papers as explained in Chapter 10. The name of the particular court within the county is also noted in the Appendix.

What Will be the Grounds for Your Divorce?

Your divorce will be based on the particular no-fault basis that is allowed in your own state. Some states have more than one basis for filing. In general however, there are four basic types of no-fault grounds: (1) irretrievable breakdown of the marriage; (2) irreconcilable differences; (3) incompatibility; and (4) living separate and apart for a certain time period. The grounds for filing for a no-fault divorce in your state are listed in the Appendix. Most states have only one type of available grounds for a no-fault divorce and it is this type that you will use. However, a few states have available a choice of no-fault grounds. You must choose the grounds that most closely fit your particular circumstances. (Residents of Louisiana: Please note that Louisiana has instituted the most liberal system for divorce grounds in the U.S. In Louisiana, it is now grounds for a divorce if one spouse simply "desires" not to be married. In addition, Louisiana has also eliminated all defenses to a divorce requested on such grounds. The only way to prevent such a divorce in Louisiana is to reconcile with the spouse desiring to divorce.)

> **Toolkit Tip!**
>
> You will also need to consult your own state's listing of the grounds for a no-fault divorce in the Appendix to determine which type of no-fault divorce your state has enacted.

In states that have "irretrievable breakdown of the marriage," "irreconcilable differences," or "incompatibility" as grounds, it is generally easy to satisfy the grounds. If either spouse decides that the marriage should be ended, it is very difficult for the other spouse to prevent the divorce. If both spouses agree on the no-fault grounds or if the other spouse does not deny that the marriage is broken, the grounds are generally satisfied. There may be a court-enforced mediation attempt or a counseling session required if the other spouse does deny that the marriage is irretrievably broken or that there are irreconcilable differences. Any such denial of the breakdown of the marriage will only delay the divorce for a specific period of time while an attempt at reconciliation is made. The divorce will proceed after the mediation period is over, usually after about 30 to 90 days. A few states have certain specific ways to prove that the marriage is irretrievably broken. Two states (New York and Tennessee) allow proof of the grounds by use of a written agreement reached between the spouses. One state (Texas) uses a unique type of grounds that is very similar to the other general no-fault grounds. The different states' requirements are listed in the Appendix. In any states with these type of no-fault grounds, the couple may separate prior to the actual divorce. During the time of separation, the spouses can live under the terms of the marital settlement agreement that may be prepared by using this book.

☀ Toolkit Tip!

A few states provide for both a 'marital breakdown' and a 'separation-based' grounds for divorce. If you live in one of these states, you and your spouse will have to decide which type to use for your divorce.

The fourth type of grounds for obtaining a divorce is "living separately and apart" for a specific length of time. This type of grounds is able to be shown by objective evidence and is proven merely by showing that the spouses did not live together or sleep together for the required time limit. There is no requirement that either spouse be at fault for the separation. The necessary time limit for living apart ranges from six months to five years. During the time of separation, the spouses can live under the terms of the marital settlement agreement that may be prepared using this book. Please refer to the Appendix to see if your state requires this type of grounds.

As noted, a few states will show two or more no-fault grounds. Generally, if there is more than one type of no-fault grounds for divorce, there is a general marital breakdown grounds and a separation-based grounds. Which grounds that you and your spouse choose will depend on your individual circumstances and an agreement between you and your spouse.

Tax Consequences of Divorce

There are various tax consequences to your divorce or separation that must be considered as you prepare your marital settlement agreement. Among these are:

• Whether you will file joint or separate returns for the current year

• Who will be liable for any taxes due for the current year

• Who will have a right to any refund due for the current year

• Who will receive the tax exemption for any dependent children

The full details regarding the potential tax aspects of divorce and separation are beyond the scope of this book. Tax laws are among the most complex and rapidly changing laws in existence. Detailed information regarding current federal income tax laws may be found in IRS Publication 504: *Divorced or Separated Individuals*. For information on your individual state's treatment of divorce for tax purposes, please consult the instructions or regulations available from your state's department of taxation or revenue. For further information, you should consult a competent accountant, attorney, or other qualified tax professional. There are, however, some general taxation guidelines that may assist you in determining your personal income tax situation before and after your divorce or separation.

> **☼ Toolkit Tip!**
>
> You can find *IRS Publication 504: Divorced or Separated Individuals* on the internet at: **www.irs.gov**.

Property Transfers

The most important rule regarding federal income taxes relating to property is that any transfers of property between you and your spouse that are related to your divorce or separation are not taxable. There will be no recognition of any gain or loss on the transfer of any property, regardless of who actually owned the property. The transfer of property related to a divorce is considered a gift from one spouse to the other for tax purposes as long as the property is actually transferred within one year after the date of the actual final divorce. The spouse who receives the property is not required to report any gain or income as the result of the receipt of any such property. However, there may be future tax consequences for a spouse who receives property that has increased in value while it was held during the marriage. In general, the spouse who receives such property in a divorce settlement and later sells the property will be liable for any taxes due on any gain in the value of the property.

For example, as a result of their divorce negotiations, Spouse A agrees to sign a deed transferring full ownership of their jointly-owned home to Spouse B. The original equity in the home at the time of original purchase was $10,000.00 (their down payment). Therefore, the value of Spouse A's one-half share at the time of purchase was $5,000.00. The equity value of the home is now $40,000.00. The current market value of Spouse A's one-half share of the equity value of the home is $20,000.00. Upon transfer of Spouse A's share to Spouse B, Spouse B is not required to report any gain or income related to the transfer. However, if Spouse B later sells the home, the $15,000.00 gain in value that is attributable to Spouse A's share ($20,000.00 - $5,000.00 = $15,000.00) may be considered as taxable gain to Spouse B. Spouse B's own share of the equity may also be taxable as gain on the sale of the home.

Additionally, there are some relatively complex tax regulations that relate to the treatment of community property in the 9 community-property states (Arizona, California, Idaho, Louisiana, Nevada, New Mexico, Texas, Washington, and Wisconsin). (*Note*: Alaska is considered an "equitable distribution state" but allows married couples to designate, by written agreement, which of their property they wish to be considered "community property"). In general, the IRS may choose to disregard community-property rules in certain specific tax situations. Although these situations seldom arise under normal circumstances, IRS Publication 504: *Divorced or Separated Individuals* should be referred to for more information on this aspect of taxation.

> **☼ Toolkit Tip!**
> If you have specific questions regarding the tax consequences of your divorce, you may need to consult an accountant.

Alimony

In general, alimony payments are treated as income to the spouse who receives them. Conversely, the spouse who actually pays the alimony may deduct such payments as an expense. The spouse paying alimony can (at the present time) deduct the alimony payments from income for tax purposes whether or not deductions are itemized on the federal tax forms. In order for alimony payments to qualify for this tax treatment for federal income tax purposes, there are certain conditions. For payments based on agreements, the following requirements must be met:

• The alimony payment must be the result of a written settlement agreement or a divorce decree or judgment

• The payment must be by cash, check, or money order

• The spouses do not live together when the payment is made

• The payment is not for child support

• The payments may not continue after death

The terms of the marital settlement agreement clause included in this book relating to the continuing payment of alimony would qualify under current federal tax law as long as: (1) the payments are terminated on the death of the recipient; (2) they are not a one-time lump-sum payment; and (3) all of the other above conditions are met.

A one-time lump-sum alimony payment is treated as a simple transfer of funds from one spouse to the other. Such a lump-sum alimony payment is neither taxable to the spouse receiving it nor deductible by the spouse paying it. Life insurance premium payments that are made by an ex-spouse for a policy that names the other ex-spouse as sole irrevocable beneficiary are also considered to be alimony, as long as the payments also meet the above qualifications. Any other voluntary payments in excess of the amount required under the marital settlement agreement or divorce decree, however, will not qualify as alimony and may not be deducted as alimony expenses for tax purposes. For example, under the terms of their marital settlement agreement, Spouse A has agreed to pay Spouse B $500.00 per month for three years or until Spouse B's death, whichever occurs first. The spouses currently have separated and live apart. Spouse A makes the required payments for a full year. For income tax purposes, Spouse A may deduct the full $6,000.00 from his income, even if other deductions are not itemized. Spouse B must report the entire $6,000.00 as income for federal income tax purposes.

> **♀ Toolkit Tip!**
>
> Alimony and child support payments are treated differently for federal tax purposes.

Child Support and Custody

For federal income tax purposes, child support payments are treated differently from alimony payments. In general, any amount that is fixed in your marital settlement agreement or in your final divorce decree as child support will not be treated as income to the parent who receives it. In addition, unlike alimony payments, the parent who makes such child support payments cannot deduct this payment as an expense for federal income tax purposes.

For example, Parent A has custody of one child and Parent B has agreed to pay $400.00 per month in child support. The payments are made on time for a full year. Parent B may not deduct any of the amount of the child support payments from income and Parent A is not required to report any of the payments as income for tax purposes. Which parent receives the benefit of the tax exemption for a dependent child is also subject to IRS regulations. In general, the parent with physical custody of the child for over one-half of the year will have the right to the exemption if the following qualifications are also met:

Toolkit Tip!

You can find IRS Form 8332: *Release of Claim to Exemption for Child of Divorced or Separated Parents* on the internet at: **www.irs.gov**.

- You are divorced, separated, or live apart for at least the last six months of the current tax year

- You and your spouse together provided over one-half of the total support for the child (as opposed to support being provided by a non-parent)

- You and your spouse had custody of the child, either alone or together for over one-half of the current year (as opposed to a non-parent having custody)

- You have not agreed in writing that your spouse should have the right to claim the dependency exemption and have not filed a written IRS waiver form (IRS Form 8332: *Release of Claim to Exemption for Child of Divorced or Separated Parents*)

Marital Settlement Agreement Instructions

You are now ready to begin preparing a draft copy of your marital settlement agreement. Begin by printing out a blank copy of the marital settlement agreement form that is included the Forms-on-CD. You will begin by filling in the information noted below in the spaces indicated by the numbers on the sample Marital Settlement Agreement that follows. The initial information will lay the legal groundwork that identifies you, your spouse, and any children, and will satisfy the basic minimum legal requirements for a valid contract. The first 15 items to fill in are covered in this section. The following sections will cover filling in information regarding property, alimony, child custody and support, and completing the Agreement form. At the end of this section is a sample Marital Settlement Agreement noting where the numbered choices should be filled in. Note: you may use either the PDF version or the text version of the Marital Settlement Agreement. Both are included on the Forms-on-CD. Using the text version will allow you to cut and paste the various clauses that you select into the form.

① Date of agreement

② Name of wife

③ Address of wife (including county of residence)

④ Name of husband

⑤ Address of husband (including county of residence)

⑥ Date of marriage

⑦ Place of marriage (city and state)

⑧ **Children Identification Clause**: Choose the clause that applies to your particular circumstances. This clause identifies whether or not any children will be involved in the terms of the agreement. Fill in the names and birthdates of any children. One of these clauses is mandatory. If the wife is currently pregnant and there are already children, use both appropriate clauses.

[   ]   There were no children born or adopted into our marriage, and none are expected.
[   ]   The wife is currently pregnant and the expected birthdate is:

[   ] The following child(ren) was (were) born (or adopted) into our marriage:
Child's name _____
Child's birthdate _____
Child's sex _____
Child's name _____
Child's birthdate _____
Child's sex _____

⑨ **Grounds for Divorce/Separation Clause**: Choose one of the following clauses that most closely fits the divorce grounds that you have chosen in your state and your particular circumstances. Refer to your state's listing in the Appendix to determine the grounds that you will use for your divorce. One of these clauses is mandatory for your agreement. (Texas and Louisiana residents: please check the Appendix for details of the language used as grounds in your respective states.)

[   ] As a result of disputes and serious differences, we sincerely believe that our marriage is irretrievably broken and that there is no possible chance for reconciliation.

[   ] As a result of disputes and serious differences, we sincerely believe that there are irreconcilable differences between us and that there is no possible chance for reconciliation.

[   ] As a result of disputes and serious differences, we sincerely believe that there is a complete incompatibility of temperament between us and that there is no possible chance for reconciliation.

[   ] As a result of disputes and serious differences, we have separated and are now living apart and intend to continue to remain permanently apart.

⑩ and ⑪ **Marital Settlement Agreement Taxation Clause**: The following clause may be used to define your various decisions regarding the tax consequences of your divorce. If you are living apart under the terms of your marital settlement agreement or under the terms of a separation decree, but your divorce is not final by the end of the year, you may choose to file: (1) a joint tax return with your spouse; (2) a separate return; or (3) you may be considered unmarried and file a "head of household" return. You may choose to file a joint income tax return with your spouse for the current tax year *only* if your divorce has not been made final before the end of the year. If your divorce is final by the end of the year, you must file either an individual return or a "head of household" return. In addition, if your divorce is finalized prior to the end of the current tax year, you may not claim your spouse as an exemption, even if you have provided all of the support for your spouse for the year. With this clause, you will decide who will receive any tax refund that may be due for the current year and who will pay any taxes due for the current year. For more information, please refer to the section earlier in this chapter regarding the tax consequences of divorce. Where ⑩ and ⑪ appear, fill in either "Wife" or "Husband."

[   ] We both agree that we will cooperate in the filing of any necessary tax returns. We also agree that any tax refunds for the current year will be the property of the P and that any taxes due for the current tax year will be paid by the ⑪ .

⑫ and ⑬ **Name Change Clause**: Most states have specific laws that allow a person to request that his or her former name be restored upon divorce. Although many of these laws are now written to make no reference to the sex of the person requesting this type of change, it is generally a wife who desires to use either her maiden name or her former name (if her former name was a previous married name). The restoration of this name may be accomplished by a simple request in the divorce papers and a provision in the divorce decree or judgment. It is useful to have your spouse's agreement to such a name change request. Such an agreement is contained in the following clause that is part of the marital settlement agreement in this book. For ⑫ , generally fill in "Wife" and for ⑬ indicate the desired name upon divorce.

[   ] We both agree that, in the event of divorce or dissolution of marriage, the ⑫ desires to and shall have the right to be known by the name of ⑬.

Additional Marital Settlement Agreement Clauses: There are various other marital settlement agreement issues that must be dealt with in order for your agreement to have the necessary legal force. These standard legal phrases are included in the basic marital settlement agreement form in this book. They are very important and should not be altered. They cover the following points:

- That you both want the terms of your marital settlement agreement to be the basis for your court order in the event of a divorce
- That you both have prepared complete and honest Financial Statements and they are attached to your agreement
- That you both know that you have the right to see your own lawyers and that you both understand your legal rights
- That you both will sign any necessary documents
- That you both intend that your agreement is the full statement of your rights and responsibilities
- That your agreement will be binding on any of your future representatives

⑭ **Number of pages**: After you have completed your entire marital settlement agreement, fill in the total number of pages of the agreement. Then the husband and wife should initial *each and every one* of the pages of the final copy of the agreement.

The following sections will explain how to complete the remaining portions of your marital settlement agreement:

⑮ to ⑱ Property division (see Chapter 3)

⑲ Alimony (see Chapter 4)

⑳ Child custody (include this page only if you have children [see Chapter 5])

㉑ Child support (include this page only if you have children [see Chapter 6])

㉒ **Additional page**: If you should need an additional page to include further information for any section of your Marital Settlement Agreement, you may use the form on the last page of this chapter as a template. Simply fill in the appropriate information and be certain to number the page accordingly and have each spouse initial the page where noted.

㉓ Fill in the name of the state that one or both of you currently reside in.

㉔ to ㊹ Completing and signing the form (see Chapter 7)

Sample Marital Settlement Agreement

This agreement is made on ① , between ② , the Wife, who lives at ③ , and ④ , the Husband, who lives at ⑤ . We were married on ⑥ , in ⑦ .

Child Identification: ⑧

Grounds for Separation: ⑨

We both desire to settle by agreement all of our marital affairs,
THEREFORE, in consideration of our mutual promises, and other good and valuable consideration, we agree as follows:

We both desire and agree to permanently live separate and apart from each other, as if we were single, according to the terms of this agreement. We each agree not to annoy, harass, or interfere with the other in any manner.

We both agree that we will cooperate in the filing of any necessary tax returns. We also agree that any tax refunds for the current year will be the property of the ⑩ and that any taxes due for the current tax year will be paid by the ⑪ .

We both agree that, in the event of divorce or dissolution of marriage, the ⑫ desires to and shall have the right to be known by the name of ⑬ .

Page 1 of ⑭ pages   Husband's initials _____   Wife's initials _____

Division of Property

To settle all issues relating to our property, we both agree that the following property shall be the sole and separate property of the Wife, and the Husband transfers and quit-claims any interest that he may have in this property to the Wife: ⑮

We also agree that the following property shall be the sole and separate property of the Husband, and the Wife transfers and quit-claims any interest that she may have in this property to the Husband: ⑯

Page 2 of ⑭ pages   Husband's initials _____   Wife's initials _____

Division of Bills

To settle all issues relating to our debts, we agree that the Wife shall pay and indemnify and hold the Husband harmless from the following debts: ⑰

We agree that the Husband shall pay and indemnify and hold the Wife harmless from the following debts: ⑱

We also agree not to incur any further debts or obligations for which the other may be liable.

Page 3 of ⑭ pages　　　　　　Husband's initials _____　　　　Wife's initials _____

Alimony

To settle any and all issues regarding alimony and maintenance, we both agree that: ⑲

Child Custody and Visitation

To settle all issues relating to our child custody and visitation, we both agree that: ⑳

Page ___ of ⑭ pages   Husband's initials _____   Wife's initials _____

Child Support

To settle all issues relating to child support, we both agree that: ㉑

Additional Terms

We further agree to the following additional terms: ㉒

Page ____ of ⑭ pages   Husband's initials _____   Wife's initials _____

Signature

We each understand that we have the right to representation by separate lawyers. We each fully understand our rights and we each consider the terms of this agreement to be fair and reasonable. Both of us agree to execute and deliver any documents, make any endorsements, and do any and all acts that may be necessary or convenient to carry out all of the terms of this agreement.

We agree that this document is intended to be the full and entire settlement and agreement between us regarding our marital rights and obligations and that this agreement should be interpreted and governed by the laws of the State of ㉓ .

We also agree that every provision of this agreement is expressly made binding upon the heirs, assigns, executors, administrators, successors in interest, and representatives of each of us.

We both desire that, in the event of our divorce or dissolution of marriage, this marital settlement agreement be approved and merged and incorporated into any subsequent decree or judgment for divorce or dissolution of marriage and that, by the terms of the judgment or decree, we both be ordered to comply with the terms of this agreement, but that this agreement shall survive.

We have prepared this agreement cooperatively and each of us has fully and honestly disclosed to the other the extent of our assets, income, and financial situation. We have each completed Financial Statements that are attached to this agreement and incorporated by reference.

Signed and dated: ㉔

㉕
Signature of Wife

㉖
Printed Name of Wife

㉗
Signature of Husband

㉘
Printed Name of Husband

㉙
Signature of Witness #1

㉚
Printed Name of Witness #1

㉛
Signature of Witness #2

㉜
Printed Name of Witness #2

Page ___ of ⑭ pages   Husband's initials _____   Wife's initials _____

Notary Acknowledgment

State of ㉝
County of ㉞

On the ㉟ , ㊱ and ㊲ , husband and wife, and ㊳ and ㊴ , their witnesses, personally came before me and, being duly sworn, did state that they are the persons described in the above document and that they signed the above document in my presence as a free and voluntary act for the purposes stated.

㊵
Signature of Notary Public
Notary Public, In and for the County of ㊶
State of ㊷
My commission expires: ㊸   Notary Seal ㊹

Page ___ of ⑭ pages   Husband's initials _____   Wife's initials _____

Chapter 3

Property Division

In the course of your attempts to reach a marital settlement agreement with your spouse, the division of your property
is one of most likely areas in which arguments may arise. As
the change to no-fault divorce has essentially removed the rel-
evance of marital misconduct from consideration, many spouses
are unable to vent their hostilities regarding the faults of their
spouse during the course of a modern divorce proceeding. Thus,
there may often be a tendency to attempt to bring anger and
animosity to bear on the other areas left to resolve in a marital
settlement. This, however, is not a productive manner in which
to approach the division of your and your spouse's property. As
much as is possible, you should attempt to keep the discussion
of the division of your property on an amicable level. The division
of your marital property may be the most important economic
event of your lives and should be dealt with in a mature and
business-like manner.

Prior to actually making the important decisions regarding the
division of your property, it is important to have before you a
complete inventory of all of your property. Even if you feel that
you have no property to divide, in order to make sure that your
marital settlement agreement covers all of your property, you
should fill out the following Property Questionnaire. It is very

> **☼ Toolkit Tip!**
>
> The division
> of property
> is one of the
> most difficult
> areas to reach
> a decision.
> Generally, the
> more property
> that a couple
> has accrued
> during their
> marriage, the
> more difficult
> it is to divide
> it in a man-
> ner that both
> spouses are
> happy with.

easy to overlook certain types of property. In order to try to list every possible type of property, this questionnaire is very comprehensive. Many of the listings may not apply to your particular situation. Fill in only those areas which apply. Each spouse should fully answer as many of the questions that he or she is able to. You should include on this questionnaire *everything* that you and your spouse own or owe money on. This is a big task but it is crucial in understanding and properly dividing your possessions and obligations in a fair manner.

After the questionnaire there is a discussion of property laws in the individual states and various other matters which are relevant to the division of your property. Next, there is a Property Division Worksheet on which you will list the property that each spouse will retain. Following this are optional property division clauses for selection and inclusion in your marital settlement agreement. Finally, at the end of this chapter there is a Financial Statement that details your and your spouse's employment, monthly income, expenses, assets, and liabilities. Both of you will need to prepare one of these forms for attachment to your completed marital settlement agreement.

✓ Toolkit Tip!

You should print out copies of the forms from this chapter and use them as worksheets to address property division issues.

Property Questionnaire

Real Estate

Family Home

Do you lease a home or apartment? _____
    If YES, how much time is left on the lease? _____
Do you own your own home? _____
    If YES, what is the address?

When was it purchased? _____
    Was this before or during the marriage? _____
Whose money was used for the down payment?

Whose name(s) is on the deed?

How much was the down payment? .... $ _____
What was the original purchase price? .... $ _____
What is the present market value? .... $ _____
How much is left unpaid on the mortgage? .... $ _____
What is the equity (market value minus mortgage balance)? .... $ _____
How much is the monthly mortgage payment? .... $ _____
How much are the taxes? .... $ _____
How much is the homeowner's insurance? .... $ _____
Have there been any major improvements made since its purchase? _____
    If YES, please describe when and what improvements were made:

What was the total cost? .... $ _____
Whose money was used?

List the actual legal description of the home here (taken directly off the deed or mortgage:

Other Real Estate

What is the address?

When was it purchased? _____
   Was this before or during the marriage? _____
Whose money was used for the down payment? _____
Whose name(s) is on the deed?

How much was the down payment? .... $ _____
What was the original purchase price? .... $ _____
What is the present market value? .... $ _____
How much is left unpaid on the mortgage? .... $ _____
What is the equity (market value minus mortgage balance)? .... $ _____
How much is the monthly mortgage payment? .... $ _____
How much are the taxes? .... $ _____
How much is the insurance? .... $ _____
Is there any rental income? .... $ _____
Have there been any major improvements made since its purchase? _____
   If YES, please describe when and what improvements were made:

What was the total cost? .... $ _____
Whose money was used?

List the actual legal description of the home here (taken directly off the deed or mortgage:

Other Real Estate

What is the address?

When was it purchased? _____

   Was this before or during the marriage? _____
Whose money was used for the down payment? _____
Whose name(s) is on the deed?

How much was the down payment? .... $ _____
What was the original purchase price? .... $ _____
What is the present market value? .... $ _____
How much is left unpaid on the mortgage? .... $ _____
What is the equity (market value minus mortgage balance)? .... $ _____
How much is the monthly mortgage payment? .... $ _____
How much are the taxes? .... $ _____
How much is the insurance? .... $ _____
Is there any rental income? .... $ _____
Have there been any major improvements made since its purchase? _____
   If YES, please describe when and what improvements were made:

What was the total cost? .... $ _____
Whose money was used?

List the actual legal description of the home here (taken directly off the deed or mortgage:

Personal Property

The term "owner" refers to the person in whose name the account, stock, bond, etc. is held. If jointly held, write "joint."

Bank Accounts

Savings Accounts
Bank: _____
Account number _____
Owner: _____
Amount .... $ _____

Bank: _____
Account number _____
Owner: _____
Amount .... $ _____

Checking Accounts
Bank: _____
Account number _____
Owner: _____
Amount .... $ _____

Bank: _____
Account number _____
Owner: _____
Amount .... $ _____

Certificates of Deposit
Bank: _____
Account number _____
Owner: _____
Amount .... $ _____

Bank: _____
Account number _____
Owner: _____
Amount .... $ _____

Money Market Accounts

Bank: _____
Account number _____
Owner: _____
Amount .... $ _____

Bank: _____
Account number _____
Owner: _____
Amount .... $ _____

Stocks

Company: _____
CUSIP number _____
Owner: _____
Number of shares: _____
Annual dividend .... $ _____
Value .... $ _____

Company: _____
CUSIP number _____
Owner: _____
Number of shares: _____
Annual dividend .... $ _____
Value .... $ _____

Company: _____
CUSIP number _____
Owner: _____
Number of shares: _____
Annual dividend .... $ _____
Value .... $ _____

Company: _____
CUSIP number _____
Owner: _____
Number of shares: _____
Annual dividend .... $ _____
Value .... $ _____

Bonds

Company: _____
CUSIP number _____
Owner: _____
Number of shares: _____
Annual interest .... $ _____
Value .... $ _____

Company: _____
CUSIP number _____
Owner: _____
Number of shares: _____
Annual interest .... $ _____
Value .... $ _____

Company: _____
CUSIP number _____
Owner: _____
Number of shares: _____
Annual interest .... $ _____
Value .... $ _____

Company: _____
CUSIP number _____
Owner: _____
Number of shares: _____
Annual interest .... $ _____
Value .... $ _____

Names and addresses of your and your spouse's stockbrokers:

Income Tax

Did you file a joint return for the last tax year? _____
Is there a tax or refund due? _____
How much state ☐ tax or ☐ refund? .... $ _____
How much federal ☐ tax or ☐ refund? .... $ _____
How much local ☐ tax or ☐ refund? .... $ _____

Other personal property

Car

Year: _____

Make and model: _____

Who has possession? ._____

Whose name is on title? _____

License plate number and state of registration: _____

Payment .... $ _____

Amount of car loan unpaid .... $ _____

Value .... $ _____

Car

Year: _____

Make and model: _____

Who has possession? _____

Whose name is on title? _____

License plate number and state of registration: _____

Payment .... $ _____

Amount of car loan unpaid .... $ _____

Value .... $ _____

Other vehicles (boats, campers, motorcycles, etc.)

Describe:

Who has possession? _____

Value .... $ _____

Describe:

Who has possession? _____

Value .... $ _____

Describe:

Who has possession? _____

Value .... $ _____

Music system
Describe:

Who has possession? _____
Value .... $ _____

Describe:

Who has possession? _____
Value .... $ _____

Jewelry
Describe:

Who has possession? _____
Value .... $ _____

Describe:

Who has possession? _____
Value .... $ _____

Describe:

Who has possession? _____
Value .... $ _____

Tools
Describe:

Who has possession? _____
Value .... $ _____

Describe:

Who has possession? _____
Value .... $ _____

Sporting Goods
Describe:

Who has possession? _____
Value .... $ _____

Describe:

Who has possession? _____

Value .... $ _____

Furniture
Describe:

Who has possession? _____

Value .... $ _____

Describe:

Who has possession? _____

Value .... $ _____

Describe:

Who has possession? _____

Value .... $ _____

Describe:

Who has possession? _____

Value .... $ _____

Appliances
Describe:

Who has possession? _____

Value .... $ _____

Describe:

Who has possession? _____

Value .... $ _____

Describe:

Who has possession? _____

Value .... $ _____

Other property
Describe:

Who has possession? _____
Value .... $ _____

Describe:

Who has possession? _____
Value .... $ _____

Describe:

Who has possession? _____
Value .... $ _____

Describe:

Who has possession? _____
Value .... $ _____

Describe:

Who has possession? _____
Value .... $ _____

Business Assets (Corporations, Partnerships, Proprietorships)

Description: _____
Location:

Who has ownership? _____
Value .... $ _____

Description: _____
Location:

Who has ownership? _____
Value .... $ _____

Description: _____
Location:

Who has ownership? _____
Value .... $ _____

Retirement/Pension/Profit-sharing/Stock Option Plans

IRA Accounts
Bank or broker: _____
Account number _____
Owner: _____
Amount .... $ _____

Bank or broker: _____
Account number _____
Owner: _____
Amount .... $ _____

Bank or broker: _____
Account number _____
Owner: _____
Amount .... $ _____

Retirement Funds
Company: _____
Account number _____
Whose fund? _____
Value .... $ _____

Company: _____
Account number _____
Whose fund? _____
Value .... $ _____

Profit-sharing Plan
Company: _____
Account number _____
Whose fund? _____
Value .... $ _____

Company: _____
Account number _____
Whose fund? _____
Value .... $ _____

Stock Option Plan
Company: _____
Account number _____
Whose fund? _____
Value .... $ _____

Company: _____
Account number _____
Whose fund? _____
Value .... $ _____

Pension Plan
Company: _____
Account number _____
Whose fund? _____
Value .... $ _____

Company: _____
Account number _____
Whose fund? _____
Value .... $ _____

Insurance

Life Insurance
Company: _____
On whose life: _____
Beneficiary: _____
Premium .... $ _____
Cash value .... $ _____

Company: _____
On whose life: _____
Beneficiary: _____
Premium .... $ _____
Cash value .... $ _____

(On children) Company: _____
On whose life: _____
Beneficiary: _____
Premium .... $ _____
Cash value .... $ _____

Medical Insurance
Company: _____
On whom: _____
Amount .... $ _____
Premium .... $ _____

Company: _____
On whom: _____
Amount .... $ _____
Premium .... $ _____

(On children) Company: _____
On whom: _____
Amount .... $ _____
Premium .... $ _____

Disability Insurance
Company: _____
On whom: _____
Amount .... $ _____
Premium .... $ _____

Company: _____
On whom: _____
Amount .... $ _____
Premium .... $ _____

Auto Insurance
Company: _____
Which car? _____
Amount .... $ _____
Premium .... $ _____

Company: _____
Which car? _____
Amount .... $ _____
Premium .... $ _____

Homeowner's Insurance

Company: _____

Property address:

Amount .... $ _____
Premium .... $ _____

Other Insurance

Company: _____
What purpose? _____
Amount .... $ _____
Premium .... $ _____

Company: _____
What purpose? _____
Amount .... $ _____
Premium .... $ _____

Separate Property

The term "separate property" generally refers to the property that each spouse held invidiually prior to the marriage and any property acquired individually by each spouse by gift or inheritance.

Was the amount of separate personal property that you or your spouse owned at the time of your marriage valued at over $1,000.00? _____
If YES, list all specific property owned prior to marriage that is still owned (note who owns each item and its value). List property here even if listed previously:
Describe:

Owner: _____
Value .... $ _____

Describe:

Owner: _____
Value .... $ _____

Describe:

Owner: _____
Value .... $ _____

Describe:

Owner: _____
Value .... $ _____

Describe:

Owner: _____
Value .... $ _____

Describe:

Owner: _____
Value .... $ _____

Was any of your property or your spouse's received by gift or inheritance? _____
If YES, list all specific property received by gift or inheritance that is still owned (note who owns each item and its value). List property here even if it is listed previously:
Describe:

Owner: _____
Value .... $ _____

Describe:

Owner: _____
Value .... $ _____

Describe:

Owner: _____
Value .... $ _____

Describe:

Owner: _____

Value .... $ _____

Describe:

Owner: _____

Value .... $ _____

Describe:

Owner: _____

Value .... $ _____

Describe:

Owner: _____

Value .... $ _____

Bills and Debts

Credit Cards

Name of company: _____

Reason for debt: _____

In whose name: _____

Monthly payment .... $ _____

Balance due .... $ _____

Name of company: _____

Reason for debt: _____

In whose name: _____

Monthly payment .... $ _____

Balance due .... $ _____

Name of company: _____

Reason for debt: _____

In whose name: _____

Monthly payment .... $ _____

Balance due .... $ _____

Name of company: _____
Reason for debt: _____
In whose name: _____
Monthly payment .... $ _____
Balance due .... $ _____

Name of company: _____
Reason for debt: _____
In whose name: _____
Monthly payment .... $ _____
Balance due .... $ _____

Name of company: _____
Reason for debt: _____
In whose name: _____
Monthly payment .... $ _____
Balance due .... $ _____

Name of company: _____
Reason for debt: _____
In whose name: _____
Monthly payment .... $ _____
Balance due .... $ _____

Other Debts

Name of company: _____
Reason for debt: _____
In whose name: _____
Monthly payment .... $ _____
Balance due .... $ _____

Name of company: _____
Reason for debt: _____
In whose name: _____
Monthly payment .... $ _____
Balance due .... $ _____

Name of company: _____
Reason for debt: _____
In whose name: _____
Monthly payment .... $ _____
Balance due .... $ _____

Name of company: _____
Reason for debt: _____
In whose name: _____
Monthly payment .... $ _____
Balance due .... $ _____

Name of company: _____
Reason for debt: _____
In whose name: _____
Monthly payment .... $ _____
Balance due .... $ _____

Name of company: _____
Reason for debt: _____
In whose name: _____
Monthly payment .... $ _____
Balance due .... $ _____

Name of company: _____
Reason for debt: _____
In whose name: _____
Monthly payment .... $ _____
Balance due .... $ _____

Name of company: _____
Reason for debt: _____
In whose name: _____
Monthly payment .... $ _____
Balance due .... $ _____

Name of company: _____
Reason for debt: _____
In whose name: _____
Monthly payment .... $ _____
Balance due .... $ _____

Name of company: _____
Reason for debt: _____
In whose name: _____
Monthly payment .... $ _____
Balance due .... $ _____

The Law of Marital Property Division

As noted earlier, there have been many recent changes in the way that the law deals with each spouse's property upon divorce. Under prior law in most states, the property generally belonged to the person whose name was on the title. This led in many instances to the wife being left with little or no property upon divorce, since it was usually the husband whose name was used to title property. Today, there are two general sets of rules that apply to the division of property upon divorce in the United States. There are 9 *community property* states which essentially view all of the property obtained during a marriage as being owned equally by the spouses. The community property states are: Arizona, California, Idaho, Louisiana, Nevada, New Mexico, Texas, Washington, and Wisconsin. *Note*: Alaska is considered an "equitable distribution state" but allows married couples to designate, by a written agreement, which of their property they wish to be considered "community property." All of the other states are known as *equitable distribution* states. In these states, upon divorce, a couple's property is subject to being divided on a more or less fair or "equitable" basis. The Appendix will explain which laws apply to your state and will also give some detail as to which property is subject to being shared with your spouse upon divorce.

Toolkit Tip!

The following are "community property" states are: Arizona, California, Idaho, Louisiana, Nevada, New Mexico, Texas, Washington, and Wisconsin. *Note*: Alaska allows married couples to designate, by a written agreement, which of their property they wish to be considered "community property."

Bear in mind that these methods of property distribution are what a judge will use if you and your spouse cannot come to an agreement regarding the division in your situation. However, these rules are only guidelines. You and your spouse may legally divide your property in any manner that you choose and can mutually agree on. The only qualification is that the division must be relatively fair. If the division of property by your marital settlement agreement appears inherently unfair to one of the spouses, the judge in most states has the authority and power to change the division upon your ultimate divorce.

What follows is a general discussion of the method by which property is divided in "community property" states and "equitable distribution" states. Check the Appendix to see which method of property division applies to your state and then read that section carefully. The property division rules provided here are general in nature and reflect the modern trends in property division law. However, specific legal rights to particular pieces of property may not always be clear. By following the general rules and applying a sense of fairness in your attempts to reach a settlement, you should be able to reach an equitable agreement. The laws relating to property and property division, however, can get extremely complicated. If either you or your spouse has a great deal of property, your property is owned in complex manners, or you are confused about your rights, it may be wise to seek professional assistance. A lawyer, accountant, or real estate broker may be able to provide enough information for you to understand your property and continue with preparing your own settlement agreement. If you are hesitant about losing any property or feel that you and your spouse cannot agree to a fair division, you should seek the aid of a competent attorney or mediator.

Community Property States

The law in "community property" states generally stems from French or Spanish civil law. Under this type of law, it was felt that all property that a couple obtained while they were married should be shared equally by the spouses. Marriage was viewed essentially as an equal business partnership. Property owned by spouses in these states is divided into two distinct classes: *separate property* and *community property*.

Separate Property
Separate property is generally described as consisting of three types of property:

- Property that each spouse owned individually prior to their marriage

- Property that each spouse acquired by individual gift, either before or during the marriage (gifts given to both spouses together or gifts given by one spouse to the other are generally considered community property)

- Property that each spouse acquired by inheritance (legally referred to as "by bequest, descent, or devise"), either before or during the marriage

⚲ Toolkit Tip!
If you and your spouse reside in a "community property" state, you will need to determine which of your property is "separate property" and which is "community property".

79

Each spouse's separate property is treated as his or her own sole property and is generally not subject to being divided upon divorce. Typically, community property states also provide that if a spouse's particular separate property is exchanged for another piece of property, the new property continues to be separate property. Similarly, in most cases, if separate property is sold and the proceeds are used to purchase different property, this new property is also considered separate property. In order for a piece of property to remain classified as "separate property" however, generally the property must actually be kept separate from any jointly-owned property. It must not be mixed at all with community property: for example, in a joint savings account or in a joint investment. Generally, you must be able to clearly trace the whereabouts of the separate property and show that it has remained separate in order to claim it as separate. In addition, interest or profits earned by separate property and any increases in value of the separate property during the marriage are also generally considered to be separate property. Some states, however, do not classify increase in value or exchanges as separate property. Check the Appendix for your state's specific rules.

Bills and obligations that either spouse incurred prior to their marriage are also considered separate property. The spouse who incurred the debt prior to getting married is solely liable for the payment of the unpaid balance. In addition, you may agree that any debts that either of you incur after your separation are to be considered separate. Be aware, however, that even though you may have a valid legal agreement with your spouse that you will each be responsible only for your own debts, such an agreement does not bind any third party. In other words, even if you have a settlement agreement, if your spouse runs up substantial debts prior to your actual divorce, you may still be liable for payment on these debts. You will, however, generally be able to sue your spouse for reimbursement under the terms of your settlement agreement.

As a rule, if you have a clear record or understanding with your spouse that certain property is your personal separate property, then that property is not to be included in your division of community property. List each of your individual pieces of separate property on the Property Division Worksheet that follows. That property is yours to keep regardless of the division of your community property. Be aware, however, that some commu-

> ### ☀ Toolkit Tip!
>
> In a "community property" state, you and your spouse's "separate property" is not generally subject to division upon divorce (in other words, you each get to keep your own separate property).

nity property states do allow a spouse's separate property to be subject to division by a judge under certain circumstances. If there is a very lopsided amount of separate property owned by one of the spouses and it is felt that an equal division of the community property is not at all fair to the other spouse, some states will allow a court to use a spouse's separate property to provide for a more equitable division. Remember, though, that you and your spouse can agree to divide your own property in any manner that you both agree is fair. Please check the Appendix to see how your state deals with this situation. If the Appendix does not contain enough specific information for you to classify a particular piece of property, you may have to consult an attorney for that determination.

Community Property
All marital property that is not separate property is referred to as "community property." This includes anything that either spouse earned or acquired at any time during the marriage that is not separate property. The property acquired during the marriage is considered community property regardless of whose name may be on the title to the property, and regardless of who actually paid for the property (unless it was paid for entirely with one spouse's separate property funds and remains separate). All of a couple's bills and obligations that were incurred during a marriage are also considered community property and are to be divided equally upon divorce. (A few states, however, consider educational loans for one spouse to be a separate debt and not to be shared by the other spouse upon divorce).

Unless there is an agreement otherwise, and unless separate property can be clearly shown, all property that the spouses own at the time of their divorce is generally presumed to be community property. If there is no separation or settlement agreement stating otherwise, this may include any property acquired even after the couple has separated.

Most "community property" states require an equal division of all community property or start with a presumption that an *equal* division is the fairest method, although even these states will allow some leeway from an exact 50/50 division depending on the facts of the case. The remaining "community property" states provide for an *equitable* division of the community property. In

> **💡Toolkit Tip!**
> In a "community property" state, you and your spouse's "community property" is subject to division upon divorce (in other words, you will each generally receive one-half of the total community property).

this situation, "equitable" is defined to mean fair and just. An exact equal division is not necessarily required. However, in practice, judges generally begin their distribution deliberations from a 50/50 division point, adjusting the balance as the particular circumstances of the case may dictate. To deviate from an equal division of the property, judges are commonly guided by a set of statutory guidelines or factors that are to be considered. A few states, however, have no statutory guidelines to follow. The guidelines available in "community property" states are, in most cases, similar to those available in "equitable distribution" states and are discussed later in this chapter under "Factors for Consideration in Property Division."

Finally, in California and a few other states, there is a class of property that is referred to as *quasi-community* property. It is simply property that the spouses may have acquired before they moved to the particular state that would have been "community" property if they had lived in the state when they acquired it. This type of property may generally be treated as "community" property.

Equitable Distribution States

There are 41 states that abide by what is known as an "equitable distribution" method of property division. This is a relatively new property law concept which is still evolving. It has distinct similarities to the "community property" system, and yet is different in many respects. There are several versions of this system of property law in effect in various states. Check the Appendix to determine which specific method is used in your state. In "equitable distribution" jurisdictions, certain marital property is subject to division by the judge upon divorce. Which property is subject to division varies somewhat from state to state but generally follows three basic patterns:

• The most common method of classifying property in "equitable distribution" states closely parallels the method used in "community property" states. Property is divided into two basic classes: *separate* or *non-marital* property and *marital* property. What constitutes property in each class is very similar to the definitions in "community property" states.

☼ Toolkit Tip!

If you do not live in a "community property" state, then your marital property is divided according to "equitable distribution" rules.

Separate or *non-marital* property typically consists of property that either spouse brought to the marriage, property acquired by individual gift, and property that was obtained by inheritance (legally known as "by bequest, descent, or devise"). Each spouse's separate non-marital property is treated as his or her own sole property and generally is not subject to being divided upon divorce. Typically, states that use this method of property division also provide that if a spouse's particular separate non-marital property is exchanged for another piece of property, the new property continues to be separate non-marital property. Similarly, in most cases, if separate non-marital property is sold and the proceeds are used to purchase different property, this new property is also considered separate non-marital property. In order for a piece of property to remain classified as "separate non-marital property," generally however, the property must actually be kept separate from any jointly-owned property. It must not be mixed at all with marital property: for example, in a joint savings account or in a joint investment. Generally, you must be able to clearly trace the whereabouts of the separate non-marital property and show that it has remained separate in order to claim that it should not be subject to division. In addition, interest or profits earned by separate non-marital property and any increases in value of the such property during the marriage are also generally considered to be separate non-marital property. Some states, however, do not classify increase in value or exchanges as separate non-marital property. Check the Appendix for your state's particular rules.

> **🔆Toolkit Tip!**
>
> If you live in an "equitable distribution" state, there are 3 different methods used to divide property in a divorce. Please check the Appendix for the rules in place in your particular state.

Similarly to community property states, *marital* property consists of all other property; essentially all property which the spouses acquired, either jointly or individually at any time during the marriage, regardless of whose name is on the title and who actually paid for the property (unless it was paid for entirely with one spouse's separate non-marital property funds and remains separate). All of a couple's bills and obligations that are incurred during a marriage are also generally considered marital property and are to be divided equally upon divorce. Unless there is an agreement otherwise, and unless separate non-marital property can be clearly shown, all property that the spouses own at the time of their divorce is generally presumed to be marital property. If there is no separation or settlement agreement stating otherwise, this may include any property acquired even after the couple has separated.

• The second method for distribution that is used in several states is to make *all* of a couple's property subject to division upon divorce. Regardless of whether it was obtained by gift or by inheritance or was brought into the marriage, and regardless of whose name is on the title or deed, the property may be apportioned to either spouse depending upon the decision of the judge. There is no differentiation between marital, non-marital, or separate property. The property is still divided on a basis that attempts to achieve a general fairness, but all of a couple's property is available for such distribution.

• The third method for distribution is basically a hybrid of the above two methods. In several states, specific property is exempted from distribution. For example, in some states, all property except gifts may be subject to division upon divorce. In other states, only inheritances may be exempted from division. In still other states, marital property may consist of all property owned by the spouses except that property brought to the marriage by either spouse and kept separate. The rules for these states are outlined in the Appendix.

> **⁀φ⁀ Toolkit Tip!**
>
> Bills and other debts are also divided according to the same rules that apply to property in a divorce.

You will need to carefully read the rules in the Appendix that apply to your state to determine which property is subject to division and distribution in your state. Keep in mind, however, that regardless of what your state law dictates, you and your spouse may divide your property in any manner that you can agree on. If you both feel that it is fair to share in a particular gift, or divide the proceeds of an inheritance, you may accomplish this by use of your marital settlement agreement. If it seems fair for one spouse to use his or her separate funds to purchase the other spouse's share of a particular piece of jointly-held property, this may also be accomplished. The state laws and guidelines are only a starting point for discussions and negotiations.

Bills and obligations that either spouse incurred prior to their marriage are also considered separate or non-marital property (except in the few states which make all property subject to division). The spouse who incurred the debt prior to getting married is solely liable for the payment of the unpaid balance. In addition, you may agree that any debts that either of you incur after your separation are to be considered separate non-marital debts. Be aware, however, that even though you may have a valid legal agreement with your spouse that you will each be responsible only for your own debts, such an agreement does not bind any third party. In other words, even if you have a settlement agreement, if your spouse runs up substantial debts prior to your actual divorce, you may still be liable for payment on these debts. You will, however, generally be able to sue your spouse for reimbursement under the terms of your settlement agreement.

In "equitable distribution" states, you will decide which property is you or your spouse's separate non-marital property and which is marital property. In those few states that allow any property to be subject to division, this step will not be necessary. Once you have determined which of your property is subject to being divided, you must then decide exactly how you will accomplish this task. As in many community property states, a 50/50 division of property is most often the starting point for property division decisions made by courts in equitable distribution jurisdictions. Please note, however, the individual differences in your state's property division laws as shown in the Appendix.

Factors for Consideration in Property Divisions

In most states, there is a list of factors provided in the statutes for the judge to use in making any property distribution decisions. These factors are present in both "community property" and "equitable distribution" states. Each state is free to allow its judges to consider what has been determined to be relevant factors in dividing the property.

> **�
-Toolkit Tip!**
> The factors relating to property division in your state will be noted in your state's Appendix listing.

Each factor carries no specific weight in the decisions to be made. In no state is a particular preference given to each factor. Rather, the list of factors is to be used as a guideline to balance the contributions of each spouse and to attempt to arrive at a fair division of the couple's property.

Recently, there have been some substantial changes in what factors are considered relevant in dividing a couple's property. Marital fault is no longer a factor for consideration in most states. Adultery, desertion, cruelty, and other marital faults have no bearing on property decisions in a majority of states. However, in many states (even those which do not consider marital fault) economic misconduct continues to be a factor. Economic misconduct is generally viewed as one spouse attempting to hide any property from the other spouse, dissipating joint assets, cleaning out joint bank accounts and keeping the money, running up major joint bills in anticipation of divorce, or other such vengeful acts.

It is wise to close all of your joint bank accounts and cancel all joint credit cards upon your separation. This, however, should be a joint decision. The obligations and proceeds of these joint accounts will then be dealt with in your settlement agreement. If you do not trust your spouse enough to discuss the closing of a joint account, or if you fear that your spouse may attempt to clean out your accounts, you will probably not be able to cooperate enough to reach a marital settlement agreement without the aid of a lawyer or mediator. Do not try to hide or conceal any of the assets that belong to both you and your spouse. If your divorce ends up contested and before a judge, you will be required to account for these assets. Such economic misconduct may influence your right to property and support.

> **Toolkit Tip!**
> You and your spouse should close all joint bank and credit accounts prior to your divorce. This should be done only by mutual agreement, when possible.

In order to attempt to equalize the treatment of homemakers and spouses who give primary care to a couple's children, the efforts of a spouse in caring for children and homemaking are now specifically being considered as a relevant factor in a majority of states. The career and economic sacrifice that one spouse has made to put the other through school is also increasingly being considered as a factor in property divisions.

The trend is for the consideration of any relevant factors that have accounted for the economic contributions to the marriage, whether such contributions are tangible (wages, salary, etc.) or intangible (homemaking, childcare, career sacrifices, etc.). The tax consequences of your property division may also be an important factor. Refer back to the discussion of taxes in Chapter 2.

Other relevant factors that may be considered in the division of property:

- The length of the marriage
- The contribution of each spouse to the acquisition of the

marital property, including the contribution of each spouse as homemaker
- The age and health of each spouse
- The value of each spouse's separate property
- Any increase or decrease in the value of the separate property of each spouse during the marriage
- Any depletion of a spouse's separate property for marital purposes
- The economic circumstances of each spouse at the time that the division of property is to become effective
- The amount of alimony that either spouse may be awarded
- The occupation and vocational skills of each spouse
- The income and liabilities of each spouse
- The employability of each spouse
- The opportunity of each spouse for further acquisition of capital assets and income
- The time necessary for either spouse to acquire sufficient education to enable him or her to find appropriate employment
- The present and potential earning capacity of each spouse
- The presence of any retirement benefits, including social security, civil service, military, and railroad retirement benefits
- Any childcare or child support burdens
- The standard of living of both spouses during the marriage
- The tax consequences of the property division
- How and by whom the property was acquired
- The economic needs of each spouse
- Any other relevant factors

> ## ☼Toolkit Tip!
> If your state listing in the Appendix does not provide specific factors for property division, you may use this listing as a general guide.

As you can see from the above list, the division of property is generally considered to be interrelated to any provisions for alimony and child support. As you work through your agreement with your spouse, realize that all of the provisions that you discuss relate to each other. For your agreement to be a success in eliminating discord from your divorce, it must be a careful balance of all factors and considerations. In short, it must be fair to both you and your spouse. How each of these factors should be taken into account is up to you and your spouse. What is important to understand is that these detailed factors for consideration were developed in an effort to somewhat quantify the process of property distribution for judges who knew little or nothing about a couple's actual circumstances. The factors are used as an outline for the presentation of evidence to courts in an effort to show that certain elements of a couple's life together should have a bearing on how their property is divided on divorce.

If the property settlement discussions can be kept on a rational and mature level, you and your spouse are in a far better position to determine how these factors should affect your agreement on the division of property. Please carefully read the factors listed in your state's Appendix. If your state does not have any statutory factors listed, the general factors listed above may be used.

Considerations Regarding Specific Property

Regardless of what type of property division system your state uses, certain properties require individual consideration. Specific types of property will be discussed below.

The Family Home

For most people, a home is, by far, their most important possession. Any attempt to divide a single home between two divorcing spouses will be difficult. Many different factors will influence your ultimate decision on how to account for your home.

The first thing you will need to know is the current market value of the home. You can determine this by the use of a professional real estate appraisal. If you have not owned the home for very long, local real estate brokers may be able to give you a good indication of its current market value. Once you know the market value, you must subtract how much is still owed on the mortgage or trust deed (including any amounts owed on second mortgages or home-equity loans) in order to determine the "equity" in the home. For example, if your home is appraised at $150,000.00 and your mortgage balance is $135,000.00, then the "equity" in your home is $15,000.00. It is the equity value of any property that you will be dividing with your spouse.

By using the above example, we can examine the various ways to deal with the division of a house. In general, there are two main methods by which to deal with a family home.

First, the simplest method of dealing with the division of the home is to sell it and divide the net proceeds. In the example above, a couple might sell the $150,000.00 home, pay off the mortgage, and have a gross profit of $15,000.00. Out of this would come any real estate commission, usually about seven percent or $3,500.00. This would leave a net profit of $11,500.00. Divided equally, each spouse would receive

$5,750.00 from the sale and division of their home. There may also be tax consequences to the sale of your home and any tax liabilities should be considered and shared in an equal manner. A marital settlement agreement clause defining the sale of property and the division of the proceeds is included later in this chapter.

Next, you may wish for one spouse to keep the home. If there are minor children who have lived in the home, serious consideration should be given to finding a method of division which will allow the spouse who retains physical custody of the children to remain in the family home. This is highly favored by most judges and is generally considered to be in the best interests of the children. In addition, it lessens the severe economic burdens that may be placed on the spouse with custody. Although it may seem one-sided for one spouse to have custody of the children and to have possession of the family home, in reality, in nearly every divorce situation involving children, it is the spouse without custody who fares better economically.

Whether there are children or not, you may decide that one of the spouses will retain possession of the house. To accomplish this, there are several standard methods. First, title to the home may be transferred to the spouse who wishes to retain possession. When there are children, this will normally be the spouse with physical custody. This transfer is generally made in a trade or exchange for something worth the one-half value of the equity of the home. Again, using the example above, if the equity of the home is $15,000.00, and the home is to be transferred to one spouse, the other spouse should receive a trade-off of cash or property worth $7,500.00. This trade can be accomplished in a number of ways. If there is sufficient cash or property available, it is a relatively simple matter.

Two other methods may be: (1) for the spouse retaining possession to take out a second mortgage and pay off the other spouse from the proceeds; and (2) for the spouse retaining possession to give the other spouse a note for payment of the one-half equity interest and either defer payment until the house is sold, make payments directly to the other spouse, or agree to pay off the note when the children are grown. Marital settlement agreement clauses relating to these rather complex methods are *not* included in this book. A real estate professional or an attorney should be consulted for assistance in structuring these particular deals. However, clauses regarding a trade-off or exchange of a property are provided later in this chapter.

Another less common method would be for both spouses to retain shared ownership of the home as tenants-in-common, with the spouse with custody of the children retaining possession. An agreement allowing possession until the children are grown and an agreement on when the home will be sold should be reached if this method is chosen. Because of the continuing joint ownership under this method, it is more likely to cause later problems and is therefore less favored and no settlement agreement clauses for use in this situation are included.

To transfer the ownership of the home to one spouse, a deed (usually a quit-claim deed) will be necessary. To transfer the title from joint marital ownership (usually referred to on the deed as "joint tenancy with right of survivorship" or "tenancy-by-the-entireties") to a third party upon a sale of the home will generally require a warranty deed. If there is to be a note taken back by one spouse (where one spouse agrees to pay the other for his or her share of the home), this should be secured by a Deed of Trust or Mortgage. Any deeds or mortgages must be recorded in the office of your county recorder. For assistance in transferring real estate, you may wish to use a real estate broker, title or escrow company, attorney, or bank. In Chapter 2, a general mandatory marital settlement agreement clause is included which obligates both you and your spouse to cooperate in signing any necessary documents to implement any of the provisions under the terms of your agreement. Various deeds and other real estate legal forms and instructions for use are contained in the Nova Publishing book *Real Estate Forms Simplified*, by Daniel Sitarz.

Retirement and Pension Plans

A majority of states now consider the value of benefits in retirement and pension plans that were accumulated during a marriage to specifically be subject to division by the court upon divorce. Realistically, if the benefits were earned during the course of the marriage, there is no reason why such benefits should not be considered as part of a spouse's income or assets that should be shared with the other spouse. The most difficult aspect of attempting to divide the value of a pension or retirement plan is actually determining what the current present value is. There are many different types of pension plans and each may have a slightly different method for determining what benefits are available and when they are due. Some common retirement arrangements are:

• Individual Retirement Accounts (IRAs or Roth IRAs)
• Self-Employed Person's IRAs (SEP-IRAs)
• HR-10 Retirement Plans (KEOGHs)
• IRS 401(K) Retirement Plans
• Tax Sheltered Annuities (TSAs)
• Employee Stock Option Plans (ESOPs)

In order to determine a plan's value for division, an estimate of the current value of benefits that accrued during your marriage is necessary. The assistance of the administrators of the plan will probably be necessary to determine how much money was contributed and when the contributions were made. You may also ask them to give you an estimate of the current value of the plan or tell you how much would be due if the plan was immediately terminated. For an actual detailed valuation, a professional actuary skilled in pensions, an accountant, CPA, or attorney may be necessary.

If you have not been married for very long, the value of the retirement plan may be very little and a rough estimate of its value may be used for purposes of division. If, however, you have been married for a considerable time and you or your spouse have substantial contributions to retirement funds or pension plans, you should get expert assistance in valuing these funds. For many older Americans, the value of pension or retirement funds may be the largest single asset that they own.

If you feel that the value of your share of your spouse's pension or retirement plan may be significant or you are unable to accurately value the benefits, you may wish to consult an attorney to be certain that you do not lose any rights to this benefit. If the value of the plan can be ascertained, division of the benefits can be accomplished by trade-off. Since a retirement plan is very difficult to divide without actually terminating it and cashing it in, the easiest method for division is for the spouse who owns it to retain the full interest in the plan. If there is a family home, the spouse retaining the home may trade his or her share of the pension plan for the other spouse's share of the home. If there are other assets available, these also may be used in a trade-off.

An example of a trade-off of retirement benefits would be as follows: Spouse A has benefits in a retirement plan that are valued at $5,000.00, and all of the benefits were earned while the couple was married. Spouse B has no retirement benefits. The only other property that the couple owns is a car worth $3,000.00 and which is fully paid off. They also have $2,000.00 in a joint bank account. The couple's joint marital property, thus, is valued at $10,000.00 ($5,000.00 retirement benefits + $3,000.00 car + $2,000.00 cash = $10,000.00). Using an equal 50/50 division, each spouse should get $5,000.00 worth of their marital assets on divorce. Spouse A may retain his or her entire interest in the retirement fund by trading off his or her interests in the bank account and car. Spouse A would then retain the entire retirement fund ($5,000.00) and Spouse B would keep the car and cash ($2,000.00 + $3,000.00 = $5,000.00).

Stock-option or Profit-sharing Plans

Like pension and retirement funds, these assets are a clear benefit accrued as a result of a spouse's employment. If you or your spouse were participants in such a plan during your marriage, the benefits that were earned during the marriage should be considered as property to be shared and divided. Again, the most difficult problem may be in determining the value of such benefits. With most of these type of plans, however, the value should be easier to ascertain than with pension plans. Check with the employer or administrator of the plan for assistance in determining the value of the benefits that accrued to the spouse during the time of the marriage. The value of any such plans should then be included in the total amount of marital property which is available for division.

Social Security Benefits

Social Security benefits are not community or marital property and are not subject to division by a court upon divorce. They are federal benefits and are not governed by state law. You will need to contact your local Social Security office to determine your rights to benefits after divorce. If you have been married for 10 years or more, you will have a right to Social Security benefits that accrued during your marriage even though you become divorced. You will also generally be eligible for Social Security survivor benefits if you and your spouse have been married for at least 10 years. If you are approaching being married for 10 years, be aware that divorce from your spouse before you reach the 10-year deadline may cost you significant Social Security benefits.

In addition, even though Social Security benefits are not subject to division in a divorce, the value of such benefits may be taken into account in any considerations regarding the amount of alimony or property to be allocated to a spouse.

Military and Federal Pensions and Benefits

Although military retirement pensions and federal civil service annuity benefits are also federally administered, they are subject, in most cases, to division upon divorce. Military *disability* pay is not, however, subject to division upon divorce. For military retirement benefits, there is a requirement that your marriage has lasted 10 years in order to share in the benefits which have accrued to your spouse. In addition, certain other benefits (such as PX and commissary rights) will be retained on divorce if your marriage lasted through 20 years of military service.

If you or your spouse are currently in military service, you will probably need to seek legal advice in order to obtain a divorce. Many states have specific legal requirements that must be met in order to obtain a divorce from a person on active military service. If you or your spouse are no longer in the service, but have military benefits that accrued while you were both married, you will need to determine the value of these benefits in much the same manner as outlined previously in the section on pension and retirement plans. You will need to contact the agency or service branch that administers the plan or benefits.

As with standard retirement benefits, an actual division of military and federal benefits will generally be difficult. A trade-off for something of equivalent value is typically the most effective method for dealing with such benefits.

Cars and Other Vehicles

The division of a car or other vehicle may be accomplished by selling the vehicle and dividing the proceeds, or by a trade-off of one spouse's share of the car's value. For the trade-off method, first determine the equity value of the car. This is determined by subtracting the amount owed on the car from its current market value. You can check with a car dealer or bank to find approximate values (Blue Book) of cars or trucks. The equity value should then be divided between the spouses. If you or your spouse desire to keep the car, a trade of something of a value equal to the other spouse's share must be made. Transfer of title and registration (license plates) should then be made to the spouse who will retain the vehicle.

Educational Degrees

Many states now consider the value of a professional educational degree that was earned during the marriage to be part of the marital or community property and subject to division. The rationale behind this is that, in many cases, the spouse who did not earn the degree has sacrificed important career or educational opportunities of his or her own in order to assist the other spouse in earning the degree. The intention of most couples in such a situation was that the spouse who earned the degree would then be in a better position to bring income into the family. Upon divorce and in order to equalize the potential earning power of the degree-holder with that of the spouse who made the sacrifices for the attainment of the other's degree, a value is placed on the degree and it is considered as property to be divided. If you feel that the value of a professional degree is an important factor in your particular situation, it may be prudent to seek professional assistance from either a qualified accountant or attorney.

Property Division Worksheet Instructions

With the various differences between state laws in mind, you must make certain decisions regarding the division of your property. You and your spouse should use the information that you previously filled in on the Property Questionnaire to examine your total property holdings. The first step in filling in your worksheet should be to list the property that you both agree is the *separate* property of each. For this worksheet, we will use the term "separate" to mean any property that you and your spouse agree is not to be subject to division, either because of your state's law on the matter or simply because of your agreement as such. Generally, this is property that either of you owned prior to your marriage and any property that either of you acquired by gift or inheritance. If you are unclear on this, refer to the specific discussion of your state's laws in the Appendix.

The next step will be to list, in the general areas provided, the type and value of all of your *marital* property. For the purpose of this worksheet, the term "marital" property will be used to refer to all property that you and your spouse agree should be subject to division. This should include all of your property that is not listed in the *separate* property section. Be aware that various states may refer to such property by differing terms, such as "community" property. At this same time, you should make a general listing of all of the bills that you and your spouse have accumulated. These, too, will need to be divided.

The next step will generally be the most difficult. You will need to divide all of the listed marital property and bills into two equal or equitable shares. Your jointly-owed bills will be used as an offset against any property. As a general rule, you should begin with an equal division of the marital property and bills. Most "community property" states require an equal division of property and many "equitable division" states also tend to use an equal division. An equal division is perhaps the easiest and most fair method of division to apply in most cases. Courts have found that the equal division method eliminates much of the confusion that may result from trying to value many of the intangible items that are relevant to the decision, such as the value of homemaking, childrearing, and career sacrifices. If an exact equal division is not possible, attempt to reach agreement on a division that is as close to equal as is reasonably possible. On a piece-by-piece basis, divide and list the property as being given to that spouse who wishes to retain it.

Certain pieces of property will not be easily subject to division. For those pieces, there are various ways to reach a fair settlement. If one spouse truly desires the property, other property or cash may be traded for that particular property in order to essentially equalize the division. If an agreement cannot be reached on a particular piece of property, the property can be sold and the proceeds simply divided in half. If a specific value cannot be readily attached to a particular piece of property, it is wise to have an independent appraisal made of the property.

Certain mediators have used a method of equal division to assure that each spouse is satisfied with the conclusion. Simply attempt to reach a division of property settlement in which either spouse would be satisfied with either share of the marital property. If you or your spouse would be content with either share of the divided property, you can be relatively assured that a generally fair division has been achieved.

Here is an example of a couple's property division: The couple had the following assets: Spouse A had cash from an inheritance of $3,000.00. Spouse B had a boat that he owned prior to the marriage worth $2,000.00. They bought a $5,000.00 car during the marriage (which is now worth $3,000.00) and still owe $1,000.00 on it. They have furniture worth $1,000.00, a $500.00 music system, and $2,500.00 in a joint checking account. Their joint bills (mostly credit card balances) amount to $1,000.00.

Spouse A's separate property would be the $3,000.00 inheritance funds. Spouse B's separate property would be the $2,000.00 boat. Their marital property would consist of the equity of $2,000.00 in the car, the furniture and music system worth $1,500.00, and the $2,500.00 cash in the bank for a subtotal of $6,000.00. From this would be subtracted the $1,000.00 in bills for a total of $5,000.00. Each would be entitled to about a $2,500.00 share of the total marital property.

Their agreement is that Spouse A would keep the car and music system for her share ($2,000.00 car equity + $500.00 stereo = $2,500.00). Spouse A would also be liable to pay off the remaining balance due on the car loan. Spouse B would keep the furniture and the cash in the bank and pay off the credit card bills ($1,000.00 furniture + $2,500.00 cash - $1,000.00 bills = $2,500.00). Any number of other agreements could have been reached to divide the property but the method is essentially the same in any instance.

The next method is to first determine what property you both have. First, take out the separate property that you will each keep and which will not be subject to your marital property division. Then determine the total value of all of your marital property that remains. Finally, agree on a method that apportions approximately one-half of the value of the remaining marital property and bills to each party.

If at this point you are not clear about what property you own or your rights to that property, or are unable to reach a fair agreement with your spouse regarding the division of your property, it may be wise to consider consulting a mediator or an attorney. Once you are clear on your position, you may still be able to proceed with preparing your own settlement agreement.

Property Division Worksheet

Separate Property

Name of Spouse #1: _____

Description: _____ Value $ _____

Description: _____ Value $ _____

Description: _____ Value $ _____

Description: _____ Value $ _____

Description: _____ Value $ _____

Description: _____ Value $ _____

Description: _____ Value $ _____

Description: _____ Value $ _____

Description: _____ Value $ _____

Description: _____ Value $ _____

Description: _____ Value $ _____

Total of Separate Property .... (Spouse #1) $ _____

Name of Spouse #2: _____

Description: _____ Value $ _____

Description: _____ Value $ _____

Description: _____ Value $ _____

Description: _____ Value $ _____

Description: _____ Value $ _____

Description: _____ Value $ _____

Description: _____ Value $ _____

Description: _____ Value $ _____

Description: _____ Value $ _____

Description: _____ Value $ _____

Description: _____ Value $ _____

Total of Separate Property .... (Spouse #2) $ _____

Marital Property of Both Spouses

Real estate: _____ Value $ _____

Auto: _____ Value $ _____

Furniture: _____ Value $ _____

Cash: _____ Value $ _____

Jewelry: _____ Value $ _____

Tools: _____ Value $ _____

Other: _____ Value $ _____

Stocks: _____ Value $ _____

Bonds: _____ Value $ _____

Total Amount of Marital Property ....(A) $ _____

Marital Bills and Obligations

Creditor: _____ Balance $ _____

Creditor: _____ Balance $ _____

Creditor: _____ Balance $ _____

Creditor: _____ Balance $ _____

Creditor: _____ Balance $ _____

Creditor: _____ Balance $ _____

Creditor: _____ Balance $ _____

Total Amount of Marital Bills ....(B) $ _____

Value of Marital Property to Be Divided

Total Amount of Marital Property .... (A) $ _____
Minus (-) Total Amount of Marital Bills ....(B) $ _____
Equals (=) *Total Value to be Divided* [A - B = C] .... (C) $ _____

Approximate Value to Each Spouse (One-half of C or C÷2) .... $ _____

Agreed Share of Marital Property and Bills for Each Spouse

Name of Spouse #1: _____

Description: _____ Value $ _____

Description: _____ Value $ _____

Description: _____ Value $ _____

Description: _____ Value $ _____

Description: _____ Value $ _____

Description: _____ Value $ _____

Description: _____ Value $ _____

Description: _____ Value $ _____

Description: _____ Value $ _____

Total Marital Property ....(Spouse #1) $ _____

Name of Spouse #2: _____

Description: _____   Value $ _____

Description: _____   Value $ _____

Description: _____   Value $ _____

Description: _____   Value $ _____

Description: _____   Value $ _____

Description: _____   Value $ _____

Description: _____   Value $ _____

Description: _____   Value $ _____

Description: _____   Value $ _____

Total Marital Property ....(Spouse #2) $ _____

Property and Bills Division Marital Settlement Agreement Clauses

⑮ and ⑯ **Division of Property Clauses**: Once you have reached an agreement on the division of your property and bills that you are both satisfied with, you are ready to fill in your settlement agreement clause relating to property.

Division of Property (Basic): The following two clauses are already included in the Marital Settlement Agreement. In these clauses, you are to specifically list the property that each of you will retain, both each spouse's separate property and his or her individual share of the marital property, as agreed to in your Property Division Worksheet. This clause provides that both of you have transferred the property mentioned and quit-claimed it to the other spouse. For each item of property, provide a complete description. For real estate, list the legal description as shown on the deed to the property. For other property, list the serial number, if available, or a clear description. If either of you has a pension plan or retirement plan, list that plan under the appropriate spouse's clause and describe it fully.

> *To settle all issues relating to our property, we agree that the following property shall be the sole and separate property of the Wife, and the Husband transfers and quit-claims any interest that he may have in this property to the Wife: (Here list Wife's property)*

> *We also agree that the following property shall be the sole and separate property of the Husband, and the Wife transfers and quit-claims any interest that she may have in this property to the Husband: (Here list Husband's property)*

Division of Property (by Sale): This clause should be used *only* if there is marital property that is to be sold and the proceeds of the sale are to be divided between you and your spouse. It may be used for the disposition of anything from items to be sold at a yard sale to the sale of your home. An exact description of the property to be sold should be included. If the property is real estate, the description should be the legal description as shown on the deed to the property. This clause provides for an equal division of the proceeds of the sale after any expenses of the sale are deducted. In the case of the sale of a home, this would allow for any appraisal expenses and real estate broker fees to be deducted from the proceeds of the sale before dividing the profits. This clause may be used in conjunction with the previous clause. *Note*: If used, this clause must be added to the Agreement, on a separate sheet. Please see instructions in Chapter 8.

[   ]   We agree that the following property will be sold as soon as possible and any

proceeds from the sale of this property, after the deduction of any expenses of the sale, will be divided equally between us: (Here list a description of the property to be sold)

⑭ Fill in the total number of pages of the agreement and each spouse initials the page space.

⑰ and ⑱ **Division of Bills Clauses**: These two clauses are also in the Marital Settlement Agreement. These clauses are used to specifically divide your bills. It provides that you will each individually assume and pay the bills listed after your name and not hold the other liable for the debts ("hold harmless and indemnify"). It also provides that neither of you will incur any more debts for which the other spouse would be liable. For each bill, list to whom the bill is owed and the amount to be paid.

> *We agree that the Wife shall pay and indemnify and hold the Husband harmless from the following debts: (Here list debts that Wife will pay. If none, state "None.")*

> *We agree that the Husband shall pay and indemnify and hold the Wife harmless from the following debts: (Here list debts that Husband will pay. If none, state "None.")*

⑭ Fill in the total number of pages of the agreement and each spouse initials the page.

Financial Statement Instructions

The following Financial Statement will be your record of the disclosures that you and your spouse have made to each other regarding your joint and individual economic situations. Each spouse will complete a separate Financial Statement that will detail each individual spouse's monthly income and expenses and his or her overall net worth (assets and liabilities). The information that you include on this form should be current and should be based upon your economic situation immediately *after* your settlement agreement takes effect. The monthly income that you list should be based on your current job and sources of income, but should not include any income derived from child support payments or alimony from your current spouse. The expenses that you include on this statement should be based on your estimated or actual expenses while you are living separate from your spouse. If you have physical custody of any children, any expenses related to their care should also be included. The assets and liabilities listed should be your separate and marital property and bills as you and your spouse have agreed to in your Marital Settlement Agreement. Fill in only those items that apply to your circumstances.

The Financial Statement of each of you will become a permanent part of your Marital Settlement Agreement and will also become a part of your final divorce papers. Both you and your spouse will need to prepare an individual copy of this statement. This Financial Statement is mandatory for you to fill out and is required, in some form, in most states. Some states have similar mandatory Financial Statement forms and you should use such forms. Check the Appendix. This form assures that both you and your spouse are fully aware of each other's economic circumstances and that you have made your decisions and agreements based on full knowledge of all of the facts relating to your property and income.

The method for preparation is as follows:

1. Make two photocopies of the entire blank Financial Statement.

2. Each spouse should then take a copy of the Financial Statement and fill in all of the items that apply to his or her personal situation. Use information that will apply on the day that you sign your Marital Settlement Agreement. In other words, describe your employment, ownership of property, and debts, as of the day that you and your spouse sign your agreement.

3. Each filled-in Financial Statement should then be typed neatly and double-spaced on one side of white 8 ½" x 11" paper. You should then make two photocopies of each of the completed, but unsigned, original Financial Statements. Note: If you are using the Forms-on-CD, you may complete your financial statements on your computer and print them out. (References to "originals" in this book refer to any *unsigned* documents, even if they are photocopies. "Copies" refer to photocopies of *signed* documents).

4. You and your spouse will then sign all three original copies of your own individual Financial Statement in front of a notary public and have the final Financial Statements notarized at the same time that you sign your final Marital Settlement Agreement as explained in Chapter 8.

Financial Statement of _____

Employment

Occupation: _____
Employed by: _____
Address of Employer:

Pay period: _____
Next pay day: _____
Rate of pay .... $ _____

Average Monthly Income

Gross monthly salary or wages .... $ _____
    Deductions from paycheck on monthly basis
        Social Security .... $ _____
        Income tax .... $ _____
        Insurance .... $ _____
        Credit Union .... $ _____
        Union dues .... $ _____
        Other deductions .... $ _____
        Total Deductions .... $ _____
Net monthly salary or wages (gross minus [-] total deductions) .... $ _____

Monthly income from other sources
    Commissions, bonuses, etc. .... $ _____
    Unemployment, welfare, etc. .... $ _____
    Dividends, interest, etc. .... $ _____
    Business income .... $ _____
    Rents, royalties .... $ _____
    Other monthly income .... $ _____
Net monthly income from other sources................................ $ _____

Total Average Monthly Income .... (A) $ _____

Average Monthly Expenses

Mortgage or rental payment .... $ _____
Property taxes .... $ _____
Homeowner's insurance .... $ _____
Electricity .... $ _____
Water, garbage, sewer .... $ _____
Cable television .... $ _____
Telephone .... $ _____
Fuel oil and natural gas .... $ _____
Cleaning and laundry .... $ _____
Repairs and maintenance .... $ _____
Pest control .... $ _____
Housewares .... $ _____
Food and grocery items .... $ _____
Meals outside home .... $ _____
Clothing .... $ _____
Medical, dental, prescriptions .... $ _____
Education .... $ _____
Childcare/babysitter .... $ _____
Entertainment .... $ _____
Gifts or donations .... $ _____
Vacation expenses .... $ _____
Public transportation .... $ _____
Automobile
    Gasoline and oil .... $ _____
    Repairs .... $ _____
    License .... $ _____
    Insurance .... $ _____
    Payments .... $ _____
Insurance
    Health .... $ _____
    Disability .... $ _____
    Life .... $ _____
    Other .... $ _____
Any other expenses (list)
    _____ $ _____
    _____ $ _____
    _____ $ _____
    _____ $ _____

Fixed debts on a monthly basis
    Creditor _____ Monthly payment $ _____
    Creditor _____ Monthly payment $ _____
    Creditor _____ Monthly payment $ _____

Creditor _____ Monthly payment $ _____
Creditor _____ Monthly payment $ _____
Creditor _____ Monthly payment $ _____
Creditor _____ Monthly payment $ _____

Any other debts
  Creditor _____ Monthly payment $ _____
  Creditor _____ Monthly payment $ _____
  Creditor _____ Monthly payment $ _____
  Creditor _____ Monthly payment $ _____
  Creditor _____ Monthly payment $ _____

Total Average Monthly Expenses .... (B) $ _____

Assets

Cash .... $ _____
Stocks .... $ _____
Bonds .... $ _____
Real estate .... $ _____
Automobiles .... $ _____
Contents of home or apartment .... $ _____
Jewelry .... $ _____
Any other assets (list)

_____ $ _____
_____ $ _____
_____ $ _____
_____ $ _____
_____ $ _____

Total Assets .... (C) $ _____

Liabilities

  Creditor _____ Total balance due $ _____
  Creditor _____ Total balance due $ _____
  Creditor _____ Total balance due $ _____
  Creditor _____ Total balance due $ _____
  Creditor _____ Total balance due $ _____
  Creditor _____ Total balance due $ _____
  Creditor _____ Total balance due $ _____

Total Liabilities .... (D) $ _____

Summary of Income and Expenses

Total Average Monthly Income .... (A) $ _____
Total Average Monthly Expenses .... (B) $ _____

Summary Of Assets And Liabilities

Total Assets .... (C) $ _____
Total Liabilities .... (D) $ _____

Signed and dated: _____ .

_____
Signature

_____
Printed Name

State of _____
County of _____

On this day, before me, the undersigned authority, in and for and residing in the above county and state, personally appeared _____ , who is personally known to me to be the same person whose name is subscribed to the foregoing document, and, being duly sworn, verified that the information contained in the foregoing document is true and correct on personal knowledge and acknowledged that said document was signed as a free and voluntary act.

Subscribed and sworn to before me on _____ .

_____
Signature of Notary Public
Notary Public, In and for the County of _____
State of _____
My commission expires: _____   Notary Seal

Chapter 4

Alimony, Maintenance, and Spousal Support

Alimony has been a subject of both fear and confusion for many people considering divorce. For some, there is an unfounded fear that they will be forced to make exorbitant alimony payments to their former spouse for the rest of their life. For others approaching divorce, there is a fear that they will be left stranded without any income, job skills, or support. For most people, confusion is the likely response to questions regarding alimony. The best way to approach a consideration of alimony is to try and forget all of your preconceived notions about it. The laws regarding alimony have changed drastically in the last few years and the common understandings regarding alimony no longer apply. The modern trends in the awarding of alimony will be discussed in this chapter.

ᦀ Toolkit Tip!

Alimony is not generally awarded unless the spouse in question requires support for a period in order to become self-sufficient.

Alimony Questionnaire Instructions

Before the general discussion of alimony, however, please complete the following Alimony Questionnaire regarding the desirability and need for alimony in your divorce situation. A copy should be filled out by each spouse. The comparison of the answers on the two forms will form the basis for the beginning of

☆ Toolkit Tip!

Use the following Alimony Questionnaire to pinpoint any facts that might indicate that alimony is an important issue in your specific situation.

your discussions regarding alimony. The responses to the questions should be openly and honestly discussed by both spouses during the conversations relating to alimony. The purpose of this questionnaire is to isolate and present the facts relating to your circumstances that are relevant to alimony. This will give both you and your spouse the information necessary to reach a rational decision on this difficult subject. Please note that all of the information that is listed on both the Property Questionnaire and the Financial Statement in the previous chapter is relevant to any discussion of alimony and may be necessary for filling in this alimony questionnaire. Please refer to those previous forms when necessary.

Alimony Questionnaire

Name of Spouse Filling out Form _____

How long have you been married? _____
Are you presently employed? _____
  If YES, where?

  For how long? _____
  What rate of pay? $ _____
  What education was necessary? _____
Prior to that what was your former job? _____
  Where?

  For how long? _____
  What rate of pay? $ _____
  What education was necessary? _____
Prior to that what was your former job? _____
  Where?

  For how long? _____
  What rate of pay? $ _____
  What education was necessary? _____
Prior to that what was your former job? _____
  Where?

  For how long? _____
  What rate of pay? $ _____
  What education was necessary? _____
If you are not now employed, when was your last job? _____
  Where?

  For how long? _____
  What rate of pay? $ _____
  What education was necessary? _____

Were you employed at the time of your marriage? _____
  If YES, where?

  For how long? _____
  What rate of pay? $ _____
  What education was necessary? _____
What was the level of education that you had attained at the time of your marriage?
_____
What level of education have you attained now? _____
What job skills, training, or experience did you have at the time of your marriage?

What job skills, training, or experience do you now have?

What is your usual occupation? _____
What will be your monthly income at the time of your separation?
                                                     $ _____
What will be your monthly expenses at the time of your separation?
                                                     $ _____
What will be the value of your property at the time of your separation?
                                                     $ _____
How long would it take you to achieve the education or skills necessary to be able to
  individually attain the standard of living that you enjoyed during your marriage?
_____
At any time during your marriage, did your spouse attend college or a special or profes-
  sional training course? _____
Did you sacrifice any career opportunities in order to allow your spouse to attend school
  or achieve success in his or her occupation? _____
Do you feel that you will be able to be self-sufficient after your divorce?

Do you anticipate any unusual expenses or circumstances in the near future which may
  affect your ability to become self-supporting?

Do you and your spouse have any type of written premarital agreement? _____
   If YES, what are the details that relate to alimony?

Do you feel that you deserve alimony? _____
   If YES, how much? $ _____
   Should it be paid in a lump-sum? _____
   Should it be paid in monthly payments? _____
     If YES, how long should the payments continue? _____

The Law of Alimony

The laws relating to alimony have undergone enormous changes in recent years. Most of these changes have been in response to the phenomenal changes in our society in the last few decades. Much of prior alimony law was based on the stereotypical subservient role of the wife in a marriage. This traditional role pattern has been irrevocably altered. As more women are seeking and finding employment outside of the home during a marriage, the role of alimony in a divorce has shifted. In the past, alimony was paid almost exclusively to the wife and was used, in many cases, to enable the wife to continue to live in the lifestyle to which she had become accustomed to during the marriage.

Alimony has evolved from this traditional pattern to a modern method that enables the spouse in the least secure economic position to become self-supporting. The right to alimony in a modern divorce setting is no longer the sole province of the wife. Both spouses are considered to be equally eligible to receive alimony under the laws in all states. Although it is still far more common for a husband to provide alimony to the wife, in some cases, husbands have been awarded alimony. In situations where the wife is the sole support of the family or the husband is incapable of self-support, the law ignores the gender of each spouse and awards alimony on the basis of need.

Alimony awards are not commonly awarded to either spouse, however. Such awards are only made in approximately 15 percent of all divorces. Thus, only in about one out of every seven divorces is alimony even considered necessary. Spousal support after marriage is definitely not common, and you should approach your discussion of alimony with this fact firmly in mind. In certain situations, however, alimony is an important and valuable right. The length of time during which alimony payments are typically paid after a divorce has also been decreasing in recent years. The average duration of alimony payments is now approximately two to five years. This is because the emphasis for economic support has been shifting away from providing periodic alimony payments toward awarding the non-working spouse a larger share of the marital assets. By providing a larger lump-sum share of marital assets as a form of alimony rather than periodic payments, the continued involvement between the spouses is terminated much sooner.

Misconduct by either spouse during the marriage is also no longer an important factor in alimony awards. It is the economic and not the moral aspects of divorce that have acheived prominence in the legal process. Although most states no longer consider marital fault relevant to the awarding of alimony, a few states continue to allow misconduct to play a role in alimony decisions. Please check the Appendix to determine how the laws of your state approach this aspect of alimony.

Alimony is not generally favored when the marriage has been of short duration. If you have not been married for at least two years, it is very unlikely that a court would award any alimony. Where there are no children and both spouses are healthy and have the ability to be self-sufficient, there is also far less chance that a court will order either spouse to provide alimony to the other. If the marriage has been of long duration (at least ten years), however, and one spouse is essentially without the ability to become self-sufficient in a reasonable length of time, alimony of long duration may be necessary to prevent injustice.

If one spouse has been a homemaker or has provided full-time childcare for the couple's children, there is a likelihood that he or she will have difficulty in making the transition from a position as a supported married person to that of a self-sufficient single person. The difficulty can stem from lack of formal education, lack of necessary job skills, the age of the spouse, and any number of other factors. In such situations, alimony is a necessary aspect of the divorce. Neither spouse should be forced to accept a dramatically lower standard of living upon divorce than he or she was accustomed to during the marriage. There is, however, generally no realistic way that one spouse's income can continue to support two households at the same level of comfort and in the same manner that was established during the marriage. The additional expenses of providing for the utilities, maintenance, and cost of two separate living spaces when spouses separate will automatically increase the total cost of living for the spouses.

Somewhat related to alimony is the problem of a divorced spouse obtaining health insurance protection. For those spouses who were formerly covered by the other spouse's employer-sponsored group health insurance, obtaining sufficient health insurance coverage at a reasonable rate may be a serious problem. This is particularly true if the spouse who will lose the coverage is not presently employed in a job that provides health insurance. In an effort to alleviate this problem, recent federal legislation now requires that employer-sponsored group health plans must offer the option to continue health insurance coverage at group rates for up to three years after divorce to divorced spouses of employees with coverage. If you are in this situation, contact the office of the insurance company that provides the group coverage for your spouse.

Generally, in modern divorce law, an award of alimony is made in an effort to allow a spouse the time and education or training to become self-supporting. However, for those spouses who have dedicated a large portion their lives to caring for their home and families, alimony will continue to provide important compensation and will allow them to lead a secure life after divorce.

Factors for Consideration

The approach that most courts have taken to making decisions about alimony has been to review a list of factors that are relevant to support of a spouse. Other than these lists of factors, there have generally been no set guidelines provided for use in determining the actual amount of alimony to award. This decision is difficult to quantify and must be made on a case-by-case basis. Whether alimony is required and if so, how much alimony is necessary and how long it should be provided, are decisions that you and your spouse will have to work out between yourselves.

The general factors that a court will consider are listed below. No set weight is given to any particular factor and how much importance each item should be afforded depends on the particular circumstances of your situation. The Appendix regarding your state contains a review of your state's particular law on alimony and should be referred to for guidance. Some states, however, do not provide any list of factors for consideration. In those states, you may use the general list below for a basis of discussion. Remember that these factors are only a general outline for a judge's deliberations and that any relevant factor may be considered. Recall also that you and your spouse may reach any decision regarding alimony that you both feel is fair and satisfactory to both of you. The general factors that a judge would use when considering an award of alimony are:

- The time necessary for a spouse to acquire sufficient education and training to enable the spouse to find appropriate employment
- Both spouse's future earning capacities
- The standard of living established during the marriage
- Whether the spouse seeking support is the custodian of a child
- Whether the spouse with child custody should be required to seek employment outside the home
- The duration of the marriage
- The financial ability of the spouse from whom alimony is sought to meet his or her needs while also meeting those of the spouse seeking alimony
- The financial resources of the spouse seeking alimony, including any marital (or community) property apportioned to the spouse and the spouse's ability to meet his or her own needs independently
- The comparative financial resources of the spouses, including their comparative earning abilities in the labor market
- The contribution of each spouse to the marriage, including services rendered in homemaking, childcare, education, and career-building of the other spouse
- The educational level of each spouse at the time of the marriage and at the time the alimony is requested

- The tax consequences of alimony payments to each spouse
- The age of both spouses
- The physical and emotional conditions of both spouses
- The usual occupation of the spouses during the marriage
- The vocational skills and employability of the spouse seeking alimony
- The probable duration of the need for alimony

Each of these factors that are relevant to your situation should be considered in arriving at a fair agreement regarding alimony. If you and your spouse cannot reach an agreement regarding alimony, you may need to seek legal assistance in order to protect your rights to sufficient future alimony. In cases where you decide that alimony is not necessary or in situations where you and your spouse are able to decide upon the amount and duration of the alimony payments, a lawyer is generally not needed.

If your marriage has been of long duration and one of you will be reasonably incapable of self-support in the future, it is recommended that you seek the assistance of a competent attorney. In such cases, alimony may be the most important economic factor in the divorce and may be the only method by which a spouse who is not self-sufficient will be able to achieve a secure life. In cases where alimony will be a major factor and will constitute the primary economic support for one spouse, many other factors (for example: cost-of-living adjustments and long-term tax consequences) become important. The advice of a lawyer is highly recommended in such situations.

Alimony Marital Settlement Agreement Clauses

⑲ **Clauses for Alimony**: One of the following clauses should be selected for inclusion in every marital settlement agreement. There are clauses for use if: (1) neither spouse is to receive alimony; (2) one spouse is to receive monthly alimony payments for a set period of time; or (3) one spouse is to receive a one-time lump-sum payment of alimony. Choose the clause that most closely fits your particular situation:

No Alimony to Either Spouse Clause: This clause should be used only if, after careful consideration, both you and your spouse agree that neither of you should be required to pay any alimony to the other. You are also agreeing that neither of you will remain as beneficiaries of any life insurance policies held by the other spouse. By using this clause, you will be giving up forever any rights that you may have to alimony. However, if this is what you have both decided is fair, then you should use this clause.

[   ]   We both agree to waive any rights or claims that we may have now or in the future to receive alimony, maintenance, or spousal support from the other. We both also agree that neither of us shall remain as the beneficiary on any insurance policy carried by the other. We both fully understand that we are forever giving up any rights that we may have to alimony, maintenance, or spousal support.

Alimony Payable in Monthly Payments Clause: This clause should be used if you and your spouse have agreed that one of you should receive alimony and one of you should pay alimony to the other in the form of periodic monthly payments. You will need to decide the amount of each payment, the day of the month that each payment will be due, and the date on which the payments should begin. You will also need to decide when the payments are to end. You may wish the payments to end upon remarriage, death, or on a particular date. Or you may decide that the alimony payments should end upon the first happening of any one of these events. In addition, in this clause you agree that your decisions may be modifiable by a court in the future. This allows for a court to alter the alimony arrangements if there is a change in circumstances that makes the agreement unfair in the future.

Finally, if using this clause, you will need to choose a method by which the payments should be made. Some states have enacted legislation that allows or requires any support payments to be made through the court or certain state agencies and then be passed on to the spouse who is to receive the payment. This indirect method of payment, although generally slower, has the benefit of allowing for immediate action to be taken if any payments are missed. There is a clear record of payment in the hands of the appropriate state authorities. In fact, some states automatically take direct action against any spouse who is late with a payment. That action may include garnishing wages, requiring a bond or deposit, or actually seizing a delinquent spouse's property. However, in virtually all states that allow this indirect method of payment, there are provisions that allow the spouses to opt out of the state requirement. In this clause, you and your spouse agree that the payments may be made directly to the spouse who is to receive them, but that the arrangement may be modifiable by a court at a later date. By making the clause subject to court modification, the spouse receiving the payments will retain the right to have the payments made through the court or state at a later date should any problems in late or delinquent payments arise.

In addition, this clause specifies that you and your spouse have agreed that one of you will remain as a beneficiary on a life insurance policy of the other. Retaining a position as beneficiary on the other's life insurance is generally a good idea if there are continuing support payments to be paid. The spouse who pays the alimony will be the spouse who maintains the insurance. The spouse who receives the alimony will be the spouse who is designated as beneficiary. In the event of the supporting spouse's death, this allows the spouse to whom the support is due to collect the benefits of any insurance and apply it to the continuing maintenance or child support obligations.

[   ]   We both agree that, as alimony and maintenance, the (Husband or Wife) shall pay to the other spouse, the sum of $ (amount of payment) per month, payable on the (date when due each month) day of each month. The first payment will be due on (date first payment due) and the payments shall continue until the first of the following occurrences: (Select two or more of the following phrases: [1] the date that either of us dies; [2] the date that the spouse receiving alimony remarries; or [3] any specific date that you both agree upon [for example: May 5, 2008].)

We both intend that the amount and the duration of the payments may be modified by a court in the future. We also both agree that these payments should be made directly to the spouse to whom they are due, but that this payment method may be modified by a court in the future and that, if appropriate and in the event of divorce or dissolution of marriage, the payments may be made through the appropriate court or state agency for payment to the spouse by such court or state agency.

The life of the (Husband or Wife) is currently insured by (name of insurance company) in the amount of $ (amount of coverage) and the (Husband or Wife) agrees to keep this policy in full force until the first of the following

117

occurrences: (Select two or more of the following phrases: [1] the date that either of us dies; [2] the date that the spouse receiving alimony remarries; or [3] any specific date that you both agree upon [for example: May 5, 2008]. Note: This date should correspond to the date in the first paragraph of this clause.) We agree that the [Husband or Wife] shall be designated as irrevocable sole beneficiary of this policy. The spouse obligated to provide such insurance will provide the other spouse with annual proof of such coverage.

Alimony Payable in a Lump-Sum Payment Clause: This clause should be used if you and your spouse agree that the fairest method of dealing with the payment of alimony is for one spouse to pay the other a one-time lump-sum payment. The funds may then be used by the spouse who receives the payment to obtain education, job skills, or training to become self-supporting. This lump-sum payment is separate from and in addition to any shift in funds or property under the terms of your property settlement. To be fair, this alimony lump-sum payment should be taken out of a spouse's share of separate and marital property after all of the couple's property has been equally or equitably divided. This method of spousal support has the benefit of lessening the future ties between you and your spouse and, thus, lessening the opportunities for problems to develop. It also has the benefit of not leaving one spouse subject to overdue payments from the other spouse. This method, however, is not workable if the spouse who is to pay the lump-sum payment does not currently have the assets by which to pay. In this clause, you are also agreeing that neither of you will remain as beneficiary of any life insurance policy held by the other spouse.

[   ]   We both agree that in full payment of any claims or rights to alimony, spousal support, or maintenance, the [Husband or Wife] shall pay to the other the sum of $ [amount of lump sum payment], which shall be paid on or before [date payment due]. We both also agree that neither of us shall remain as the beneficiary on any insurance policy carried by the other.

⑭ Fill in the total number of pages and each spouse initial the page.

Chapter 5

Child Custody and Visitation

Each year, over one million children experience the divorce of their parents. Too often, when children are part of a divorcing family, a devastating legal battle is waged over the right to retain custody. The emotional and psychological scars that children receive in these fierce custody wars are perhaps the most tragic results of divorce. Unfortunately, in too many instances, children become pawns in a destructive game of revenge and vindictiveness between their divorcing parents. If you and your spouse have children, the decisions that you will face regarding their custody and visitation will perhaps be the most difficult of the entire divorce process. But in many respects, they may also be the most important. Your children's future well-being will depend directly on your ability to come to a reasonable agreement with your spouse regarding custody and visitation. If you have children, you must understand that your divorce will not end the relationship between you and your spouse. You will both still continue to be parents, even though you will no longer be wife and husband. Because of the necessity for this ongoing relationship, it is very important to keep your settlement discussions regarding your children on a calm and peaceful level. In many cases there is a temptation to allow personal animosity toward your spouse to enter into the discussions regarding your children. If you personally no longer

⚡ **Warning!**

Do not attempt to use your children as bargaining chips in any of your divorce discussions. Judges do not look kindly on any such attempts.

wish to live with your spouse, you may feel that you don't want your children to live with him or her either. There may also be a tendency to attempt to vent your frustration at the prospect of divorce through a battle over custody. For your children's sake, you must make every effort to keep your discussions about custody on a reasonable and mature basis. Your children will have to live the rest of their lives with the results of you and your spouse's custody decisions.

Child Custody Questionnaire Instructions

☼Toolkit Tip!

Use the answers that each parent completes on the following Questionnaire to assist you both in ap-proaching the child custody issue with the same informa-tion clearly in mind.

On the next page is the Child Custody Questionnaire. Two copies should be made of this form, one for each spouse to complete. This form is designed to assist you in understanding what fac-tors are pertinent to your discussions regarding custody and visitation. Each of you should complete your questionnaire by honestly and completely answering the questions. Although the questions relate to one child, if you have more than one child please include answers on the form relating to each child. Many of the questions relate to which parent in general currently provides the primary care for the children. Your answers will be the basis for your custody discussions with your spouse and will allow both of you to focus on the relevant issues. After each of you have completed the questionnaire and read this section, you will then confer with your spouse and jointly complete a Custody and Visitation Worksheet that is explained later in this chapter.

Child Custody Questionnaire

Name of Spouse Filling out Form _____

What is your child's full name? _____

What is your child's birth date? _____

In what city and state was your child born?

Have there ever been any previous court proceedings regarding custody of your child? _____

   If YES, describe in full; indicating dates, city, state, name of court, and outcome:

Where does your child currently live?

   With whom? _____

   For how long? _____

What is your educational level? _____

   Your spouse's? _____

Do you or your spouse have any children by a previous marriage? _____

   If YES, list names, ages, and whereabouts:

Do you have any specific physical or emotional health problems? _____

   If YES, please describe:

   Your spouse?

Your child?

Does your child have any special medical needs? _____
   If YES, please describe:

   Is any special treatment required? _____
      If YES, please describe:

   Is any special medication needed? _____
      If YES, please describe:

Who is your child's doctor?

Who is your child's dentist?

Who takes the child to the doctor/dentist? _____
Does your child have any special educational needs? _____
   If YES, please describe:

What school or daycare does your child currently attend?

   For how long? _____
   Who is your child's teacher? _____
   Who takes your child to school or daycare? _____
   Who helps with homework? _____
   Who attends parent/teacher conferences? _____

Who prepares the child's meals? _____

  What is your child's favorite food? _____

  Who does the grocery shopping? _____

  Who does the dishes? _____

Do you read to your child? _____

  What is your child's favorite story? _____

Is your child involved in any sports activities? _____

  If YES, please describe:

  Who goes to the games? _____

  Who is the coach or teacher? _____

Is your child involved in any music, crafts, or art activities? _____

  If YES, please describe:

  Who takes your child or participates? _____

  Who is the teacher? _____

What is your religious affiliation? _____

  Your spouse's? _____

  Your child's? _____

  Does your child attend church? _____

When was the last time that you or your spouse took your child to the following?
(Indicate when, and which parent[s]):

    Library _____

    Museum _____

    Zoo _____

    Movie _____

    Ballgame _____

    Playground _____

    Your work _____

    Bike ride/hike _____

For the following questions, please answer and explain in detail in your own words regarding both you and your spouse:

Which of you is more likely to allow the child frequent and continuing contact with the other parent?
You:

Your spouse:

Describe the love, affection, and other emotional ties which exist between each of you and your child:
You:

Your spouse:

Describe the ability of each of you to provide for your child's basic needs (food, clothing, shelter, medical care):
You:

Your spouse:

How long has your child lived with you in a stable environment?
You:

Your spouse:

In your opinion, in which home will your child receive better ethical, moral, and spiritual guidance?
You:

Your spouse:

In your opinion, in which home will your child find the most love and affection?
You:

Your spouse:

In your opinion, in which home will your child have the most educational enrichment and opportunities?
You:

Your spouse:

In your opinion, in which home is the child most familiar with the schools, neighborhood, and community?
You:

Your spouse:

Describe each of your efforts at the discipline of your child:
You:

Your spouse:

Has there ever been any evidence of spouse or child abuse?
You:

Your spouse:

Describe the physical, mental, and moral fitness of both you and your spouse:
  You:

  Your spouse:

If your child is of sufficient intelligence and understanding to form an opinion, do you feel that your child has a preference regarding who should retain custody?
  You:

  Your spouse:

Which of you has been the parent who has provided the primary day-to-day care for the child?
  You:

  Your spouse:

Do you feel that you should have custody of your child? _____
  If YES, please describe:

Do you feel that you and your spouse would be able to effectively and peacefully share in making the major decisions regarding your child in the future? (For example: which school to attend, which doctor to visit, etc.)

What visitation should be allowed to the parent who does not have physical custody of your child?
(Include times and dates):
Contact during the week?

Contact on weekends?

Contact on school holidays?

Which holidays?

Contact on winter vacation?

Contact on spring vacation?

Contact on summer vacation?

The Law of Child Custody and Visitation

⋅�miⵀ⋅ Toolkit Tip!

Determing child custory can often be a very difficult part of the divorce process. You should approach such discussions calmly and with an open mind. Remember that if you and your spouse are unable to reach a decision, the decision will be made by a judge who is unfamiliar with your child or children.

Determining which parent is to have custody of a minor child is one of the most difficult decisions that you will encounter in your divorce. Judges and legislators have also grappled extensively with the difficulty of this decision. In recent years, certain legal trends have emerged regarding how an impartial judge might decide which parent is to be awarded custody of a minor child. These relatively new legal doctrines are a clear break with many of the traditional methods that were previously used to determine custody. In the past, there were several legal doctrines that governed child custody decisions. Most notably, there was a very strong presumption that a mother should be awarded custody of any child. This presumption stemmed directly from the traditional, though not universal, role of the mother as homemaker in our society at that time. The younger the child was, the stronger the presumption that custody should be given to the mother. This doctrine was known as the "tender years doctrine" and carried very considerable weight in legal custody decisions. If the child in question was a girl, the presumption that custody be awarded to the mother was almost insurmountable. Effectively, the only method by which a father could get custody of a minor child was to prove in open court that the mother was totally unfit to care for the child. This required, in most instances, that the father and his attorney attempt to paint as negative a picture as possible of the mother for the court. Innocent past actions and harmless present circumstances were often distorted and misrepresented to the court in attempts to have a mother declared unfit. This type of custody battle provided a forum for some of the most psychologically and emotionally damaging court proceedings in our society's history. The traumatic effects on the children involved in these proceedings were particularly tragic.

In an attempt to overcome the type of proceeding that encouraged the dredging up of irrelevant details of each parent's private life, a doctrine known as the "best interests of the child" was developed. Under this legal theory, the mental, physical, and emotional well-being of the child was considered paramount in any legal proceeding regarding custody. Theoretically, a parent's actions were pertinent only to the extent that they had an impact on the child. In practice, however, much irrelevant testimony and evidence were still allowed in custody battles. Detailed lists of factors were also developed to guide a court in determining what was actually important in making decisions regarding the custody of a child. Most states continue to provide these guidelines for custody decisions and these factors for consideration are discussed later in this chapter.

In the 1970s, extensive legal battles were waged in attempts to overturn the "tender years" doctrine and allow fathers an equal footing in custody disputes. For the most part, the battles were successful. Fathers do have an equal legal ability now to obtain custody of any minor children. However, despite the changes in the law that provide that both parents have an equal right to custody, mothers are still overwhelmingly the parent who retains custody. In over 90 percent of all custody cases, it is the mother who is awarded custody of the children. There is also an unhappy consequence of the legal changes that make it easier for fathers to request custody. Some fathers and their attorneys have unscrupulously used this right as a weapon to pressure the mother into trading her property, alimony, or child support rights for uncontested custody of a child. Fathers who have no desire at all to actually have custody have used this manipulative tactic to prey upon the maternal fear of losing a child. In order to be certain that they do not lose custody of their child, many mothers have given up their rights to substantial property and support. Any attempts to engage in this tactic are highly disfavored by courts. If you feel that this tactic is being used in your situation, you should immediately consult an attorney for legal guidance.

> **♀ Toolkit Tip!**
>
> The former legal doctrine that highly favored mothers in custody battles has been overturned. However, mothers still obtain custody in the vast majority of cases.

Another legal doctrine has emerged recently however, that allows both parents much greater flexibility in sharing parental responsibility. Joint or shared custody has been developed in an effort to allow a child reasonable access to both parents while growing up. Some confusion has resulted from the use of this phrase and it is important to understand exactly what joint custody is and is not. Some definitions are offered here in an attempt to clear up this confusion. Unfortunately, some people (lawyers and judges included) will use some of these terms interchangeably or incorrectly. Be certain in your discussions regarding custody that you both agree on exactly what you are taking about.

Types of Custody Arrangements

✎ Definition:

Sole Custody:
One parent
has both
the physical
custody of the
child and the
right to make
all major deci-
sions relating
to the child's
upbringing.

In the past, *sole custody* by one parent was the standard form of custody. Under sole custody, one parent was awarded both the *physical* custody of the child (the right to have the child live with the custodial parent) and the *legal* custody (the right to make all of the major decisions relating to the upbringing of the child). Decisions regarding which school the child should attend, whether the child should have medical attention, what religion the child should be taught, and all decisions regarding the child's activities, conduct, and well-being are the responsibility of the parent with sole custody. In most sole custody arrangements, the non-custodial parent is afforded some type of reasonable visitation rights unless there is a danger of harm to the child. This form of custody arrangement, with sole custody to one parent and liberal visitation for the other parent, is still the predominant method used in the majority of divorce situations involving children.

✎ Definition:

**Joint or
Shared
Custody:** Both
parents are
given some
rights to
share in both
the physical
custody and
major deci-
sion-making
for the child.

Joint or *shared custody*, on the other hand, is an attempt to allow both parents a voice in the major decisions involved in the raising of a child. Joint custody is generally divided into two separate rights: joint *physical* custody (actual custody of the child), and joint *legal* custody (rights to share in important decisions regarding the child). While both parents may be awarded joint physical custody of a child, generally one parent is still awarded sole physical custody of the child, with the other parent being allowed reasonable visitation privileges. However, both parents are awarded joint legal custody of the child. This rather confusing terminology simply means that both parents will continue to share the rights and responsibilities that come with parenthood. They will both have a right to jointly make the major decisions that will affect the child's life: religious, educational, medical, and social decisions. Naturally, the parent with actual physical custody for the majority of the time is allowed individual control over the minor day-to-day decisions that must be made. In many joint custody situations, the actual physical custody time a child spends with each parent mirrors sole custody situations. It is the decision-making process affecting the child that is the responsibility shared by the parents.

Divided or *alternating custody* is another form of custody (in some areas this is referred to as *split custody*; in others, as *joint physical custody*). Under this form of custody, each parent is awarded actual physical and legal custody for alternating periods of time. A child may be awarded to each parent for six months out of a year, or for alternating months or weeks. This type of custody arrangement is not generally favored by either the courts or child psychologists. It is seen as emotionally difficult for a child to be continually shifted back and forth between each parent, without a sense of where his or her "home" is truly located. In some situations, however, it may be appropriate.

Another alternative that has also proved to be difficult for the children involved is also known as *split custody*. This type of custody has been used in the past to attempt to achieve a technical fairness when there is more than one child by giving each parent physical custody of one or more of the children. For the children involved, however, this constitutes not only a splitting up of one's parents, but also a forced separation from one's siblings. Arrangements of this type are not favored by courts.

Currently, there seems to be a general national trend towards approval of joint custody arrangements. The encouragement of frequent and continuing contact with both parents is clearly preferable to fostering single-parent childhoods for children of divorce. These types of arrangements work well and are a benefit to the child, however, only if both parents can cooperate maturely in the necessary decision-making. For joint custody to be successful, both parents must be willing to compromise for the sake of the child and to consider the well-being of the child as the most important factor. In situations where there is genuine hostility between the parents, however, one parent should generally be granted sole physical and legal custody. This is often the clearest and most definite method to establish which parent has the necessary authority to make the major decisions. Some states have established a legal preference for joint custody, while others clearly state that there is no preference for one particular type of custody. Most states specifically allow for joint custody, while others have no particular statutory authorization for any type of shared custody. In all states, however, there is legal precedent to allow custody arrangements that are most beneficial to the children involved.

⊘ Definition:

Divided or Alternating Custody:

Each parent is awarded custody of the child for alternating periods of time. This type of custody is not generally favored by courts.

⊘ Definition:

Split Custody:

Dividing the custody of multiple children between the parents. This type of arrangement is not favored by courts.

The most recent trend in custody legislation and court decisions provides one of the most common-sense approaches to the problem. Increasingly, courts are looking at a child's day-to-day circumstances in an effort to determine which parent has been the primary caregiver of the child. The parent who has provided most of the day-to-day care for the child during the marriage is then considered to be the most likely candidate to continue on as the primary custodian of the child after the divorce. The preference is given to the parent who has actively participated in caring for the child and performed the majority of the parenting activities: preparing meals, readying the child for sleep, sharing in his or her playtime, dealing with medical problems, participating in the child's education, etc. This method does not presuppose that either parent has an entitlement to being awarded custody, but rather is based on an examination of the reality of the burdens of parenthood. The decision is based on the practical considerations of which parent has provided the most time, care, and guidance to the child prior to the actual divorce. It allows each parent an equal right to earn the custody of a child by providing care for the child before the divorce proceeding begins. This method of selection of the parent to have physical custody places the greatest emphasis on which one has been providing the most parental care for the child prior to the divorce. Selection of the primary caregiver as continuing custodian generally fosters a home life of stability and continuity for the child. In the family upheaval caused by divorce, this factor deserves considerable attention.

> **♀ Toolkit Tip!**
>
> In making child custody decisions, courts are increasingly examining which parent provided the primary care for the child.

Visitation

In any custody arrangement, and in all states, the parent who is not awarded actual physical custody of a child has a legal right to reasonable and frequent visitation with the child. Unless there is a genuine and substantiated fear of emotional or physical harm to the child, such visitation is generally allowed on an unsupervised basis and in the non-custodial parent's home. A court does have the authority to completely deny any visitation to a parent who has abused a child. In most cases, however, reasonable visitation is standard. When, where, and how long such visitation should be is one of the major decisions that you and your spouse will have to work out as you discuss your children's future. Visitation should be structured to allow frequent contact between the non-custodial parent and the child and should attempt to fit into the child's normal schedule. The schedule should be firm enough to allow for a degree of long-term planning, but flexible enough to allow for reasonable changes. Remember that any visitation schedule is only a starting point. Reasonable adjustments can be made as you and your spouse become more comfortable in your roles as divorced parents. Visitation is as much the child's right as it is the parents'. As you approach the decisions on visitation, you should remember certain points. You should keep in mind that:

> **·V· Toolkit Tip!**
>
> Unless it can be shown that a child may be in danger during visitation, each parent has a legal right to obtain visitation rights.

- Visitation with the other parent is necessary and helpful for your child's normal development and future welfare
- Visitation should be a pleasant and positive experience for both the parents and the child
- Visitation is a time for the parent and child to be with each other and enjoy each other's company and should be maintained on a clear schedule and without interference
- Visitation exchanges may be the only time that you see your spouse after the divorce. Both of you should show mutual respect for the other while in the child's presence

As you and your spouse discuss specific visitation terms, you should make every effort to insure that both of you are treated fairly regarding visitation. As you discuss the amount of visitation, put yourself in the other's place. Imagine that your only contact with your child will be the visitation that is agreed upon. You would want it to be as liberal and as frequent as possible. An agreement that is fair and reasonable for both parents will generally be the best for your child.

Modification of Custody and Visitation Terms

Finally, in all states, any custody and visitation agreements that are reached between parents remain subject to court modification. Of all the terms of your Marital Settlement Agreement, the terms that relate to the care and custody of your children will receive the closest scrutiny by a court. The court has total authority in this area and has the power to totally disregard any

⊘ **Definition:**

Guardian Ad Litem:
A court-appointed legal guardian of a child's rights in any legal proceeding.

agreement that is felt to be harmful to the children. In fact, in many states the court has the authority to appoint a lawyer who will represent the interests of the child in a contested custody situation. This court-appointed legal guardian of a child's legal rights is generally referred to as a *guardian ad litem*. In the vast majority of cases, however, a court will accept reasonable custody and visitation provisions contained in marital settlement agreements, particularly if it appears that such agreements were obtained through thoughtful and mature negotiation. Most judges, however, are conservative when it comes to the rights of children and will not favor any unusual custody arrangements that fall outside of the traditional boundaries. Recognize also that although the court that handles your divorce will have the right to modify your custody agreement at any time in the future, it is much more difficult to have such modifications made after your divorce is finalized. For the sake of promoting a sense of stability in a child's life, courts are somewhat reluctant to make changes in settled custody arrangements. For this reason, you and your spouse should work diligently to attempt to initially fashion a fair agreement for custody and visitation. As you examine your own lives and consider the realities of custody and visitation, keep these legal trends in mind. They are what guide most courts in their deliberations of custody disputes. Decisions on custody and visitation, however, are best made by both parents in a cooperative manner without the involvement of courts and lawyers. Cooperating parents can adopt any practical arrangement that provides a reasonable resolution to the difficult problems of dividing a child's time between two parents who no longer desire to live together.

Both parents deserve an opportunity to interact with their child during childhood. More importantly, your child deserves to have both of you available for love, affection, and guidance as he or she grows up. You should make every possible attempt to work out a reasonable child custody arrangement that is satisfactory to both of you and your child. However, if you and your spouse are unable to reach an agreement, the use of an impartial mediator may be useful. In child custody disputes, mediation is the preferred first alternative for providing a solution. If personal negotiation and mediation both fail to help you achieve an agreement, a resort to the legal process may be necessary. However, keep in mind the tremendous psychological and emotional toll that a bitter court battle over custody can have on both you and your child. If your spouse hires a lawyer to engage in a custody battle, you should, however, seek legal assistance immediately.

Factors for Consideration

In most states, judges are provided with a specific list of items that have been determined to be relevant to custody decisions. The factors are provided only as guidelines and there are generally no mandatory requirements that each factor be considered. These factors are used as a framework by which to approach the complex set of circumstances that influence the decision of which parent should be awarded custody of a child. The wishes of the parents and of the child are almost universally considered to be relevant, particularly if the child is old enough to have a mature and intelligent choice. Marital misconduct is not considered at all in many states to be relevant, unless the misconduct has a direct bearing on the parent's relationship with the child. The tax aspects of child custody and visitation may be an important factor in your particular situation. The following is a list of the most important factors that are in use in courts throughout the United States:

🔆Toolkit Tip!

The factors relating to child custody in your state will be noted in your state's Appendix listing.

- The age and sex of the child
- The physical, emotional, mental, religious, and social needs of the child
- Which parent provides the primary care for the child
- The capability and desire of each parent to meet the child's needs
- The preference of the child, if the child is of sufficient age and capacity to form a meaningful opinion
- The love and affection existing between the child and each parent
- The length of time the child has lived in a stable and satisfactory environment and the desirability of maintaining continuity
- The desire and ability of each parent to allow an open, loving, and frequent relationship between the child and the other parent
- The wishes of the parents
- The child's adjustment to his/her home, school, and community
- The mental and physical health of all individuals involved

⚬Toolkit Tip!

If your state listing in the Appendix does not provide specific factors for child custody decisions, you may use this listing as a general guide.

- The relationship of the child with parents, siblings, and other significant family members
- The material needs of the child
- The stability of the home environment likely to be offered by each parent
- The education of the child
- The advantages of keeping the child in the community where the child resides
- The optional time for the child to spend with each parent
- Any findings or recommendations of a neutral mediator
- A history of violence between the parents or of child abuse
- A need to promote continuity and stability in the life of the child

In addition, there are other factors that a court will take into consideration when joint or shared custody is an issue. These factors relate to the ability of the parents to cooperate and to the practical aspects of allowing joint custody and are as follows:

- The ability of the parents to cooperate and make decisions jointly
- The ability of the parents to encourage the sharing of love, affection, and contact between the child and the other parent
- Whether the past pattern of involvement of the parents with the child reflects a system of values and mutual support that indicates the parents' ability as joint custodians to provide a positive and nourishing relationship with the child
- The physical proximity of the parents to each other as this relates to the practical considerations of where the child will reside
- Whether an award of joint custody will promote more frequent or continuing contact between the child and each of the parents
- The permanence as a family unit, of the existing or proposed custodial home
- The nature of the physical and emotional environment in the home of each of the persons awarded joint custody
- The willingness and ability of the persons awarded joint custody to communicate and cooperate in advancing the child's welfare
- Whether the child has established a close and beneficial relationship with both of the persons awarded joint custody
- Whether both parents have actively cared for the child before and since the separation
- Whether one or both parents agree to, or are opposed to joint custody

As you examine your particular situation, use the above factors to attempt to realistically assess what type of child custody and visitation arrangements would be best suited to your family. Remember that you and your spouse are in the best position to clearly understand the particular circumstances that influence your lives and the life of your child. Although a judge will use a list of factors similar to those presented here to make custody decisions in contested cases, a court decision will never be as meaningful to a child as one that his or her parents have worked out in an amicable and loving manner.

The Child's Bill of Rights

In addition to the various factors that courts consider, an outline of the rights of children was developed from Wisconsin Supreme Court decisions and is now used throughout the United States. Delaware recently enacted legislation that makes it a requirement for parents to sign an affidavit stating that they have read and understand these rights. This Child's Bill of Rights is useful in reminding parents involved in a divorce that their children are entitled to have certain important rights considered during any discussions relating to custody and visitation. A review of these rights can help each of the parents to better view the effects of their divorce through the eyes of their child. Of all of the factors that you and your spouse will consider in your discussions on child custody and visitation, these are the most important. The Child's Bill of Rights is as follows:

- The right to a continuing relationship with both parents
- The right to be treated as an important human being, with unique feelings, ideas, and desires
- The right to continuing care and guidance from both parents
- The right to know and appreciate what is good in each parent without one parent degrading the other
- The right to express love, affection, and respect for each parent without having to stifle that love because of disapproval of the other parent
- The right to know that a parent's decision to divorce was not the responsibility of the child
- The right not to be a source of argument between the parents

> ☀️ **Toolkit Tip!**
>
> Read the Child's Bill of Rights carefully to understand the important rights that you should uphold regarding your child and his or her position in your family throughout the divorce process and beyond.

- The right to honest answers about the changing family relationships
- The right to be able to experience regular and consistent contact with both parents and the right to know the reason for any cancellation of time or change of plans
- The right to have a relaxed, secure relationship with both parents without being placed in a position to manipulate one parent against the other

Child Custody Jurisdiction

♀ Toolkit Tip!

If either parent has previously been involved in any type of child custody litigation, you will need to consult an attorney.

Related to the actual custody decisions is the issue of which specific state has the proper authority and jurisdiction to hear a child custody case. All 50 states and Washington D.C. have now enacted a uniform law relating to jurisdiction in custody matters: The Uniform Child Custody Jurisdiction Act. This legislation was passed in an effort to create a uniform nationwide system for determining which individual state should be the proper forum for custody decisions in every situation. It is an attempt to deal with the problems of child-snatching by parents who are dissatisfied with a particular state's custody decision. In the past, some parents who have lost custody battles have taken their children across state lines in an attempt to have another state's court award custody to them. This new uniform legislation provides a set of standardized guidelines to determine which single state should have the sole power and authority to decide the custody of a child in all situations. The decision as to which state will have jurisdiction is based on a variety of factors, such as: the length of time the child has resided in the state, whether there have been any previous court proceedings concerning the child's custody, the residency of both parents, etc. If you and your spouse: (1) have never before been involved in any child custody proceedings concerning your children; (2) are both able to agree upon the arrangements regarding your child's care; and (3) both live in the same state; then you may assume that the state that you both live in presently is the state with the proper jurisdiction to decide your child's custody. If, however, you, your spouse, or your child have previously been involved in child custody litigation in another state, you will need to consult a lawyer for advice relating to the court with proper jurisdiction in your particular situation.

Custody and Visitation Worksheet Instructions

With all of the various factors that influence the decisions regarding child custody firmly in mind, you and your spouse should be ready to approach the actual mechanics of custody and visitation arrangements. The following Child Custody Worksheet sets out the most common questions that arise in custody situations. You and your spouse should fill in this Worksheet together as the decisions that are made regarding custody and visitation must be arrived at in as amicable a manner as possible. As parents, you will both spend the rest of your lives under the terms of the agreement that you reach regarding custody and visitation rights. After completing the worksheet, various clauses are listed outlining custody and visitation arrangements. Several are provided, ranging from very simple statements of general rights to detailed provisions regarding times and dates. You and your spouse may not wish to make as detailed an arrangement as this worksheet provides. In such case, you may choose to use the simplified version of the custody and visitation clause.

Custody and Visitation Worksheet

Which parent will have actual primary physical custody of the child? (In other words, with whom will the child generally live?) _____

Will both parents share in the major decisions regarding the child? _____

    If YES, do you desire a joint custody arrangement? _____

    If YES, on what decisions will you both jointly confer?

        Education/school choice _____

        Medical care _____

        Dental care _____

        Religious training _____

        Vacation dates _____

    If YES, does the non-custodial parent have the right to be notified in advance of any upcoming decisions? _____

    If YES, does either parent have veto power over the decisions of the other? _____

Will the custodial parent have the right to move out of the state with the children without the other parent's consent? _____

Will both parents have the right to be informed of any change of address or telephone number of the other? _____

On what dates and times will the non-custodial parent have visitation?

    Weekends:

    Weekdays:

    Holidays (New Year's Day, Martin Luther King Jr.'s Birthday, Valentine's Day, Easter, Mother's Day, Memorial Day, Father's Day, 4th of July, Labor Day, Halloween, Thanksgiving, Christmas/Hanukkah, the child's birthday, any other special days):

    Vacations (Winter, Spring Break, Summer):

Will the non-custodial parent be allowed to see the child at any other times if reasonable notice is provided? _____
If YES, please describe:

Will the non-custodial parent have the right to be informed about the child's activities, illnesses, school, etc.?
If YES, please describe:

Will the non-custodial parent have the right to obtain the child's school, medical, or dental records?
If YES, please describe:

Will there be any visitation privileges for grandparents? _____
If YES, when?

What last name will the child use? _____

Child Custody and Visitation Marital Settlement Agreement Clauses

㉑ **Marital Settlement Agreement Clauses for Child Custody and Visitation**: On the following pages are various clauses that may be used for completing your Marital Settlement Agreement. There are many possible arrangements that may be made for custody and visitation. They can range from very brief to extremely complex and lengthy statements. Listed below are four separate child custody and visitation clauses. The first is a very simplified clause, the second moderately-detailed, and the third and fourth are very comprehensive. According to your particular situation, you and your spouse should read through each of these clauses and choose the one with which you feel most comfortable. In each of the two more detailed clauses, you will be given various choices regarding specific provisions of your arrangements. You may wish to add other specific provisions to these clauses that you both agree are important. You may do so if you use simple straightforward language that you both agree clearly states your agreements. The particular child custody and visitation clause that you choose will be used when you prepare your actual Marital Settlement Agreement. Please refer back to this section at that time. Fill in the appropriate choices for the clause that you have chosen and type (or cut and paste from the text clauses) this clause into your Agreement where indicated on the sample agreement form.

Sole Custody and Visitation Clause (Basic Agreement): The following clause is a very simplified and straightforward agreement relating to your child's custody arrangements. It provides for sole custody to be given to one parent. It should be used only if both you and your spouse are cooperative and amicable in your relationship and it is likely that you will remain that way in the future. This approach allows a wide range of flexibility in setting up visitation and vacation arrangements. Such arrangements are not spelled out at all in this clause, but are left for you and your spouse to structure as they arise. The very flexibility of this approach has some inherent dangers, however. Since there are no definite details or dates and times of visitation provided, there is a danger that arguments may erupt regarding interpretation of this clause. This clause should, therefore, be used only if you both feel that you have a clear understanding of each other's views and feelings regarding custody and visitation and have complete faith that you and your spouse will be able to agree on the details of visitation in the future. Even if you and your spouse are currently on friendly terms, it may be wise to use a clause with a more detailed schedule of visitation terms. Then you can always mutually agree after the divorce to allow different visitation, but you will at least have a written base of minimum terms. If you wish to provide for joint custody, you will need to use one of the more detailed clauses later in this section.

[   ]   We both agree that it is in the best interests of our child(ren) that the (Wife

or Husband) have sole physical and legal custody of our child(ren). We also agree that the other parent has the right to be with our child(ren) on a frequent and liberal basis through reasonable visitation, at such times as we and the child(ren) can agree upon. We agree that we will share as equally as possible the right to be with our child(ren) on holidays, birthdays, and during the child(ren)'s school vacations. We agree that our child(ren)'s time with either of us should not interfere with his or her (their) attendance at school. We also agree that the parent with custody should have the right to make the major decisions regarding the care and upbringing of the child(ren), but that the other parent has the right to be notified of any major decisions. We both also agree that, in the event of divorce or dissolution of marriage, our child(ren) will be known by the last name of (desired name).

Sole Custody and Visitation Clause (with Visitation Schedule): This clause is somewhat more detailed than the above clause. In particular, it allows for provisions to be made for specific times and dates for visitation with the non-custodial parent. This detailed schedule has the advantage of putting your agreements in writing as to how to deal with visitation. This will generally lessen the opportunity for future disagreements to arise over what was actually agreed upon during your discussions. This clause also provides for sole physical and legal custody to be given to one parent with reasonable visitation rights for the non-custodial parent. If you and your spouse have agreed that joint custody is preferable, you should use one of the more detailed clauses that follow later in this section.

[   ] We both agree that it is in the best interests of our child(ren) that the (Wife or Husband) have sole physical and legal custody of our child(ren). We also agree that the other parent has the right to be with our child(ren) on a frequent and liberal basis through reasonable visitation, at such times as we and the child(ren) can agree upon. If in the future we are unable to agree upon visitation, the (Wife or Husband) will have the right to be with our child(ren) as follows:

1. On the following holidays during even-numbered years:

2. On the following holidays during odd-numbered years:

3. On the following dates and times each (every other) weekend:

4. On the following dates and times during each (every other) week:

5. For the following vacation periods each year:
We agree that our child(ren)'s time with either of us should not interfere

with attendance at school. We also agree that the parent with custody should have the right to make the major decisions regarding the care and upbringing of our child(ren), but that the other parent should have the right to be notified of any major decisions. We both also agree that, in the event of divorce or dissolution of marriage, our child(ren) will be known by the last name of (desired name).

Custody and Visitation Clause (Joint Legal and Sole Physical Custody): The following clause provides a very detailed and comprehensive agreement for joint custody. It should be used in all situations in which both you and your spouse have decided that joint decision-making but sole physical custody with one parent is the best alternative. In some states, a detailed agreement of this nature is a requirement for both parents being awarded joint or shared custody. This agreement provides for both parents to share in the major decisions and lists the general categories of such decisions. It provides that the home of one parent shall be the primary residence of the child, but that the other parent be allowed frequent and liberal visitation and contact with the child. Specific visitation provisions are also included. In addition, various other rights and responsibilities of the parents are spelled out in detail in this clause.

[   ] We both agree that it is in the best interests of our child(ren) that we both have joint legal custody of our child(ren). We also agree that it is in the best interests of our child(ren) that the (Wife or Husband) have sole physical custody of our child(ren). We acknowledge that our child(ren) presently live(s) with the (Wife or Husband) and that the actual physical residence of our child(ren) may be changed at any time as we may mutually agree. All decisions pertaining to the education, discipline, health, extracurricular and summer activities, religious training, medical and dental care, and welfare of our child(ren) will be decided by both of us after reasonable and adequate discussion. We also agree that the parent with physical custody shall have control over the minor day-to-day decisions affecting the child(ren), including any medical or dental emergencies. We agree that if, after reasonable attempts, we are unable to reach an agreement on any of the decisions affecting our child(ren), we will jointly seek professional mediation to resolve our differences. We also agree that each of us has the right to know of any circumstances or decisions that affect our child(ren) and that each of us has the right to any medical, dental, or school records of our child(ren). Neither of us will do anything to hamper or interfere with the natural and continuing relationship between our child(ren) and the other parent. We both also agree that, in the event of divorce or dissolution of marriage, our child(ren) will be known by the last name of (desired name). We both realize that the well-being of our child(ren) is of paramount importance and, therefore, we

agree that our child(ren) should have as much contact as possible with the parent who does not have physical custody and that our child(ren) may visit that parent as often as may be agreed upon. We additionally agree to use our very best efforts to insure that our child(ren) receive(s) the most care, love, and affection possible from both parents throughout his or her (their) entire childhood. Although visitation may be scheduled more often, the parent who does not have physical custody will have the right to be with our child(ren) at least as follows:

1. On the following holidays during even-numbered years:

2. On the following holidays during odd-numbered years:

3. On the following dates and times each (every other) weekend:

4. On the following dates and times during each (every other) week:

5. For the following vacation periods each year:

Custody and Visitation Clause (Joint Legal and Physical Custody): This clause is the most detailed and comprehensive provided. This does not necessarily mean that this is the most appropriate clause in all situations. The following clause provides for both parents to share the physical and legal custody of their child. This clause still designates one parent's home as the primary residence of the child and provides for visitation with the other parent. Most of the other terms of this clause are identical to the preceding clause. For practical purposes, the day-to-day lives of parents and children under this clause would be very similar to their lives under the terms of the preceding clause. Legally, however, there are slight differences between these clauses. Under this clause, both parents have the right to retain the actual physical custody of the child. For this reason, there is an agreement included in this clause regarding taking the child out of the state in which you both live. Where there is a genuine and honest joint effort and agreement to cooperate in raising a child, this clause may provide the most even and equal division of the rights to the upbringing and custody of the child.

[   ]   We both agree that it is in the best interests of our child(ren) that we both have joint legal and physical custody of our child(ren). We also agree that it is in the best interests of our child(ren) that the home of the (Wife or Husband) be the primary residence of the child(ren). We acknowledge that our child(ren) presently live(s) with the (Wife or Husband) and that the actual physical residence of our child(ren) may be changed at any time as we may mutually agree. All decisions pertaining to the place of residence, dis-

cipline, education, health, extracurricular and summer activities, vacations, religious training, medical and dental care, and welfare of our child(ren) will be decided by both of us after reasonable and adequate discussion. We also agree that the parent with physical custody shall have control over the minor day-to-day decisions affecting the child(ren), including any medical or dental emergencies. We agree that if, after reasonable attempts, we are unable to reach an agreement on any of the decisions affecting our child(ren), we will jointly seek professional mediation to resolve our differences. We also agree that each of us has the right to know of any circumstances or decisions that affect our child(ren) and that each of us has the right to any medical, dental, or school records of our child(ren). Neither of us will do anything to hamper or interfere with the natural and continuing relationship between our child(ren) and the other parent. We both also agree that, in the event of divorce or dissolution of marriage, our child(ren) will be known by the last name of (desired name). We both agree that frequent and continuing contact with both parents is vital to our child(ren), and therefore we both agree that neither of us will permanently remove our child(ren) from this state without the express written permission of the other parent. We additionally agree to use our very best efforts to insure that our child(ren) receive(s) the most care, love, and affection possible from both parents throughout his or her (their) entire childhood. We both realize that the well-being of our child(ren) is of paramount importance and, therefore, we agree that our child(ren) should have as much contact as possible with the parent who does not have physical custody and that our child(ren) may visit that parent as often as may be agreed upon. Although contact may be scheduled more often, the parent who does not live in the primary physical residence of the child(ren) will have the right to be with our child(ren) at least as follows:

1. On the following holidays during even-numbered years:

2. On the following holidays during odd-numbered years:

3. On the following dates and times each (every other) weekend:

4. On the following dates and times during each (every other) week:

5. For the following vacation periods each year:

⑭ Fill in the total number of pages and have each spouse initial the page.

Chapter 6

Child Support

Closely related to the decisions that must be made regarding child custody are those decisions relating to the support of a child. In most instances, the parent who does not have physical custody of a child must provide child support to the parent who has custody. Child support agreements are essentially financial in nature. Much of the information that you and your spouse have already provided each other in the Financial Statements will be used in determining the proper support amounts. However, a Child Support Worksheet is provided to allow you to gather the necessary information for these decisions.

Before you and your spouse consider the legal aspects of child support, you should both understand that child support terms are the provisions of marital settlement agreements and divorce orders that are most often defaulted upon or ignored. Tragically, this has resulted in the creation of a new class of poverty-level individuals: children of divorced parents. The majority of court-ordered child support payments are neither paid in full nor on time. Nearly one-third of the children entitled to child support receive no support at all. The reasons for this tragedy are many, but perhaps the most important stems from the frustration of the non-custodial parent having to pay for the support for children that he or she does not live with or raise. If

☉ Toolkit Tip!

Use the answers that each parent completes on the following Questionnaire to assist you both in approaching the child custody issue with the same information clearly in mind.

you and your spouse can come to a reasonable and workable agreement regarding the custody and visitation arrangements for your child, there will be a far greater chance that your child support agreement will also be seen as reasonable. As you approach your child support discussions, please keep these tragic statistics firmly in mind.

The Law of Child Support

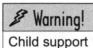

Warning!

Child support obligations continue for both parents until the child reaches adulthood. Judges take these legal obligations extremely seriously.

Both natural parents of a minor child have a legal obligation to provide adequate support for the child until the child reaches 18 years of age (21 in some states). This legal duty includes providing food, clothing, shelter, medical care, and education for a child. This is the law in every state. Parents of adopted children also have this same obligation. Child support, however, is not merely the delivery of a monthly support payment. It is a legal, moral, and ethical obligation to provide full care and support for your offspring. Divorce does not end this legal obligation for support. It merely complicates the duty. Both parents have an equal duty to support their children. In the vast majority of divorces that involve children however, the mother is awarded physical custody of those children. Also, in the majority of family situations, it is the mother who earns a disproportionately lower income than the father. Thus, in most divorce situations involving children, there will be an immediate and definite need for considerable child support to be provided by the father. Regardless of which parent has physical custody and even when the incomes of both parents are equal, both parents still need to provide their fair share of support for the child. A child should not be forced to suffer economically because of the divorce of his or her parents.

When a single family unit is divided into two households upon divorce, the total living costs will naturally escalate. Two homes must be maintained instead of one. Two sets of furniture, appliances, and housewares must be provided. Two cars, two televisions, two of almost every household item will need to be purchased and maintained. Unfortunately, the income of the divorced family will not increase. In many cases, in fact, it may actually decrease as the parent with custody may find it more difficult to maintain a full-time job. Because both parents are no longer able to share their time with the child as easily, child care costs may also increase. The goals of child support laws are to achieve a fair division of the income of both parents in order to provide for the satisfactory support of the children of a marriage. As much as is possible, a child should be entitled to share in the income of both parents, despite their divorce.

Federal legislation (the Family Support Act of 1988) requires each state to provide some type of formula or guidelines for the determination of child support awards. In the attempt to provide specific financial guidelines for child support provisions, many states have adopted detailed legislation and rules regarding how to arrive at a fair support amount. Some states have provided only simple formulas. Included in this book is a general set of guidelines for determining child support. In recent years, these child support guidelines have tended to become more detailed, specific, and mathematical. The newest versions of child support legislation are full of various charts and financial formulas for determining the correct amount of support. These detailed guidelines are an attempt to take the mystery out of the manner in which a court determines how much child support to award. In most states that have such guidelines, however, the rules are only to be used to provide a structure for determining a minimum amount of child support. A court has the authority to order more or less child support if necessary.

> **☼ Toolkit Tip!**
> Federal law provides that each state must provide a clear and understandable method for determining child support amounts.

While each state's guidelines may be somewhat different, they all generally require that if the non-custodial parent has sufficient income, he or she must provide a specific level of monthly support to the parent who has custody of the child. Increasingly, states are adopting legislation that goes beyond simply providing a monthly payment for child support. Some of these recent laws may require various non-monetary forms of support: that a parent provide health insurance, dental insurance, and life insurance for the parent with the child as sole beneficiary, or that the family home not be sold for a particular period of time. All of these provisions are an attempt to provide sufficient security for a child of divorce to prevent the child from requiring welfare or other social service support from the state. Please check the Appendix for information on your state's specific statutory child support guidelines.

Factors for Consideration

:ᵜ:Toolkit Tip!

The factors relating to child support in your state will be noted in your state's Appendix listing.

In addition to any specific detailed statutory child support guidelines, most states also provide a list of factors that are considered relevant in child support cases. A judge will determine how much weight to give each factor depending on the unique circumstances of each case. Following is a general listing of the basic factors that are most commonly used by judges. You and your spouse should use this general list of factors to focus your discussions regarding child support. The factors that are considered pertinent in most states revolve around two specific areas: the needs of the child and the ability of the parents to pay support. Each of these basic factors has many subfactors, which are outlined below. Aspects of the first main factor, the needs of the child, are generally used to determine the minimum amount of child support that is necessary to provide the child with the basic comforts of life. Considerations regarding the second major factor, the ability of the parents to pay, are then often used to establish the maximum amount that the supporting parent should pay. The standard of living of both parents is considered in this decision. The general factors that are considered pertinent to decisions relating to child support are as follows:

- The financial resources of the child
- The age and health of the parents
- The standard of living the child would have enjoyed if the marriage had not been dissolved
- The physical and emotional conditions and educational needs of the child
- The financial resources, needs, and obligations of both the non-custodial and the custodial parent
- Any excessive expenditures, destruction, or concealment of assets
- The occupation of each parent
- The earning capacity of each parent
- The amount and sources of income of each parent
- The vocational skills and employability of each parent
- The age and health of the child
- The child's occupation (if old enough to work)
- The vocational skills of the child (if old enough to work)
- The employability of the child (if old enough to work)

- The needs of the child
- The standard of living and circumstances of each parent
- The relative financial means of the parents
- The need and capacity of the child for education, including higher education
- The responsibility of the parents for the support of others
- The value of services contributed by the custodial parent
- The desirability of the parent having either sole custody or physical care of the child remaining in the home as a full-time parent

- The cost of daycare to the parent having custody or physical care of the child if that parent works outside the home, or the value of the childcare services performed by that parent if the parent remains in the home
- The tax consequences of child support to each parent

☼ Toolkit Tip!

If your state listing in the Appendix does not provide specific factors for child support decisions, you may use this listing as a general guide.

A very important factor that is not listed here, but that you and your spouse must take into consideration, is that the court always has absolute authority over child support decisions. This power is retained regardless of any agreement that you may reach. The obligation for child support cannot be bargained away in your negotiations. Courts are very protective of the rights of a child to be supported by both parents and will not accept the terms of any settlement agreement that does not provide for reasonable levels of support. Although courts will often accept the child support terms to which parents agree in settlement negotiations, the courts can and will ignore any agreements they find unreasonable. Ultimately, it is the court that has final authority to issue support orders for dependent children and they take that power very seriously. Much as you cannot trade away the custody of your child for monetary rewards, you cannot bargain away your child's rights to support. The marital settlement agreement that you and your spouse sign will bind the two of you, but will not bind your children. Their rights to reasonable support may be enforced by a court if necessary, despite your and your spouse's agreement.

Enforcement and Modification of Child Support

Of all the provisions of a final divorce, child support obligations are, unfortunately, the ones that are most often ignored. Over

Federal law now requires that all states cooperate in the enforcement of child support obligations.

one-half of court-ordered child support payments are not paid in full or on time. Nearly one-third of qualifying children receive no child support at all. Recent studies have shown that the income level of the divorced parents has no bearing on whether a child will receive adequate child support. Unfortunately, wealthy parents are just as likely to default on child support payments as poor parents. There is now a concerted national effort to collect and enforce overdue child support payments. This effort is backed by very comprehensive and powerful laws that are beginning to turn the tide of non-payment of child support. In recent years, all 50 states have enacted legislation to deal with this problem: the Uniform Reciprocal Enforcement of Support Act. Many states have also enacted other strict laws dealing with methods to enforce child support obligations. In addition, the federal government has enacted very tough child support enforcement legislation. Child support provisions in a marital settlement agreement or final divorce order are always subject to modification, regardless of any attempt to limit such future modification. The courts always have the authority to increase or decrease the amount of the support. However, modifying a child support order in the future involves a showing of changed circumstances and an often lengthy lawsuit and court hearing. It is far easier to attempt to anticipate any lifestyle and income changes in advance than to resort to the courts to keep changing the amount of child support.

General Child Support Guidelines

The guidelines provided here are just that: guidelines. They are not intended to be an ultimate method for determining support payments in all cases. They should be reviewed and used while considering all of the other relevant factors in your particular situation. The determination of the proper amount of child support in each case will always be difficult. A careful balance must be obtained between providing an adequate level of support and overburdening the parent who must pay the support. If the support payments are set at a level that becomes a tremendous financial burden to the paying parent, there will be a tendency and temptation to default on the payments. On the other hand, if the payments are too low, the child will suffer the consequences. Both parents must work together carefully to actually determine a fair and reasonable amount of support. Care must be taken to keep the negotiations on a mature and rational basis. Discussions involving child support have the very real potential of deteriorating into hostile arguments. Of all the aspects of divorce, child support obligations have spawned more post-divorce lawsuits than any other.

Many different methods of determining the amount of child support payments have been utilized around the country. A mathematical formula method of determining child support has been adopted recently in many states. Generally, this method consists of determining the actual monthly needs of the child based on the particular circumstances of the family and the ability of the parents to pay. Other methods rely upon charts of child support amounts. The method of determining the proper amount of child support that is provided in this book was adapted from the guidelines used in many different states and is a combination of the most common methods in use. It attempts to take both parents' economic situations into account. Your particular state may use a similar method or a variation. You should refer to the Appendix for information regarding your state's specific requirements. In addition, you may wish to check with the clerk of the court in the county where you live to see if there are any local child support guidelines or rules in effect. In addition, many states have specific child support worksheets that are to be used. Check the Appendix and with your court clerk.

> **̣ᆞ Toolkit Tip!**
> Check your state's listing in the Appendix to determine where to find information regarding your state's child support guidelines.

Child Support Worksheet and Child Support Guidelines Instructions

☀️Toolkit Tip!

Use the answers that each parent completes on the following Worksheet to assist you both in approaching the child support issue with the necessary information before you.

To determine the figures necessary for the calculations on the Child Support Worksheet, please refer back to the Financial Statement that you and your spouse prepared when you negotiated the division of your property. The Child Support Guidelines Chart is provided on page 140 as an example of how various states have decided to calculate minimum child support amounts. You should use the highest amount provided by the calculations as a starting point for your discussions. Other factors, in addition to income and deductions, may then be used to adjust the amount accordingly. To use this method, you must first determine the monthly net income of each parent. To obtain this figure, combine all of the income of each parent from any source. Then, subtract the mandatory deductions from this income as shown on the following worksheet. This will give you the monthly net income of each parent for child support purposes. If there are seasonal or monthly fluctuations in the parent's income or deductions, you may wish to determine the income and deductions on an annual basis and then divide that amount by 12 for the net monthly income.

Next, combine the two monthly net income amounts for a total net family income. Using this combined net monthly family income, consult the child support chart to determine the total minimum amount of child support that is necessary. Always go to the next higher level if your combined monthly income falls in between the amounts shown. As with all decisions concerning children, the courts will always favor the decision that benefits the children the most. Remember, the amount shown is only the general minimum amount necessary and the actual amount of support required may be higher (or even lower) than this amount, depending on the particular circumstances of your situation. Federal law requires that if a judge decides to award less child support than is warranted by a state's guidelines, the specific reasons must be stated. Also remember that your particular state may have a slightly different set of guidelines or various other charts for determining support. Note also that the amount shown on the chart is the amount of support required by *both* parents together.

The amount of the non-custodial parent's individual share is determined as explained in the next paragraph.

After the amount on the chart is determined, the non-custodial parent's share must be determined. Divide the net monthly income of the parent without custody by the total net monthly family income to determine the fractional or percentage share of the total child support. This figure multiplied times the figure from the support guideline chart will be the minimum monthly support required to be paid by the non-custodial parent. To this amount should then be added any childcare costs that are required to enable the parent with custody to obtain employment. This final general minimum figure should be adjusted up or down based on the following factors and any other relevant information:

- Any extraordinary medical, dental, or health expenses
- Any independent income of the child
- Any seasonal variations in a parent's income
- The age of the child, taking into consideration the greater needs of older children
- Any special needs that have previously been met by the family budget
- The total assets available to the parents and the child
- The custody arrangements for the child

In situations where there is joint physical custody, the actual amount of time the child spends with each parent may be particularly relevant. The amount of the actual payment as calculated using this method depends upon the income, deductions, and childcare expenses of both parents. If the income of the parent with custody is very low, the non-custodial parent will be required to pay all or the bulk of the amount of child support shown on the chart. On the other hand, if the income of the parent with custody is very high and that of the non-custodial parent is low, the required child support payment may be very low.

☀ Toolkit Tip!

Use the Child Support Guidelines Chart to determine a general amount of child support. You will, however, need to use the guidelines that your state provides for the final amount determination.

Child Support Worksheet

Net Monthly Income of Parent with Custody

Gross Monthly Income

Wages, salary, bonuses .... $ _____
Interest and dividends .... $ _____
Business income .... $ _____
Unemployment/Social Security .... $ _____
Income from other sources .... $ _____

Total Gross Monthly Income .... $ _____

Monthly Deductions

Income taxes withheld .... $ _____
Social Security withheld .... $ _____
Union dues withheld .... $ _____
Children's insurance premiums .... $ _____
Mandatory retirement withheld .... $ _____

Total Monthly Deductions .... $ _____

Total Net Monthly Income of Parent With Custody

Total Gross Monthly Income .... $ _____
Minus (-) Total Monthly Deductions .... $ _____
Equals (=) *Total Net Monthly Income* .... (A) $ _____

Net Monthly Income of Parent without Custody

Gross Monthly Income

Wages, salary, bonuses .... $ _____
Interest, dividends .... $ _____
Business income .... $ _____
Unemployment/Social Security .... $ _____
Income from other sources .... $ _____

Total Gross Monthly Income .... $ _____

Monthly Deductions

Income taxes withheld .... $ _____
Social Security withheld .... $ _____
Union dues withheld .... $ _____
Mandatory retirement withheld .... $ _____
Children's insurance premiums .... $ _____

Total Monthly Deductions .... $ _____

Total Net Monthly Income of Parent Without Custody

Total Gross Monthly Income .... $ _____
Minus (-) Total Monthly Deductions .... $ _____
Equals (=) *Total Net Monthly Income* .... (B) $ _____

Total Combined Net Monthly Family Income

Net Monthly Income of Parent With Custody ....(A) $ _____
Plus (+) Net Monthly Income of Parent Without Custody ..... (B) $ _____
Equals (=) *Combined Net Monthly Family Income* ....(C) $ _____

Use the Combined Net Monthly Family Income figure (C) above to find the total minimum amount of child support required on the following chart. If this figure is over $4,200.00, please use the percentages listed following this chart. To this amount is added any child care expenses that are required in order that the parent with custody may obtain employment.

Minimum Child Support from Both Parents .... $ _____
Plus (+) Required Monthly Child Care Expenses .... $ _____
Equals (=) *Minimum Total Child Support* .... $ _____

Use the Minimum Total Child Support figure above to determine the minimum child support necessary from the parent without custody as follows:

Monthly Net Income of Parent Without Custody ....(B) $ _____
Divided by (÷) Combined Net Monthly Family Income ....(C) $ _____
Equals (=) *Non-Custodial Parent's Percentage Share* (%) .... $ _____
Times (X) Minimum Total Child Support from Both Parents ..... $ _____
Equals (=) *Monthly Minimum Child Support to be Paid* .... $ _____

Remember that this final figure is a general minimum amount and is subject to adjustment based on the other factors in your particular situation.

Child Support Guideline Chart

This chart is similar to charts used in various states throughout the country. In nearly all cases, if the figures in this chart are used for your calculations, your child support decisions will be accepted by the court.

Combined Monthly Income	One Child	Two Children	Three Children	Four Children	Five Children	Six Children
$ 500	$ 48	$ 48	$ 49	$ 49	$ 50	$ 50
750	177	274	279	282	285	288
1000	231	359	450	507	520	525
1100	251	390	489	551	600	620
1200	271	421	528	595	648	693
1300	291	452	566	638	695	744
1400	311	483	605	682	742	794
1500	332	516	645	728	792	847
1600	353	548	686	773	842	901
1700	374	580	726	819	892	954
1800	395	612	767	865	942	1007
1900	416	645	807	910	992	1060
2000	437	677	847	956	1042	1113
2100	457	709	887	1000	1091	1166
2200	476	739	924	1042	1136	1215
2300	495	768	961	1084	1182	1264
2400	514	798	999	1126	1228	1313
2500	532	828	1036	1167	1274	1362
2600	551	857	1073	1209	1319	1411
2700	570	887	1110	1251	1365	1460
2800	589	917	1147	1292	1411	1509
2900	607	945	1176	1332	1 453	1554
3000	624	972	1209	1370	1495	1598
3100	642	999	1243	1408	1536	1643
3200	659	1026	1276	1446	1578	1687
3300	677	1052	1310	1484	1619	1731
3400	694	1079	1343	1521	1660	1775
3500	712	1106	1377	1559	1702	1819
3600	729	1133	1410	1597	1743	1863
3700	747	1160	1444	1635	1785	1907
3800	764	1187	1477	1673	1826	1951
3900	778	1208	1510	1704	1859	1986
4000	791	1227	1534	1731	1889	2018
4100	804	1246	1559	1758	1919	2050
4200	817	1265	1583	1785	1949	2082

For combined net monthly income amounts over $4,200.00, use the following percentages to determine the minimum child support payments:

1 Child:	20% of the net monthly combined income
2 Children:	30% of the net monthly combined income
3 Children:	38% of the net monthly combined income
4 Children:	43% of the net monthly combined income
5 Children:	47% of the net monthly combined income
6 or More Children:	50% of the net monthly combined income

Child Support Marital Settlement Agreement Clauses

㉑ **Clauses for Child Support**: Once you have determined the specific amount that the monthly child support payments should be, it is a relatively simple matter to include that provision in a clause for your Marital Settlement Agreement. A standard clause for this purpose is set out below. There is also a provision regarding insurance that requires that, as additional child support, the parent who is to pay the support must maintain a life insurance policy naming the children as beneficiaries and health insurance coverage for the children. This provision is highly recommended and is required in some states. Federal law mandates that states require a parent responsible for child support to include any children under a health and dental insurance plan if such a plan is available to the parent through their place of employment or otherwise at a relatively low cost. The life insurance provision provides some measure of security and insurance protection for the children in the event of death of the paying parent. The health insurance protection provides the child with protection in case of illness or injury. Fill in the appropriate choices and then type this clause into your Agreement where indicated on the sample form.

[   ] We both agree that the (Wife or Husband) will pay to the other spouse, for child support, the amount of $ (amount of each child's support payment) per child per month, for a total monthly payment of $ (total monthly combined child support payment amount). The payments will begin on the (date of first payment) and will continue for each child until that child has reached the age of majority, died, become self-supporting, or married. We both agree that this obligation is subject to modification by a court at any time. We both further agree that should the parent obligated to pay the support receive a salary or income increase in the future, the amount of child support due per child per month shall be increased proportionately. The parent obligated to pay support agrees to notify the other parent immediately of any salary or income increase. As additional child support, we both agree that as long as support payments are due, the (Wife or Husband) will carry and maintain life insurance in the amount of $ (amount of life insurance coverage), naming our child(ren) as sole irrevocable beneficiary(ies). The parent obligated to provide such insurance will provide the other parent with annual proof of such coverage. As additional child support, we both agree that as long as support payments are due, the (Wife or Husband) will carry and maintain adequate health, dental, and hospitalization insurance for the child(ren)'s benefit, pay any required deductible amount, and pay for any necessary medical or dental expenses of the child(ren) that are not covered by such insurance. The parent obligated to provide such insurance will provide the other parent with annual proof of such coverage.

In addition to selecting the amount of the payment, another child support issue must be addressed. A decision must be reached on how the payment is to be made. In response to the enormous rate of default on child support payments, all states in recent years and in response to federal legislation have adopted various methods to attempt to insure that the payments will continue to be paid and paid on time. These methods range from automatic wage assignments and withholding of wages, to having the support payments made through the clerk of the court or some other government agency. The most common arrangement is for the paying parent to be required to make the payments directly to the clerk of the court. Once the payment is received, the clerk then pays the parent to whom the payment is due. There are several benefits to having the payments made in this indirect way. By having the payment made through an official government body instead of directly to the other parent, there is an official documented record of the amount and date the payment is made. Furthermore, many states have programs to collect past due payments that will automatically go into effect when a payment is missed. This takes much of the burden of enforcement off the parent who is to be paid the support.

This book offers two alternatives for this situation. The first alternative is for the payments, in the event of a divorce, to be made to an official state agency or court official for disbursement to the other parent. The other alternative is for the payments to be made directly to the other parent. Most courts will allow a couple to waive any requirement that the payments be made through the state if the agreement to make the child support payments directly to the parent is in the form of a marital settlement agreement. To allow the payments to be made directly to the parent, there must be valid reason why the parents wish to avoid the indirect payment method. Good reasons might be that the parent who is to make the payments is very reliable or has established a clear record of making the payments on time while the parents were separated. However, if there is any doubt as to whether the payments may be paid late or not at all after a divorce, you should choose the alternative that requires the payments to be made through an official state agency or court official. The clause that provides for direct payment to the other spouse also allows the payments to be switched to collection by the court or state if problems arise in the future. Remember that there is a definite tendency for child support payments to be paid late or not at all in the majority of cases. Choose the clause below that you and your spouse agree would be most appropriate in your circumstances:

[   ]   We agree that the required child support payments should be made directly to the parent to whom they are due. However, in the event of a divorce or dissolution of marriage, we agree that the required child support payments are to be paid directly to the court or state official or agency so designated by the laws of this state to receive and disburse such payments. We both further agree that, in the event of a divorce or dissolution of marriage, we

will cooperate in obtaining any necessary income withholding orders or income assignments if required to guarantee this obligation.

[   ] We agree that the required child support payments should be made directly to the parent to whom they are due and should not be required to be paid through any court or state agency or official. The parent receiving the payments, however, does not waive the right to request, at any time and in his or her sole discretion, that such payments be made directly through a court or state agency or official in the future. We both further agree that, in the event of a divorce or dissolution of marriage, we will cooperate in obtaining any necessary income withholding orders or income assignments if required to guarantee this obligation.

Additional Child Support Clause: Finally, a general clause is provided for those parents who wish to provide a written agreement on any other provisions regarding the support of their children. This clause may be used, for example, to indicate that the non-custodial parent will contribute additional amounts for the college education of the child. Generally, a parent's legal support obligation ends when the child reaches the age of majority (usually 18 years old). However, parents may legally agree to provide support beyond this minimum cutoff date. You and your spouse may also desire to use this clause to provide additional sums for other needs of your children, such as summer camp fees, special educational costs, or religious training. For any such additional support provisions, use clear explanatory language to define the obligations that you have agreed upon.

[   ] As additional child support, we both agree that the (Wife or Husband) will provide: (here include the terms of the agreed upon provision [for example: one-half of the amount necessary for the child's college education]).

Federal Income Tax Dependency Exemption: You and your spouse will also have an opportunity to choose which of you will receive the federal income tax dependency exemption. Generally, the parent with custody should receive the exemption. This is true even if the non-custodial parent provides over one-half of the actual monetary support for the child. If the non-custodial parent is given the right to claim the exemption, IRS Form 8332: *Release of Claim to Exemption for Child of Divorced or Separated Parents* must be signed by the custodial parent and filed with the non-custodial parent's tax return in order to officially waive the right to the exemption.

[   ] We also agree that the (Wife or Husband) may claim the federal dependency tax exemption for the child(ren).

⑭ Fill in the total number of pages and have each spouse initial the page.

164

Chapter 7

Marital Settlement Agreement

On the following pages is the Marital Settlement Agreement.

Fill in each of the appropriate blanks, using the information you have collected from the previous chapters. You will then complete the preparation of all your forms following the instructions in Chapter 8. *Please note*: The following agreement pages are for you to use as a guide; the actual agreement should be prepared following the instructions in Chapter 8.

Please note that you should carefully read all of the instructions and all of the information in the Appendix of this book that relates to the details of your state's laws prior to attempting to complete your marital settlement agreement. In addition, it may be a good idea to look over the state-specific divorce legal forms that are provided on the enclosed CD before your finalize your agreement. There may be information on those forms that are relevant to your particular situation that should be considered before you sign your settlement agreement and proceed with your actual divorce.If there are any issues that you are unsure about or any aspects of your agreement that you do not understand, you are advised to consult a competent divorce attorney prior to signing your ageement. Your settlement agreement is a valid contract and it may be very difficult and expensive to change any terms of your agreement after you have signed it.

Toolkit Tip!

Before you prepare your final marital settlement agreement, you should carefully consider all of the details of your state's listing in the Appendix.

Marital Settlement Agreement

This agreement is made on _____ , between
_____ , the Wife, who lives at
_____ , and
_____ , the Husband, who lives
at _____ . We
were married on _____ , in
_____ .

Child Identification:

Grounds for Separation:

We both desire to settle by agreement all of our marital affairs,
THEREFORE, in consideration of our mutual promises, and other good and valuable
consideration, we agree as follows:

   We both desire and agree to permanently live separate and apart from each other,
   as if we were single, according to the terms of this agreement. We each agree not to
   annoy, harass, or interfere with the other in any manner.

   We both agree that we will cooperate in the filing of any necessary tax returns. We also
   agree that any tax refunds for the current year will be the property of the _____
   and that any taxes due for the current tax year will be paid by the _____ .

   We both agree that, in the event of divorce or dissolution of marriage, the _____
   desires to and shall have the right to be known by the name of
   _____ .

Page 1 of _____ pages   Husband's initials _____   Wife's initials _____

Division of Property

To settle all issues relating to our property, we both agree that the following property shall be the sole and separate property of the Wife, and the Husband transfers and quit-claims any interest that he may have in this property to the Wife:

We also agree that the following property shall be the sole and separate property of the Husband, and the Wife transfers and quit-claims any interest that she may have in this property to the Husband:

Page 2 of _____ pages   Husband's initials _____   Wife's initials _____

Division of Bills

To settle all issues relating to our debts, we agree that the Wife shall pay and indemnify and hold the Husband harmless from the following debts:

We agree that the Husband shall pay and indemnify and hold the Wife harmless from the following debts:

We also agree not to incur any further debts or obligations for which the other may be liable.

Page 3 of _____ pages   Husband's initials _____   Wife's initials _____

Alimony

To settle any and all issues regarding alimony and maintenance, we both agree that:

Child Custody and Visitation

To settle all issues relating to our child custody and visitation, we both agree that:

Page _____ of _____ pages   Husband's initials _____   Wife's initials _____

Child Support

To settle all issues relating to child support, we both agree that:

Page _____ of _____ pages   Husband's initials _____   Wife's initials _____

Additional Terms

We further agree to the following additional terms:

Page _____ of _____ pages   Husband's initials _____   Wife's initials _____

Signature

We each understand that we have the right to representation by separate lawyers. We each fully understand our rights and we each consider the terms of this agreement to be fair and reasonable. Both of us agree to execute and deliver any documents, make any endorsements, and do any and all acts that may be necessary or convenient to carry out all of the terms of this agreement.

We agree that this document is intended to be the full and entire settlement and agreement between us regarding our marital rights and obligations and that this agreement should be interpreted and governed by the laws of the State of _____ .

We also agree that every provision of this agreement is expressly made binding upon the heirs, assigns, executors, administrators, successors in interest, and representatives of each of us.

We both desire that, in the event of our divorce or dissolution of marriage, this marital settlement agreement be approved and merged and incorporated into any subsequent decree or judgment for divorce or dissolution of marriage and that, by the terms of the judgment or decree, we both be ordered to comply with the terms of this agreement, but that this agreement shall survive.

We have prepared this agreement cooperatively and each of us has fully and honestly disclosed to the other the extent of our assets, income, and financial situation. We have each completed Financial Statements that are attached to this agreement and incorporated by reference.

Signed and dated: _____

_____   _____
Signature of Wife   Printed Name of Wife

_____   _____
Signature of Husband   Printed Name of Husband

_____   _____
Signature of Witness #1   Printed Name of Witness #1

_____   _____
Signature of Witness #2   Printed Name of Witness #2

Page _____ of _____ pages   Husband's initials _____   Wife's initials _____

Notary Acknowledgment

State of _____
County of _____

On the _____ ,
_____ and
_____ , husband and
wife, and _____ and
_____ , their witnesses,
personally came before me and, being duly sworn, did state that they are the persons
described in the above document and that they signed the above document in my presence as a free and voluntary act for the purposes stated.

_____
Signature of Notary Public
Notary Public, In and for the County of _____
State of _____
My commission expires:_____   Notary Seal

Page _____ of _____ pages   Husband's initials _____   Wife's initials _____

Chapter 8

Completing Your Marital Settlement Agreement

After you and your spouse have reached all of the necessary decisions and have chosen the appropriate clauses in the preceding sections, you are ready to assemble your final Marital Settlement Agreement. After it is assembled, you will be given instructions on signing and having your agreement notarized. Once you have reached this step in your divorce process, you may relax somewhat with the knowledge that the most difficult decisions in your divorce are behind you. You and your spouse have essentially worked out all of the matters relating to your marriage that require agreement. The divorce procedure now becomes the rather routine matter of preparing and processing the necessary paperwork.

Before you begin to actually assemble your agreement, you should both carefully review each clause that you and your spouse have chosen and be certain that it embodies your complete agreement.

Preparing Your Marital Settlement Agreement

If you are both satisfied that your choices are complete, you are ready to complete and finalize the agreement. The actual preparation of your Marital Settlement Agreement will be accomplished in four easy steps. These steps are as follows:

1. Using a word processor (or Adobe Acrobat Reader®), carefully type or prepare each page of the Marital Settlement Agreement, being certain to include the

proper words or clauses where indicated by the numbers (①) to (44)) on the sample form. The only blank lines that should appear on your typed Agreement should be:

- the date of the agreement
- the spaces for each spouse's initials at the bottom of each page
- the spaces for the signatures on the signature page
- the Notary Acknowledgment information

Both you and your spouse should then carefully proofread your entire Marital Settlement Agreement when it is completed. If any corrections are necessary, you will need to redo the entire page that requires the correction. Make sure that, on each page of the Agreement, you have indicated the correct page number and the total number of pages of the Agreement.

2. When you are satisfied that the Agreement is complete, make two photocopies of the unsigned original, so that you will have three original unsigned Agreements. Using a pen, each spouse should then initial each page at the bottom in the space provided.

3. Attach to each of the three unsigned Agreements an unsigned version of each of your Financial Statements that you prepared earlier. Staple the upper left-hand corner of all of the pages of each original together. (References to *originals* in this book refer to any *unsigned* documents, even if they are photocopies. *Copies* refer to photocopies of *signed* documents). You should now have three identical unsigned "original" documents. Each document will consist of a complete Marital Settlement Agreement, a Financial Statement completed by you, and a Financial Statement completed by your spouse.

4. Take all three original Agreement documents along with two witnesses to the office of a local notary public or other similar authority for signing. The witnesses may be family or friends, as long as they are over 18 years old. There may also be acceptable people available to use as witnesses at the office of the notary. Call in advance and check. In front of the notary public, both you and your spouse should complete all three versions of your Marital Settlement Agreement as follows:

(24) Fill in the date on which the Agreement is actually being signed

(25) Wife should sign in front of the notary public and witnesses

(26) Print the Wife's name

㉗ Husband should sign in front of the notary public and witnesses

㉘ Print the Husband's name

㉙ Witness #1 should sign in front of the notary public

㉚ Print Witness #1's name

㉛ Witness # 2 should sign in front of the notary public

㉜ Print Witness #2's name

㉝ to ㊹ The notary public should complete these items and sign where indicated

5. Additionally, each spouse should also sign the last page of his or her individual Financial Statement where indicated and the notary public should also complete, sign, and notarize these documents that have been stapled to each of the three original Marital Settlement Agreements.

Thus each spouse will have signed each of the three full sets of documents in two places, for a total of six signatures each (once on each Marital Settlement Agreement and once on each Financial Statement times three).

After Signing Your Martial Settlement Agreement

You should each retain one of the complete signed originals of your agreement. The third original signed Agreement will be filed with your divorce papers when and if you should file for divorce. You will also need to make at least three photocopies of the already-signed original for later use when you file for your divorce. Place the original agreement and the photocopies in a safe place.

The final signed and notarized Marital Settlement Agreement (with its attached Financial Statements) will be a valid legal contract between you and your spouse that is enforceable in a court of law if either of you break your promises in the agreement. Under the terms of your agreement, you may proceed to fulfill the promises that you made to each other. You may begin to live separately. You may divide your property and sell any property that you have agreed to sell. Any necessary papers for transferring property may be signed (for example: car titles, quit-claim deeds, etc.). The custody and visitation provisions of your agreement should go into effect and you may begin to make and receive any alimony or child support payments. Essentially, under the terms of your Marital Settlement Agreement, you may begin to live your life as a single person again. However, you are not yet free to remarry and you cannot yet legally have sexual relations with other people. You are not yet divorced.

Chapter 9

Preparing Your Divorce Papers

Once you and your spouse have completed and signed your Marital Settlement Agreement and your individual Financial Statements, you are ready to begin preparation of your actual divorce documents. This section will take you through the process and steps necessary to complete this portion of the divorce procedure. As stated previously, divorce is governed by individual state law. Even individual counties within a single state may have certain local legal rules that will govern your divorce process. Although the basic general pattern followed in divorce proceedings is similar throughout all 50 states, there are significant minor differences between the particular documents that you will be required to submit to a court and the specific procedures to follow in each state or county. The information given in this section will instruct you on how to prepare documents that will satisfy the legal requirements in the vast majority of all states and counties. Please refer to the listing for your individual state in the Appendix for the specific requirements in your state.

Steps in the Divorce Process

The process of divorce is similar in all jurisdictions. Although the legal terminology and procedure may be difficult to understand at times, the process itself is not complicated. If you understand the process, you will be able to approach your divorce with much less fear and concern about the outcome. In general, by filing for a divorce you will be asking a court to formally declare that your marriage is over. In order to make this legal request and have it granted, you must prepare certain legal documents and follow certain court procedures. There are, generally, five basic steps that must be followed in order to obtain a divorce:

① Prepare all of the necessary legal documents. You have already prepared your Marital Settlement Agreement and Financial Statements. Preparation of the other necessary documents will be explained later in this section.

② File a first set of divorce documents with the clerk of the court that has the proper authority to decide on your case.

③ File a second set of divorce documents with the clerk of the same court.

④ Schedule and attend a short court hearing on your divorce.

⑤ Have the judge sign the final court document that declares your marriage is over.

The preparation of this document will be explained in this section and the procedure to follow in court will be discussed next. Courts handle over 1.7 million divorce cases every year. It is the most common legal proceeding in the nation. Because of this enormous volume of cases, the procedures and process for uncontested divorces have become relatively routine. Although it will be an entirely new experience for you and your spouse, the judges and clerks with whom you will be dealing have handled, literally, thousands of divorce cases. The divorce papers prepared using the instructions in this kit are very basic and routine and should be processed without difficulty.

General Considerations

There are certain general instructions that will apply to the preparation and use of all of the legal documents that you will file with the court. By following these instructions, your legal documents will look like and be treated like every other legal document that a court examines. For all of the legal forms that you prepare using this kit, you should follow these instructions:

① The legal forms that you will prepare for court use must be prepared on clean white 8½" x 11" paper. There are state-specific legal forms contained on the enclosed CD for some of the necessary documents. Each form that you complete should be filled in by neatly typing or printing double-spaced on only one side of the form. Some courts may require various other localized practices such as having holes punched in the papers, or attaching your documents to blue paper backing sheets. Check with the court clerk.

② Keep all of your papers neat, clean, orderly, and in one place. Each document you file that has more than one page should be stapled together in the upper left-hand corner of the pages.

③ Each of the documents that you prepare must be signed and notarized (if necessary) according to the instructions at the end of this section.

④ The original of each document (with the actual signatures) will be filed with the court. You should, however, make at least two copies of each document that you prepare: one copy for you and one copy for your spouse. Your complete file of all documents should be brought with you at the time of your court appearance. The Appendix also contains information that you will need to prepare the court documents in the proper format. Each state and often each county may have a slightly differing form for court papers that they will use. Check your state's listing in the Appendix and also the state-specific forms on the CD.

⑤ The top portion of the first page of each court document will consist of specific information that the courts have standardized to some extent to aid in the filing and referencing of court records. This is known as the *caption* of the document. Each document must have this information present or the court clerk will not accept the document for filing. This information is: (1) the name of the court; (2) the name of the parties involved; (3) the case number assigned to the case by the clerk; and (4) the title of the document. The Appendix will contain the data that you need to prepare your own document caption. If you have obtained court records for a divorce in your county (as explained in the next section), you should prepare the caption of your documents exactly as shown on the official court records.

⑥ The documents that you prepare will be legal court documents and will generally be acceptable in all courts. Most judges are glad to see situations in which a potential legal battle has been settled outside of court. Many judges will provide considerable guidance as you negotiate your way through the legal process. Be aware, however, that in certain areas of the country and in certain courts, there may still be strong resistance to allowing self-help divorces to take place. Some judges may be very strict in the interpretation of laws and may allow no deviation at all in the precise legal wording of court documents. If you encounter resistance of this nature, try to understand what the problem is and make every attempt to correct it. If you cannot successfully correct the difficulty, you will need to see a lawyer for assistance.

The Necessary Documents

In addition to your Marital Settlement Agreement and Financial Statements, there four or five relatively short legal documents that you will need to prepare for submission to the court. These documents, in general, are:

- Petition (or Complaint)
- Appearance, Consent, and Waiver form
- Child Custody Jurisdiction form (if children are involved)
- Proposed Final Judgment or Decree
- Certificate of Divorce (or Dissolution of Marriage)

Some states or counties may require one or more other routine forms. For example, some California counties require couples to submit a short form that indicates that they desire or have declined marriage counseling services. Other states may require forms that outline child support calculations or other information relating to child support. The most common type of other form required will relate to the payment of child support payments. If you and your spouse have agreed to have any child support payments paid through a court or government agency or official, there will be certain required forms that will need to be filled out. In addition, many states have procedures and forms available for use if there will be an automatic wage withholding order or assignment of wages when there are child support payments involved. Any of these types of forms should be available from the office of the clerk of the court where you will file your divorce papers.

Although the legal method outlined in this kit does not require the use of a summons or citation, some states may still require that a summons or citation be used as a formality. A summons/citation is a document that is officially delivered to a person against whom a lawsuit has been filed. The initial court papers that are filed in a lawsuit are also delivered with the summons/citation. The summons/citation notifies the person that the suit has been filed and specifies a time limit in which the person must respond to the lawsuit. Since you and your spouse are cooperating in the filing of your divorce, your spouse will file an Appearance, Consent, and Waiver form that takes the place of the summons/citation in the vast majority of states. When you file your actual divorce papers, you should, however, ask the clerk of the court if a summons/citation will be required if your spouse files the written waiver of service of process. The Appearance, Consent, and Waiver form is explained later in this section.

In order for the judge to properly handle your case, you must file all of the documents that are required in your jurisdiction. Refer back to the decision that you made earlier regarding where to file for your divorce. The specific forms and procedure for that state and county (or parish) are what you will need to adhere to. There are three steps that you should take initially to determine exactly what documents must be filed:

① You should carefully read through the Appendix regarding your state's laws to see if any specific additional forms are mentioned. Most states have specific mandatory fill-in-the-blank type forms for use in filing for your divorce. **If your state has official forms available, you** *must* **use them. Most mandatory official forms are included on the CD.** If not, the forms are generally available directly from the clerk of the court where you will file for your divorce. If there are mandatory forms, they will usually contain their own instructions and these should be followed carefully. The information that you have compiled in your questionnaires and in your Marital Settlement Agreement and Financial Statements should be all that you will need to easily prepare most forms of this nature. The instructions for filling in these types of forms will be the same as for the forms contained in this kit. Simply follow the instructions for preparing and signing the divorce forms as explained in this section.

② **You should ask the clerk of the court where you intend to file your divorce papers if any other forms are required, beyond the basic forms listed earlier.** Some courts may have specific state or local forms in use that may be required. You can easily do this by phone or in person. Most court clerks are very helpful and will be glad to assist you. Remember to be courteous and respectful when you deal with the clerk. Court clerks, however, are not attorneys and are not allowed to provide any legal advice. They can and often will assist you in being certain that the forms that you file are the correct ones, but do not ask them for answers to specific legal questions. They are not authorized to offer legal assistance. You may also wish to inquire with the court clerk at this time about the general procedure that is followed in divorce cases. The clerk should be able to inform you regarding any time limits, waiting periods, filing requirements, the customary order in which the documents are filed, how much the filing fees are, and other technical information regarding your case. You should write down any information that you receive from the court clerk. If you run into a particular clerk who is less than helpful, be polite and try to determine if there is a problem. If you cannot correct the problem, try again later with a different clerk.

③ Finally, you may wish to request and obtain from the court clerk a copy of another couple's divorce papers that were filed recently in an uncontested divorce in the county where you intend to file for your divorce. Legal documents filed with the court clerk are public records and are generally available to the public for a small copying fee. A few states, however, seal divorce records. In most jurisdictions, you have the right to obtain a copy of the court file for any other divorce that has been filed. You will have to make your request and pick up the copies in person. The documents in these other court records can be very useful in the preparation of your own divorce papers. They will show you the exact format that is in use in your particular county. Copies of any other required forms will also be included in any such records. They will provide you with a basic outline of the set of documents that are necessary in your particular county to obtain a divorce. To obtain such court records, ask the clerk of the court for "a copy of the court file of any uncontested divorce that was made final within the last six months." They should easily be able to fill this request. There will usually be a small charge per page for copying the documents in the file. Lawyers often obtain court records for exactly this same purpose. The clerk may require that you provide the specific names of the people involved in another case in order to find a proper court file. In that case, you should consult your local newspaper to determine the names of couples who were recently divorced. Most newspapers will list such names in a legal listing or notice section.

By using the above methods, you should be able to determine the exact documents that are required for your divorce. A simple list of the documents that are necessary in your county should be compiled. The preparation of these documents is explained next. After each instruction section, a sample document is included with the numbered areas that are to be filled in indicated clearly. Use these samples to determine where the required information must be filled in on the actual blank forms.

Petition or Complaint Instructions

The main document that you will file with the court may be titled a "petition" or "complaint." A few states may refer to this document as an "action," "application," "bill of complaint," or "declaration:" check the Appendix. The names of the two spouses on this and the other court documents will be either the petitioner and respondent (for petitions) or the plaintiff and defendant (for complaints). The Appendix listing for your state will give you the proper titles to use. (A few states allow the filing of a Joint Petition for Divorce or Dissolution of Marriage. In these cases, the spouses are both referred to as co-petitioners).

The petition/complaint form included in this book begins with the words "This action is brought by ... ," following the caption section of the document. The petition/complaint will contain your formal request to the court that your marriage be terminated. It will also include your request that the terms of your marital settlement agreement be used as the terms of your divorce. It will contain all of the basic information that a court will need to decide your case. The information that you have compiled in the various questionnaires throughout this book should be used when completing this form. Your questionnaire answers should contain all of the necessary facts for your petition/complaint. You will now need to decide which of you will be the petitioner/plaintiff in your case and which of you will be the respondent/defendant. The spouse who will be the respondent/defendant will have no duties other than signing documents. The spouse who is the petitioner/ plaintiff will sign documents, file the papers with the court, and attend the court hearing, if one is necessary. Legally, it will make no difference which of you serves as petitioner/plaintiff and which of you serves as respondent/defendant. Your particular state procedures relating to which county (or parish) to file your divorce papers in may have bearing on which spouse is chosen as petitioner/plaintiff. You may decide to allow either spouse to be petitioner/plaintiff if it will result in the court proceedings being held in the most convenient county (or parish) for you and your spouse. For preparing your own documents, you should use either the title/caption information that is contained in the Appendix for your state or follow the format as shown on the divorce record files that you have obtained from the clerk of the court. Once you have determined the exact information for the caption, you will use the same caption for each court document.

The basic Petition/Complaint document in this book should be generally acceptable in every jurisdiction in the United States. However, you should always use the state-specific form that is contained on the CD. **You must use the state-specific form if available.** In addition, consult your local court clerk in advance to determine any local rules that may result in slight differences in this form. At most, you may be required to add a sentence or two of further information to this form or change the wording slightly. You should always substitute the official legal terminology that is in use in your state wherever appropriate as shown in the Appendix. You may, for example, need to substitute "dissolution of marriage" for "divorce;" or "maintenance" for "alimony," etc. **Of course, if mandatory official forms are in use in your state or county, you *must* use them instead.**

Fill in the appropriate information on a blank copy of the form from the CD and then type Do not make any alterations in the wording of this form unless it is to comply with wording in an actual sample that you have obtained from the court or to comply with information contained in the Appendix of this book. Instructions for signing this document and the rest of the documents in this chapter and filing them with the court clerk are included at the end of this section. For preparing your petition/complaint, you will need the following specific information:

① The exact name of the court as shown in the Appendix for your state
② The name of the county in which you will file your divorce papers
③ The name of the state that you have determined is the proper one for your divorce
④ The exact name of the spouse who will be the one filing for the divorce, followed by the correct title for that person (either "Petitioner" or "Plaintiff"). Check the Appendix for your state
⑤ The exact name and title of the other spouse (either "Respondent" or "Defendant")
⑥ If children are involved, type "And in the interests of: [name of each child]"
⑦ Exact title as shown in Appendix (generally, "Petition for Dissolution of Marriage" or "Complaint for Divorce")
⑧ Exact full name of spouse filing
⑨ Title of spouse filing ("Petitioner" or "Plaintiff")
⑩ Age of spouse filing
⑪ Full address of spouse filing
⑫ Social Security number of spouse filing
⑬ Enter occupation, place of employment, complete address and state of employer
⑭ Title of other spouse ("Respondent or Defendant")
⑮ Exact full name of other spouse
⑯ Age of other spouse
⑰ Full address of other spouse
⑱ Social Security number of other spouse
⑲ Enter occupation, place of employment, complete address and state of employer
⑳ Title of spouse filing ("Petitioner" or "Plaintiff")
㉑ Title of spouse filing ("Petitioner" or "Plaintiff")
㉒ State of residency and how many months resiging in that state
㉒ County of residency and how many months resiging in that county
㉓ County of residency
㉔ Title of other spouse ("Respondent or Defendant")
㉕ Title of other spouse ("Respondent or Defendant")
㉖ Title of spouse filing ("Petitioner" or "Plaintiff")
㉗ Title of other spouse ("Respondent or Defendant")
㉘ Date of marriage
㉙ State of marriage
㉚ Date of separation
㉛ One or more of the following statements:

No children were born or adopted to the marriage and the wife is not now pregnant.

There [was or were] [number of children] born or adopted to this marriage and [his, her, or their] name[s] and date[s] of birth [is or are] as follows: [List names and dates of birth of all children].

㉜ Type the word "wife" and name of wife

㉝ In a complete sentence, state the grounds that apply to your marriage using the language in the Appendix that applies to your state. For example: "There are irreconcilable differences between the spouses which has led to an irretrievable breakdown of this marriage."

㉞ Title of spouse filing ("Petitioner" or "Plaintiff")

㉟ Title of other spouse ("Defendant" or Respondent")

㊱ Date document was signed

㊲ Title of other spouse ("Respondent or Defendant")

㊳ Title of other spouse ("Respondent or Defendant")

㊴ Title of spouse filing ("Petitioner" or "Plaintiff")

㊵ Date document was signed

㊶ Signature and title of spouse filing

㊷ This information should be completed by the notary public

㊸ Repeat signature and title of other spouse and notary section (Not shown on sample form)

In the ① _____ Court for ② _____ County, State of ③ _____

In re: The Marriage of:

④ _____ , _____)
)
)
and)   Case #:_____
⑤ _____ , _____)
)
⑥ _____)
)
_____)
_____)
_____

⑦ _____ FOR _____

This action is brought by ⑧ _____ , ⑨ _____ , age
⑩ _____ , who resides at ⑪ _____ , City of
⑪ _____ , whose Social Security # is ⑫ _____ , and
who is employed as a ⑬ _____ at ⑬ _____ ,
located at ⑬ _____ , City of ⑬ _____ , State of
⑬ _____ .

The ⑭ _____ in this action is ⑮ _____ ,
age ⑯ _____ , who resides at ⑰ _____ , City of
⑰ _____ , whose Social Security # is ⑱ _____ , and
who is employed as a ⑲ _____ at ⑲ _____ , located at ⑲ _____ , City of ⑲ _____ ,
State of ⑲ _____ .

The undersigned ⑳ _____ states, under oath, the following:

1. RESIDENCY. ㉑ _____ has been a resident of and domiciled
in the State of ㉒ _____ for the preceding ㉒ _____ and the County
of ㉓ _____ for the preceding ㉓ _____ .

2. SERVICE OF PROCESS. The ㉔ _____ has agreed to file a
Waiver of Service of Process in this cause and, therefore, no service of process is necessary at this time.

3. JURISDICTION. The court has proper jurisdiction to hear this cause. The
㉕ _____ has agreed to file an Appearance in this cause. Neither party
has ever been involved in any other domestic relations proceeding involving the other

party in this or any other jurisdiction. Neither party is currently an active member of any branch of the Armed Forces of the United States.

4. MARRIAGE. The ㉖ _____ and ㉗ _____ were married on the ㉘ _____ day of ㉘ _____ , ㉘ ____ , in the State of ㉙ _____ and lived together as husband and wife until on or about the ㉚ _____ day of ㉚ _____ , ㉚ ____ , at which time they separated and ceased to live together and they have lived separate and apart without cohabitation ever since.

5. CHILDREN.

㉛

and the ㉜ _____ is not now pregnant.

6. GROUNDS.

㉝

7. AGREEMENT. This proceeding is uncontested. The ㉞ _____ and ㉟ _____ have both signed a Marital Settlement Agreement, dated the ㊱ _____ day of ㊱ _____ , 20 ㊱ ____ , which is attached and incorporated by reference. By the terms of this Marital Settlement Agreement they have settled all of the issues relating to their marriage, including the division of all of their property, the disposition of all of their bills and obligations, the need for any alimony, maintenance or spousal support, and the custody, visitation, care, and support of their children]. A Financial Statement has been prepared by each of the parties listing their respective income, expenses, assets, and liabilities and the individual Financial Statements are attached and incorporated by reference. The Marital Settlement Agreement and Financial Statements were signed under no duress or force and without collusion.

8. CONSENT. The (37) _____ has agreed to file a Consent to the incorporation and merger of said Marital Settlement Agreement into a Final Judgement of Divorce.

9. WAIVER. The (38) _____ hereby waives any rights to findings of fact and conclusions of law, a record of testimony, motion for a new trial, notice of entry of final judgement or decree, and the right to appeal, but does not waive any rights to the future modification of any judgement or decree in this cause.

The (39) _____ respectfully requests and prays:

1. That a Divorce be granted by the court dissolving and terminating forever the marriage between the parties.

2. That all of the terms and conditions of the party's Marital Settlement Agreement, which is attached, be approved and be incorporated, merged into, and made part of a Final Judgement of Divorce , and that the parties be ordered to comply with all terms and conditions of the Marital Settlement Agreement, but that the Marital Settlement Agreement survive.

3. That the court award the parties any other further relief as may be just and equitable.

Dated this (40) _____ day of (40) _____, 20 (40) ___ .

(41)
_____
Signature of (41) _____

(42) State of _____
County of _____

On _____, 20 ____ , _____ personally came before me and, being duly sworn, did state that he/she is the person described in the above document and that he/she signed the above document in my presence and verified that the information contained in the foregoing document is true and correct on personal knowledge and acknowledged that the document was signed as a free and voluntary act for the purposes stated.

_____
Notary signature

(43)

Appearance, Consent, and Waiver Instructions

This form will need to be filed in all cases, except those in which a state allows a petition for divorce or dissolution of marriage to be filed jointly. The form serves several functions. First, by using the form, the requirement for a formal serving of the divorce papers on one of you is made unnecessary. The delivery of the divorce papers is formally known as *service of process.* Filing this form effectively waives the right to have papers served formally by a sheriff or some other process server. Also with this document, the spouse who is not designated as the petitioner/plaintiff officially makes a legal appearance and consents to the jurisdiction and venue of the court. This means that he or she agrees that the court has the proper authority to grant your divorce. The other spouse (officially the respondent/defendant) also offers his or her consent to the adoption of the Marital Settlement Agreement into the final divorce order. He or she also waives his or her right to findings of fact, conclusions of law, a record of testimony, motion for a new trial, notice of entry of final judgment or decree, and right to appeal. These rights were also waived by you in the petition/complaint in an effort to eliminate any unnecessary and extraneous legal proceedings and technicalities. The purpose of the entire document is to streamline and speed up the legal process when you have both agreed to the results desired. It is a formality that is required in states that require that only one spouse file the petition or complaint for divorce. This form is basically an agreement by the other spouse to join in the effort to obtain a divorce. Filing this form generally eliminates much paperwork and often considerable expense from the process of obtaining a divorce. Once the spouse who will act as respondent/defendant has signed this form, no further action by that spouse should be necessary for the remainder of the divorce process. The title to this document will normally always be "Appearance, Consent, and Waiver." The rest of the caption portion of this document should be identical to that used in your petition/complaint information:

① The exact name of the court as shown in the Appendix for your state
② The name of the county in which you will file your divorce papers
③ The name of the state that you have determined is the proper one for your divorce
④ The exact name of the spouse who will be the one filing for the divorce, followed by the correct title for that person (either "Petitioner" or "Plaintiff"). Check the Appendix for your state
⑤ The exact name and title of the other spouse (either "Respondent" or "Defendant")
⑥ If children are involved, type "And in the interests of: [name of each child]"
⑦ Title of the other spouse ("Respondent" or "Defendant")
⑧ State of residency

⑨ Number of months of residency in state
⑩ County of residency
⑪ Number of months residency in county
⑫ Petition or Complaint
⑬ Date of Marital Settlement Agreement
⑭ Petition or Complaint Judgment or Decree
⑮ Judgment or Decree
⑯ Petition or Complaint
⑰ Signature of other spouse (signed in front of notary public)
⑱ Title of other spouse ("Respondent" or "Defendant")
⑲ Printed name of other spouse
⑳ Title of other spouse ("Respondent" or "Defendant")
㉑ To be completed by the notary public (not shown)

In the ① Court for ② County, State of ③

In re: The Marriage of:

    ④

and

    ⑤
    ⑥

APPEARANCE, CONSENT, AND WAIVER

The undersigned ⑦ states on oath, that:

1. RESIDENCY. I have been a resident of and domiciled in the State of ⑧ for the preceding ⑨ and the County of ⑩ for the preceding ⑪ .

2. ADMISSION. I have received a copy of the ⑫ which was filed in this cause and I have read and understand it and admit all of the allegations contained in it.

3. APPEARANCE AND WAIVER. I waive all objections to venue and the issuance, service, and return of process in this cause and voluntarily enter my general appearance in this cause and submit personally to the jurisdiction of the court. I have never been involved in any other domestic relations proceeding involving the other party in this or any other jurisdiction. I am not currently an active member of any branch of the Armed Forces of the United States.

4. AGREEMENT. I have freely and voluntarily entered into a Marital Settlement Agreement, dated ⑬ , and a Financial Statement which are attached to and incorporated into the original ⑭ . The Marital Settlement Agreement and Financial Statements were signed under no duress or force and without collusion.

5. CONSENT. I consent to said Marital Settlement Agreement and Financial Statements being approved and incorporated, merged into, and made part of a Final ⑮ , and that the parties be ordered to comply with all terms and conditions of the Marital Settlement Agreement, but that the Marital Settlement Agreement survive.

6. ADDITIONAL CONSENT. I agree that this proceeding is uncontested. I further consent that this cause be heard on any day convenient to the court without further notice to me and that the court enter an Order granting the relief prayed for in the ⑯.

7. ADDITIONAL WAIVER. I further waive my rights to notice of trial, findings of fact and conclusions of law, a record of testimony, motion for a new trial, notice of entry of final judgment or decree, and right to appeal, but do not waive any rights to the future modification of any judgment or decree in this cause.

⑰
Signature of ⑱
⑲
Printed Name of ⑳

㉑

Child Custody Jurisdiction Form Instructions

This particular form should only be used if there are minor children who were born or adopted during the marriage. If there are no children involved in your divorce, skip this section. The purpose of this form is to provide the court with information relevant to the jurisdiction of the court to issue orders concerning the children. If you have minor children, the information on this form is mandatory under the Uniform Child Custody Jurisdiction Act in all states. This form and the law on which it is based is an attempt to be certain that only one court will exercise jurisdiction over the issue of child custody for a particular child. If you or your spouse have been involved in prior custody proceedings involving any of your children or if you are aware of any current proceedings or persons claiming custody, you should consult a competent lawyer. You and your spouse will be making an official declaration under oath to the court about the following information:

① The exact name of the court as shown in the Appendix for your state

② The name of the county in which you will file your divorce papers

③ The name of the state that you have determined is the proper one for your divorce

④ The exact name of the spouse who will be the one filing for the divorce, followed by the correct title for that person (either "Plaintiff" or "Petitioner"). Check the Appendix for your state

⑤ The exact name and title of the other spouse (either "Defendant" or "Respondent")

⑥ "And in the interests of: [name of each child]

⑦ Title of spouse filing ("Plaintiff" or "Petitioner")

⑧ Title of the other spouse ("Defendant" or "Respondent")

⑨ Number of children of your marriage

⑩ For each child, state the name, sex, Social Security number, date and place of birth, time and place of residence, and name and relationship of person child lived with for the past five years

⑪ Date document was signed

⑫ Signature of spouse filing (signed in front of notary public)

⑬ Title of spouse filing ("Plaintiff" or "Petitioner")

⑭ Printed name of spouse filing

⑮ Title of spouse filing ("Plaintiff" or "Petitioner")

⑯ To be completed by notary public

⑰ Repeat signature and title of other spouse and notary section

In the ① Court for ② County, State of ③

In re: The Marriage of:

     ④

and

     ⑤
     ⑥

DECLARATION UNDER THE UNIFORM CHILD CUSTODY JURISDICTION ACT

We, the undersigned, ⑦ and ⑧ , are both parties to this proceeding to determine the custody of a minor child, and upon oath state:

1. The number of minors subject to this proceeding is ⑨ . For each child, the name, sex, Social Security number, date and place of birth, and time and place of residence, and name and relationship of person child lived with for the past 5 years, is as follows: ⑩

2. Neither of us have participated as a party or a witness or in any other capacity in any other litigation or custody proceeding in this state or elsewhere, concerning the custody of a child subject to this proceeding.

3. Neither of us have any information concerning any other litigation or custody proceeding in this state or elsewhere, concerning the custody of a child subject to this proceeding.

4. Neither of us knows of any other person who is not a party to this proceeding who has physical custody or claims to have custody or visitation rights of any child subject to this proceeding.

Dated ⑪.

⑫
Signature of ⑬
⑭
Printed Name of ⑮

⑯ State of
County of

On   ,   personally came before me and, being duly sworn, did state that he or she is the person described in the above document and that he or she signed the above document in my presence and verified that the information contained in the foregoing document is true and correct on personal knowledge and acknowledged that the document was signed as a free and voluntary act for the purposes stated.

  Notary public signature
  Notary Public
  In and for the County of
  State of
  My Commission expires   Notary Seal
⑰

Final Judgment or Decree Instructions

This particular document is actually the ultimate goal you are seeking in your divorce. It is the legal court order that declares that your marriage is officially over. It will also include the formal court order regarding all of the other terms of your divorce. This final court order may be called a Judgment of Divorce, Judgment of Dissolution of Marriage, Decree of Divorce, Decree of Dissolution of Marriage, or some other similar title. Check the Appendix and with the clerk of the court to determine the title in your jurisdiction. As you prepare this document, be very careful and take your time. It must be prepared to reflect exactly what you and your spouse have agreed upon in your Marital Settlement Agreement. It should also parallel exactly what you have requested in the last section of your petition/complaint. Most judges will allow some deviation from strict technical application of legal terminology if it is clear what is intended by the particular language used. However, some judges are very strict in this regard. To be safe, you should try to comply as closely as possible to the particular legal language used in your locale.

Judges in some localities may require that the actual judgment or decree contain all of the terms of the court's order. In other words, these judges want to have all of the various terms and conditions that are in your Marital Settlement Agreement actually typed into the judgment/decree form. There should be no problem with this, other than a little more work typing this form. If your particular area has this requirement, simply delete those portions of the judgment/decree form that state that your property, custody, child support, alimony, and name change will be according to or as set forth in the Marital Settlement Agreement. Then actually type into the judgment/decree the relevant portions of your Marital Settlement Agreement that apply. Although this document will not be signed by the judge until the end of your divorce hearing, it should be prepared in advance. In an uncontested divorce proceeding that is based on a written and signed marital settlement agreement (as yours will be), a pre-prepared final judgment/decree is common. In the vast majority of cases, the judge will sign this document at the close of your court hearing. Although it is unlikely, there is a slight possibility that the judge may make some changes in the final version of the decision. For example, the amount of child support may be increased or decreased by the judge. If this happens, the judge will orally inform you of such a change during your hearing. Any such changes must be noted carefully at the time of your hearing. Your judgment/decree must then be retyped and resubmitted to the court clerk for the judge's signature.

① The exact name of the court as shown in the Appendix for your state
② The name of the county in which you will file your divorce papers

③ The name of the state that you have determined is the proper one for your divorce

④ The exact name of the spouse who will be the one filing for the divorce, followed by the correct title for that person (either "Plaintiff" or "Petitioner"). Check the Appendix for your state

⑤ The exact name and title of the other spouse (either "Defendant" or "Respondent")

⑥ If children are involved, type "And in the interests of: [name of each child]"

⑦ Title of final document ("Judgment of Divorce," "Decree of Dissolution of Marriage," or other). Check your state's requirements in the Appendix

⑧ Date of final hearing

⑨ Title of spouse filing ("Plaintiff" or "Petitioner")

⑩ Title of other spouse ("Defendant" or "Respondent")

⑪ Petition or Complaint (whichever applies)

⑫ Judgment or Decree (whichever applies)

⑬ Judgment or Decree (whichever applies)

⑭ Plaintiff or Petitioner

⑮ Defendant or Respondent

⑯ Date of Marital Settlement Agreement

⑰ to ⑲ Will be completed by the Judge

⑳ Signature of spouse filing

㉑ Title of spouse filing ("Plaintiff" or "Petitioner")

㉒ Printed name of person filing

㉓ Title of spouse filing ("Plaintiff" or "Petitioner")

㉔ Signature of other spouse

㉕ Title of other spouse ("Defendant" or "Respondent")

㉖ Printed name of other spouse

㉗ Title of other spouse ("Defendant" or "Respondent")

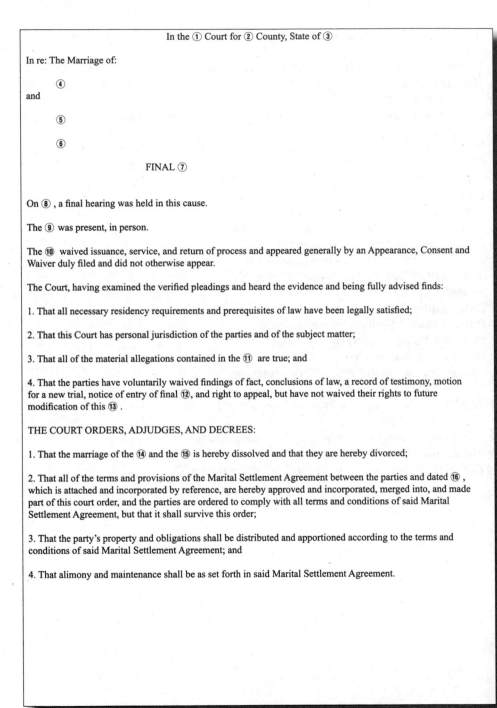

In the ① Court for ② County, State of ③

In re: The Marriage of:

④

and

⑤

⑥

FINAL ⑦

On ⑧ , a final hearing was held in this cause.

The ⑨ was present, in person.

The ⑩ waived issuance, service, and return of process and appeared generally by an Appearance, Consent and Waiver duly filed and did not otherwise appear.

The Court, having examined the verified pleadings and heard the evidence and being fully advised finds:

1. That all necessary residency requirements and prerequisites of law have been legally satisfied;

2. That this Court has personal jurisdiction of the parties and of the subject matter;

3. That all of the material allegations contained in the ⑪ are true; and

4. That the parties have voluntarily waived findings of fact, conclusions of law, a record of testimony, motion for a new trial, notice of entry of final ⑫, and right to appeal, but have not waived their rights to future modification of this ⑬ .

THE COURT ORDERS, ADJUDGES, AND DECREES:

1. That the marriage of the ⑭ and the ⑮ is hereby dissolved and that they are hereby divorced;

2. That all of the terms and provisions of the Marital Settlement Agreement between the parties and dated ⑯ , which is attached and incorporated by reference, are hereby approved and incorporated, merged into, and made part of this court order, and the parties are ordered to comply with all terms and conditions of said Marital Settlement Agreement, but that it shall survive this order;

3. That the party's property and obligations shall be distributed and apportioned according to the terms and conditions of said Marital Settlement Agreement; and

4. That alimony and maintenance shall be as set forth in said Marital Settlement Agreement.

Signed and Entered on ⑰.

⑱
Signature of Presiding Judge
⑲
Printed Name of Presiding Judge

Approved as to form and content:

⑳
Signature of ㉑
㉒
Printed Name of ㉓

㉔
Signature of ㉕
㉖
Printed Name of ㉗

㉘

Certificate of Divorce or Dissolution of Marriage Instructions

Most states require that a certificate be filed upon the granting of the final divorce. This certificate is similar to a birth certificate and will generally be filed with the state's Bureau of Vital Statistics or some similar agency. It is prepared on an official form and is, generally, very simple to fill out. Since you must use the official forms for your state, no form for this purpose is contained in this kit. The official forms for this purpose should be available from the clerk of the court where you file for your divorce. This form should be filled out and taken with you to the court hearing in your case.

STATE OF UTAH - DEPARTMENT OF HEALTH

CERTIFICATE OF DIVORCE, DISSOLUTION OF MARRIAGE, OR ANNULMENT

HUSBAND

1. HUSBAND'S NAME (First, Middle, Last)

2a. RESIDENCE - CITY, TOWN OR LOCATION   2b. COUNTY

2c. STATE | 3. BIRTHPLACE (State or Foreign Country) | 4. DATE OF BIRTH (Month, Day, Year)

5. NUMBER OF THIS MARRIAGE - First, Second, etc. (Specify below) | 6. IF NOT FIRST MARRIAGE, LAST MARRIAGE ENDED: By Death, Divorce, Dissolution, or Annulment (Specify Below) Date (Mo., Day, Yr.) | 7. RACE: White, Black, Amer. Indian, etc. (Specify below) | 8. EDUCATION: (Specify only highest grade completed) Elementary/Secondary (0 - 12) College (13-16 or 17+)

WIFE

9a. WIFE'S NAME (First, Middle, Last)   9b. MAIDEN LAST NAME

10a. RESIDENCE - CITY, TOWN OR LOCATION   10b. COUNTY

10c. STATE | 11. BIRTHPLACE (State or Foreign Country) | 12. DATE OF BIRTH (Month, Day, Year)

13. NUMBER OF THIS MARRIAGE - First, Second, etc. (Specify below) | 14. IF NOT FIRST MARRIAGE, LAST MARRIAGE ENDED: By Death, Divorce, Dissolution, or Annulment (Specify Below) Date (Mo., Day, Yr.) | 15. RACE: White, Black Amer. Indian, etc. (Specify below) | 16. EDUCATION: (Specify only highest grade completed) Elementary/Secondary (0 - 12) College (13-16 or 17+)

MARRIAGE

17a. PLACE OF THIS MARRIAGE - CITY, TOWN, OR LOCATION | 17b. COUNTY | 17c. STATE OR FOREIGN COUNTRY | 18. DATE OF THIS MARRIAGE (Month, Day, Year)

19. DATE COUPLE LAST RESIDED IN SAME HOUSEHOLD (Month, Day, Year) | 20. NUMBER OF CHILDREN UNDER 18 IN THIS HOUSEHOLD AS OF THE DATE IN ITEM 19. Number _____ ☐ None | 21. PETITIONER ☐ Husband ☐ Wife ☐ Both ☐ Other, Specify _____

ATTORNEY

22a. NAME OF PETITIONER'S ATTORNEY (Type/Print) | 22b. ADDRESS (Street and Number or Rural Route Number, City or Town, State Zip Code)

DECREE

23. I CERTIFY THAT THE MARRIAGE OF THE ABOVE NAMED PERSONS WAS DISSOLVED ON (Month, Day, Year) | 24. TYPE OF DECREE, Divorce, Dissolution, or Annulment (Specify) | 25. DATE RECORDED (Month, Day, Year)

26. NUMBER OF CHILDREN UNDER 18 WHOSE PHYSICAL CUSTODY WAS AWARDED TO: Husband _____ Wife _____ Joint _____ Other _____ ☐ No Children ☐ Not Determined Yet | 27. COUNTY OF DECREE | 28. TITLE OF COURT

29. SIGNATURE OF CERTIFYING OFFICIAL | 30. TITLE OF CERTIFYING OFFICIAL | 31. DATE SIGNED (Month, Day, Year)

UDOH OVRS Form 14 Rev 12/03

Instructions for Signing and Filing the Documents

Once you have properly filled in all of the draft versions of the preceding forms, you will need to recheck your list of documents to be certain that you have all of the necessary papers on hand. If you have previously determined that there are other documents required in your jurisdiction, you will need to check those documents and fill in the appropriate information on them. Most additional documents are self-explanatory and should be easy to complete. In general, there are five easy steps necessary to complete and file the forms:

① Every document that is over one page should have the pages numbered at the bottom in this manner: Page 1 of [*fill in the total number of pages in your form*] pages; Page 2 of [*total number of*] pages; etc. After preparing the forms, two copies should be made of each document. Each original document and the copies should then be individually stapled together if there is more than one page. Do not, however, staple any of the documents to any other documents. You will now have before you three original copies of each of at least three different documents: your Petition/Complaint; your Appearance, Consent, and Waiver form, and your final Judgment/Decree form. You may, of course, also have various other forms depending on your circumstances and any local or state requirements: a Child Custody Jurisdiction form, a Certificate of Divorce or Dissolution of Marriage, a Withholding of Wages Order, an Assignment of Wages, etc. (Recall that references to "originals" or "original copies" in this book refer to any unsigned documents, even if they are photocopies. "Copies" refer to photocopies of signed documents).

② All of the various documents should now be taken to a notary public or similar official for signing. Although some states do not specifically require that all of these forms be signed before a notary, it is a good idea to do so. The Judgment/ Decree form does not require a notary. Any statistical Certificate of Divorce or Dissolution of Marriage will also not generally require notarization. In addition, unlike the Marital Settlement Agreement, none of these forms will require the use of witnesses. In front of the notary, you and your spouse should each sign all three original copies of each of the necessary documents, except the Appearance, Consent, and Waiver. (The Appearance, Consent, and Waiver form will be signed later). You should then have the notary sign all original copies of the forms (except the Judgment/Decree and Certificate of Divorce) where indicated and fill in the appropriate date and information regarding his or her authority. The notary should affix a seal to each original copy if required in your state.

③ To each of the three original copies of the Petition/Complaint you should now staple one original copy of the signed and notarized Marital Settlement Agreement and one original copy of each of your signed and notarized Financial Statements. You will now have three complete original signed and notarized copies of a rather large main document, consisting of the Petition/Complaint, the Marital Settlement Agreement, and two versions of the individual Financial Statement. One original copy of this master document will be for you and one original copy should be given to your spouse. The third original copy will be the one that you will file with the court. Assemble all of the other original documents and give one original copy of each to your spouse, keep one original copy for yourself, and set aside one original copy for filing with the clerk of the court.

④ The complete third original copy of the signed notarized main document (consisting of the Petition/Complaint, the Marital Settlement Agreement, and two versions of the individual Financial Statement) should now be brought to the office of the clerk of the appropriate court. This will be the only document that you file with the clerk at this time. At the clerk's office, you should tell the clerk that you wish to file the Petition/Complaint and ask that a case number be assigned to your divorce case. There will be a filing fee that must be paid at this time. The clerk will assign a case number to your case. Make careful note of the number and write it in ink on all copies of your other court documents. You may also request at this time that a final hearing be scheduled on the court calendar. If this is the practice in your area, the clerk will assign you a court date and time. In some jurisdictions, there will be a waiting period before a court date is actually scheduled. Make note of the waiting period and contact the clerk of the court at the appropriate time to schedule a hearing. If there is any difficulty in filing the forms, or if the clerk tells you that other forms should be filed, try to determine exactly what is necessary and make every effort to comply.

⑤ Your spouse must now return to the notary and sign the three original copies of the Appearance, Consent, and Waiver form. Once this form is completed and notarized, you are ready to file all of your other forms with the clerk of the court. Assemble one complete signed and notarized original copy of each document. (A notary may not be necessary on all of your additional documents). You may also need to file a certified copy of your Marriage Certificate with the clerk at this time. (Check with the clerk in advance). Take all of these documents to the clerk of the court and request that they be filed with your case records. You will need to tell the clerk the case number that was assigned to your case. The clerk may not accept your unsigned (by the judge) Final Judgment/Decree form for filing or your incomplete Certificate of Divorce/Dissolution of Marriage form. Don't worry. Some jurisdictions do not allow the filing of incomplete, unsigned forms. Just be sure to take these forms with you to your court hearing. You will use them at that time. Once you have completed these steps, you will have completed all of the paperwork necessary for your divorce. Instructions on how to conduct yourself during your court appearance are explained next.

Chapter 10

Sample Divorce Forms

In this chapter you will find a complete set of sample divorce documents similar to those which you will prepare for filing with a court. These forms are provided only as examples of how the actual completed court documents should look when they have been properly prepared according to the instructions in the previous chapter. The titles, captions, and actual contents of these sample forms will not be appropriate for your particular jurisdiction. They should not be used other than as an example. You should prepare your own forms according to the instructions in the previous chapter and the information as shown in the Appendix. However, as you prepare and type your own documents, you may wish to consult these forms for reference regarding the form and style of typical divorce documents.

The actual forms required in your particular state and county will differ from the forms contained here and generally several additional local or state forms will be necessary to complete your divorce. The sample forms which are included in this chapter are:

❑　Petition for Divorce

❑　Appearance, Consent, and Waiver

❑　Declaration Under the Uniform Child Custody Jurisdiction Act

❑　Judgement of Divorce

In the Circuit Court for Washington County, State of Superior

In re: The Marriage of:	)	
Mary Ellen Smith,	)	
Petitioner, and	)	
John William Smith,	)	
Respondent	)	Case #: ABC123
	)	
	)	
And in the interest of:	)	
Alice Mary Smith	)	
James John Smith	)	

PETITION FOR DIVORCE

This action is brought by Mary Ellen Smith, Petitioner, age 30, who resides at 150 Emerald Lane, Centerville, Superior, whose Social Security # is 333-33-3333, and who is employed as a homemaker at 150 Emerald Lane, Centerville, Superior.

The Respondent in this action is John William Smith , age 32, who resides at 2000 Main Street, Apartment #2, Centerville, Superior, whose Social Security # is 444-44-4444, and who is employed as a mechanic at Town Garage, located at 14 Broadway, Centerville, Superior.

The undersigned Petitioner states, under oath, the following:

1. RESIDENCY. Petitioner has been a resident of and domiciled in the State of Superior for the preceding 12 months and the County of Washington for the preceding 6 months.

2. SERVICE OF PROCESS. The Respondent has agreed to file a Waiver of Service of Process in this cause and, therefore, no service of process is necessary at this time.

3. JURISDICTION. The court has proper jurisdiction to hear this cause. The Respondent has agreed to file an Appearance in this cause. Neither party has ever been involved in any other domestic relations proceeding involving the other party in this or any other jurisdiction. Neither party is currently an active member of any branch of the Armed Forces of the United States.

4. MARRIAGE. The Petitioner and Respondent were married on the 1st day of January, 1999, in the State of Superior and lived together as husband and wife until on or about the 1st day of May, 2002, at which time they separated and ceased to live together and they have lived separate and apart without cohabitation ever since.

5. CHILDREN. There were 2 children born to the marriage and their names and dates of

birth are as follows:

Alice Mary Smith, born April 21, 2001

James John Smith, born October 26, 1999

and the Petitioner is not now pregnant.

6. GROUNDS. The marriage between the Petitioner and the Respondent is irretrievably broken and there is no possible chance for reconciliation.

7. AGREEMENT. This proceeding is uncontested. The Petitioner and Respondent have both signed a Marital Settlement Agreement, dated the 1st day of May, 2001, which is attached and incorporated by reference. By the terms of this Marital Settlement Agreement they have settled all of the issues relating to their marriage, including the division of all of their property, the disposition of all of their bills and obligations, the need for any alimony, maintenance or spousal support, and the custody, visitation, care, and support of their children. A Financial Statement has been prepared by each of the parties listing their respective income, expenses, assets, and liabilities and the individual Financial Statements are attached and incorporated by reference. The Marital Settlement Agreement and Financial Statements were signed under no duress or force and without collusion.

8. CONSENT. The Respondent has agreed to file a Consent to the incorporation and merger of said Marital Settlement Agreement into a Final Judgement of Divorce in this cause.

9. WAIVER. The Petitioner hereby waives any rights to findings of fact and conclusions of law, a record of testimony, motion for a new trial, notice of entry of final judgement or decree, and the right to appeal, but does not waive any rights to the future modification of any judgement or decree in this cause.

The Petitioner respectfully requests and prays: That a Divorce be granted by the court dissolving and terminating forever the marriage between the parties.

2. That all of the terms and conditions of the party's Marital Settlement Agreement, which is attached, be approved and be incorporated, merged into, and made part of a Final Judgement of Divorce, and that the parties be ordered to comply with all terms and conditions of the Marital Settlement Agreement, but that the Marital Settlement Agreement survive.

3. That the court award the parties any other further relief as may be just and equitable.

Dated this _____ day of _____ , 20 _____ .

_____

Mary Ellen Smith, Petitioner

State of Superior

County of Washington

On June 4 , 2005 , Mary Ellen Smith personally came before me and, being duly sworn, did state that he/she is the person described in the above document and that she signed the above document in my presence and verified that the information contained in the forego-ing document is true and correct on personal knowledge and acknowledged that the docu-ment was signed as a free and voluntary act for the purposes stated.

_____

Notary signature

Notary Public
In and for the County of Washington
State of Superior
My Commission expires January 1, 2006

_____

John William Smith, Respondent

State of Superior
County of Washington

On June 4, 2005 , John William Smith personally came before me and, being duly sworn, did state that he/she is the person described in the above document and that he signed the above document in my presence and verified that the information contained in the forego-ing document is true and correct on personal knowledge and acknowledged that the docu-ment was signed as a free and voluntary act for the purposes stated.

_____

Notary signature

Notary Public
In and for the County of Washington
State of Superior
My Commission expires January 1, 2006

In the Circuit Court for Washington County, State of Superior

In re: The Marriage of:)
   Mary Ellen Smith,   )
   Petitioner, and   )
   John William Smith,   )
   Respondent   )   Case #: ABC123
)
)
And in the interest of:)
   Alice Mary Smith   )
   James John Smith   )

APPEARANCE, CONSENT, AND WAIVER

The undersigned Respondent, John William Smith, states on oath, that:

1. RESIDENCY. I have been a resident of and domiciled in the State of Superior for the preceding 12 months and the County of Washington for the preceding 6 months.

2. ADMISSION. I have received a copy of the Petition which was filed in this cause and I have read and understand it and admit all of the allegations contained in it.

3. APPEARANCE AND WAIVER. I waive all objections to venue and the issuance, service, and return of process in this cause and voluntarily enter my general appearance in this cause and submit personally to the jurisdiction of the court. I have never been involved in any other domestic relations proceeding involving the other party in this or any other jurisdiction. I am not currently an active member of any branch of the Armed Forces of the United States.

4. AGREEMENT. I have freely and voluntarily entered into a Marital Settlement Agreement, dated the 1st day of May, 2005, and a Financial Statement which are attached to and incorporated into the original Petition [or Complaint]. The Marital Settlement Agreement and Financial Statements were signed under no duress or force and without collusion.

5. CONSENT. I consent to said Marital Settlement Agreement and Financial Statements being approved and incorporated, merged into, and made part of a Final Judgement [or Decree] of Divorce [or Dissolution of Marriage], and that the parties be ordered to comply with all terms and conditions of the Marital Settlement Agreement, but that the Marital Settlement Agreement survive.

6. ADDITIONAL CONSENT. I agree that this proceeding is uncontested. I further consent that this cause be heard on any day convenient to the court without further notice to me and that the court enter an Order granting the relief prayed for in the Petition.

7. ADDITIONAL WAIVER. I further waive my rights to notice of trial, findings of fact and conclusions of law, a record of testimony, motion for a new trial, notice of entry of final judgement or decree, and right to appeal, but do not waive any rights to the future modification of any judgement or decree in this cause.

_____
John William Smith, Respondent

State of Superior
County of Washington

On June 5, 2005, John William Smith personally came before me and, being duly sworn, did state that he/she is the person described in the above document and that he/she signed the above document in my presence and verified that the information contained in the foregoing document is true and correct on personal knowledge and acknowledged that the document was signed as a free and voluntary act for the purposes stated and that a copy of the Petition has been received.

_____
Notary signature

Notary Public
In and for the County of Washington
State of Superior
My Commission expires January 1, 2006

In the Circuit Court for Washington County, State of Superior

In re: The Marriage of:)
   Mary Ellen Smith,)
   Petitioner, and)
   John William Smith,)
   Respondent)   Case #: ABC123
)
)
And in the interest of:)
   Alice Mary Smith)
   James John Smith)

DECLARATION UNDER THE UNIFORM CHILD CUSTODY JURISDICTION ACT

We, the undersigned, Mary Ellen Smith and John William Smith, are both parties to this proceeding to determine the custody of a minor child, and upon oath state:

1. There are 2 minor children subject to this proceeding. For each child, the name, sex, Social Security number, date and place of birth, and time and place of residence and name and relationship of person child lived with for the past 5 years, is as follows:

A. Child's Name: Alice Mary Smith   Sex of Child: Female
   Place of Birth: Centerville, Superior   Date of Birth: April 21, 2002
   Child's Social Security Number: 555-44-3333

   Present residence: 150 Emerald Lane, Centerville, Superior
   Person child lives with: Mary Ellen Smith and John William Smith
   Relationship: Parents
   Dates of Residence: April 21, 2002 to Present

   Previous residence: none

B. Child's Name: James John Smith   Sex of Child: Male
   Place of Birth: Centerville, Superior   Date of Birth: October 26, 1999
   Child's Social Security Number: 333-44-5555

   Present residence: 150 Emerald Lane, Centerville, Superior
   Person child lives with: Mary Ellen Smith and John William Smith
   Relationship: Parents
   Dates of Residence: October 26, 1999 to Present

2. Neither of us have participated as a party or a witness or in any other capacity in any other litigation or custody proceeding in this state or elsewhere, concerning the custody of a child subject to this proceeding.

3. Neither of us have any information concerning any other litigation or custody proceeding in this state or elsewhere, concerning the custody of a child subject to this proceeding.

4. Neither of us knows of any other person who is not a party to this proceeding who has physical custody or claims to have custody or visitation rights of any child subject to this proceeding.

Dated this 4th day of June, 2005.

_____
Mary Ellen Smith, Petitioner

State of Superior
County of Washington

On June 4, 2005, Mary Ellen Smith personally came before me and, being duly sworn, did state that he/she is the person described in the above document and that he/she signed the above document in my presence and verified that the information contained in the foregoing document is true and correct on personal knowledge and acknowledged that the document was signed as a free and voluntary act for the purposes stated.

Notary signature

Notary Public
In and for the County of Washington
State of Superior
My Commission expires January 1, 2006

_____
John William Smith, Respondent

State of Superior
County of Washington

On June 4, 2005, John William Smith personally came before me and, being duly sworn, did state that he/she is the person described in the above document and that he/she signed the above document in my presence and verified that the information contained in the foregoing document is true and correct on personal knowledge and acknowledged that the document was signed as a free and voluntary act for the purposes stated.

Notary signature

Notary Public
In and for the County of Washington
State of Superior
My Commission expires January 1, 2006

In the Circuit Court for Washington County, State of Superior

In re: The Marriage of:) 　Mary Ellen Smith,) 　Petitioner, and) 　John William Smith,) 　Respondent)	Case #: ABC123

In re: The Marriage of:　　　　　　)
　Mary Ellen Smith,　　　　　　　　)
　Petitioner, and　　　　　　　　　)
　John William Smith,　　　　　　　)
　Respondent　　　　　　　　　　　)　　　Case #: ABC123
　　　　　　　　　　　　　　　　　)
　　　　　　　　　　　　　　　　　)
And in the interest of:　　　　　　　)
　Alice Mary Smith　　　　　　　　)
　James John Smith　　　　　　　　)

FINAL JUDGEMENT OF DIVORCE

On the 6th day of July, 2005, a final hearing was held in this cause.

The Petitioner Mary Ellen Smith was present, in person.

The Respondent waived issuance, service, and return of process and appeared generally by an Appearance, Consent and Waiver duly filed and did not otherwise appear.

The Court, having examined the verified pleadings and heard the evidence and being fully advised finds:

1. That all necessary residency requirements and prerequisites of law have been legally satisfied;

2. That this Court has personal jurisdiction of the parties and of the subject matter;

3. That all of the material allegations contained in the Petition [*or Complaint*] are true; and

4. That the parties have voluntarily waived findings of fact, conclusions of law, a record of testimony, motion for a new trial, notice of entry of final Judgement, and right to appeal, but have not waived their rights to future modification of this Judgement.

THE COURT ORDERS, ADJUDGES, AND DECREES:

1. That the marriage of the Petitioner and the Respondent is hereby dissolved and that they are hereby divorced;

2. That all of the terms and provisions of the Marital Settlement Agreement between the parties and dated the 1st day of May, 2005, which is attached and incorporated by reference, are hereby approved and incorporated, merged into, and made part of this court order, and the parties are ordered to comply with all terms and conditions of said Marital Settlement Agreement, but that it shall survive this order;

3. That the party's property and obligations shall be distributed and apportioned according to the terms and conditions of said Marital Settlement Agreement;

4. That alimony and maintenance shall be as set forth in said Marital Settlement Agreement;

5. That the custody, visitation, care, and support of the parties children shall be as set forth in said Marital Settlement Agreement;

6. That the Petitioner's name be restored to Mary Ellen Carter as set forth in said Marital Settlement Agreement.

Signed and Entered this 6th day of July, 2005.

Signature of Presiding Judge

Approved as to form and content:

Signature of Petitioner

Signature of Respondent

Chapter 11

Appearing in Court

The court appearance is the part of the divorce procedure that usually produces the most fear and uneasiness. There are many reasons for this: fear of the unknown, the general lack of understanding of the often arcane courtroom procedures, or the unfamiliar surroundings of a courtroom atmosphere. In most states, there are procedures in place that allow for the required court appearance to be short and straightforward. Some states allow the court appearance to be held in a judge's office (or chambers). Other states have entirely eliminated court appearances in certain uncontested no-fault divorce cases. Still other states have procedures for your hearing to be held informally before a *master* (or lesser court official). In some states, there are different rules for each county. Some counties may require a short five-minute hearing in uncontested cases, while others may require no hearing at all. Generally, there has been an attempt to streamline and modernize the court proceedings relating to divorce in many jurisdictions. The actual procedure for the court hearing (if one is required) may also be somewhat different in different locales. Some courts will only require that you state under oath that the information in your petition/complaint is true and correct. Judges in other courts may ask a few simple questions to verify the information. Some counties or states will require that you bring a witness to court with you to testify that you have been a resident of the state for the required time and, perhaps, to answer a few other simple questions. A few courts may insist that both you and your spouse attend the court hearing. (The Appearance, Consent, and Waiver form that you filed should eliminate the necessity that both of you attend, however.) In general, in most states and counties, only the spouse who is the plaintiff/petitioner will be required to attend. The actual time of the court hearing may range from a few minutes to an hour. The average time for a hearing in an uncontested divorce that is based on a marital settlement agreement is, perhaps, fifteen minutes. You will need to check with the clerk of the court in your particular county (or parish) to determine the local procedure for uncontested divorce court hearings. Although each county and state may have slightly differing procedures and slightly different rules, there are certain basic guidelines that apply generally to all courtroom situations.

General Court Appearance Rules

① Once you have filed all of the proper papers with the court (your Petition/Complaint, Appearance, Consent, and Waiver form, Marriage Certificate, etc.) you should ask the court clerk to schedule a date and time for a hearing for your case. In some states, there is a mandatory waiting period before the hearing is scheduled. Check the Appendix or ask the clerk of the court. If no hearing is necessary, they will inform you. They will also generally know how much time will be required for the hearing, based on previous cases that are similar to yours. The clerk will note your particular hearing time on the court calendar or court docket. The daily court calendar or docket sheet should be posted in the court house or the court clerk's office. Make a note of the courtroom number and time of the hearing.

② In addition, you should ask the court clerk if a witness is normally required. If there is any doubt or question as to whether a witness will be required, you should arrange for a witness to accompany you to the court hearing. Your witness should be an adult who has known you and your spouse for at least as long as the required residency time in your particular state. The witness should also be able to testify truthfully regarding the few questions noted under section 15 in the Testimony Worksheet found later in this section.

③ Well before the time of the hearing, you should assemble all of your documents. You should bring with you to the court all of the documents that were noted as mandatory in the document checklist, as well as any important documents relating to property (deeds, titles, etc.). These documents should be neatly placed in a file folder in a manner that allows you to find them immediately, if necessary. You should also assemble your original copies of all of the documents that were filed with the court. Unless it is already filed with the clerk, be certain that you have an original and several copies of your judgment/decree of divorce/dissolution with you when you arrive in court. This is the document that the judge will sign to finalize your divorce.

④ You should review the testimony guidelines and your actual testimony that you have prepared using the instructions later in this section. It is highly recommended that, a few days before your own hearing is scheduled, you attend a hearing for another uncontested divorce being held before the same judge as yours. This will greatly aid you in understanding what will be required for your own hearing. It will allow you to see how the hearing is handled, what questions are likely, and what documents are generally necessary. You will see that the hearing is relatively straightforward and not frightening.

⑤ You should arrive early on the day of your scheduled hearing to determine the location of the courtroom and find your place. Many courts prefer that you check in with the court clerk in advance of the hearing. Some will require you to pick up your own official case file from the clerk before going to the courtroom. Again, you will need to ask the court clerk for instructions before the day of your hearing.

⑥ In every court in the land, the judge will require that all participants show respect for the court. The courtroom judge has extremely wide powers inside a courtroom. In the extreme, a disrespectful and disruptive person can, potentially, be immediately removed from the courtroom and imprisoned for contempt of court. Since you and your spouse are attempting to obtain a divorce with as little hostility as possible, you should make certain that your courtroom behavior is courteous and respectful. You should dress appropriately in a business-like manner. The judge should always be referred to as "Your Honor." You should be patient, speak firmly and directly, and try to remain relaxed and calm.

⑦ Once in the courtroom, you should be seated and wait patiently until your name is called. The amount of time that you wait will most likely be longer than your actual hearing. When your name or the name of your case is called, state "Ready, Your Honor" to the judge and take your documents and your case file with you to the place where the clerk or judge directs. You may take a seat in a witness stand, directed to sit at a table, or asked to stand before the judge. You will normally be sworn in. Take a deep breath and relax.

⑧ As your hearing begins, you may be asked direct questions by the judge relating to the information that is in your petition/complaint. The judge will not try to confuse you or embarrass you. He or she just wants the facts of your situation. Answer any questions concisely and truthfully. In most locales, the judge will want you to present your case in the manner outlined later in this section under *Guide to Court Testimony*. You should have with you a written or typed copy of the testimony guidelines. You shouldn't take a copy of this kit to court with you, however. In all cases where there is a court hearing, the intent is to be certain that the statements that you and your spouse made in your court papers are true and correct and that you understand the proceedings. If you have gotten this far in the divorce procedure, you should be confident that you understand the laws relating to divorce much better than most people. You should be as brief and as clear as possible in your answers. If the judge wants more information, he or she will ask for it. Your testimony or questions/answers will generally follow the outline of your petition/complaint. You do not need to elaborate on any of the information, unless the judge specifically asks you to.

⑨ When you have finished your own testimony and if a witness is required to testify regarding your residency, etc., you should tell the judge: "Your Honor, I would now like to call _____ (name of witness) to testify." If no witness is required, your case is finished and the judge will generally announce his or her decision immediately. Carefully read through your judgment/decree to be certain that it exactly follows what the judge states as his or her decision. If the judge's decision is exactly what is contained in your prepared judgment/decree, this final document will generally be signed immediately by the judge. If there are differences between what the judge states and your document, you will need to take the judgment/decree home with you and type a new version that exactly states the judge's decision. Once the judgment/decree is correct, bring it back to the courthouse and the judge will sign it. Some states may have a waiting period before your divorce becomes effective. The judge or court clerk will inform you if this is the case.

Court Testimony Worksheet Instructions

The following is a general guide to the testimony that is most often required in uncontested divorce hearings. As you can see, the information required is merely a restatement of the information that is contained in your various court documents. When you have filled in this information, you should be certain to have it with you when you attend your hearing. Although the judge may ask you direct questions instead of allowing you to present your testimony, this testimony worksheet will provide you with an outline that will aid you in any hearing setting. Lawyers commonly use prepared testimony sheets similar to the one you will prepare. If the judge does not begin by asking you direct questions, you should begin your case by stating the following information as contained on your prepared testimony sheets. Speak directly to the judge, go carefully, and don't skip anything. If the judge interrupts you, answer his or her questions and then ask if you should continue. In the vast majority of situations, the hearing will be over in a few minutes.

In certain instances, however, you may encounter problems. If you become confused, ask the judge to explain. If the judge feels that your paperwork is not in order, ask the judge exactly what is necessary to correct the problem. Take very careful notes regarding what the judge tells you. If you feel that the hearing is going very badly or you simply do not understand what the difficulty is, you have an escape route. Simply state to the judge: "Your Honor, I would like a continuance to seek advice and to further prepare my case. I would like this hearing to be rescheduled, please." This will allow you time to seek out advice from an attorney or other legal professional as to the difficulty. In most cases, the problem relates to some legal formality for your locale that has not been satisfied. When you return, start at the beginning of your testimony and proceed. To complete this form, fill in the following information, on the Testimony Worksheet found on the CD that accompanied this book.

1. Full name of spouse filing
2. Plaintiff or Petitioner
3. Petition or Complaint
4. Petition or Complaint
5. Number of months of residency in state
6. Number of months of residency in county
7. Name of other spouse
8. Defendant or Respondent
9. Date of marriage
10. State of marriage
11. Defendant or Respondent
12. Date of separation
13. Divorce or Dissolution of Marriage
14. Grounds used in Petition or Complaint
15. Petition or Complaint
16. Defendant or Respondent
17. Petition or Complaint
18. Title of final document ("Final Judgment" or "Decree")
19. Divorce or Dissolution of Marriage
20. Final Judgment or Decree
21. Final Judgment or Decree
22. and 23. Select and complete statement regarding alimony
24. through 26. Select and complete statement regarding children
27. (Plaintiff's or Petitioner's) or (Defendant's or Respondent's)
28. List desired name upon divorce or dissolution of marriage
29. Petition or Complaint
30. Name of witness
31. Plaintiff or Petitioner

㉜ Plaintiff or Petitioner
㉝ Plaintiff or Petitioner
㉞ Plaintiff or Petitioner
㉟ Defendant or Respondent
㊱ Defendant or Respondent
㊲ Defendant or Respondent
㊳ Defendant or Respondent
㊴ Defendant or Respondent
㊵ Plaintiff or Petitioner
㊶ Defendant or Respondent
㊷ Plaintiff or Petitioner
㊸ Defendant or Respondent

Sample Testimony Worksheet

1. "Your Honor, my name is ① , and I am the ② in this case."

2. "All of the facts stated in my verified ③ are true and correct."

3. "Immediately prior to filing the ④ , I had continually been a resident of and domiciled in this state for more than ⑤ , and this county [or parish] for more than ⑥ ."

4. "I am now married to ⑦ , who is the ⑧ in this case. We were married on ⑨ , in the State of ⑩, and a copy of our marriage certificate has been filed with the court. *[Here hold up the Marriage Certificate]*. I am familiar with the marriage certificate and recognize it as the certificate of my marriage to the ⑪. We separated on ⑫, and have lived separate and apart without cohabitation since that time."

5. "I seek a ⑬ on the grounds that: ⑭ ."

6. "Your Honor, my spouse and I have signed a written Marital Settlement Agreement resolving all of our differences. Attached to and incorporated into this agreement are two individual Financial Statements that my spouse and I have signed and verified. The information contained in my Financial Statement is true and correct. The original of this agreement and the Financial Statements were attached to and incorporated into the ⑮ that was filed. *[Here hold up the Marital Settlement Agreement and Financial Statements.]* I am familiar with the signature of my spouse on both of those documents and can state that it is genuine. I request that the Marital Settlement Agreement and attached Financial Statements be admitted into evidence and approved by this court."

7. "My spouse, the ⑯, has also signed an Appearance, Consent, and Waiver that was filed in this case. *[Here hold up the Appearance, Consent, and Waiver form]*. I am familiar with the signature of my spouse and can state that it is genuine. By the terms of this Appearance, Consent, and Waiver, my spouse admitted all of the allegations as contained in the ⑰, waived all objections to venue, waived issuance, return, and service of process, entered a general appearance, and consented to the entry of judgment in this case."

8. "Your Honor, I have prepared and submitted a ⑱ that prays for a ⑲ and that our Marital Settlement Agreement be approved, incorporated, and merged into

the ⑳ and that we both be ordered to comply with all terms and conditions. The ㉑ has been approved by my spouse, whose signature is on the last page. [*Here hold up the proposed Judgment or Decree.*] I am familiar with the signature of my spouse and can state that it is genuine."

9. "My spouse and I have agreed to the division of all of our property and debts under the terms of our Marital Settlement Agreement that I have submitted."

10. *Select the statement that applies:* ㉒

> "My spouse and I have agreed that neither of us should receive any alimony or maintenance from the other and we have forever waived our claims to such support. We have both agreed to this in our Marital Settlement Agreement, that I have submitted."
>
> *Or:*
>
> "My spouse and I have agreed in our Marital Settlement Agreement that ㉓ should receive the alimony and maintenance as set forth in that document."

11. *Select the statement that applies:* ㉔

> "Your Honor, my spouse and I have no minor children and none are expected."
>
> *Or:*
>
> "Your Honor, my spouse and I are the parents of ㉕ child(ren). [His, Her, or Their] name[s], age[s], birthdate[s], and birthplace[s] are as follows: ㉖

12. *If you have children, also state:*

> "Apart from personal possessions, no property is owned by the child[ren]. My spouse and I have both signed a Declaration regarding Child Custody Jurisdiction that is true and correct and that was filed in this case. [*Here hold up the Declaration regarding Child Custody Jurisdiction.*] I am familiar with the signature of my spouse and can state that it is genuine. I request that this Declaration be admitted into evidence."

"Your Honor, my spouse and I have agreed on all issues concerning the care, custody, and support of our children and our agreement is contained in our Marital Settlement Agreement, that was submitted. We both believe that it would be in the best interests of our child[ren] that these terms be approved by this court."

The provisions that you and your spouse have made regarding your children will be the most likely area in which the judge will question you carefully. Be prepared to answer questions relating to how your custody and visitation provisions will actually be instituted and how the child support payments may be guaranteed. The judge may insist that the payments be made though the clerk of the court or other state agency. If so, ask the judge what additional forms will be necessary. The judge may also inquire into your health insurance coverage. Be prepared to answer as to how the child will be covered. The judge may also insist that automatic wage withholding or some other method to guarantee the child support payments be used. If so, ask the judge what forms will be necessary. Take careful notes and later ask the court clerk for any of the necessary forms.

13. *If desired, state*: "Your Honor, I request that the ㉗ name be restored to ㉘ , as set forth in the Marital Settlement Agreement."

14. "I respectfully request that our marriage be dissolved and that the relief prayed for in the ㉙ be granted."

15. *If no witness will be required, state*: "That concludes my testimony, your Honor."

If a witness is required in your situation, state: "Your Honor, I would now like to call ㉚ to testify."

Have your witness come forward and be sworn in. Then ask the following questions:

    a. "What is your name, please?"

    b. "Where do you live and how long have you lived there?"

    c. "Are you personally familiar with the ㉛ in this case?"

    d. "How long have you known ㉜?"

e. "Where does the ㉝ live?"

f. "To your own knowledge, how long has ㉞ lived in this State and in this County [or Parish]?"

g. "Are you personally familiar with the ㉟ in this case?"

h. "How long have you known ㊱?"

i. "Are you familiar with where the ㊲ currently lives?"

j. "Where does the ㊳ currently live?"

k. "To your own knowledge, how long has ㊴ lived in this State and in this County [or Parish]?"

l. "Are you familiar with the marital status of the ㊵ and the ㊶ ?"

m. "To your own knowledge, what is their marital status?"

n. [*If the grounds for your divorce are based on separation for a specific period of time, ask the following two questions*]:

> "To your knowledge, do the ㊷ and the ㊸ currently live together?"
>
> "On your own knowledge, how long have they not lived together?"

o. [*In all cases, state:*] "Thank you very much, you are excused."

16. *In those few jurisdictions in which the testimony of both spouses is necessary, your spouse should prepare a testimony sheet substantially the same as yours. It should, of course, be altered to be read from the point of view of your spouse. After you have concluded your testimony, your spouse should stand, ask the court when to begin, and then begin his or her own testimony.*

At the end of his or her testimony, or at the end of your testimony or your witnesses', you should state: "Your Honor, that concludes my testimony."

Then be seated and wait for the judge's decision.

Chapter 12

After Your Divorce

Once your divorce decree or judgement has been officially entered, you are legally a single person again. A few states have a short waiting period before you may remarry. Check with the court clerk in your county if this is an immediate consideration in your situation. Although you are both now single, there are some very important steps that you and your ex-spouse must take to complete the divorce process. Essentially, you must do all of the things that you agreed to do in your Marital Settlement Agreement and you must begin to satisfy those parts of the Agreement that are ongoing obligations. These final steps are required to actually complete the total separation of you and your ex-spouse's affairs and to transfer any property that has not yet been properly transferred.

This final chapter will provide you with a basic checklist of items that you should consider as you wrap up the last loose ends of your divorce. There may be a tendency to put off dealing with these concluding steps. It is important that you attend to these final considerations as promptly as possible. Go through the checklist item by item until you and your ex-spouse are both satisfied that all of the appropriate final steps have been accomplished. Take care that no important detail is overlooked.

Following the final checklist, there are some basic legal guidelines that apply to various post-divorce situations. An overview is provided of methods available for the: (1) enforcement child support or alimony orders; (2) modification of support orders; (3) enforcement of visitation provisions; (4) modification of custody rights; and (5) issuance of domestic violence protective orders.

Final Divorce Checklist

❑ From the court clerk, you should order several certified copies of your final Judgement or Decree for each of you. You and your ex-spouse may need these documents for an transfers of property, bank accounts, loan releases, etc.

❑ Be certain that you have filed a Certificate of Divorce or Dissolution of Marriage with the clerk of the court or your state's department of vital statistics. This is required in most states. Check with the court clerk in your jurisdiction.

❑ If there is any personal or household property that has not yet been exchanged, you should do so at this time. Arrange for delivery or pickup of any items that you and your spouse have agreed will be the property of the other: furnishings, jewelry, tools, appliances, music systems, etc.

❑ If you have not yet closed all of your personal joint bank accounts, you should do so at this time. Verify the balance in any joint accounts and then divide any proceeds of the accounts according to the terms of your Marital Settlement Agreement.

❑ If you have any joint credit accounts that still remain open, these should also now be closed. The payment of the remaining outstanding bills should be arranged according to the terms you and your spouse have set out in your Agreement. You should determine what the exact balance is on the date of your signing of the Marital Settlement Agreement. If there are utility bills or other bills that you must split, determine the pro-rated amount for each spouse. Change any addresses as necessary to be sure that future bills are delivered to the proper person. For joint credit card accounts, you should destroy the cards or surrender them back to the company. You should advise all of your joint creditors of your divorce that from now on, you will only be liable for your own debts. You and your spouse should furnish each other with any necessary account records regarding your joint debts.

❑ If you and your spouse have any outstanding joint loans, you should notify the lending institution of your divorce. You may need to supply them with a copy of your Marital Settlement Agreement if it contains a hold-harmless and indemnification agreement from your spouse. If possible, the spouse whose duty to pay is being taken over by the other spouse should try to obtain a release from the lending institution relieving him or her of liability for the debt. Be sure to notify the lender of any address or billing changes.

☐ If you have cars or other property for which ownership is determined by a title, you should make any appropriate transfers of title. Be sure to also change over the registration and license plates to the appropriate spouse at this time, if necessary. Recall that you each agreed to take any necessary steps and sign any documents required to complete all of the terms of your Marital Settlement Agreement.

☐ If you have real estate that will need to be transferred between the two of you, you will need to complete any necessary deeds to accomplish this task. You may need to contact a real estate professional or attorney for assistance in preparing the required paperwork. If there is a mortgage on the property, you should contact the lending institution regarding any changes required in the mortgage documents. Again, you may need to supply them with a certified copy of your Marital Settlement Agreement if it contains a hold-harmless and indemnification agreement from your spouse. If possible, the spouse whose duty to pay is being taken over by the other spouse should try to obtain a release from the lending institution relieving him or her of liability for the mortgage. Any documents relating to real estate will need to be recorded in the appropriate office (usually the county recorder's) in the county or parish where the real estate is located. Forms and instructions for various real estate transfer documents that you may need can be found in the Nova Publishing Company book *Real Estate Forms Simplified*.

☐ If any of your jointly-owned property is to be sold and the proceeds divided, you and your spouse will now need to arrange for this. If the property is real estate, you will need to contact a broker or list the property for sale your-selves. Keep a record of any expenses that are required to complete the sale (for example: appraisal fees, surveys, advertising charges, brokerage fees, etc.). These expenses will be deducted from the gross proceeds of the sale to determine the profits to be divided. Again, any documents relating to real estate will need to be recorded in the appropriate office (usually the county recorder's) in the county or parish where the real estate is located.

❑ Each of your insurance policies should be reviewed. Any beneficiary changes should be directed to the insurance company or agent who handles your policy. The policies that should be reviewed include: any life insurance policies; health or hospitalization policies; homeowner or personal property policies; auto insurance policies; and any insurance policies pertaining to children. If you or your spouse are required to maintain life or health insurance as part of your agreement or decree, you should furnish the other spouse with proof of the policy. If you are converting from group to individual coverage under a group health insurance plan, you must generally do so quickly. There may be a time limit for doing this (often 30 days).

❑ Be certain that both you and your spouse understand how your income tax situation is to be handled. If you have agreed to file a final joint return, arrange to do so. (Remember, that in order to file a joint return, you need to have still been legally married on the last day of the year for which you will file). If you have agreed on who will actually pay the tax or receive any tax refund, you should go over these terms with your spouse. If you will file separate returns, you should supply each other with any tax information that will be necessary for completing the returns. Each of you should keep copies of all of the tax returns that you filed while you were married. You should discuss and clarify the tax status of any required property settlement, alimony, or child support payments.

❑ Finally, if you or your spouse has a will, it needs to be revised. Individual states deal with the effect of divorce on a will in various manners. Some states consider any provisions for an ex-spouse in a will as automatically revoked by the divorce. Other states do not. Some states have provisions that declare the entire will of either ex-spouse to be revoked upon divorce. To be absolutely safe, a new will should be prepared reflecting your and your spouse's new relationship. If you have children, preparing a will that contains adequate provisions for their future is especially important. If you don't presently have a will, you should consider preparing one. Compared with obtaining your own divorce, preparing a will is a very easy legal task. Nova Publishing Company provides an excellent reference on this topic: *Estate Planning Toolkit*.

Post-Divorce Legal Problems

Various legal problems relating to your divorce can confront you and your ex-spouse well after your divorce has become final. These legal difficulties fall into two general categories: (1) enforcement of provisions in your divorce decree or judgement; or (2) modification of provisions in your divorce decree or judgement.

The need for legal action in either of these situations is much more likely to occur to a divorced couple who have minor children. Divorced couples without children typically go their own separate ways and begin to lead fully independent lives with little or no interaction with an ex-spouse. The situation is different if children are involved. There will necessarily be continued contact with an ex-spouse who is also a parent of a child due to the continuing obligations of child support and the ongoing responsibilities of custody.

Enforcement of Child Support

The most common legal difficulty encountered after a divorce is the need to collect overdue child support payments. The delinquency of child support payments is a massive problem and a national disgrace. In the last few years, both federal and state governments have taken major steps in an effort to correct this problem. All states have passed the Uniform Reciprocal Enforcement of Support Act which coordinates state efforts at enforcement. The passage of federal legislation in this area has been a large step in the efforts to correct this problem. The federal Family Support Act of 1988 mandates that each state must establish a formula for child support award amounts. Earlier federal legislation, most notably the 1984 Child Support Enforcement amendments to Title IV-D of the Social Security Act, established guidelines and requirements for states to follow in the area of child support collection and enforcement.

There is a wide range of weapons now available to states in the battle to collect child support. The use of these techniques has been simplified and, in most cases, can be arranged without the aid of a lawyer. Court clerks and child support enforcement agency personnel should be able to provide assistance in obtaining and filing the proper forms. Many of the necessary forms for the enforcement of child support obligations are now simplified and pre-printed for easy use without a lawyer.

States may use *wage or payroll deductions* or *wage withholding orders*. This type of court order will require that an employer must take a direct withholding out of a delinquent employee's wages and that the employer must then make the child support payments to either the custodial parent, a court clerk, or the local support agency. Every state now has laws in effect which grant similar powers to the local support enforcement agencies or courts. Some states refer to this method as a *wage* or *income assignment*, in which a portion of the future wages or income of the parent ordered to pay is actually legally transferred to the parent entitled to receive the support. "Wages" are generally defined broadly to include income from pensions, retirement funds, annuities, Social Security, unemployment compensation, and other benefits.

Under current federal law, employers are now required to withhold wages from parents of children receiving Aid to Families with Dependent Children. Beginning in 1994, income withholding became mandatory for all parents required to pay child support, *unless* the non-custodial parent who receives the support formally waives the protection of withholding. In addition, under the federal Child Support Enforcement Amendments of 1984, child support offenders can be tracked across state lines with powerful government computer networks.

Another very powerful method of collection of unpaid support payments is the *tax refund intercept*. This legal device allows the delinquent support payments to be taken directly out an ex-spouse's federal or state income tax refund, before the refund is ever sent out. The ability to collect overdue payments from an ex-spouse in any state is a particularly attractive aspect of this legal weapon. In addition, if all other means of collection of overdue child support payments have failed, the IRS may also use all of its tax-collecting powers to collect the delinquency, including seizing property and money from the parent.

Other weapons in the support enforcement arsenal include: (1) *attachments*: this amounts to a claim or lien which is legally "attached" to a specific piece of property. If the property is sold, the claim for overdue support is paid off first. Variations of this legal device can be used to impound funds in bank accounts; (2) *garnishment of wages*: similar to a wage withholding order, this method is available for any money-based legal judgment; (3) *security or bond*: this method requires a parent to post bond to guarantee the future payments; (4) *no discharge in bankruptcy*: a defaulting parent can not be relieved of a child support obligation by filing for bankruptcy; (5) *no retroactive judicial reduction of child support obligations*; a defaulting parent can not convince a court that the past-due payments were too high and have them reduced; (6) *civil contempt of court*: this method can result in imprisonment of an ex-spouse for failure to obey a court order which requires child support payments; and (7) *criminal prosecution*: many states make it a crime to fail to provide child support, punishable by fines and/or imprisonment.

If you need immediate assistance regarding collection of child support, check your phone book for the nearest office of the federal Child Support Enforcement Administration or your state's own child support enforcement agency. They will be able to provide assistance with enforcement and collection of your overdue payments.

Enforcement of Alimony

In the past, when alimony awards of long duration were more common, alimony payments were more likely to be overdue or totally delinquent. The trend to providing alimony on a short-term basis and often solely for the education or training of an ex-spouse has, to some extent, lessened the problems of collecting alimony payments over long periods of time.

Many of the same weapons available in child support enforcement situations are also available for the collection of overdue alimony payments. If the alimony and child support payments are lumped together into a single payment, all of the enforcement techniques mentioned above are available. If the alimony is a separate payment, tax intercepts are not available. However, wage withholding, income assignments, attachments, liens, garnishment of wages, and contempt of court orders are all generally available to aid in the collection of delinquent alimony payments.

Enforcement of Custody and Visitation

Visitation and custody can often create legal difficulties between ex-spouses. One parent may deny visitation on the grounds of overdue child support payments. Another parent may intentionally withhold support payment because of interference with visitation rights. A parent with custody may wish to move across the country with the child, effectively denying the other parent the right to reasonable visitation.

Courts and legislatures have been struggling with these problems and have yet to resolve them in a uniform manner. Each state may view the denial of visitation somewhat differently. In most states, however, you may seek various court relief from failure to abide by the court-ordered custody and visitation terms of your divorce judgment/decree. That relief may take the form of: (1) a contempt of court order against the offending ex-spouse; (2) an actual change in the custody or visitation terms of your divorce; (3) a court-order suspending support payments until visitation is allowed; (4) a court order requiring visitation; or (5) fines and imprisonment for failure to comply with a court order.

Child-snatching is a separate problem which has come under increasing scrutiny of the courts and legislatures. Parental kidnapping by a non-custodial parent is a major problem and has resulted in two powerful pieces of national legislation: The Uniform Child Custody Jurisdiction Act (which has been adopted by all states); and the federal Parental Kidnapping Prevention Act. These laws mandate which single state will have continuing jurisdiction and control over the custody of a child and are designed to prevent conflicting awards of custody. The court which issued the original custody award generally retains all authority over the case, regardless of where the child is taken.

In addition, in interstate child-snatching situations, the FBI can be brought into the case. For in-state situations, local district attorney or the state attorney general can often intervene. The advice and assistance of a lawyer in such situations is highly recommended.

Domestic Violence

One of the most negative aspects of the modern ease of divorce is the increasing frequency of domestic violence directed against an ex-spouse. Every state now has specific laws which attempt to deal with this problem. Many states have instituted programs for simplified and immediate issuance of restraining orders against domestic violence, whether the abuse is directed against a spouse, ex-spouse, parent, or child. Such protective orders are also being taken much more seriously by local law enforcement agencies who must enforce them.

In most states, there are simplified and standardized forms available from court clerks, social service, or law enforcement agencies which may be filled in without the aid of a lawyer. Courts are, in many cases, required to respond immediately with the issuance of emergency court orders to provide protection to an abused or battered spouse, ex-spouse, or child. The court orders can be very powerful weapons, giving police the authority to immediately arrest a person without a warrant on the basis of violation of a court order. Check with your local police, court clerk, any local domestic violence shelters, or social service agencies for more information.

Modification of Support and Custody Provisions

After your divorce, your life will change to some extent. If you have children, the changes may be extensive. Unanticipated events may also occur in the future which will influence your life and the lives of your children. There are legal provisions in every state for the future modification of child support and custody provisions. The changes may be to provide for an increased or decreased amount of support or to provide for alterations in the amount of custody and visitation. The ex-spouses or parents may mutually consent to the changes without a lengthy court proceeding. In addition, the court that issued the original order always retains jurisdiction to make necessary changes in child support, custody, or visitation provisions of a final divorce decree or judgement.

The legal basis for receiving a modification to a prior support or custody award is, generally, a "significant change in circumstances". The change must be substantial enough to warrant a court proceeding to alter a previous court order. The changes must generally: (1) not have been considered when the original judgement was entered; (2) be permanent and substantial; (3) affect one's current standard of living.

Various situations can be the basis for an attempt to have a court modify support or custody awards. A substantial increase or decrease in one's income or expenses; remarriage of one of the ex-spouses; a serious illness or injury of an ex-spouse or child; bankruptcy; inheritance; and many other significant changes can be grounds to seek a modification of the terms of a divorce judgement or decree. In all cases, however, a court will not be receptive to making changes in a prior court order unless there is an actual demonstrated need for the modification and a provable substantial change in the circumstances which affect the family.

Any of the court orders in your divorce judgment/decree regarding child custody and visitation are never actually final. They may be altered at any time, if your circumstances have changed substantially. Courts, however, are somewhat reluctant to alter settled custody arrangements unless there is a dramatic change or extraordinary reason. The basis for any modification in custody is the same as it was in the original divorce proceeding: the best interests of the child. Factors which may influence a court are: (1) remarriage; (2) any spouse or child abuse; (3) any drug or alcohol abuse; (4) interference with visitation rights; (5) the child's safety; and (6) any of the factors originally listed in the chapter on **Child Custody and Visitation**. An attorney may be necessary to assist in dealing with any of these legal difficulties. However, you may be able to handle many of them yourself with the proper guidance.

Appendix

State Divorce Laws

The following Appendix contains a summary of the divorce laws of all states and the District of Columbia. It has been compiled directly from the most recently-available statute books and updates for each state. Every effort has been made to assure that the information contained in this Appendix is accurate and complete. However, laws are subject to constant change. Therefore, those legal points which are particularly important in your situation should be checked directly in the appropriate law book or state legislative Internet site to be certain that the law has not changed since this book was written. After each section of information, the exact name of the law book and the chapter or section number of where the information can be found is noted. Any of these official statute books should be available at any public library. A librarian will be glad to assist you in locating the correct book and in finding the appropriate pages. The Internet also has all state statues available online. There is a listing in this Appendix for each state's legislative Internet site.

The correct terminology for each state is used in these listings. However, some states use certain language interchangeably. In those states, the most commonly-used language is stated. Although it has been simplified to some extent, you will find that the language in the Appendix is somewhat more complicated than the language used in the rest of this book. This is due to the fact that much of the language in the Appendix has been taken directly from the laws and statutes of each state. We apologize for this. We feel, however, that, as a reference, the technical details of the laws should be provided. The following information is listed for each state:

STATE WEBSITE: This listing provides the internet website address of the location of the state's statutes relating to divorce law. The addresses were current at the time of this book's publication; however, like most websites, the page addresses are subject to change. If an expired state webpage is not automatically redirected to a new site, laws can be searched at http://www.findlaw.com.

DOWNLOAD STATE FORMS: Most states have recently made certain official state divorce forms available online. Nearly all states have child support guidelines and forms available online. This listing provides a link to the state website from which you should be able to download any divorce-related state forms that may be required.

FORMS PROVIDED ON CD: The forms in this category are necessary for filing for divorce in each state. The forms listed can be found on the CD provided with this book. The types of forms included are petitions or complaints for divorce, forms for simplified divorce procedures, financial statements and cover sheets.

FORMS AVAILABLE ONLINE: The forms in this category are miscellaneous forms that may not be necessary to file for a divorce, but may be helpful for particular situations. These forms can be found at the website provided under Download State Forms. The types of forms included will aid with filing for child custody, child support, mediation, or alimony.

RESIDENCY REQUIREMENTS AND WHERE TO FILE: The specific time limits that you or your spouse must have lived in your state (and possibly county) are explained. Which particular county (or parish) that you should file for your divorce is also listed. This is technically referred to as the *venue*.

LEGAL GROUNDS FOR DIVORCE: The specific language of the grounds for divorce in each state are listed. Some states have more than one no-fault ground. If this is the case, they are specified by numbering each particular ground. Some states have also retained some fault-based divorce grounds. These are referred to as "General" grounds and are only for your information. You will be using a "No-fault" ground.

NAME OF COURT IN WHICH TO FILE FOR DIVORCE: The information under this heading shows the name of the correct court in which to file your papers for divorce. It may also show the exact wording necessary for the court name in the caption of your divorce court papers.

TITLE OF DIVORCE ACTION: The correct language for the title of your request for divorce is listed. This is generally either a Petition for Dissolution of Marriage or a Complaint for Divorce. In some states, the language used to describe the case are also noted. For example: "In the Matter of the Marriage of _____ and _____."

NAME USED TO DESCRIBE SPOUSE FILING FOR DIVORCE: This refers to the person who will officially be the one filing for divorce. Generally, this will either be the Plaintiff or Petitioner, although some states allow joint Co-Petitioners.

NAME USED TO DESCRIBE OTHER SPOUSE IN DIVORCE: This refers to the title of the other spouse, technically the one against whom the divorce is filed. Generally, this will be either the Defendant or Respondent, although some states allow joint Co-Petitioners.

TITLE OF FINAL DIVORCE PAPERS: This is the actual title of the document that will declare you divorced. You will prepare this and submit it to the judge for his or her signature.

LEGAL SEPARATION: This information explains the situation in your state relating to legal court-ordered separation. You may live separate and apart under the terms of your Marital Settlement Agreement *without* obtaining a legal court-ordered separation. The grounds and residency requirements for court-ordered separations are included.

SIMPLIFIED OR SPECIAL DIVORCE PROCEDURES: Many states now have instituted procedures which allow for simplified procedures to be used in obtaining a divorce. In addition, some states have mandatory forms which are required to be used. Other states have specific provisions relating to shortening the divorce process. All of the details of any specific methods to shorten or streamline the divorce process are contained under this heading.

MEDIATION OR COUNSELING REQUIREMENTS: Most states have now instituted voluntary mediation or conciliation services that are available to spouses on request or on the order of the judge. The details regarding this aspect of divorce are listed here.

PROPERTY DISTRIBUTION: A description of which property is subject to division upon divorce and what factors are considered in the distribution are contained in this section. Community, separate, non-marital, and marital property are defined for each state.

ALIMONY/MAINTENANCE/SPOUSAL SUPPORT: The laws and factors for consideration relating to the awarding of alimony are discussed under this heading.

SPOUSE'S NAME: Each state's laws regarding the restoration of a spouse's name are included.

CHILD CUSTODY: The details of how child custody decisions are made are contained under this heading. Each state's particular factors for consideration are explained. Specific state provisions for joint custody are also detailed.

CHILD SUPPORT: The various laws relating to child support are outlined. In recent years, this area has become the most complex aspect of divorce. Virtually all states now have detailed child support guidelines that are to be applied in child support situations. The availability of specific state child support guidelines and general state requirements to guarantee child support payments are noted.

235

ALABAMA

STATE WEBSITE: http://alisdb.legislature.state.al.us/acas/CodeOfAlabama/1975/coatoc.htm

DOWNLOAD STATE FORMS: No state forms available online.

FORMS PROVIDED ON CD: Alabama Complaint for Divorce

FORMS AVAILABLE ONLINE: None

RESIDENCY REQUIREMENTS AND WHERE TO FILE: When 1 of the spouses is a nonresident of the state, the spouse filing for divorce must have been a resident of the state for at least 6 months before filing for divorce. The divorce may be filed for in any of the following: (1) the county where the defendant resides; (2) the county where the spouses both resided at the time of their separation; or (3) the county where the plaintiff resides if the defendant is a non-resident of Alabama. [Code of Alabama; Title 30, Chapters 2-4 and 2-5].

LEGAL GROUNDS FOR DIVORCE: No-Fault: (1) Irretrievable breakdown of the marriage; (2) complete incompatibility of temperament such that the parties can no longer live together; (3) voluntary separation for over 1 year. [Code of Alabama; Title 30, Chapter 2-1].
General: (1) Adultery; (2) living separate and apart without cohabitation for over 2 years without the husband supporting the wife (divorce must be filed by wife); (3) imprisonment (for over 2 years if the total sentence is over 7 years); (4) unnatural sexual behavior before or after the marriage; (5) alcoholism; (6) drug abuse; (7) confinement for incurable insanity for over 5 years; (8) wife pregnant by another at the time of the marriage without the husband's knowledge; (9) physical abuse or reasonable fear of physical abuse; (10) lack of physical ability to consummate marriage. [Code of Alabama; Title 30, Chapters 2-1 and 2-2].

NAME OF COURT IN WHICH TO FILE FOR DIVORCE: Circuit Court. "In the Circuit Court for _____ _____ County, Alabama." [Code of Alabama; Title 30, Chapter 2-1].

TITLE OF DIVORCE ACTION: Complaint for Divorce. "In Re the Marriage of: _____ and _____."

NAME USED TO DESCRIBE SPOUSE FILING FOR DIVORCE: Plaintiff.

NAME USED TO DESCRIBE OTHER SPOUSE IN DIVORCE: Defendant.

TITLE OF FINAL DIVORCE PAPERS: Judgment of Divorce.

LEGAL SEPARATION: Legal Separation requirements repealed 1/1/99.

SIMPLIFIED OR SPECIAL DIVORCE PROCEDURES: There is no legal provision in Alabama for summary divorce. In addition, specific evidence must be presented at a court hearing to support a default judgment in a divorce case. However, acceptance and waiver of service is allowed if signed by the defendant and a credible witness. There is a 30-day waiting period after the filing of the summons and complaint before a judge may issue a final judgment of divorce. Testimony in uncontested divorces may be taken before a court clerk, by sworn statements, or by transcripts of oral depositions. A standardized Child Support Guidelines form and Child Support Income Statement/Affidavit must be filed in every case in which child support is requested. [Code of Alabama: Title 30, Chapter 2-8.1; Alabama Rules of Civil Procedure; Rules 4, 43(a), 53, and 55 and Alabama Rules of Judicial Administration: Rule 32].

MEDIATION OR COUNSELING REQUIREMENTS: There is no legal provision in Alabama for mediation.

PROPERTY DISTRIBUTION: There is no statutory provision in Alabama for property division. Under Alabama case law, Alabama is an "equitable distribution" state and the judge has full discretion to divide any jointly-owned real estate or personal property, but does not have the authority to award the wife's separate property to the husband (regardless of whether the wife's separate property was obtained before or after the marriage). Gifts and inheritances are considered separate property and are not subject to division unless they have been used for the common benefit of both spouses. The property division need not necessarily be exactly equal, but it must be equitable. Marital fault may be considered in the division of property. [Alabama Case Law].

ALIMONY/MAINTENANCE/SPOUSAL SUPPORT: The judge has full discretion to award an allowance for maintenance to either spouse, if such spouse has insufficient property to provide for his or her own maintenance. This award may be made out of the property belonging to the other spouse, unless it is separate property (acquired by gift or inheritance, or acquired prior to the marriage) and was never used for the common benefit of the marriage. The factors to be considered are: (1) the value of the estate of both spouses; and (2) the condition of the spouse's family. Up to 50% of a spouse's retirement benefits may be used for alimony if the retirement was accumulated during a marriage of 10 years or more. Misconduct of either spouse may be considered in the determination as to whether to award maintenance and may totally bar the right to any maintenance. Any award of maintenance will be terminated if the recipient is living openly with a member of the opposite sex or has remarried. [Code of Alabama: Title 30, Chapters 2-51, 2-52, and 2-55].

SPOUSE'S NAME: An ex-wife may be prevented from using the last name of the ex-husband. Under general common law principles, a wife may resume the use of her maiden or former name upon divorce. [Code of Alabama: Title 30, Chapter 2-11].

CHILD CUSTODY: Custody of any children of the marriage may be granted to either parent. Factors to be considered are: (1) the age and sex of the child; (2) the safety and well-being of the child; and (3) the moral character of the parents. The wishes of the child are also a factor to be considered. There is a legal presumption against giving custody to any person who has inflicted any violence against either a spouse or a child. In abuse cases, the judge is required to consider any history of domestic abuse and may not consider the fact that a parent or spouse has relocated to avoid abuse. Alabama officially favors joint custody (but not equal physical custody) if in the best interests of the child and the parents agree. Factors to be considered are: (1) parental custody agreement; (2) parental cooperation; (3) parental ability to encourage love and sharing; (4) any history of abuse; and (5) geographic proximity of parents. Joint custody may be awarded. However, if the wife abandons the husband and the children are over 7 years old, the husband is granted custody if he is suitable. Grandparents may be given visitation rights. [Code of Alabama: Title 30, Chapters 3-5 to 3-6.1,3-60 to 3-71,3-110 to 3-115, 3-170 to 3-179, 3-190 to 3-200; and Alabama Case Law].

CHILD SUPPORT: The court may order either parent to provide child support. There are official Child Support Guidelines contained in the Alabama Rules of Judicial Administration: Rule 32. These guidelines are presumed to be correct unless there is a showing that the amount would be unjust or inappropriate under the particular circumstances of a case. A written agreement between the parents for a different amount with a reasonable explanation for the deviation from the guidelines will also be allowed. A standardized Child Support Guidelines form and Child Support Income Statement/Affidavit must be filed in every case in which child support is requested. There is also a procedure for expedited processing in child support cases. Alabama driver's licenses may be suspended for failure to pay child support. [Code of Alabama: Title 30, Chapters 3-5 to 3-6.1,3-60 to 3-71,3-110 to 3-115, 3-170 to 3-179, 3-190 to 3-200 and Alabama Rules of Judicial Administration: Rules 32 and 35].

ALASKA

STATE WEBSITE: http://www.legis.state.ak.us/folhome.htm

DOWNLOAD STATE FORMS: http://www.state.ak.us/courts/selfhelp.htm

FORMS PROVIDED ON CD: Petition for Dissolution of Marriage with Children, Petition for Dissolution of Marriage without Children When Filing Together, Petition for Dissolution of Marriage without Children When One Spouse is Filing Alone, Complaint for Divorce with Minor Children, Complaint for Divorce without Minor Children, Financial Declaration

FORMS AVAILABLE ONLINE: Petition for Dissolution of Marriage with Children, Petition for Dissolution of Marriage without Children When Filing Together, Petition for Dissolution of Marriage without Children When One Spouse is Filing Alone, Complaint for Divorce with Minor Children, Complaint for Divorce without Minor Children, Financial Declaration, Child Support Order, Complaint for Child Custody

RESIDENCY REQUIREMENTS AND WHERE TO FILE: The spouse filing for a divorce/dissolution of marriage must be a resident. No residency time limit is specified. [Alaska Statutes; Sections 22.10.030, 25.24.080, and 25.24.090].

LEGAL GROUNDS FOR DIVORCE/DISSOLUTION OF MARRIAGE: No-Fault: Incompatibility of temperament which has caused the irremediable breakdown of the marriage. [Alaska Statutes; Section 25.24.200].
General: (1) Adultery; (2) incurable mental illness and confinement to an institution for 18 months; (3) drug abuse; (4) failure to consummate marriage; (5) conviction of a felony; (6) willful desertion of over 1 year; (7) cruel and/or inhuman treatment; (8) personal indignities; and (9) habitual drunkenness. [Alaska Statutes; Section 25.24.050].

NAME OF COURT IN WHICH TO FILE FOR DIVORCE/DISSOLUTION OF MARRIAGE: Superior Court. "Superior Court for the State of Alaska; #_____ Judicial District." [Alaska Rules of Court Procedure and Administration.]

TITLE OF DIVORCE/DISSOLUTION OF MARRIAGE ACTION: Petition for Dissolution of Marriage, if filed on no-fault grounds (see below under *Simplified or Special Dissolution of Marriage Procedures*). "In the Matter of the Dissolution of the Marriage of _____ and _____." Complaint for Divorce, if filed on fault-based grounds.

NAME USED TO DESCRIBE SPOUSE FILING FOR DIVORCE/DISSOLUTION OF MARRIAGE: Petitioner, if filed on no-fault grounds (see below under *Simplified or Special Dissolution of Marriage Procedures*). Plaintiff, if filed on fault-based grounds.

NAME USED TO DESCRIBE OTHER SPOUSE IN DIVORCE/DISSOLUTION OF MARRIAGE: Respondent, if filed on no-fault grounds (see below under *Simplified or Special Dissolution of Marriage Procedures*). Defendant, if filed on fault-based grounds.

TITLE OF FINAL DIVORCE/DISSOLUTION OF MARRIAGE PAPERS: Decree of Dissolution of Marriage, if filed on no-fault grounds (see below under *Simplified or Special Dissolution of Marriage Procedures*). Judgment of Divorce, if filed on fault-based grounds.

LEGAL SEPARATION: There is no specific legal provision in Alaska for legal separation.

SIMPLIFIED OR SPECIAL DISSOLUTION OF MARRIAGE PROCEDURES: The spouses may jointly petition the court for a dissolution of marriage of their marriage on the grounds of incompatibility of temperament which has caused the irremediable breakdown of the marriage, under the following conditions: (1) if there are minor children or the wife is pregnant, the spouses have agreed on the custody, visitation, and support of the child or children. They must also have agreed on whether the child support payments should be made through the state child support enforcement agency and on the tax consequences of the agreement regarding the child or children; (2) the spouses have agreed to the distribution of all jointly-owned property (including retirement benefits) and the payment of spousal support, if any and the tax consequences of these payments, if any (the amount of the property distributed to each spouse must be fair and just); and (3) the spouses have agreed as to the payment of all unpaid obligations incurred by either or both of them, and to the payment of obligations incurred jointly in the future. The petition for dissolution of marriage may be made by 1 spouse individually if: (1) the grounds for the dissolution of marriage is the incompatibility of temperament, evidenced by extended separation of the spouses, which has caused the irremediable breakdown of the marriage; (2) the petitioning spouse has been unable to ascertain the other spouse's position regarding the dissolution of marriage of their marriage, the division of their property, and the division of their obligations, custody, support, and visitation of any child or children, because the whereabouts of the other spouse is unknown to the petitioning spouse, after reasonable efforts to locate the absent spouse; and (3) the other spouse cannot be personally served with process inside or outside the state. Filing for a dissolution of marriage does not preclude filing for a divorce. Official state forms for obtaining a dissolution of marriage under these provisions may be obtained from the Clerk of any Superior Court, or from the Division of Social Services of the Alaska Department of Health and Social Services. [Alaska Statutes; Sections 25.24.200 to 25.24.260].

MEDIATION OR COUNSELING REQUIREMENTS: Either spouse may request mediation of an attempt to reach a settlement. If no request is made, the judge may order the spouses to submit to mediation if it is felt that a more satisfactory settlement may be achieved. The court will appoint a mediator. [Alaska Statutes; Section 25.24.060].

PROPERTY DISTRIBUTION: Alaska is an "equitable distribution" state. Both joint and separate property which has been acquired during the marriage will be divided in a "just" manner. Any fault of the spouses shall not be taken into account. If necessary, to achieve a fair result in a "fault-based" divorce action, property acquired before the marriage may be divided also. In a "no-fault" dissolution of marriage action, property acquired prior to the marriage will not be divided unless the spouses agree or it is in the best interests of any children to do so. Gifts and inheritances are also subject to division by the court. Factors considered are: (1) length of marriage; (2) position in life of the parties during marriage; (3) the age and health of the parties; (4) the earning capacity of each spouse; (5) the financial condition of each spouse; (6) the parties' conduct regarding their assets; (7) the desirability of awarding the family home to the spouse with primary physical custody of children; (8) the time and manner of acquisition of their property; (9) the income-producing capacity of the property and its value; and (10) all other relevant factors. Non-monetary contributions to the marriage (for example: home-making) are also considered. If property is considered "community property" under a community property agreement or trust under Alaska Statutes, Section 34.77, the court may divide such property in a just and equitable manner based on all factors, including: (1) the nature and extent of the community property; (2) the nature and extent of the spouse's separate property; and (3) the duration of the marriage. [Alaska Statutes; Sections 25.24.160 and 25.24.230].

ALIMONY/MAINTENANCE/SPOUSAL SUPPORT: Maintenance may be awarded to either spouse for support. The award may be made as a lump-sum or may be ordered paid in installments. Any fault of the spouses may not be taken into account. Factors considered are: (1) length of marriage; (2) position in life of the parties during marriage; (3) the age and health of the parties; (4) the earning capacity of each spouse; (5) the financial condition of each spouse; (6) the parties conduct regarding their assets; (7) the division of the spouse's property; and (8) all other relevant factors. Non-monetary contributions to the marriage (for example: home-making) are also considered. [Alaska Statutes; Section 25.24.160].

SPOUSE'S NAME: The name of either spouse may be changed in the Judgment for Divorce or in the Decree for Dissolution of Marriage. [Alaska Statutes; Sections 25.24.165 and 25.24.230].

CHILD CUSTODY: Custody is determined with the best interests of the child in mind. Factors to be considered are: (1) the capability and desire of each parent to meet the child's needs; (2) the physical, emotional, mental, religious, and social needs of the child; (3) the preference of the child (if the child is of sufficient age and capacity); (4) the love and affection between the child and each parent; (5) the length of time the child has lived in a stable, satisfactory environment and the desirability of maintaining continuity; (6) the desire and ability of each parent to allow an open and loving frequent relationship between the child and the other parent; (7) any evidence of domestic violence, child abuse, neglect, or spousal abuse; and (8) any evidence of substance abuse that affects the emotional or physical well-being of the child. Neither parent is considered to be entitled to custody. [Alaska Statutes; Section 25.24.150].

Joint/shared custody may be awarded, if it is in the best interests of the child. For shared custody to be awarded, the court considers the following factors: (1) the child's needs and education; (2) any special needs of the child that may be better met by 1 parent; (3) any findings of a neutral mediator; (4) the optimal time for the child to be with each parent; (5) the physical proximity of the parents as it relates to where the child will reside and where the child will attend school; (6) the advantage of keeping the child in the community where he or she presently resides; (7) whether shared custody will promote more frequent or continuing contact between the child and the parents; (8) the length of time the child has lived in a stable, satisfactory environment and the desirability of maintaining continuity; (9) the fitness and suitability of each of the parents (including any evidence of substance abuse); (10) any history of violence by either parent; (11) the preference of the child (if the child is of sufficient age and capacity); (12) the stability of the home of each parent; and (13) any other relevant factors. [Alaska Statutes; Section 25.20.090].

CHILD SUPPORT: Either or both parents may be ordered to provide child support. Child support payments may be ordered paid to a court-appointed trustee or through the state child support enforcement agency. There are official Child Support Guidelines contained in Alaska Rules of Civil Procedure; Rule 90.3. These guidelines are presumed to be correct unless there is a showing that the amount would be manifestly unjust under the particular circumstances in a case. Factors for deviation from the guidelines are: (1) especially large family size; (2) significant income of the child; (3) health or other extraordinary expenses; (4) unusually low expenses; (5) the parent with the child support obligation has an income below Federal poverty level; and (6) any other unusual circumstances. For parents with income over $72,000, the above 6 factors do not apply. In those instances, the factors are: (1) that an increased award is just and proper; (2) the needs of the children; (3) the standard of living of the children; and (4) the extent to which the standard of living of the children should be reflective of the parent's ability to pay. Each parent must file a verified statement of income. There is a Child Support Guidelines Worksheet contained in Alaska Rules of Civil Procedure; Rule 90.3. [Alaska Statutes; Sections 25.24.160 and 25.27.120 to 25.27.900, and Alaska Rules of Civil Procedure; Rule 67 and 90.3].

ARIZONA

STATE WEBSITE: http://www.azleg.state.az.us/ArizonaRevisedStatutes.asp

DOWNLOAD STATE FORMS: http://supreme.state.az.us/

FORMS PROVIDED ON CD: PETITION FOR DISSOLUTION OF MARRIAGE

FORMS AVAILABLE ONLINE: State-wide forms not available. Check county websites for forms. For example; http://www.mohavecourts.com/court%20forms/forms.htm.

RESIDENCY REQUIREMENTS AND WHERE TO FILE: One of the spouses must have lived in the state at least 90 days before filing for dissolution of marriage. The divorce should be filed in the county in which the petitioner resides at the time of filing. There is also a 60-day waiting period after the service of process on the Respondent (or after the Respondent's acceptance of service). [Arizona Revised Statutes Annotated; Title 12, Chapter 401 and Title 25, Chapters 312 and 329].

LEGAL GROUNDS FOR DISSOLUTION OF MARRIAGE: No-Fault: Irretrievable breakdown of the marriage. [Arizona Revised Statutes Annotated; Title 25, Chapter 312].
General: Irretrievable breakdown of the marriage is the only grounds for dissolution of a "standard" marriage in Arizona. However, Arizona recognizes what is termed a "covenant marriage," which is presumably a higher standard of marriage. The grounds for dissolution of a covenant marriage are: (1) adultery; (2) conviction of a felony which mandates imprisonment or death; (3) abandonment for over 1 year; (4) commission of domestic violence against spouse, child, or relative; (5) living separately and continuously and without reconciliation for over 2 years; (6) living separately for over 1 year after a legal separation is obtained; (7) habitual use of drugs or alcohol; and (8) both spouses agree to a dissolution. [Arizona Revised Statutes Annotated; Title 25, Chapters 312, 901, and 903].

NAME OF COURT IN WHICH TO FILE FOR DISSOLUTION OF MARRIAGE: Superior Court. "In the Superior Court in and for the County of _____, Arizona." [Arizona Revised Statutes Annotated; Title 25, Chapter 311].

TITLE OF DISSOLUTION OF MARRIAGE ACTION: Petition for Dissolution of Marriage. "In Re the Marriage of _____ and _____." [Arizona Revised Statutes Annotated; Title 25, Chapter 311].

NAME USED TO DESCRIBE SPOUSE FILING FOR DISSOLUTION OF MARRIAGE: Petitioner.

NAME USED TO DESCRIBE OTHER SPOUSE IN DISSOLUTION OF MARRIAGE: Respondent.

TITLE OF FINAL DISSOLUTION OF MARRIAGE PAPERS: Decree of Dissolution of Marriage.

LEGAL SEPARATION: Irretrievable breakdown of the marriage or if 1 spouse desires to live separate and apart are the grounds for legal separation in Arizona. However, if the marriage is a "covenant marriage," the grounds for legal separation are the same as the grounds for a general dissolution of a "covenant marriage" listed above, under *Legal Grounds for Dissolution of Mar-*

riage. One of the spouses must live in the state of Arizona when the action for legal separation is filed. No residency time limit is specified. If 1 spouse objects to a legal separation, the case will be amended to be an action for dissolution of the marriage. [Arizona Revised Statutes Annotated; Title 25, Chapters 313, 901, and 903].

SIMPLIFIED OR SPECIAL DISSOLUTION OF MARRIAGE PROCEDURES: Acceptance and waiver of service is allowed. In addition, Arizona law expressly encourages separation agreements. Also, dissolution of marriage petitions may be heard before a court commissioner if an appearance and waiver is filed. [Arizona Revised Statutes Annotated; Title 25, Chapter 317, Arizona Rules of Civil Procedure; Rule 4(f), and Arizona Rules of the Supreme Court; Rule 91].

MEDIATION OR COUNSELING REQUIREMENTS: Prior to filing for dissolution of marriage, either spouse may ask the court to order mediation for the purpose of a reconciliation to save the marriage or to obtain an amicable settlement and avoid further litigation. After a dissolution of marriage has been filed, either spouse may request that the dissolution of marriage proceedings be transferred to the Conciliation Court for mediation. Official forms for requesting this transfer are available from the clerk of any Superior Court. In addition, if 1 spouse denies that the marriage is irretrievably broken, the court may delay the case for up to 60 days and order the spouses to attend a conciliation conference. In addition, a judge may require spouses to attend conciliation conferences. Finally, there is a required delay of 60 days after the service of papers on the respondent spouse before any hearing may be held for a dissolution of marriage. [Arizona Revised Statutes Annotated; Title 25, Chapters 312, 316, 329, and 381.09+].

PROPERTY DISTRIBUTION: Arizona is a "community property" state. Separate property is retained by the owner of the property. Community or marital property (property acquired during the marriage) is divided and awarded equitably. Marital misconduct is not considered in the division. The court may consider excessive or abnormal expenditures of community property, and any destruction, concealment, or fraudulent disposition of community property in making the division. The court may place a lien upon a spouse's separate property in order to secure payment of child support or spousal support. A special Notice regarding debts and creditors is provided by statute and must be included on any materials served to the respondent. In addition, at the request of either spouse, the court shall order the spouses to submit a "debt distribution plan" which allocates the responsibilities for debts. Forms for this are included in Arizona Revised Statutes; Title 25, Chapter 318. [Arizona Revised Statutes Annotated; Title 25, Chapter 318].

ALIMONY/MAINTENANCE/SPOUSAL SUPPORT: Maintenance can be awarded to either spouse, if the spouse seeking maintenance: (1) lacks sufficient property to provide for his or her reasonable needs; (2) is unable to support himself or herself through appropriate employment; (3) is the custodian of a child whose age and condition is such that the custodian should not be required to seek employment outside the home; (4) lacks earning ability in the labor market to adequately support himself or herself; (5) contributed to the educational opportunities of the other spouse; or (6) had a marriage of long duration and is of an age which may preclude the possibility of gaining employment adequate to support himself or herself. Marital misconduct is not a factor to be considered. The factors to be considered are: (1) the contribution of the spouse seeking maintenance to the earning ability of the other spouse and the extent that the seeking spouse reduced his or her income or career opportunities to benefit the other spouse; (2) the time for the spouse to acquire education and training for suitable employment; (3) the spouse's future earning capacity; (4) the spouse's standard of living during the marriage; (5) the duration of the marriage; (6) the ability of the spouse providing maintenance to meet his or her needs while providing the maintenance to the other; (7) the financial resources of the spouse seeking maintenance (including marital property awarded and the spouse's ability to meet his or her needs independently); (8) any destruction, concealment, fraudulent disposition, or excessive expenditures of jointly-held property; (9) the comparative financial resources of the spouses including their comparative earning capacities; (10) the age of the spouses; (11) the physical and emotional condition of the spouses; (12) the usual occupations of the spouses during the marriage; (13) the vocational skills of the spouse seeking maintenance; (14) the ability of both parties to contribute to the future educational costs of any children; and (15) any other factors the court may deem just and equitable. Awards of maintenance are to be paid through the court unless the spouses agree otherwise. Maintenance agreements may be made non-modifiable by agreement of both spouses. [Arizona Revised Statutes Annotated; Title 25, Chapters 319 and 322].

SPOUSE'S NAME: A spouse's former or maiden name may be restored upon request. [Arizona Revised Statutes Annotated; Title 25, Chapter 325].

CHILD CUSTODY: In awarding custody, the court considers the best interests of the child and the following factors: (1) the preference of the child; (2) the desire and ability of each parent to allow an open, loving, and frequent relationship between the child and the other parent; (3) the wishes of the parents; (4) the child's adjustment to his or her home, school, and community; (5) the mental and physical health of the child and the parents; (6) the relationship between the child and the parents and any siblings; (7) any evidence of significant spouse or child abuse; (8) any coercion or duress in obtaining a custody agreement; and (9) which parent(s) have provided primary care of the child. No preference is to be given on the basis of the parent's sex. If custody is contested, all other issues in the case are decided first. Joint custody may be awarded if the parents submit a written agreement providing for joint or shared custody and it is found to be in the best interests of the child, after a consideration of the general child custody factors (above) and the following additional factors: (1) that neither parent was coerced or influenced by duress into withholding or granting his or her agreement to joint custody; (2) that the parents can sustain an ongoing commitment to the child; and (3) that the joint custody agreement is logistically possible. Grandparents and great-grandparents may be awarded visitation rights. [Arizona Revised Statutes Annotated; Title 25, Chapters 401-415 and Arizona Case Law].

CHILD SUPPORT: Either parent may be ordered to pay child support, without regard to marital misconduct, based on the following factors: (1) the financial resources of the child; (2) the standard of living of the child during the marriage; (3) the physical and emotional needs of the child; (4) the financial resources and obligations of both parents; (5) any destruction, concealment, fraudulent disposition, or excessive expenditure of jointly-held property; (6) the needs of the child; and (7) the duration of parenting time and any related expenses. Awards of child support are to be paid through the court unless the spouses agree otherwise. In addition, there are specific Arizona Supreme Court guidelines for child support payments available from the Clerk of any Superior Court. The amount of support established by using the official guidelines will be the required amount of child support, unless the court finds such an amount would be inappropriate or unjust. Every child support order must assign 1 or both of the parents responsibility for providing medical insurance coverage for the child and for payment of any medical expenses not covered by insurance. Unless there is contrary evidence presented in court, the court will assume that the non-custodial parent is capable of full-time work at the Federal minimum wage (unless the parent is under 18 years of age and attending high-school). [Arizona Revised Statutes Annotated; Title 25, Chapters 320, 322, and 500-527].

ARKANSAS

STATE WEBSITE: http://www.arkleg.state.ar.us/

DOWNLOAD STATE FORMS: http://courts.state.ar.us/courts/aoc_forms.html

FORMS PROVIDED ON CD: Cover Sheet

FORMS AVAILABLE ONLINE: Cover Sheet, Child Support Forms

RESIDENCY REQUIREMENTS AND WHERE TO FILE: A spouse must reside in the state for 60 days to file for divorce and for 3 months before a divorce will be finalized. The divorce should be filed in the county of the plaintiff's residence. However, if the plaintiff is a non-resident of Arkansas, the divorce may be filed in the county where the defendant resides. The venue requirements may be waived in Arkansas. [Arkansas Code of 1987 Annotated; Title 9, Chapters 12-301 and 12-303].

LEGAL GROUNDS FOR DIVORCE: No-Fault: Voluntarily living separately without cohabitation for 18 months. [Arkansas Code of 1987 Annotated; Title 9, Chapter 12-301].
General: (1) Impotence; (2) adultery; (3) confinement for incurable insanity or separation caused by mental illness for a period of 3 years; (4) conviction of a felony; (5) cruel and inhuman treatment which endangers the life of the spouse; (6) personal indignities; (7) habitual intemperance (drunkenness) for 1 year; (8) commission and/or conviction of an infamous crime; and (9) nonsupport whereby the spouse is able to provide support but willfully fails to provide suitable maintenance for the complaining spouse. [Arkansas Code of 1987 Annotated; Title 9, Chapter 12-301].

NAME OF COURT IN WHICH TO FILE FOR DIVORCE: Circuit Court. "In the Circuit Court of _____ Arkansas." [Arkansas Code of 1987 Annotated; Title 9, Chapter 12-301].

TITLE OF DIVORCE ACTION: Complaint for Divorce.

NAME USED TO DESCRIBE SPOUSE FILING FOR DIVORCE: Plaintiff.

NAME USED TO DESCRIBE OTHER SPOUSE IN DIVORCE: Defendant.

TITLE OF FINAL DIVORCE PAPERS: Decree of Divorce.

LEGAL SEPARATION: Legal separation may be granted for the following reasons: (1) Impotence; (2) adultery; (3) confinement for incurable insanity or separation caused by mental illness for a period of 3 years; (4) conviction of a felony; (5) willful desertion for 1 year; (6) cruel and inhuman treatment which endangers the life of the spouse; (7) personal indignities; (8) habitual intemperance (drunkenness) for 1 year; (9) commission and/or conviction of an infamous crime; (10) voluntary separation for 18 months; and (11) nonsupport whereby the spouse is able to provide support but willfully fails to provide suitable maintenance for the complaining spouse. [Arkansas Code of 1987 Annotated; Title 9, Chapter 12-301].

SIMPLIFIED OR SPECIAL DIVORCE PROCEDURES: In an uncontested divorce, proof of a spouse's residency, proof of separation, and proof of no cohabitation may be provided by a signed affidavit from a third party. In addition, in an uncontested divorce, proof of the grounds for divorce need not be corroborated by a third party. [Arkansas Code of 1987 Annotated; Title 9, Chapters 12-306, 12-313, and 12-316].

MEDIATION OR COUNSELING REQUIREMENTS: There is no legal provision in Arkansas for mediation.

PROPERTY DISTRIBUTION: Arkansas is an "equitable distribution" state. All of the marital property acquired during the marriage is divided equally between the spouses. However, if the court finds the division to be unfair, it may redistribute the property, after consideration of the following factors: (1) the contribution of each spouse to the preservation, appreciation, or acquisition of the marital property, including the contribution of each spouse as homemaker; (2) the length of the marriage; (3) the age, health, and station in life of the spouses; (4) the occupation of the spouses; (5) the amount and sources of income of the spouses; (6) the vocational skills of the spouses; (7) the employability of the spouses; (8) the estate, liabilities, and needs of each spouse and the opportunity of each for further acquisition of capital assets and income; (9) and the federal income tax consequences of the court's division of the property. The separate property of each spouse, consisting of property acquired prior to the marriage, and any gifts or inheritances, is retained by the spouse owning it, unless the court finds it necessary to divide the separate property in order to achieve an equitable distribution. [Arkansas Code of 1987 Annotated; Title 9, Chapter 12-315].

ALIMONY/MAINTENANCE/SPOUSAL SUPPORT: Alimony may be granted to either spouse in fixed installments for a specific period of time and subject to automatic termination upon the death of either spouse, remarriage of the receiving spouse, or the establishment by the receiving spouse of a relationship that produces a child or children. Where the grounds for divorce are voluntary separation for 3 years, fault may be considered in dividing the property. The factors for consideration specified in the statute are that the amount be reasonable based on the circumstances of the parties and the nature of the case. Alimony payments may be ordered to be paid through the registry of the court. [Arkansas Code of 1987 Annotated; Title 9, Chapter 12-312].

SPOUSE'S NAME: The court may restore the wife's pre-marriage name. [Arkansas Code of 1987 Annotated; Title 9, Chapter 12-318].

CHILD CUSTODY: Child custody is awarded based on the welfare and best interests of the child, after a consideration of the following factors: (1) the circumstances of the parents and child; (2) the nature of the case; (3) which parent is most likely to allow frequent and continuing contact with the other parent; and (4) any acts of domestic violence. Joint or shared custody may been awarded if it is found to be in the best interests of the child. The sex of the parent is not a factor for decisions relating to child custody. A grandparent of a child may petition the court to request continuing contact with the child. [Arkansas Code of 1987 Annotated; Title 9, Chapter 13-101 and Arkansas Case Law].

CHILD SUPPORT: In awarding a reasonable amount of child support, the court is to consider the following factors: (1) the circumstances of the parents and child, and (2) the nature of the case. Child support payments may be ordered to be paid through the registry of the court and the court may require that a bond securing payment be required. There is an official Arkansas Family Support guidelines chart which is presumed to be correct, unless the court finds that the amount would be inappropriate or unjust, considering the following factors: (1) any necessary medical, dental, or psychological care or insurance; (2) the creation or maintenance of trust fund for the child; (3) daycare expenses; (4) extraordinary time spent with the non-custodial parent; and (5) any additional support provided by the parent obligated to pay support. This chart should be available from the Clerk of any Chancery Court. In addition, an official Affidavit of Financial Means must be filed with divorce cases which involve issues relating to child support. [Arkansas Code of 1987 Annotated; Title 9, Chapters 12-312 and 14-105 and Addendum to 1997 Arkansas Code Supplement].

CALIFORNIA

STATE WEBSITE: http://www.leginfo.ca.gov/calaw.html

DOWNLOAD STATE FORMS: http://www.courtinfo.ca.gov/cgi-bin/forms.cgi

FORMS PROVIDED ON CD: Joint Petition for Summary Dissolution, Petition for Dissolution of Marriage, Financial Statement

FORMS AVAILABLE ONLINE: Joint Petition for Summary Dissolution, Petition for Dissolution of Marriage, Financial Statement, Order/Notice to Withhold Income for Child Support

RESIDENCY REQUIREMENTS AND WHERE TO FILE: A spouse filing for dissolution of marriage must have been a resident of the state for 6 months and a resident of the county for 3 months where the dissolution of marriage is filed. In addition, there is a waiting period of 6 months after the service of process or the appearance by the respondent before the dissolution of marriage becomes final. Partners of a "domestic partnership" under California Family Code Section 297 may terminate their partnership by using forms available from any county clerk or the office of the Secretary of State. [Annotated Family Code; Sections 297, 298, 2320, and 2339].

LEGAL GROUNDS FOR DISSOLUTION OF MARRIAGE: No-Fault: Irreconcilable differences which have caused the irremediable breakdown of the marriage. [Annotated California Family Code; Section 2310]. General: Incurable insanity. [Annotated California Family Code; Section 2310].

NAME OF COURT IN WHICH TO FILE FOR DISSOLUTION OF MARRIAGE: Superior Court. "Superior Court of California, County of _____." [Annotated California Family Code; Section 2330.3].

TITLE OF DISSOLUTION OF MARRIAGE ACTION: Petition for Dissolution of Marriage. "In Re the Marriage of _____ and _____." (Official mandatory and optional forms for filing a Dissolution of Marriage are available from the County Clerk of any county). [Annotated California Family Code; Section 2330 and Judicial Council Forms #FL-100] See *Simplified Dissolution Procedures* below.

NAME USED TO DESCRIBE SPOUSE FILING FOR DISSOLUTION OF MARRIAGE: Petitioner.

NAME USED TO DESCRIBE OTHER SPOUSE IN DISSOLUTION OF MARRIAGE: Respondent.

TITLE OF FINAL DISSOLUTION OF MARRIAGE PAPERS: Final Judgment of Dissolution of Marriage.

LEGAL SEPARATION: The grounds for obtaining a legal separation in California are: (1) irreconcilable differences and (2) incurable insanity. A spouse filing for legal separation must have been a resident of the state for 6 months and a resident of the county for 3 months where the action for legal separation is filed for. [Annotated California Family Code; Sections 2310 and 2320].

SIMPLIFIED OR SPECIAL DISSOLUTION OF MARRIAGE PROCEDURES: A marriage of 5 years or less may be dissolved by summary action. A Joint Petition for Summary Dissolution of Marriage may be filed if: (1) either spouse has met the residency requirement for a standard dissolution of marriage; (2) there is an irremediable breakdown of the marriage due to irreconcilable differences; (3) there are no children born of or adopted during the marriage; (4) the wife is not pregnant; (5) neither spouse owns any real estate, (6) there are no unpaid debts exceeding $4,000 incurred during the marriage; (7) the total value of the community property (including any deferred compensation or retirement plans but excluding cars and loans) is less than $25,000; (8) neither spouse has separate property (excluding cars and loans) exceeding $25,000 in value [On January 1 of every odd-numbered year, the dollar amounts in this section may be revised]; (9) the spouses have signed an agreement regarding the division of their assets and the assumption of their liabilities and have signed any documents or given proof of any transfers necessary to effectuate the agreement; (10) the spouses waive any rights to spousal support [maintenance]; (11) the spouses waive their right to appeal the dissolution of marriage and their right to a new trial upon entry of the final dissolution of marriage judgment; (12) the spouses have read and understand the summary dissolution of marriage brochure available from the county clerk; and (13) both spouses desire that the marriage be dissolved. Official mandatory and optional forms for filing for a Summary Dissolution of Marriage are available from the County Clerk of any county. [Annotated California Family Code; Sections 2400 to 2406, and Judicial Council Forms].

MEDIATION OR COUNSELING REQUIREMENTS: When spouses seek a no-fault dissolution of marriage (on the grounds of irremediable breakdown of the marriage) and it appears to the court that there is a reasonable possibility of reconciliation, the court will stay the dissolution of marriage proceedings for 30 days. If there is no reconciliation at the end of this 30-day period, either spouse may move for a dissolution of marriage or legal separation. In addition, a confidential counseling statement must be filed in any county that has a Conciliation Court. Official forms to this effect are available from the County Clerk of any county that has a Conciliation Court. In addition, if child custody is contested, a mediation conference will be ordered at which the mediator may choose to exclude any attorneys of the parents. [Annotated California Family Code; Sections 2334(a), 2334(c), 3170, and 3182(a) and California Family Law Court Rule 1224].

PROPERTY DISTRIBUTION: California is a "community property" state. Any jointly-held property is presumed to be "community" property, unless it is clearly stated in a deed or written agreement that the property is "separate" property. Unless the spouses agree otherwise, all community and quasi-community property is divided equally between the spouses. If economic circumstances warrant, however, the court may award any asset to 1 spouse on such conditions as it feels proper to provide for a substantially equal distribution of property. In addition, if 1 of the spouses has deliberately misappropriated community property, the court may make an unequal division of the community property. Marital contributions to the education and training of the other spouse that substantially increases or enhances the other spouse's earning capacity are reimbursable to the community property. Each spouse shall be responsible for the following debts: (1) those incurred prior to marriage; (2) any separate debts during the marriage that were not incurred to benefit the community (marriage); (3) their equitable share of any community debts made during the marriage; and (4) any debts incurred after separation and before dissolution of marriage if the debts were for non-necessities and an equitable share of debts incurred during this period if the debts were for necessities. [Annotated California Family Code; Sections 2502, 2581, 2601, 2602, 2620, 2621, 2623, 2625, and 2641].

ALIMONY/MAINTENANCE/SPOUSAL SUPPORT: The court may award support to either spouse in any amount and for any period of time that the court deems just and reasonable, based on the standard of living achieved during the marriage. The factors considered are: (1) whether the spouse seeking support is the custodian of a child whose circumstances make it appropriate for that spouse not to seek outside employment; (2) the time necessary to acquire sufficient education and training to enable the spouse to find appropriate employment and that spouse's future earning capacity; (3) the standard of living established during the marriage; (4) the duration of the marriage; (5) the comparative financial resources of the spouses, including their comparative earning abilities in the labor market; (6) the needs and obligations of each spouse; (7) the contribution of each spouse to the marriage, including services rendered in homemaking, childcare, education, and career-building of the other spouse; (8) the age and health of the spouses; (9) the physical and emotional conditions of the spouses; (10) the tax consequences to each spouse; (11) the ability of the supporting spouse to pay, taking into account that spouse's earning capacity, earned and unearned income, assets, and standard of living; (12) the balance of hardships to each party; and (13) any other factor the court deems just and equitable. Marital misconduct is not a factor to be considered in determining the amount of support, except for a criminal conviction of an abusive spouse. The goal is specifically to make the supported spouse self-supporting in a reasonable period of time (generally considered to be half the length of the marriage). [Annotated California Family Code; Section 4320, 4324, and 4330].

SPOUSE'S NAME: On a party's request, the court shall restore a spouse's former or birth name, regardless of the last name of any custodial child. [Annotated California Family Code; Sections 2401, 2080 and 2081].

CHILD CUSTODY: Joint or sole custody may be awarded based on the best interests of the child and the following factors: (1) the preference of the child, if the child is of sufficient age and capacity; (2) the desire and ability of each parent to allow an open and loving frequent relationship between the child and the other parent; (3) the child's health, safety, and welfare; (4) any history of child or spouse abuse by anyone seeking custody or who has had any caretaking relationship with the child, including anyone dating the parent; (5) the nature and amount of contact with both parents; and (6) any habitual and continued use of alcohol or illegal controlled substances. Marital misconduct may also be considered. Custody is awarded in the following order of preference: (1) to both parents jointly; (2) to either parent; (3) to the person in whose home the child has been living; or (4) to any other person deemed by the court suitable to provide adequate and proper care and guidance for the child. However, it is not presumed that joint custody is necessarily the preferred choice, unless there is an agreement between the parents regarding joint custody. No preference in awarding custody is to be given because of parent's sex. The court may order a parent to give the other parent 30-days' notice of any plans to change the residence of a child. [Annotated California Family Code; Sections 3011, 3020, 3024, 3040, and 3042].

CHILD SUPPORT: Either parent may be ordered to pay an amount necessary for the support, maintenance, and education of the child. Child support payments may be awarded on a temporary basis during custody or child support proceedings. There is a mandatory minimum amount of child support which is determined by official forms which are available from the County Clerk of any county. These minimum payment amounts will apply unless there is a reasonable agreement between the parents providing otherwise that states that: (1) the parents state that they are fully informed of their rights regarding child support under California law; (2) that the child support amount is being agreed to without coercion or duress; (3) that both parents declare that their children's needs will be adequately met; and (4) that the right to child support has not been assigned to the county and that no public assistance is pending. A parent may be required to provide medical insurance coverage for a child if such coverage is available at a reasonable cost. An applicant for child support must complete and submit to the court: (1) an application for an expedited child support order; (2) an income and expense declaration from both parents; (3) a worksheet setting forth the basis of the amount of child support requested; and (4) a proposed expedited child support order. The parent required to pay may be required to give reasonable security for the support payments. In addition, there are detailed and extensive statutory provisions in California relating to the securing of child support payments. Please consult the statutes directly if this is an important factor. [Annotated California Family Code; Sections 3024, 3622, 4001, 4050, Judicial Council Forms, and California Rules of Court].

COLORADO

STATE WEBSITE: http://www.leg.state.co.us/

DOWNLOAD STATE FORMS: http://www.courts.state.co.us/chs/court/forms/domestic/domestic.html

FORMS PROVIDED ON CD: Petition for Dissolution of Marriage, Sworn Financial Statement, Case Information Sheet

FORMS AVAILABLE ONLINE: Petition for Dissolution of Marriage, Sworn Financial Statement, Case Information Sheet, Parenting Plan, Order/Notice to Withhold Income for Support

RESIDENCY REQUIREMENTS AND WHERE TO FILE: One spouse must have been a resident of Colorado for 90 days prior to filing for dissolution of marriage. The dissolution of marriage may be filed for in: (1) the county where the respondent resides or (2) the county in which the petitioner resides if the respondent has been served in the same county or is a non-resident of Colorado. [Colorado Revised Statutes; Article 10, Section 14-10-106 and Colorado Rules of Civil Procedure, Rule 98].

LEGAL GROUNDS FOR DISSOLUTION OF MARRIAGE: No-Fault: Irretrievable breakdown of the marriage. [Colorado Revised Statutes; Article 10, Section 14-10-106].

General: Irretrievable breakdown of the marriage is the only grounds for dissolution of marriage in Colorado. [Colorado Revised Statutes; Article 10, Section 14-10-106].

NAME OF COURT IN WHICH TO FILE FOR DISSOLUTION OF MARRIAGE: District Court. "In the District Court in and for the County of _____ and State of Colorado." [Colorado Revised Statutes; Article 10, Section 14-10-106].

TITLE OF DISSOLUTION OF MARRIAGE ACTION: Petition for Dissolution of Marriage.

NAME USED TO DESCRIBE SPOUSE FILING FOR DISSOLUTION OF MARRIAGE: Petitioner.

NAME USED TO DESCRIBE OTHER SPOUSE IN DISSOLUTION OF MARRIAGE: Respondent.

TITLE OF FINAL DISSOLUTION OF MARRIAGE PAPERS: Decree of Dissolution of Marriage.

LEGAL SEPARATION: If there has been an irretrievable breakdown of the marriage, the spouses may file for a legal separation. One spouse must have been a resident of Colorado for 90 days prior to filing for legal separation. [Colorado Revised Statutes; Article 10, Section 14-10-106].

SIMPLIFIED OR SPECIAL DISSOLUTION OF MARRIAGE PROCEDURES: A dissolution of marriage may be obtained by affidavit of either or both of the spouses if: (1) there are no minor children and the wife is not pregnant or both spouses are represented by counsel and have entered into a separation agreement granting custody and child support; (2) there are no disputes; (3) there is no marital property or the spouses have agreed on the division of marital property; and (4) the adverse party (non-filing spouse) has been served with the dissolution of marriage papers. A signed affidavit stating the facts in the case and a copy of any separation agreement must be filed with the petition. [Colorado Revised Statutes; Article 10, Section 14-10-120.3].

MEDIATION OR COUNSELING REQUIREMENTS: At the request of either spouse or their attorney, or at the discretion of the court, the court may appoint a marriage counselor in any dissolution of marriage or legal separation proceeding and delay the proceedings for 30 to 60 days to allow for counseling. In addition, the court may order a parent of a child under 18 years of age to attend a program concerning the impact of separation and dissolution on children. Finally, a court may appoint an arbitrator to resolve disputes between parents concerning child support and custody. [Colorado Revised Statutes; Article 10, Sections 14-10-110, 14-10-123.7, 14-10-128.5, and 14-12-106].

PROPERTY DISTRIBUTION: Colorado is an "equitable distribution" state. The separate property of each spouse which was owned prior to the marriage or obtained by gift or inheritance is retained by that spouse. All other property acquired during the marriage will be divided, without regard to any fault, based on the following: (1) the contribution of each spouse to the acquisition of the marital property, including the contribution of each spouse as homemaker; (2) the value of each spouse's separate property; (3) the economic circumstances of each spouse at the time the division of property is to become effective, including the desirability of awarding the family home or right to live in it to the spouse having custody of any children; and (4) any increase or decrease in the value of the separate property of the spouse during the marriage or the depletion of the separate property for marital purposes. [Colorado Revised Statutes; Article 10, Section 14-10-113].

ALIMONY/MAINTENANCE/SPOUSAL SUPPORT: Either spouse may be awarded support for a just period of time, without regard to any marital fault. If the spouses' combined income is over $75,000.00, the monthly temporary maintenance to the lower-earning spouse will be 40% of the higher-earning spouse's income less 50% of the lower-earning spouse's income. If the spouses' combined income is over $75,000.00, maintenance is only allowed if the spouse seeking maintenance: (1) lacks sufficient property, including his or her share of any marital property, to provide for his or her needs and (2) is unable to support himself or herself through appropriate employment, or has custody of a child and the circumstances are such that the spouse should not be required to seek employment outside the home. For couples with over $75,000.00 joint income, the award of maintenance is based upon the following factors: (1) the time necessary to acquire sufficient education and training to enable the spouse to find appropriate employment and that spouse's future earning capacity; (2) the standard of living established during the marriage; (3) the duration of the marriage; (4) the ability of the spouse from whom support is sought to meet his or her needs while meeting those of the spouse seeking support; (5) the financial resources of the spouse seeking maintenance, including marital property apportioned to such spouse and such spouse's ability to meet his or her needs independently; (6) the age of the spouses; (7) the physical and emotional conditions of the spouses; and (8) any custodial and child support responsibilities. Maintenance payments may be ordered to be paid directly to the court for distribution to the spouse. [Colorado Revised Statutes; Article 10, Sections 14-10-114 and 14-10-117].

SPOUSE'S NAME: There is no legal provision in Colorado for restoration of the spouse's name upon divorce. However, there is a general statute which allows for the change of a person's name upon petition to the court. [Colorado Revised Statutes; Article 10, Section 13-15-101].

CHILD CUSTODY: Joint or sole custody will be determined with regard to the best interests of the child, without regard to the sex of the parent, and after considering the following factors: (1) the preference of the child; (2) the desire and ability of each parent to allow an open and loving froquont rolationship betwoon the child and the other parent; (3) the wishes of the parents; (4) the child's adjustment to his or her home, school, and community; (5) the mental and physical health of all individuals involved; (6) the relationship of the child with parents, siblings, and other significant family members; (7) any child abuse or spouse abuse by either parent; (8) whether a parent's past involvement with the child reflects a system of values, time commitment, and mutual support; (9) the physical proximity of the parties to each other; and (10) the ability of each party to place the needs of the child ahead of his or her own needs. Visitation may be restricted if there is a danger to the child.

Joint custody may be awarded on the petition of both parents if they submit a reasonable plan for custody. The plan submitted to the court for joint custody should address the following issues: (1) the location of each parent; (2) the periods of time during which each parent will have physical custody of the child; (3) the legal residence of the child; (4) the child's education; (5) the child's religious training, if any; (6) the child's health care; (7) finances to provide for the child's needs; (8) holidays and vacations; and (9) any other factors affecting the physical or emotional health or well-being of the child. The actual joint custody award is based on all of the factors involved in standard custody decisions and on the following additional factors: (1) the ability of the parents to cooperate and make decisions jointly; (2) whether the past pattern of involvement of the parents with the child reflects a system of values and mutual support which indicates the parent's ability as joint custodians to provide a positive and nourishing relationship with the child; and (3) whether an award of joint custody will promote more frequent or continuing contact between the child and each of the parents. [Colorado Revised Statutes; Article 10, Sections 14-10-123, 14-10-124, and 14-10-129].

CHILD SUPPORT: The court may order reasonable and necessary child support to be paid by either or both parents, without regard to marital fault, after considering the following factors: (1) the financial resources of the child; (2) the financial resources of the custodial parents; (3) the standard of living the child would have enjoyed if the marriage had survived; (4) the physical and emotional conditions and educational needs of the child; and (5) the financial resources, needs, and obligations of both the noncustodial and the custodial parent. Provisions for medical insurance and medical care for any children may be ordered to be provided. There are specific child support guidelines specified in the statute. In addition, standardized child support guideline forms are available from the Clerk of any District Court. Child support payments may be ordered to be paid through the Clerk of the Court. Child support must continue through high school graduation, unless certain factors are met. [Colorado Revised Statutes; Article 10, Sections 14-10-115 and 14-10-117].

The No-Fault Divorce Toolkit

CONNECTICUT

STATE WEBSITE: http://www.cslib.org/psaindex.htm

DOWNLOAD STATE FORMS: http://www.jud2.state.ct.us/webforms/

FORMS PROVIDED ON CD: Divorce Complaint, Financial Affidavit

FORMS AVAILABLE ONLINE: Divorce Complaint, Financial Affidavit, Order/Notice to Withhold Income for Child Support, Proposed Parental Responsibility Plan

RESIDENCY REQUIREMENTS AND WHERE TO FILE: The dissolution of marriage may be filed by either spouse if a resident. However, the dissolution of marriage will not be finalized until 1 spouse has been a resident for 1 year; unless 1 of the spouses was a resident of Connecticut at the time of the marriage and returned with the intention of permanent residence; or if the grounds for the dissolution of marriage arose in Connecticut. In cases which involve support, the dissolution of marriage is to be filed in the county in which the plaintiff resides. In all other cases, the dissolution of marriage may be filed in any county which is most convenient to both spouses. [Connecticut General Statutes Annotated; Title 46b, Chapter 815j Section 44, and Title 51, Chapter 890 Section 349].

LEGAL GROUNDS FOR DISSOLUTION OF MARRIAGE: No-Fault: (1) Irretrievable breakdown of the marriage; (2) incompatibility and voluntary separation for 18 months with no reasonable prospect for reconciliation. [Connecticut General Statutes Annotated; Title 46b Chapter 815j Section 40]. General: (1) Adultery; (2) life imprisonment; (3) confinement for incurable insanity for a total of 5 years; (4) willful desertion and nonsupport for 1 year; (5) 7 years absence; (6) cruel and inhuman treatment; (7) fraud; (8) habitual intemperance (drunkenness); and (9) commission and/or conviction of an infamous crime involving a violation of conjugal duty and imprisonment for at least 1 year. [Connecticut General Statutes Annotated; Title 46b Chapter 815j Section 40].

NAME OF COURT IN WHICH TO FILE FOR DISSOLUTION OF MARRIAGE: Superior Court. [Connecticut General Statutes Annotated; Title 46b Chapter 815j Section 42].

TITLE OF DISSOLUTION OF MARRIAGE ACTION: Complaint for Dissolution of Marriage.

NAME USED TO DESCRIBE SPOUSE FILING FOR DISSOLUTION OF MARRIAGE: Plaintiff.

NAME USED TO DESCRIBE OTHER SPOUSE IN DISSOLUTION OF MARRIAGE: Defendant.

TITLE OF FINAL DISSOLUTION OF MARRIAGE PAPERS: Decree of Dissolution of Marriage.

LEGAL SEPARATION: A legal separation may be granted on the following grounds: (1) irretrievable breakdown of the marriage; (2) incompatibility and voluntary separation; (3) adultery; (4) life imprisonment; (5) confinement for incurable insanity for a total of 5 years; (6) willful desertion and nonsupport for 1 year; (7) cruel and inhuman treatment; (8) fraud; (9) habitual intemperance (drunkenness); and (10) commission and/or conviction of an infamous crime involving a violation of conjugal duty and imprisonment for at least 1 year. There is no residency requirement noted in the statute. [Connecticut General Statutes Annotated;Title 46b Chapter 815j Section 40].

SIMPLIFIED OR SPECIAL DISSOLUTION OF MARRIAGE PROCEDURES: Proof of the breakdown of the marriage can be made by: (1) the spouses signing an agreement or statement that their marriage io irrotriovobly broken or (2) both spouses stating in court that their marriage is irretrievably broken and submitting an agreement concerning the care, custody, visitation, maintenance, support, and education after custody of their children, if any, and concerning alimony and the disposition of any property. [Connecticut General Statutes Annotated; Title 46b Chapter 815j Section 51].

MEDIATION OR COUNSELING REQUIREMENTS: Within 90 days after the dissolution of marriage has been filed, either spouse or the attorney for any minor children may submit a request for conciliation to the clerk of the court. Two mandatory counseling sessions will be ordered. Mediation services may also be available from the court for property, financial, custody, and visitation issues. [Connecticut General Statutes Annotated; Title 46b Chapter 815j Section 53 and 53a].

PROPERTY DISTRIBUTION: Connecticut is an "equitable distribution" state. The court may assign to either spouse all or part of the property of the other spouse, including any gifts and inheritances, based on the following factors: (1) the contribution of each spouse to the acquisition of the marital property, including the contribution of each spouse as homemaker; (2) the length of the marriage; (3) the age and health of the spouses; (4) the occupation of the spouses; (5) the amount and sources of income of the spouses; (6) the vocational skills of the spouses; (7) the employability of the spouses; (8) the estate, liabilities, and needs of each spouse and the opportunity of each for further acquisition of capital assets and income; (9) the circumstances that contributed to the estrangement of the spouses; and (10) the causes of the dissolution of marriage. [Connecticut General Statutes Annotated; Title 46b Chapter 815j Section 81].

ALIMONY/MAINTENANCE/SPOUSAL SUPPORT: Alimony may be awarded to either spouse, based on the following factors: (1) the causes for the dissolution of marriage, including any marital fault; (2) the distribution of the marital property; (3) whether the spouse seeking support is the custodian of a child whose condition or circumstances make it appropriate for that spouse not to seek outside employment; (4) the duration of the marriage; (5) the age of the spouses; (6) the physical and emotional conditions of the spouses; (7) the usual occupation of the spouses during the marriage; (8) the needs of each spouse; and (9) the vocational skills and employability of the spouse seeking support and alimony. [Connecticut General Statutes Annotated; Title 46b Chapter 815j Section 82 and 86].

SPOUSE'S NAME: Either spouse's birth name shall be restored upon request. [Connecticut General Statutes Annotated; Title 46b Chapter 815j Section 63].

CHILD CUSTODY: Joint or sole custody is awarded based upon the best interests of the child and the following factors: (1) the causes for the dissolution of marriage if such causes are relevant to the best interests of the child and (2) the wishes of the child if the child is of sufficient age and is capable of forming an intelligent choice. There are no other specific state guidelines for consideration. There is a presumption that joint custody is in the best interests of the child if both parents have agreed to joint custody. [Connecticut General Statutes Annotated; Title 46b Chapter 815j Section 56,56a,56b,and 84].

CHILD SUPPORT: Either parent may be ordered to contribute child support, based on the following factors: (1) the financial resources of the child; (2) the age, health, and station of the parents; (3) the occupation of each parent; (4) the earning capacity of each parent; (5) the amount and sources of income of each parent; (6) the vocational skills and employability of each parent; (7) the age and health of the child; (8) the child's occupation; (9) the vocational skills of the child; (10) the employability of the child; (11) the estate and needs of the child; and (12) the relative financial means of the parents. Either parent may be ordered to provide health insurance for the child. There are official Child Support Guidelines. These guidelines are presumed to be correct unless there is a showing that the amount would be inequitable or inappropriate under the particular circumstances in a case. [Connecticut General Statutes Annotated; Title 46b Chapter 815j Section 84].

DELAWARE

STATE WEBSITE: http://delaware.gov/

DOWNLOAD STATE FORMS: http://courts.state.de.us/Courts/Family%20Court/

FORMS PROVIDED ON CD: Petition for Divorce, Financial Report

FORMS AVAILABLE ONLINE: Petition for Divorce, Financial Report, Petition for Custody, Petition for Support

RESIDENCY REQUIREMENTS AND WHERE TO FILE: One spouse must have been a resident for 6 months immediately prior to filing for divorce. The divorce may be filed for in a county where either spouse resides. [Delaware Code Annotated; Title 13 Chapter 15 Section 1504 and 1507].

LEGAL GROUNDS FOR DIVORCE: No-Fault: (1) Irretrievable breakdown of the marriage and reconciliation is improbable [a marriage is considered "irretrievably broken" when it is characterized by 1 of the following: (a) voluntary separation; (b) separation caused by the other spouse's misconduct or mental illness; or (c) separation caused by incompatibility; and (2) living apart for 6 months because of incompatibility]. [Delaware Code Annotated; Title 13 Chapter 15 Section 1505].

General: Separation caused by mental illness. [Delaware Code Annotated; Title 13 Chapter 15 Section 1505].

NAME OF COURT IN WHICH TO FILE FOR DIVORCE: Family Court. "In the Family Court for the State of Delaware, in and for _____ County." [Delaware Code Annotated; Title 13 Chapter 15 Section 1504 and 1507].

TITLE OF DIVORCE ACTION: Petition for Divorce. "In Re the Marriage of _____ and _____."

NAME USED TO DESCRIBE SPOUSE FILING FOR DIVORCE: Petitioner.

NAME USED TO DESCRIBE OTHER SPOUSE IN DIVORCE: Respondent.

TITLE OF FINAL DIVORCE PAPERS: Decree of Divorce.

LEGAL SEPARATION: There is no legal provision in Delaware for legal separation.

SIMPLIFIED OR SPECIAL DIVORCE PROCEDURES: The respondent may file an appearance which will fulfill the requirement of service of process. In addition, a sample Petition for Divorce is contained in Delaware Code Annotated; Title 13, Chapter 1507. [Delaware Code Annotated; Title 13 Chapter 15 Section 1508].

MEDIATION OR COUNSELING REQUIREMENTS: In a contested divorce, the court may delay the proceedings for 60 days to allow the spouses to seek counseling or order a mediation conference. In addition, there are mediation/arbitration units attached to the Delaware Family Court. Finally, the court may require parents seeking divorce to participate in a certified "parenting education course." If the parent has a history of domestic violence, he or she may be required to attend additional, more intensive courses. [Delaware Code Annotated; Title 13 Chapter 15 Section 1507 and 1517].

PROPERTY DISTRIBUTION: Delaware is an "equitable distribution" state. A spouse's separate property is that which is: (1) obtained prior to the marriage; (2) obtained by inheritance; (3) specified as separate property by an agreement between the spouses; or (4) property acquired in exchange for separate property or an increase in value of separate property. All separate property is retained by the spouse who owns such property. Marital property acquired during the marriage, including any property acquired by gift, is to be divided equitably, without regard to fault, based on the following factors: (1) the contribution of each spouse to the acquisition of the marital property, including the contribution of each spouse as homemaker; (2) the value of each spouse's personal property; (3) the economic circumstances of each spouse at the time the division of property is to become effective; (4) the length of the marriage; (5) the age and health of the spouses; (6) the occupation of the spouses; (7) the amount and sources of income of the spouses; (8) the vocational skills of the spouses; (9) the employability of the spouses; (10) the estate, liabilities, and needs of each spouse and the opportunity of each for further acquisition of capital assets and income; (11) the federal income tax consequences of the court's division of the property; (12) liabilities of the spouses; (13) any prior marriage of each spouse; (14) whether the property award is instead of or in addition to maintenance; (15) how and by whom the property was acquired; and (16) any custodial provisions for the children. [Delaware Code Annotated; Title 13 Chapter 15 Section 1513].

ALIMONY/MAINTENANCE/SPOUSAL SUPPORT: Either spouse may be awarded alimony if he or she: (1) is dependent on the other spouse; (2) lacks sufficient property, including any award or marital property, to provide for his or her reasonable needs; and (3) is unable to support himself or herself through appropriate employment or is the custodian of a child whose condition or circumstances make it appropriate that he or she not be required to seek employment. Either spouse may be awarded alimony for no longer than a a period of time equal to 50% of the length of the marriage. There is, however, no time limit if the marriage lasted for over 20 years. Marital misconduct is not a factor to be considered in an award or alimony. The factors to be considered are: (1) the time necessary to acquire sufficient education and training to enable the spouse to find appropriate employment and that spouse's future earning capacity; (2) the standard of living established during the marriage; (3) the duration of the marriage; (4) the ability of the spouse from whom support is sought to meet his or her needs while meeting those of the spouse seeking support; (5) the financial resources of the spouse seeking alimony, including marital property apportioned to such spouse and such spouse's ability to meet his or her needs independently; (6) the tax consequences to each spouse; (7) the age of the spouses; (8) the physical and emotional conditions of the spouses; (9) any custodial and child support responsibilities; (10) whether either spouse has foregone or postponed economic, education, or other employment opportunities during the course of the marriage; and (11) any other factor that the court finds just and appropriate. Any party awarded alimony has a duty to make an effort to seek vocational training and employment unless the court finds that it would be inequitable to require this because of: (1) a severe physical or mental disability; (2) his or her age; or (3) the needs of any children living with the spouse receiving alimony. Unless the spouses agree otherwise, alimony is terminated upon death, remarriage, or cohabitation with another person. [Delaware Code Annotated; Title 13 Chapter 15 Section 1512].

SPOUSE'S NAME: Upon request, the wife may resume her former or maiden name. [Delaware Code Annotated; Title 13 Chapter 15 Section 1514].

CHILD CUSTODY: Joint or sole child custody is awarded based on the best interests of the child and after considering the following factors: (1) preference of the child; (2) the wishes of the parents; (3) the child's adjustment to his or her home, school, and community; (4) the mental and physical health of all individuals involved; (5) the relationship of the child with parents, siblings, and other significant family members; and (6) the past and present compliance by both parents with the duty to support the child. The conduct of the proposed guardian is to be considered only as it bears on his or her relationship with the child. No preference is to be given because of parent's sex.

In addition, in any case involving minor children, the petitioning parent must submit with the petition a signed affidavit that states that the parent has been advised of or has read the following list of children's rights. The list of rights must be included in the affidavit. The children's rights are: (1) the right to a continuing relationship with both parents; (2) the right to be treated as an important human being, with unique feelings, ideas, and desires; (3) the right to continuing care and guidance from both parents; (4) the right to know and appreciate what is good in each parent without 1 parent degrading the other; (5) the right to express love, affection, and respect for each parent without having to stifle that love because of disapproval by the other parent; (6) the right to know that the parents' decision to divorce was not the responsibility of the child; (7) the right not to be a source of argument between the parents; (8) the right to honest answers to questions about the changing family relationships; (9) the right to be able to experience regular and consistent contact with both parents and the right to know the reason for any cancellation of time or change of plans; and (10) the right to have a relaxed, secure relationship with both parents without being placed in a position to manipulate 1 parent against the other. [Delaware Code Annotated; Title 13 Chapter 15 Section 1507 and Title 13 Chapter 7 Section 722].

CHILD SUPPORT: Each parent has an equal duty to support any children. The following factors are considered in awards of child support: (1) the financial resources of the child; (2) the standard of living the child would have enjoyed if there had been no divorce; (3) the age and health of the parents; (4) the earning capacity of each parent; (5) the amount and sources of income of each parent; (6) the age, health, or station of the child; (7) the estate and needs of the child; and (8) the relative financial means of the parents. [Delaware Code Annotated; Title 13 Chapter 5 Section 501 and 514. Title 13 Chapter 7 Section 701].

DISTRICT OF COLUMBIA (Washington D.C.)

STATE WEBSITE: http://www.dc.gov/

DOWNLOAD STATE FORMS: http://www.dccourts.gov/dccourts/superior/family/domestic.jsp

FORMS PROVIDED ON CD: Complaint for Absolute Divorce, Marital Property and Marital Debt

FORMS AVAILABLE ONLINE: Complaint for Absolute Divorce, Marital Property and Marital Debt, Complaint for Child Custody, Petition to Establish Child Support, Motion for Temporary Alimony

RESIDENCY REQUIREMENTS AND WHERE TO FILE: One of the spouses must have been a resident of Washington D.C. for 6 months immediately prior to filing for divorce. Military personnel are considered residents if they have been stationed in Washington D.C. for 6 months. [District of Columbia Code Annotated; Title 16, Chapter 9, Section 902].

LEGAL GROUNDS FOR DIVORCE: No-Fault: (1) Mutual voluntary separation without cohabitation for 6 months; (2) living separate and apart without cohabitation for 1 year. "Living separate and apart" may be accomplished under the same roof, if the spouses do not share bed or food. [District of Columbia Code Annotated; Title 16, Chapter 9, Sections 904, 905, and 906].

General: (1) Mutual voluntary separation without cohabitation for 6 months and (2) living separate and apart without cohabitation for 1 year are the only grounds for divorce in Washington D.C. [District of Columbia Code Annotated; Title 16, Chapter 9, Sections 904 to 906].

NAME OF COURT IN WHICH TO FILE FOR DIVORCE: Superior Court–Family Division. "In the Superior Court of the District of Columbia–Family Division." [District of Columbia Court Rules; Volume 2, Appendix I].

TITLE OF DIVORCE ACTION: Complaint for Divorce.

NAME USED TO DESCRIBE SPOUSE FILING FOR DIVORCE: Plaintiff.

NAME USED TO DESCRIBE OTHER SPOUSE IN DIVORCE: Defendant.

TITLE OF FINAL DIVORCE PAPERS: Final Decree of Divorce.

LEGAL SEPARATION: Legal separation (from bed and board) may be granted on the following grounds: (1) adultery; (2) cruelty; (3) voluntary separation; and (4) living separate and apart without cohabitation. One of the spouses must have been a resident for 6 months prior to filing for legal separation. Military personnel are considered residents if they have been stationed in Washington D.C. for 6 months. [District of Columbia Code Annotated; Title 16, Chapter 9, Sections 902 and 904-906].

SIMPLIFIED OR SPECIAL DIVORCE PROCEDURES: There are no legal provisions in Washington D.C. for simplified divorce.

MEDIATION OR COUNSELING REQUIREMENTS: The court may order either or both spouses to attend parenting classes in those cases in which child custody is an issue. [District of Columbia Code Annotated; Title 16, Chapter 9, Section 914].

PROPERTY DISTRIBUTION: Washington D.C. is an "equitable distribution" jurisdiction. If there is no valid property distribution agreement, each spouse retains his or her separate property (acquired before the marriage or acquired during the marriage by gift or inheritance) and any increase in such separate property and any property acquired in exchange for such separate property. All other property, regardless of how title is held, shall be divided equitably and reasonably, based on relevant factors, including: (1) the contribution of each spouse to the acquisition of the marital property, including the contribution of each spouse as homemaker; (2) the length of the marriage; (3) the occupation of the spouses; (4) the vocational skills of the spouses; (5) the employability of the spouses; (6) the estate, liabilities, and needs of each spouse and the opportunity of each for further acquisition of capital assets and income; (7) the assets and debts of the spouses; (8) any prior marriage of each spouse; (9) whether the property award is instead of or in addition to alimony; (10) any custodial provisions for the children; (11) the age and health of the spouses; and (12) the amount and sources of income of the spouses. The conduct of the spouses during the marriage is not a factor for consideration. [District of Columbia Code Annotated; Title 16, Chapter 9, Section 910].

ALIMONY/MAINTENANCE/SPOUSAL SUPPORT: Either spouse may be awarded alimony, during the divorce proceeding or after, if it is just or proper. Specific factors listed in the statute are: (1) ability of the party seeking alimony to wholly or partly self-supporting; (2) time necessary for the party seeking alimony to gain sufficient education or training; (3) standard of living that the parties established during their marriage; (4) duration of the marriage; (5) circumstances which contributed to the estrangement of the parties; (6) age of each party; (7) physical and mental condition of each party; (8) ability of the party from whom alimony is sought to meet his or her needs while meeting the needs of the other party; and (9) the financial needs and financial resources of each party. [District of Columbia Code Annotated; Title 16, Chapter 9, Sections 911 and 913].

SPOUSE'S NAME: Upon request, the birth name or previous name may be restored. [District of Columbia Code Annotated; Title 16, Chapter 9, Section 915].

CHILD CUSTODY: Sole or joint custody may be granted during and after a divorce proceeding based on the best interests of the child, without regard to spouse's sex or sexual orientation, race, color, national origin, or political affiliations. The following factors shall also be considered: (1) the preference of the child, if the child is of sufficient age and capacity; (2) the wishes of the parents; (3) the child's adjustment to his or her home, school, and community; (4) the mental and physical health of all individuals involved; (5) the relationship of the child with parents, siblings, and other significant family members; (6) the willingness of the parents to share custody; (7) the prior involvement of the parent in the child's life; (8) the geographical proximity of the parents; (9) the sincerity of the parent's request; (10) the age and number of children; (11) the demands of parental employment; (12) the impact on any welfare benefits; (13) any evidence of spousal or child abuse; (14) the capacity of the parents to communicate and reach shared decisions affecting the child's welfare; (15) the potential disruption of the child's social and school life; (16) the parent's ability to financially support a joint custody arrangement and; (17) the benefit to the parents. There is a rebuttable presumption that joint interest is in the best interests of the child unless child abuse, neglect, parental kidnapping or other intrafamily violence has occurred. The court may order the parents to submit a written parenting plan for custody. [District of Columbia Code Annotated; Title 16, Chapter 9, Sections 911 and 914].

CHILD SUPPORT: Either parent may be ordered to pay reasonable child support during and after a divorce proceeding. Detailed specific child support guidelines are contained in Title 16, Chapter 9, Sections 916.01 and 916.02. Applications of the guidelines is to be gender neutral. Variations from the official child support guidelines are allowed based on the following factors: (1) the child's needs are exceptional; (2) the non-custodial parent's income is substantially less than the custodial parent's income; (3) a property settlement between the parents provides resources for the child above the minimum support requirements; (4) the non-custodial parent provides support for other dependents and the guideline amounts would cause hardship; (5) the non-custodial parent needs a temporary reduction [of no longer than 12 months] in support payments to repay a substantial debt; (6) the custodial parent provides medical insurance coverage; (7) the custodial parent receives child support payments for other children and the custodial parent's household income is substantially greater than that of the non-custodial parent; and (8) any other extraordinary factors. Child support may be ordered to be paid through the Clerk of the Superior Court. [District of Columbia Code Annotated; Title 16, Chapter 9, Sections 911, 916, 916.01, and Title 46, Section 201].

The No-Fault Divorce Toolkit

FLORIDA

STATE WEBSITE: http://www.leg.state.fl.us/statutes/

DOWNLOAD STATE FORMS: http://www.flcourts.org/gen_public/family/forms_rules/index.shtml

FORMS PROVIDED ON CD: Petition for Dissolution of Marriage with Children, Petition for Dissolution of Marriage without Children, Petition for Simplified Dissolution of Marriage, Financial Affidavit, Financial Affidavit Short Form

FORMS AVAILABLE ONLINE: Petition for Dissolution of Marriage with Children, Petition for Dissolution of Marriage without Children, Petition for Simplified Dissolution of Marriage, Financial Affidavit, Financial Affidavit Short Form, Petition for Support

RESIDENCY REQUIREMENTS AND WHERE TO FILE: One of the spouses must have been a resident for 6 months prior to filing for dissolution of marriage. The dissolution of marriage should be filed in either: (1) the county where the defendant resides or (2) the county where the spouses last lived together prior to separating. [Florida Case Law and Florida Statutes Annotated; Chapter 61.021].

LEGAL GROUNDS FOR DISSOLUTION OF MARRIAGE: No-Fault: Irretrievable breakdown of the marriage. [Florida Statutes Annotated; Chapter 61.052].

General: Mental incapacity for at least 3 years. [Florida Statutes Annotated; Chapter 61.052].

NAME OF COURT IN WHICH TO FILE FOR DISSOLUTION OF MARRIAGE: Circuit Court. "In the Circuit Court in and for the County of _____, Florida." [Florida Rules of Civil Procedure].

TITLE OF DISSOLUTION OF MARRIAGE ACTION: Petition for Dissolution of Marriage. "In Re the Marriage of _____, Husband, and _____, Wife." [Florida Statutes Annotated; Chapter 61.043].

NAME USED TO DESCRIBE SPOUSE FILING FOR DISSOLUTION OF MARRIAGE: Petitioner.

NAME USED TO DESCRIBE OTHER SPOUSE IN DISSOLUTION OF MARRIAGE: Respondent.

TITLE OF FINAL DISSOLUTION OF MARRIAGE PAPERS: Final Judgment of Dissolution of Marriage.

LEGAL SEPARATION: A spouse may file for separate maintenance and child support. [Florida Statutes Annotated; Chapter 61.09].

SIMPLIFIED OR SPECIAL DISSOLUTION OF MARRIAGE PROCEDURES: Florida has a procedure for a Simplified Dissolution of Marriage. In order to qualify to use this procedure, the spouses must certify that: (1) there are no minor or dependent children of the spouses and the wife is not pregnant; (2) the spouses have made a satisfactory division of their property and have agreed as to payment of their joint obligations; (3) that 1 of the spouses has been a resident of Florida for 6 months immediately prior to filing for dissolution of marriage; and (4) that their marriage is irretrievably broken. The spouses must appear in court to testify as to these items and file a Certificate of a Corroborating Witness as to the residency requirement. Each must also attach a financial affidavit to the Simplified Dissolution Petition. Specific forms and an instruction brochure are available from the Clerk of any Circuit Court. In addition, sample forms for various aspects of a standard dissolution of marriage are available in the Florida Family Law Rules of Procedure. [Florida Family Law Rules of Procedure Appendix 1; Rules 12.105 and 12.285 and Family Law Forms 12.900+].

MEDIATION OR COUNSELING REQUIREMENTS: If there are minor children involved, or if 1 of the spouses denies that the marriage is irretrievably broken, the court may delay the proceedings for up to 3 months and may order the spouses to seek counseling, order the spouses to attempt reconciliation, or order the spouses to attend mediation sessions. [Florida Statutes Annotated; Chapters 61.052 and 61.183].

PROPERTY DISTRIBUTION: Florida is an "equitable distribution" state. The spouse's non-marital property will be retained by each spouse. Non-marital property is all property acquired prior to the marriage, property acquired by gift or inheritance, and any property considered to be non-marital according to a written agreement between the spouses. The court is required to begin with the premise that all marital property should be equally divided, based on the following factors: (1) the contribution of each spouse to the acquisition of the marital property, including the contribution of each spouse as homemaker; (2) the length of the marriage; (3) the age and health of the spouses; (4) the amount and sources of income of the spouses; (5) the estate, liabilities, and needs of each spouse and the opportunity of each for further acquisition of capital assets and income; (6) the standard of living established during the marriage; (7) the time necessary for a spouse to acquire sufficient education to enable the spouse to find appropriate employment; and (8) any other factor necessary to do equity and justice between the spouses. Marital misconduct is not specified as a factor. All retirement, pension, profit-sharing and insurance are considered There are also specific rules which govern whether a party is entitled to setoffs or credits upon the sale of the marital home, based on the following factors: (1) the contribution to the marriage by each spouse, including the care and education of the children and services as homemaker; (2) the economic circumstances of the parties; (3) the duration of the marriage; (4) any interruption of personal career or educational opportunity of the other spouse; (5) the contribution of one spouse to the career or educational opportunity of the other spouse; (6) the desirability of retaining any asset, including an interest in a business, from any interference by the other party; (7) the contribution of each spouse to the acquisition, enhancement, and production of income or the improvement of both the marital assets and the nonmarital assets of the parties; (8) the desirability of retaining the marital home as a residence for any dependent child; (9) the intentional dissipation, waste. depletion, or destruction of marital assets after the filing of the petition or within 2 years prior to the filing; and (10) any other factors. [Florida Statutes Annotated: Chapters 61.075 to 61.077].

ALIMONY/MAINTENANCE/SPOUSAL SUPPORT: The court may grant rehabilitative or permanent alimony to either spouse in either lump-sum or periodic payments or both. Adultery is a factor in the award. Other factors which are considered are: (1) the time necessary to acquire sufficient education and training to enable the spouse to find appropriate employment and that spouse's future earning capacity; (2) the standard of living established during the marriage; (3) the duration of the marriage; (4) the comparative financial resources of the spouses, including their comparative earning abilities in the labor market; (5) the contribution of each spouse to the marriage, including services rendered in homemaking, childcare, education, and career-building of the other spouse; (6) the age of the spouses; (7) the physical and emotional conditions of the spouses; (8) each spouse's share of marital assets and liabilities; and (9) any other factor the court deems just and equitable.

Alimony payments made be ordered to be paid through a state depository. [Florida Statutes Annotated; Chapter 61.08].

SPOUSE'S NAME: There is a general statutory provision that allows for a person to change his or her name by petition filed with the court. [Florida Statutes Annotated; Chapter 68.07].

CHILD CUSTODY: Joint or sole custody may be granted. Joint custody is referred to as "shared parental responsibility" and is preferred over sole custody. Both parents are given equal consideration in any award of custody. Custody is granted according to the best interests of the child, based on the following factors: (1) which parent is more likely to allow the child frequent and continuing contact with the non-residential parent; (2) the love, affection, and other emotional ties between the parents and the child; (3) the ability and desire of the parents to provide the child with food, clothing, medical or remedial care, and other material needs; (4) the length of time the child has lived in a stable, satisfactory environment and the desirability of maintaining continuity; (5) the permanence, as a family unit, of the existing or proposed custodial home; (6) the mental, physical, and moral fitness of the parents; (7) the home, school, and community record of the child; (8) the preference of the child if old enough to understand and express a preference; (9) the willingness of each parent to encourage a close and continuing parent-child relationship with the other parent; (10) any evidence that a parent has supplied false information to a court regarding domestic violence; (11) any evidence of spouse or child abuse; and (12) any other relevant factors. No preference is to be given because of parent's sex. Grandparents may be awarded visitation. Custody and visitation may not be denied based on the fact that a parent or grandparent may be infected with human immunodeficiency virus. [Florida Statutes Annotated; Chapter 61.13].

CHILD SUPPORT: The court may order either parent to pay child support, based on the nature and circumstances of the case. There are specific child support guidelines set out in Florida Statutes Annotated; Chapter 61.30. In addition, there are specific factors for consideration upon which the child support guidelines may be adjusted: (1) extraordinary medical, psychological, educational, or dental expenses; (2) independent income of the child; (3) the custodial parent receiving both child support and spousal support; (4) seasonal variations in a parent's income or expenses; (5) the age of the child, taking into consideration the greater needs of older children; (6) any special needs of the family; (7) the terms of any shared parental arrangement; (8) the total assets of the parents and the child; (9) the impact of any IRS Dependency Exemption; (10) any other reason that should be considered in order to make the child support payments equitable; and (11) when the child support guidelines require a person to pay 55% or more of a personal income. Health insurance for the child and life insurance covering the life of the parent ordered to pay support may be required by the court. Child support payments may be ordered to be paid through a state depository. [Florida Statutes Annotated; Chapters 61.13 and 61.30].

GEORGIA

STATE WEBSITE: http://www.legis.state.ga.us/cgi-bin/gl_codes_detail.pl?code=1-1-1

DOWNLOAD STATE FORMS: http://www.georgiacourts.org/

FORMS PROVIDED ON CD: Domestic Relations Case Filing Information Form

FORMS AVAILABLE ONLINE: Domestic Relations Case Filing Information Form

RESIDENCY REQUIREMENTS AND WHERE TO FILE: The spouse filing must have been a resident of Georgia for 6 months and file for divorce in the county of residence. However, a non-resident may file for divorce against a spouse who has been a resident of Georgia for 6 months. In such cases, the divorce must be filed for in the county in which the respondent resides. [Code of Georgia Annotated; 19-5-2 and 19-5-5].

LEGAL GROUNDS FOR DIVORCE: No-Fault: Irretrievable breakdown of the marriage. [Code of Georgia Annotated; 19-5-3].

General: (1) Impotence; (2) adultery; (3) conviction of and imprisonment of over 2 years for an offense involving moral turpitude; (4) alcoholism and/or drug addiction; (5) confinement for incurable insanity; (6) separation caused by mental illness; (7) willful desertion; (8) cruel and inhuman treatment which endangers the life of the spouse; (9) habitual intemperance (drunkenness); (10) consent to marriage was obtained by fraud, duress, or force; (11) spouse lacked mental capacity to consent (including temporary incapacity resulting from drug or alcohol use); (12) the wife was pregnant by another at the time of the marriage unknown to the husband; and (13) incest. [Code of Georgia Annotated; 19-5-3].

NAME OF COURT IN WHICH TO FILE FOR DIVORCE: Superior Court. "In the Superior Court of _____ County, Georgia." [Georgia Civil Practice Act and Code of Georgia Annotated; 19-5-1].

TITLE OF DIVORCE ACTION: Petition for Divorce.

NAME USED TO DESCRIBE SPOUSE FILING FOR DIVORCE: Petitioner.

NAME USED TO DESCRIBE OTHER SPOUSE IN DIVORCE: Respondent.

TITLE OF FINAL DIVORCE PAPERS: Final Judgment and Decree of Divorce. [Official form for final judgement and decree are in 19-5-12].

LEGAL SEPARATION: There are legal provisions in Georgia for an action for separate maintenance for spouses who are living separately, but not divorcing. The factors and conditions are the same as those listed below under *Alimony/Maintenance/Spousal Support*. [Code of Georgia Annotated; 19-6-10].

SIMPLIFIED OR SPECIAL DIVORCE PROCEDURES: There are no legal provisions in Georgia for simplified divorce.

MEDIATION OR COUNSELING REQUIREMENTS: The court may refer any contested divorce to alternative dispute resolution. [Code of Georgia Annotated; 19-5-1].

PROPERTY DISTRIBUTION: Georgia is an "equitable distribution" state. The courts will distribute the marital property including any gifts and inheritances, equitably. There are no factors to be considered specified in the statute. [Code of Georgia Annotated; 19-5-13 and Georgia Case Law].

ALIMONY/MAINTENANCE/SPOUSAL SUPPORT: Permanent or temporary alimony may be awarded to either spouse, unless the separation was caused by that spouse's desertion or adultery. The following factors are to be considered: (1) the contribution of each spouse to the acquisition of the marital property, including the contribution of each spouse as homemaker, in childcare, education, and career-building of the other spouse; (2) the duration of the marriage; (3) the financial resources of each spouse; (4) the age and physical and emotional condition of both spouses; (5) the value of each spouse's separate property; (6) the earning capacity of each spouse; (7) any fixed liabilities of either spouse; (8) the standard of living established during the marriage; and (9) the time necessary for a spouse to acquire sufficient education to enable the spouse to find appropriate employment. [Code of Georgia Annotated; 19-6-1+].

SPOUSE'S NAME: If requested, a spouse's name may be restored. [Code of Georgia Annotated; 19-5-12 and 19-5-16].

CHILD CUSTODY: Joint or sole custody is granted, based upon the best interests of the child and a consideration of the following factors: (1) the suitability of each parent as custodian; (2) the psychological, emotional, and developmental needs of the child; (3) the ability of the parents to communicate with each other; (4) the prior and continuing care that the parents have given the child; (5) parental support for the other parent's relationship with the child; (6) the wishes of the child (considering the child's age and maturity); (7) the safety of the child; (8) the geographic proximity of the parents; (9) any custodial agreements of the parents; and (10) any history of domestic abuse. There is a presumption against awarding joint custody in Georgia when there is a history of domestic abuse. [Code of Georgia Annotated; 19-9-1 to 19-9-51].

CHILD SUPPORT: Both parents are liable for the support of minor children. The court may award child support from either parent, based on their customary needs and the parents' ability to pay. There are no specific factors for consideration set out in the statute. However, there are official child support guidelines set out in the statute that are to be followed in all cases in which the parents are not able to reach an agreement. In such cases there are factors which will be followed in special circumstances. The special circumstances include: (1) the age of the children; (2) a child's medical costs or extraordinary needs; (3) educational costs; (4) daycare costs; (5) shared physical custody arrangements; (6) a parent's support obligations to another household; (7) hidden income of a parent; (8) the income of the parent with custody; (9) contributions of the parents; (10) extreme economic circumstances; (11) a parent's own extraordinary needs; (12) historic spending levels of the family; (13) the cost of health and accident insurance coverage for the child; and (14) any extraordinary visitation travel expenses. [Code of Georgia Annotated; 19-5-12, 19-6-14, and 19-6-15.].

HAWAII

STATE WEBSITE: http://www.law.cornell.edu/states/hawaii.html

DOWNLOAD STATE FORMS: http://www.courts.state.hi.us/index.jsp

FORMS PROVIDED ON CD: Forms are different for each circuit. For Kaua'i, Fifth Circuit: Complaint for Divorce with Children, Complaint for Divorce without Children, Income and Expense Statement with Children, Income and Expense Statement without Children, Asset and Debt Statement. For Maui, Second Circuit: Complaint for Divorce with Children, Complaint for Divorce without Children, Financial Statement. For O'ahu, First Circuit: Complaint for Divorce with Children, Complaint for Divorce without Children, Income and Expense Statement, Asset and Debt Statement.

FORMS AVAILABLE ONLINE: Forms are different for each circuit. For Kaua'i, Fifth Circuit: Complaint for Divorce with Children, Complaint for Divorce without Children, Income and Expense Statement with Children, Income and Expense Statement without Children, Asset and Debt Statement. For Maui, Second Circuit: Complaint for Divorce with Children, Complaint for Divorce without Children, Financial Statement, Order/Notice to Withhold Income for Child Support. For O'ahu, First Circuit: Complaint for Divorce with Children, Complaint for Divorce without Children, Income and Expense Statement, Asset and Debt Statement, Parenting Plan, Order/Notice to Withhold Income for Child Support. Forms for Hawaii, Third Circuit, may be picked up at Circuit Court, Hilo or Circuit Court, Kona.

RESIDENCY REQUIREMENTS AND WHERE TO FILE: The spouse filing for divorce must have been present in Hawaii for 3 months. However, a final divorce will not be granted unless 1 spouse has been a resident for 6 months. The divorce should be filed in either: (1) the judicial district where the plaintiff resides or (2) the judicial district where the spouses last lived together. [Hawaii Revised Statutes; Section 580-1].

LEGAL GROUNDS FOR DIVORCE: No-Fault: (1) Irretrievable breakdown of the marriage and (2) living separate and apart without cohabitation for 2 years and it would not be harsh or oppressive to the defendant spouse to grant the divorce. [Hawaii Revised Statutes; 580-41].
General: Legal separation and there has been no reconciliation. [Hawaii Revised Statutes; 580-41].

NAME OF COURT IN WHICH TO FILE FOR DIVORCE: Family Court. [Hawaii Revised Statutes, 580-1].

TITLE OF DIVORCE ACTION: Complaint for Divorce.

NAME USED TO DESCRIBE SPOUSE FILING FOR DIVORCE: Plaintiff.

NAME USED TO DESCRIBE OTHER SPOUSE IN DIVORCE: Defendant.

TITLE OF FINAL DIVORCE PAPERS: Decree of Divorce.

LEGAL SEPARATION: The spouse filing for separation must have been a resident for 3 months. Temporary legal separation may be granted for up to 2 years on the grounds that the marriage is temporarily disrupted. [Hawaii Revised Statutes; 580-1 and 580-71].

SIMPLIFIED OR SPECIAL DIVORCE PROCEDURES: The "irretrievable breakdown of the marriage" may be shown by both spouses stating so in an affidavit or by 1 spouse stating so in an affidavit and the other spouse not denying it. The court, in such cases, may waive a hearing in uncontested divorces and grant the divorce based on the affidavit. [Hawaii Revised Statutes; 580-42]. Forms for Maui, Second Circuit are available as easy forms if; (1) you believe your spouse will not contest the divorce; and (2) no one is requesting alimony.

MEDIATION OR COUNSELING REQUIREMENTS: If 1 of the spouses denies that there has been an irretrievable breakdown of the marriage, the court may delay the proceedings for 60 days and advise the spouses to seek counseling. [Hawaii Revised Statutes; 580-42].

PROPERTY DISTRIBUTION: Hawaii is an "equitable distribution" state. The court will distribute all of the spouse's property, including the community, joint, and separate property, in a just and equitable manner, based on the following factors: (1) the burdens imposed upon either spouse for the benefit of the children; (2) the position each spouse will be left in after the divorce; (3) the relative abilities of the spouses; (4) the respective merits of the spouses; and (5) all other circumstances. [Hawaii Revised Statutes; 580-47].

ALIMONY/MAINTENANCE/SPOUSAL SUPPORT: The court may award either spouse maintenance, for either an indefinite period or a specific period to allow the receiving spouse to become self-supporting. Marital misconduct is not a factor to be considered. The factors to be considered are: (1) the standard of living established during the marriage; (2) the duration of the marriage; (3) the ability of the spouse from whom support is sought to meet his or her needs while meeting those of the spouse seeking support; (4) the ability of the spouse seeking maintenance to meet his or her needs independently; (5) the comparative financial resources of the spouses; (6) the needs of each spouse; (7) the age of the spouses; (8) the physical and emotional conditions of the spouses; (9) the usual occupation of the spouses during the marriage; (10) the vocational skills and employability of the spouse seeking support and maintenance; (11) the probable duration of the need of the spouse seeking support and maintenance; (12) any custodial and child support responsibilities; (13) the ability of the spouse from whom support is sought to meet his or her own needs while meeting the needs of the party seeking support; (14) other factors which measure the financial condition in which the spouses will be left as a result of the divorce; and (15) any other factor which measures the financial condition in which the spouses will be left in as a result of any award of maintenance. [Hawaii Revised Statutes; 580-47].

SPOUSE'S NAME: If requested, the wife may resume the use of her maiden name. [Hawaii Revised Statutes; 574-5(a)2(B)].

CHILD CUSTODY: Joint or sole child custody may be awarded to either or both of the parents or another person based on the best interests of the child and upon the wishes of the child, if the child is of sufficient age and capacity to form an intelligent choice. The parent who has had custody of the child in a wholesome home and is considered a fit and proper parent, is presumed to be preferred in custody. Joint custody will be allowed if it can be arranged to assure the child of continuing contact with both parents. The court may order a child custody investigation and report. Grandparents may be awarded visitation. Family violence committed by a parent raises the presumption that it is not in the best interests of the child for that parent to have any custody. There are no other specific factors for consideration set out in the statute. [Hawaii Revised Statutes; Title 571, Chapter 46].

CHILD SUPPORT: The court may order either or both parents to provide child support in a just and equitable manner. Factors to be considered are: (1) all earnings, income, and resources of the parents; (2) the earning potential, reasonable necessities, and borrowing capacity of the parents; (3) the needs of the child; (4) the full amount of public aid the child would receive without any child support; (5) any other dependents of the parents; (6) incentives for both parents to work; (7) an attempt to balance the standard of living of the parents and avoid placing any parent below poverty level; (8) to avoid any extreme changes in either parent's income; and (9) if a parent with school-age children is able to work and does not, 30 hours of minimum wage income will be added to that parent's presumed income. There are official Child Support Guidelines set out in the statute. [Hawaii Revised Statutes; Title 576D, Chapter 7 and Title 580, Chapter 47].

IDAHO

STATE WEBSITE: http://www2.state.id.us/legislat/legislat.html

DOWNLOAD STATE FORMS: http://www.courtselfhelp.idaho.gov/

FORMS PROVIDED ON CD: Divorce Complaint with Minor Children, Divorce Complaint with no Minor Children, Family Law Case Information Cover Sheet

FORMS AVAILABLE ONLINE: Divorce Complaint with Minor Children, Divorce Complaint with no Minor Children, Family Law Case Information Cover Sheet, Parenting Plan

RESIDENCY REQUIREMENTS AND WHERE TO FILE: The spouse filing for divorce must have been a resident of Idaho for 6 full weeks immediately prior to filing for divorce. The divorce should be filed in: (1) the county where the defendant resides or (2) if the defendant is not a resident of Idaho, the county where the plaintiff resides or designates in the complaint. [Idaho Statues; Title 5, Chapter 404 and Title 32, Chapter 701].

LEGAL GROUNDS FOR DIVORCE: No-Fault: (1) Irreconcilable differences and (2) living separate and apart without cohabitation for a period of 5 years. [Idaho Statues; Title 32, Chapters 603 and 610]. General: (1) Adultery; (2) permanent insanity; (3) conviction of a felony; (4) willful desertion; (5) extreme cruelty; (6) willful neglect; and (7) habitual intemperance (drunkenness). [Idaho Statues; Title 32, Chapters 603 to 610].

NAME OF COURT IN WHICH TO FILE FOR DIVORCE: District Court. " In the District Court of the _____ Judicial District for the State of Idaho, in and for the County of _____."

TITLE OF DIVORCE ACTION: Complaint for Divorce.

NAME USED TO DESCRIBE SPOUSE FILING FOR DIVORCE: Plaintiff.

NAME USED TO DESCRIBE OTHER SPOUSE IN DIVORCE: Defendant.

TITLE OF FINAL DIVORCE PAPERS: Decree of Divorce.

LEGAL SEPARATION: There is no legal provision in Idaho for legal court-ordered separation. However, the spouses may live separate and apart. [Idaho Statues; Title 32, Chapter 610].

SIMPLIFIED OR SPECIAL DIVORCE PROCEDURES: Divorces may be granted upon the default of the defendant. In addition, marital settlement agreements are specifically authorized. They must be in writing and notarized in the same manner as deeds. If the marital settlement agreement has any provisions which concern real estate, it must be recorded in the county recorder's office. [Idaho Statues; Title 32, Chapters 917 and 918].

MEDIATION OR COUNSELING REQUIREMENTS: There is a mandatory 20-day delay in the granting of all divorces, unless there is an agreement by the spouses. During this period, either spouse may request that there be a meeting held to determine if there is any practical chance for reconciliation. If there is determined to be a chance for reconciliation and there are minor children of the marriage, the court may delay the proceedings for up to 90 days for an attempt at reconciliation. [Idaho Statues; Title 32, Chapter 716].

PROPERTY DISTRIBUTION: Idaho is a "community property" state. Each spouse's separate property consists of: (1) all property acquired prior to the marriage, (2) property acquired by gift either before or during the marriage; and (3) property acquired by individual gift before or during the marriage. The court will divide all other property (the community property) of the spouses in a substantially equal manner, unless there are compelling reasons to provide otherwise. The court will consider the following factors: (1) any marital misconduct; (2) the length of the marriage; (3) the age and health of the spouses; (4) the occupation of the spouses; (5) the amount and sources of income of the spouses; (6) the vocational skills of the spouses; (7) the employability of the spouses; (8) any premarital agreement; (9) the present and potential earning capability of each spouse; (10) any retirement benefits, including social security, civil service, military and railroad retirement benefits; (11) the liabilities of the spouses; (12) the needs of the spouses; and (13) whether the property award is instead of or in addition to maintenance. [Idaho Statues; Title 32, Chapters 712 and 903 to 919].

ALIMONY/MAINTENANCE/SPOUSAL SUPPORT: The court may award maintenance to a spouse, if that spouse: (1) lacks sufficient property to provide for his or her reasonable needs and (2) is unable to support himself or herself through employment. The award of maintenance is based on the following factors: (1) the time necessary to acquire sufficient education and training to enable the spouse to find appropriate employment; (2) the duration of the marriage; (3) the ability of the spouse from whom support is sought to meet his or her needs while meeting those of the spouse seeking support; (4) the financial resources of the spouse seeking maintenance, including marital property apportioned to such spouse and such spouse's ability to meet his or her needs independently; (5) the tax consequences to each spouse; (6) the age of the spouses; (7) the physical and emotional conditions of the spouses; and (8) the fault of either party. [Idaho Statues; Title 32, Chapter 705].

SPOUSE'S NAME: There is no legal provision in Idaho for restoration of a spouse's name upon divorce. However, there is a general statutory provision that allows a person to apply for a name change by petition to the court. [Idaho Statues; Title 7, Chapter 801-4].

CHILD CUSTODY: Joint or sole child custody may be awarded according to the best interests of the child, and based on the following factors: (1) the preference of the child; (2) the wishes of the parents; (3) the character and circumstances of all individuals involved; (4) the relationship of the child with parents, siblings, and other significant family members; (5) the child's adjustment to his or her home, school, and community; (6) a need to promote continuity and stability in the life of the child; and (7) domestic violence, whether or not in the presence of the child. Joint custody is allowed if it can be arranged to assure the child with frequent and continuing contact with both parents. Unless shown otherwise, it is presumed that joint custody is in the best interests of the child. [Idaho Statues; Title 32, Chapters 717 and 717B and Title 39, Chapter 6303].

CHILD SUPPORT: The court may order either or both parents to provide child support until the child is 18, without regard to marital misconduct, and based upon the following factors: (1) the financial resources of the child; (2) the standard of living the child would have enjoyed if the marriage had not been dissolved; (3) the physical and emotional conditions and educational needs of the child; (4) the financial resources, needs, and obligations of both the noncustodial and the custodial parent [normally, not including the parent's community property share of the financial resources or obligations with a new spouse]; (5) the availability of reasonable medical insurance coverage for the child; and (6) the actual tax benefits achieved by the parent claiming the federal dependency exemption for income tax purposes. There are provisions in Idaho for child support payments to be paid to the clerk of the court unless otherwise ordered by the court. There are specific child support guidelines adopted by the Idaho Supreme Court which are presumed to be correct unless evidence is presented that shows that the award would be inappropriate or unjust. Finally, all child support orders issued in Idaho must contain provisions allowing enforcement of the order by income withholding. [Idaho Statues; Title 32, Chapters 706, and 1201+].

The No-Fault Divorce Toolkit

ILLINOIS

STATE WEBSITE: http://www.ilga.gov/

DOWNLOAD STATE FORMS: http://www.law.siu.edu/selfhelp/info/divorce/packets.htm

FORMS PROVIDED ON CD: Petition for Dissolution of Marriage with Minor Children, Petition for Dissolution of Marriage with Minor Children - Joint Parenting Order, Divorce Order without Children, Joint Petition for Simplified Dissolution of Marriage

FORMS AVAILABLE ONLINE: Petition for Dissolution of Marriage with Minor Children, Petition for Dissolution of Marriage with Minor Children - Joint Parenting Order, Divorce Order without Children, Joint Petition for Simplified Dissolution of Marriage, Legal Separation, Uniform Order for Support, Joint Parenting Order

RESIDENCY REQUIREMENTS AND WHERE TO FILE: The spouse filing for dissolution must have been a resident of Illinois for 90 days immediately prior to filing for dissolution of marriage. The dissolution of marriage may be filed in a county where either spouse resides. [750 Illinois Compiled Statutes Annotated; Chapter 5, Sections 104 and 401].

LEGAL GROUNDS FOR DISSOLUTION OF MARRIAGE: No-Fault: Irreconcilable differences have caused the irretrievable breakdown of the marriage *and* reconciliation has failed or further attempts at reconciliation are impractical *and* the spouses have been living separate and apart without cohabitation for 2 years. (If both spouses consent, the time period becomes 6 months). [750 Illinois Compiled Statutes Annotated; Chapter 5, Section 401].

General: (1) Impotence; (2) adultery; (3) habitual drunkenness for 2 years and/or drug addiction; (4) conviction of a felony; (5) willful desertion for 1 year; (6) cruel and inhuman treatment; (7) attempted poisoning or otherwise endangering the life of the spouse; (8) infection of the other spouse with a communicable disease; and (9) bigamy. [750 Illinois Compiled Statutes Annotated; Chapter 5, Section 401].

NAME OF COURT IN WHICH TO FILE FOR DISSOLUTION OF MARRIAGE: Circuit Court. "In the Circuit Court of the _____ Judicial District, _____ County, Illinois." [Illinois Civil Practice Act].

TITLE OF DISSOLUTION OF MARRIAGE ACTION: Petition for Dissolution of Marriage. "In Re the Marriage of _____ and _____." [750 Illinois Compiled Statutes Annotated; Chapter 5, Section 105].

NAME USED TO DESCRIBE SPOUSE FILING FOR DISSOLUTION OF MARRIAGE: Petitioner.

NAME USED TO DESCRIBE OTHER SPOUSE IN DISSOLUTION OF MARRIAGE: Respondent.

TITLE OF FINAL DISSOLUTION OF MARRIAGE PAPERS: Judgment for Dissolution of Marriage.

LEGAL SEPARATION: The residency requirement specified in the statute is that an action for legal separation must be brought where the Respondent resides. Any person living separate and apart from his or her spouse, without fault, may obtain a legal separation with provisions for reasonable support and maintenance. [750 Illinois Compiled Statutes Annotated; Chapter 5, Section 402].

SIMPLIFIED OR SPECIAL DISSOLUTION OF MARRIAGE PROCEDURES: Marital settlement agreements are specifically allowed and encouraged [750 Illinois Compiled Statutes Annotated; Chapter 5, Section 502]. In addition, Illinois has an approved "Joint Simplified Dissolution" procedure and petition found in 750 Illinois Compiled Statutes Annotated; Chapter 5, Section 452. To use this simplified procedure: (1) the spouses must not have been married over 5 years; (2) the spouses must neither have had nor adopted any children; (3) the wife cannot now be pregnant by the husband; (4) neither spouse can own any real estate; (5) both spouses must certify that neither is dependent on the other for support [or must waive any type of alimony]; (6) the market value of all marital property must be less than $10,000.00; and (7) the combined gross annual income of both spouses must be less than $35,000.00. Forms are available at any Office of the Clerk of a Circuit Court. [750 Illinois Compiled Statutes Annotated; Chapter 5, Section 502 and 452].

MEDIATION OR COUNSELING REQUIREMENTS: At the request of either spouse, or on the court's own initiative, the court may order a conciliation conference if it is felt that there is a prospect of reconciliation. [750 Illinois Compiled Statutes Annotated; Chapter 5, Section 404].

PROPERTY DISTRIBUTION: Illinois is an "equitable distribution" state. Each spouse retains the non-marital (separate) property that he or she owned prior to the marriage and any property acquired by gift or inheritance during the marriage. The court will distribute all other marital property, without regard to fault, considering the following factors: (1) the contribution of each spouse to the acquisition or dissipation of the marital or non-marital property, including the contribution of each spouse as homemaker or to the family unit; (2) the value of each spouse's non-marital property; (3) the economic circumstances of each spouse at the time the division of property is to become effective, including the desirability of awarding the family home to the spouse having custody of the children; (4) the length of the marriage; (5) the age and health of the spouses; (6) the occupation of the spouses; (7) the amount and sources of income of the spouses; (8) the vocational skills of the spouses; (9) the employability of the spouses; (10) the estate, liabilities, and needs of each spouse and the opportunity of each for further acquisition of capital assets and income; (11) the federal income tax consequences of the court's division of the property; (12) any premarital agreement; (13) liabilities of the spouses (including obligations from a prior marriage); (14) whether the property award is instead of or in addition to maintenance; and (15) any custodial provisions for the children. [750 Illinois Compiled Statutes Annotated; Chapter 5, Section 503].

ALIMONY/MAINTENANCE/SPOUSAL SUPPORT: The court may award maintenance to either spouse for a period of time it considers just. Marital fault is not a factor. The factors to be considered are: (1) the time necessary to acquire sufficient education and training to enable the spouse to find appropriate employment; (2) the standard of living established during the marriage; (3) the duration of the marriage; (4) the age of the spouses; (5) the physical and emotional conditions of the spouses; (6) the income and property of each spouse; (7) whether the spouse seeking support is able to support himself or herself or is unable to seek employment because he or she is the custodian of a child; (8) any contributions or service by the spouse seeking support to the education, career, training, potential, or licensure of the other spouse; (9) any marital settlement agreement; and (10) any other just and equitable factor. [750 Illinois Compiled Statutes Annotated; Chapter 5, Section 504].

SPOUSE'S NAME: Upon the wife's request, her maiden or former name will be restored. [750 Illinois Compiled Statutes Annotated; Chapter 5, Section 413].

CHILD CUSTODY: Sole or joint custody may be awarded, based upon the best interests of the child and upon the following factors: (1) preference of the child; (2) the wishes of the parents; (3) the child's adjustment to his or her home, school, and community; (4) the mental and physical health of all individuals involved; (5) the relationship of the child with parents, siblings, and other significant family members; (6) any history of violence or threat of abuse by a parent, whether directed against the child or against another person; and (7) the willingness and ability of each parent to encourage a close and continuing relationship between the child and the other parent. Marital misconduct that does not directly affect the parent's relationship with the child is not to be considered. There is a presumption that the maximum involvement and cooperation of the parents is in the best interests of the child. However, this is not to be considered a presumption that joint custody is always in the best interests of the child.

For an award of joint custody, the court will also consider the following factors: (1) the ability of the parents to cooperate effectively and consistently; (2) the residential circumstances of each parent; and (3) any other relevant factor. The parents shall prepare a Joint Parenting Agreement (which may be part of a Marital Settlement Agreement) which will specify each parent's rights and responsibilities for: (1) personal care of the child and (2) major educational, health care, and religious training decisions. The Joint Parenting Agreement will also include provisions specifying mediation of problems and periodic review of the terms of the Agreement. Joint parenting does not necessarily mean equal parenting time. The physical residence for the child is to be determined by either: (1) an agreement between the parents or (2) a court order based on the factors listed above. [750 Illinois Compiled Statutes Annotated; Chapter 5, Sections 602, 602.1, 603, and 610].

CHILD SUPPORT: Either or both parents may be ordered to pay reasonable and necessary child support, without regard to marital fault or misconduct. However, the court may adjust property division if child has been a victim of abuse by a parent. If the official guidelines are not appropriate, the following factors are considered: (1) the financial resources and needs of the child; (2) the standard of living the child would have enjoyed if the marriage had not been dissolved; (3) the physical and emotional conditions and educational needs of the child; and (4) the financial resources, needs, and obligations of both the noncustodial and the custodial parent. The court may require support to include payment of a child's health insurance premium. Support payments may be ordered to be paid directly to the clerk of the court. There are official guidelines for the amount of support contained in the statute. Illinois Driver's licenses may be revoked if child support obligations are not met. [625 Illinois Compiled Statutes Annotated; Chapter 5, Sections 7-703 and 750 Illinois Compiled Statutes Annotated; Chapter 5, Sections 503,505, 505.2, and 507].

INDIANA

STATE WEBSITE: http://www.in.gov/legislative/ic/code/

DOWNLOAD STATE FORMS: http://www.in.gov/judiciary/selfservice/forms.html

FORMS PROVIDED ON CD: Petition for Dissolution of Marriage with Children, Petition for Dissolution of Marriage without Children

FORMS AVAILABLE ONLINE: Petition for Dissolution of Marriage with Children, Petition for Dissolution of Marriage without Children, Establishment or Modification of Child Support

RESIDENCY REQUIREMENTS AND WHERE TO FILE: One of the spouses must have been a resident of the state for 6 months and the county for 3 months in which the petition is filed for immediately prior to filing for dissolution of marriage. [Annotated Indiana Code; Title 31, Article 15, Chapter 2-6].

LEGAL GROUNDS FOR DISSOLUTION OF MARRIAGE: No-Fault: Irretrievable breakdown of the marriage. [Annotated Indiana Code; Title 31, Article 15, Chapter 2-3].

General: (1) Impotence at the time of marriage; (2) conviction of a felony; and (3) incurable mental illness for 2 years. [Annotated Indiana Code; Title 31, Article 15, Chapter 2-3].

NAME OF COURT IN WHICH TO FILE FOR DISSOLUTION OF MARRIAGE: Superior Court, Circuit Court, or Domestic Relations Court. "_____ Court of _____ County, Indiana." [Annotated Indiana Code; Title 31, Article 12, Chapter 1-1+].

TITLE OF DISSOLUTION OF MARRIAGE ACTION: Petition for Dissolution of Marriage. "In Re the Marriage of _____ and _____." [Annotated Indiana Code; Title 31, Article 15, Chapter 2-4].

NAME USED TO DESCRIBE SPOUSE FILING FOR DISSOLUTION OF MARRIAGE: Petitioner.

NAME USED TO DESCRIBE OTHER SPOUSE IN DISSOLUTION OF MARRIAGE: Respondent.

TITLE OF FINAL DISSOLUTION OF MARRIAGE PAPERS: Final Dissolution of Marriage Decree.

LEGAL SEPARATION: One of the spouses must have been a resident of the state for 6 months and the county for 3 months immediately prior to filing for legal separation. A legal separation may be granted on the grounds that it is currently intolerable for the spouses to live together, but that the marriage should be maintained. [Annotated Indiana Code; Title 31, Article 15, Chapters 2-6, 3-2 and 3-3].

SIMPLIFIED OR SPECIAL DISSOLUTION OF MARRIAGE PROCEDURES: The court may enter a summary dissolution decree without holding a court hearing in all cases in which the following requirements have been met: (1) 60 days have elapsed since the filing of a petition for dissolution;

(2) the petition was verified and signed by both spouses; (3) the petition contained a written waiver of a final hearing; and (4) the petition contained either: (a) a statement that there are no contested issues or (b) that the spouses have made a written agreement in settlement of any contested issues. If there are some remaining contested issues, the court may hold a final hearing on those remaining contested issues. In addition, marital settlement agreements are specifically authorized in Indiana. [Annotated Indiana Code; Title 31, Article 15, Chapters 2-13 and 2-17].

MEDIATION OR COUNSELING REQUIREMENTS: Upon the request of either spouse or if the court believes that there is a reasonable possibility of reconciliation, the dissolution of marriage proceedings may be delayed for up to 60 days and the spouses may be ordered to seek counseling. [Annotated Indiana Code; Title 31, Article 15, Chapters 2-10 and 9.4-1].

PROPERTY DISTRIBUTION: Indiana is an "equitable distribution" state. The court will divide all of the spouses' property in a just manner, whether jointly or separately owned and whether acquired before or after the marriage, including any gifts or inheritances. There is a presumption that an equal division is just and reasonable. Marital fault is not a factor. The following factors are considered: (1) the contribution of each spouse to the acquisition of the marital property, regardless of whether the contribution was income-producing; (2) the economic circumstances of each spouse at the time the division of property is to become effective, including the desirability of awarding the family residence to the spouse having custody of the children; (3) the actual earnings and the present and potential earning capability of each spouse; (4) the extent to which the property was acquired by each spouse prior to marriage or through gift or inheritance; (5) the conduct of the spouses during the marriage as it relates to the disposition of their property; and (6) the tax consequences of any property division. If there is insufficient marital property, the court may award money to either spouse as reimbursement for the financial contribution by 1 spouse toward the higher education of the other. [Annotated Indiana Code; Title 31, Article 15, Chapter 7].

ALIMONY/MAINTENANCE/SPOUSAL SUPPORT: Maintenance will be awarded to a spouse who: (1) is physically or mentally incapacitated to the extent that he or she is unable to support himself or herself or (2) lacks sufficient property to provide support for himself or herself and any incapacitated child and must forgo employment to care for the physically or mentally incapacitated child. Marital fault is not a factor. In addition, rehabilitative maintenance may be granted to a spouse for up to 3 years, based on the following factors: (1) the time and expense necessary to acquire sufficient education and training to enable the spouse to find appropriate employment; (2) the educational level of each spouse at the time of the marriage and at the time the action is commenced; (3) whether an interruption in the education, training, or employment of a spouse who is seeking maintenance occurred during the marriage as a result of homemaking or childcare responsibilities, or both; and (4) the earning capacity of each spouse, including educational background, training, employment skills, work experience, and length of presence or absence from the job market. [Annotated Indiana Code; Title 31, Article 15, Chapter 7].

SPOUSE'S NAME: Upon request, the wife's former name may be restored. [Annotated Indiana Code; Title 31, Article 15, Chapter 2-18].

CHILD CUSTODY: Joint or sole custody is granted based on the best interests of the child, and based upon the following factors: (1) the age and sex of the child; (2) the preference of the child; (3) the wishes of the parents; (4) the child's adjustment to his or her home, school, and community; (5) the mental and physical health of all individuals involved; and (6) the relationship of the child with parents, siblings, and other significant family members.Joint custody may be awarded if it is in the best interest of the child and based upon the following factors: (1) the physical proximity of the parents to each other as this relates to the practical considerations of where the child will reside; (2) the fitness and suitability of the parents; (3) the nature of the physical and emotional environment in the home of each of the persons awarded joint custody; (4) the willingness and ability of the persons awarded joint custody to communicate and cooperate in advancing the child's welfare; (5) the wishes of the child; and (6) whether the child has established a close and beneficial relationship with both of the persons awarded joint custody. [Annotated Indiana Code; Title 31, Article 17, Chapters 2-8, 2-8.5, and 2-15].

CHILD SUPPORT: Either parent may be ordered to pay reasonable child support, without regard to marital fault, based on the following factors: (1) the standard of living the child would have enjoyed if the marriage had not been dissolved; (2) the physical and emotional conditions and educational needs of the child; and (3) the financial resources, needs, and obligations of both the noncustodial and the custodial parent. Support may be ordered to include medical, hospital, dental, and educational support. Support payments may be required to be paid through the clerk of the court. Specific Indiana Child Support Rules and Guidelines are contained in the Indiana Supreme Court Child Support Rules. [Annotated Indiana Code; Title 31, Article 15, Chapter 6].

IOWA

STATE WEBSITE: http://www.legis.state.ia.us/

DOWNLOAD STATE FORMS: http://www.judicial.state.ia.us/families/

FORMS PROVIDED ON CD: Petition for Dissolution with no Minor Children, Cover Sheet, Financial Affidavit for Dissolution with no Minor Children,

FORMS AVAILABLE ONLINE: Petition for Dissolution with no Minor Children, Cover Sheet, Financial Affidavit, Confidential Information Sheet

RESIDENCY REQUIREMENTS AND WHERE TO FILE: If the defendant spouse is a resident of Iowa and was personally served the dissolution of marriage papers, there is no residency requirement for the spouse filing the dissolution of marriage. Otherwise, there is a 1-year residency requirement. In addition, there is a 90-day waiting period prior to the dissolution of marriage becoming final. The dissolution of marriage may be filed in a county where either spouse resides. [Iowa Code Annotated; Title XV Chapter 598 Sections 598.2, 598.5, and 598.19].

LEGAL GROUNDS FOR DISSOLUTION OF MARRIAGE: No-Fault: Breakdown of the marriage relationship to the extent that the legitimate objects of matrimony have been destroyed and there remains no reasonable likelihood that the marriage can be preserved. [Iowa Code Annotated; Title XV Chapter 598 Sections 598.5 and 598.17].

General: The only grounds for dissolution of marriage in Iowa are that there has been a breakdown of the marriage relationship to the extent that the legitimate objects of matrimony have been destroyed and there remains no reasonable likelihood that the marriage can be preserved. [Iowa Code Annotated; Title XV Chapter 598 Sections 598.5 and 598.17].

NAME OF COURT IN WHICH TO FILE FOR DISSOLUTION OF MARRIAGE: District Court. "In the District Court for the County of _____, Iowa." [Iowa Code Annotated; Title XV Chapter 598 Section 598.4].

TITLE OF DISSOLUTION OF MARRIAGE ACTION: Petition for Dissolution of Marriage. "In Re the Marriage of _____ and _____."

NAME USED TO DESCRIBE SPOUSE FILING FOR DISSOLUTION OF MARRIAGE: Petitioner.

NAME USED TO DESCRIBE OTHER SPOUSE IN DISSOLUTION OF MARRIAGE: Respondent.

TITLE OF FINAL DISSOLUTION OF MARRIAGE PAPERS: Decree of Dissolution of Marriage.

LEGAL SEPARATION: If the defendant spouse is a resident of Iowa and was personally served legal papers, there is no residency requirement for the spouse filing the legal separation. Otherwise, there is a 1-year residency requirement. The grounds for legal separation in Iowa are that there has been a breakdown of the marriage relationship to the extent that the legitimate objects of matrimony have been destroyed and there remains no reasonable likelihood that the marriage can be preserved. [Iowa Code Annotated; Title XV Chapter 598 Sections 598.5, 598.17, and 598.28].

SIMPLIFIED OR SPECIAL DISSOLUTION OF MARRIAGE PROCEDURES: There are no legal provisions in Iowa for simplified dissolution of marriage. However, sample petition captions and contents are contained in Iowa Code Annotated; Sections 598.4 and 598.5. In addition, both spouses are required to file Financial Affidavits on official forms which are available from the clerk of every district court. [Iowa Code Annotated; Title XV Chapter 598 Sections 598.4, 598.5, and 598.13].

MEDIATION OR COUNSELING REQUIREMENTS: If either spouse requests, or on the court's own initiative, the spouses may be ordered to participate in conciliation procedures for a period of 60 days. A course on children's needs is required for all parents when custody is at issue within 45 days of the commencement of the case. [Iowa Code Annotated; Title XV Chapter 598 Sections 598.16].

PROPERTY DISTRIBUTION: Iowa is an "equitable distribution" state. The court will divide all of the spouse's property whether it was acquired before or after the marriage, except any gifts and inheritances received prior to or during the marriage. A portion of the property may be set aside in a fund for the support, maintenance, and education of any minor children. Marital fault is not a factor. The following factors are considered in any division of property: (1) the contribution of each spouse to the acquisition of the marital property, including the contribution of each spouse as homemaker or in childcare; (2) the value of any property brought to the marriage; (3) the contribution by 1 party to the education, training, or increased earning capacity of the other; (4) the length of the marriage; (5) the age and physical and emotional health of the spouses; (6) the vocational skills of the spouses; (7) the time and expense necessary to acquire skills and training to become self-sufficient; (8) the federal income tax consequences of the court's division of the property; (9) any premarital or marital settlement agreement; (10) the present and potential earning capability of each spouse, including educational background, training, employment skills, work experience, and length of absence from the job market; (11) whether the property award is instead of or in addition to alimony and the amount and duration of any such alimony award; (12) the total economic circumstances of the spouses, including any pension benefits; (13) the desirability of awarding the family home to the spouse with custody of any children; (14) any custodial provisions for the children; and (15) the amount and duration of any maintenance payments; and (16) any other relevant factors. [Iowa Code Annotated; Title XV Chapter 598 Section 598.21].

ALIMONY/MAINTENANCE/SPOUSAL SUPPORT: Maintenance may be granted to either spouse for a limited or indefinite time, based on the following factors: (1) the time necessary to acquire sufficient education and training to enable the spouse to find appropriate employment and become self-supporting; (2) the duration of the marriage; (3) the financial resources of the spouse seeking alimony, including marital property apportioned to such spouse and such spouse's ability to meet his or her needs independently; (4) the tax consequences to each spouse; (5) the age of the spouses; (6) the physical and emotional conditions of the spouses; (7) the work experience and length of absence from the job market of the spouse seeking alimony; (8) the vocational skills and employability of the spouse seeking support and alimony; (9) the probable duration of the need of the spouse seeking support and alimony; (10) custodial and child support responsibilities; (11) the educational level of each spouse at the time of the marriage and at the time the action for support is commenced; (12) any premarital or other agreements; (13) the earning capacity of the spouse seeking maintenance, including the educational background, employment skills, and work experience; and (14) feasibility of spouse becoming self-supporting at the same level of the marriage; and (15) any other factor the court deems just and equitable. Marital misconduct is not a factor. Maintenance payments may be ordered to be paid through the court. [Iowa Code Annotated; Title XV Chapter 598 Sections 598.21, 598.22, and 598.32].

SPOUSE'S NAME: Upon dissolution of marriage, either spouse may request to change his or her name to a former or maiden name. [Iowa Code Annotated; Title XV Chapter 598 Section 598.37].

CHILD CUSTODY: Joint or sole custody may be awarded in the best interests of the child and in a manner which will encourage the parents to share the rights and responsibilities of raising the child. Joint custody may be awarded if either parent requests and if it is in the best interests of the child and based on the following factors: (1) the ability of the parents to cooperate; (2) the ability to support the child's relationship with the other parent; (3) the physical proximity of the parents to each other; (4) the fitness and suitability of the parents; (5) the reasonable preference of the child, if the court deems the child to be of sufficient intelligence, understanding, and experience to express a preference; (6) whether both parents have actively cared for the child before and since the separation; (7) whether the psychological and emotional needs and development of the child will suffer because of lack of contact with both parents; (8) whether the safety of the child will be jeopardized by an award of joint custody or unsupervised visitation; (9) whether 1 or both parents agree to, or are opposed to, joint custody; and (10) any history of domestic abuse. However, the court may grant joint custody even when both parents do not agree to joint custody. [Iowa Code Annotated; Title XV Chapter 598 Section 598.41].

CHILD SUPPORT: Either or both parents may be ordered to pay a reasonable and necessary amount of child support. Child support payments may be ordered to be paid directly to the court. Specific Child Support Guideline Charts are available at www.judicial.state.ia.us/. The court shall order a parent to provide a health benefit plan if available at a reasonable cost. The amount of child support determined by use of the Guideline Charts is presumed to be correct, but may be adjusted for fairness or special needs of the child. [Iowa Code Annotated; Title XV Chapter 598 Section 598.21].

KANSAS

STATE WEBSITE: http://www.kslegislature.org/cgi-bin/index.cgi

DOWNLOAD STATE FORMS: http://www.kscourts.org/ctruls/csintro.htm

FORMS PROVIDED ON CD: Petition for Divorce, Financial Affidavit, Civil Information Cover Sheet

FORMS AVAILABLE ONLINE: Petition for Divorce, Financial Affidavit, Civil Information Cover Sheet, Parenting Plan, Order for Mediation,

RESIDENCY REQUIREMENTS AND WHERE TO FILE: Either spouse must have been a resident of Kansas for 60 days immediately before filing for divorce. The divorce may be filed for in a county where either spouse resides. [Kansas Statutes Annotated; Chapter 60, Article 16, Subjects 1601 and 1603].

LEGAL GROUNDS FOR DIVORCE: No-Fault: Incompatibility. [Kansas Statutes Annotated; Chapter 60, Article 16, Subject 1601].

General: (1) Failure to perform a marital duty or obligation and (2) incompatibility due to mental illness. [Kansas Statutes Annotated; Chapter 60, Article 16, Subject 1601].

NAME OF COURT IN WHICH TO FILE FOR DIVORCE: District Court. "In the District Court in and for the County of _____, Kansas." [Kansas Statutes Annotated; Chapter 60, Article 16, Subject 1601].

TITLE OF DIVORCE ACTION: Petition for Divorce. "In the Matter of the Marriage of _____ ___ and _____." [Kansas Statutes Annotated; Chapter 60, Article 16, Subject 1604].

NAME USED TO DESCRIBE SPOUSE FILING FOR DIVORCE: Petitioner.

NAME USED TO DESCRIBE OTHER SPOUSE IN DIVORCE: Respondent.

TITLE OF FINAL DIVORCE PAPERS: Decree of Divorce.

LEGAL SEPARATION: Either spouse must have been a resident of Kansas for 60 days immediately before filing for legal separation. The grounds for legal separation are: (1) incompatibility; (2) failure to perform a marital duty or obligation; and (3) incompatibility due to mental illness. [Kansas Statutes Annotated; Chapter 60, Article 16, Subjects 1601 and 1603].

SIMPLIFIED OR SPECIAL DIVORCE PROCEDURES: Only 1 spouse need testify as to the facts in the divorce. In addition, marital settlement agreements are specifically authorized. Also, child custody and child residency agreements are specifically authorized and are presumed to be in the best interests of the child. [Kansas Statutes Annotated; Chapter 60, Article 16, Subjects 1609 and 1610].

MEDIATION OR COUNSELING REQUIREMENTS: On either spouse's request, or on its own initiative, the court may require that the spouses seek marriage and/or family counseling if marriage counseling services are available in the judicial district where the divorce is sought. Unless in emergency situations, there is a mandatory 60-day delay from the time the petition is filed until a final Decree of Divorce may be granted. [Kansas Statutes Annotated; Chapter 60, Article 16, Subjects 1608 and 1617].

PROPERTY DISTRIBUTION: Kansas is an "equitable distribution" state. The court may divide all of the spouse's property, including: (1) any gifts and inheritances; (2) any property owned before the marriage; (3) any property acquired in a spouse's own right during the marriage; and (4) any property acquired by the spouse's joint efforts. Property distribution may include actual division of the property, an award of all or part of the property to 1 spouse with a just and reasonable payment to the other, or a sale of the property and a division of the proceeds. The court considers the following factors: (1) the value of each spouse's property; (2) the length of the marriage; (3) the age of the spouses; (4) whether the property award is instead of or in addition to maintenance; (5) how and by whom the property was acquired; (6) the present and future earning capacity of the spouses; (7) family ties and obligations; (8) any dissipation of assets by a spouse; (9) the tax consequences of property distribution; and (10) any other factor necessary to do equity and justice between the spouses. [Kansas Statutes Annotated; Chapter 60, Article 16, Subject 1610].

ALIMONY/MAINTENANCE/SPOUSAL SUPPORT: Either spouse may be awarded maintenance for a period of up to 121 months. After 121 months, the recipient may apply for an extension of 1 more 121-month period. The amount awarded is whatever is judged to be fair, just, and equitable. There are no specific statutory factors for consideration. Payments are to be made through the clerk of the court or through the court trustee. [Kansas Statutes Annotated; Chapter 60, Article 16, Subject 1610].

SPOUSE'S NAME: Upon a spouse's request, a wife's maiden name will be restored. [Kansas Statutes Annotated; Chapter 60, Article 16, Subject 1610].

CHILD CUSTODY: If the parents have entered into a written agreement regarding child custody, the court will approve it if it is in the best interests of the child. Where there is no agreement, the court may award joint or sole custody based on the best interests of the child and upon the following factors: (1) the length of time and circumstances under which the child may have been under the care of someone other than a parent; (2) preference of the child; (3) the wishes of the parents; (4) the child's adjustment to his or her home, school, and community; (5) the relationship of the child with parents, siblings, and other significant family members; (6) the willingness of each parent to respect and appreciate the bond between the child and the other parent and allow for a continuing relationship between the child and the other parent; and (7) any evidence of spousal abuse. There is to be no preference given based on the sex of the parent, regardless of the age of the child. Joint custody may be awarded if the court finds both parents suitable. The court may order that a joint custody plan be submitted to the court by the parents. [Kansas Statutes Annotated; Chapter 60, Article 16, Subject 1610].

CHILD SUPPORT: Either or both parents may be ordered to pay child support, without regard to any marital misconduct, based on the following factors: (1) the financial resources of the child; (2) the physical and emotional conditions and educational needs of the child; and (3) the financial resources, needs, and obligations of both the noncustodial and the custodial parent. Child support payments are to be paid through the clerk of the court or through the court trustee, unless the court orders otherwise. There are specific Supreme Court Child Support Guidelines contained in Kansas Statutes Annotated Chapter 20, Subject 165. [Kansas Statutes Annotated; Chapter 20, Article 1 Subject 165 and Chapter 60, Article 16, Subject 1610].

KENTUCKY

STATE WEBSITE: http://www.lrc.state.ky.us/index.htm

DOWNLOAD STATE FORMS: http://www.kycourts.net/forms/

FORMS PROVIDED ON CD: PETITION FOR DISSOLUTION OF MARRIAGE

FORMS AVAILABLE ONLINE: None

RESIDENCY REQUIREMENTS AND WHERE TO FILE: The spouse filing for dissolution of marriage must have been a resident (or a member of the armed services stationed in Kentucky) for 180 days prior to filing. The dissolution of marriage may be filed in a county where either spouse usually resides. [Kentucky Revised Statutes; Title XXXV, Chapters 403, Section .140 and Title XLII, Chapter 452, Section .470].

LEGAL GROUNDS FOR DISSOLUTION OF MARRIAGE: No-Fault: Irretrievable breakdown of the marriage. A final dissolution of marriage will not be granted until the spouses have lived apart for 60 days. ("Living apart" includes living in the same house but not sharing sex). [Kentucky Revised Statutes; Title XXXV, Chapter 403, Section .170]. General: Irretrievable breakdown of the marriage is the only grounds for dissolution of marriage in Kentucky. [Kentucky Revised Statutes; Title XXXV, Chapter 403, Section .140].

NAME OF COURT IN WHICH TO FILE FOR DISSOLUTION OF MARRIAGE: Circuit Court. "____ _____ Circuit Court, Kentucky." [Kentucky Rules of Civil Procedure].

TITLE OF DISSOLUTION OF MARRIAGE ACTION: Petition for Dissolution of Marriage. "In Re the Marriage of _____ and _____."

NAME USED TO DESCRIBE SPOUSE FILING FOR DISSOLUTION OF MARRIAGE: Petitioner.

NAME USED TO DESCRIBE OTHER SPOUSE IN DISSOLUTION OF MARRIAGE: Respondent.

TITLE OF FINAL DISSOLUTION OF MARRIAGE PAPERS: Decree of Dissolution of Marriage.

LEGAL SEPARATION: Irretrievable breakdown of the marriage is the only grounds for legal separation (or divorce from bed and board) in Kentucky. The spouse filing for legal separation must have been a resident (or a member of the armed services stationed in Kentucky) for 180 days prior to filing. [Kentucky Revised Statutes; Title XXXV, Chapter 403, Section .140].

SIMPLIFIED OR SPECIAL DISSOLUTION OF MARRIAGE PROCEDURES: Marital settlement agreements and separation agreements are specifically authorized. [Kentucky Revised Statutes; Title XXXV, Chapter 403, Section .180].

MEDIATION OR COUNSELING REQUIREMENTS: If 1 spouse disagrees that the marriage is irretrievably broken, the court may delay the dissoultion of marriage proceedings for 60 days and suggest the spouses seek counseling. In addition, at a spouse's request or on the court's own initiative, a conciliation conference may be ordered by the court. [Kentucky Revised Statutes; Title XXXV, Chapter 403, Section .170].

PROPERTY DISTRIBUTION: Kentucky is an "equitable distribution" state. The spouses are allowed to keep their separate property (property acquired before the marriage and any gifts or inheritances). All other property (their marital property) is divided, without regard to any marital misconduct, in just proportions, based on the following factors: (1) the contribution of each spouse to the acquisition of the marital property, including the contribution of each spouse as homemaker; (2) the value of each spouse's separate property; (3) the economic circumstances of each spouse at the time the division of property is to become effective, including the desirability of awarding the family home to the spouse awarded custody of any children; (4) the length of the marriage; and (5) any retirement benefits. [Kentucky Revised Statutes; Title XXXV, Chapter 403, Section .190].

ALIMONY/MAINTENANCE/SPOUSAL SUPPORT: Either spouse may be awarded maintenance if: (1) that spouse lacks the property to provide for his or her own needs and (2) that spouse is unable to find appropriate employment, or is unable to work because of obligations to care for children or others in his or her custody. Marital fault is not a factor to be considered. The award is then based on the following factors: (1) the time necessary to acquire sufficient education and training to enable the spouse to find appropriate employment, and that spouse's future earning capacity; (2) the standard of living established during the marriage; (3) the duration of the marriage; (4) the ability of the spouse from whom support is sought to meet his or her needs while meeting those of the spouse seeking support; (5) the financial resources of the spouse seeking maintenance, including marital property apportioned to such spouse and such spouse's ability to meet his or her needs independently and any share of a child support award intended for the custodian; and (6) the physical and emotional conditions of the spouses. [Kentucky Revised Statutes; Title XXXV, Chapter 403, Section .200].

SPOUSE'S NAME: If there are no children, and at the wife's request, the wife's maiden name may be restored. [Kentucky Revised Statutes; Title XXXV, Chapter 403, Section .230].

CHILD CUSTODY: The court may award sole or joint custody, giving equal consideration to either spouse. Custody is awarded based on the best interests of the child and on the following factors: (1) preference of the child; (2) the wishes of the parents; (3) the child's adjustment to his or her home, school, and community; (4) the mental and physical health of all individuals involved; (5) the relationship of the child with parents, siblings, and other significant family members; (6) any evidence of domestic violence; (7) whether the child has been cared for and/or supported by a non-parent primary caregiver; and (8) the intent of the parent[s] in placing the child with a non-parent primary giver [ie., to avoid domestic violence, or to allow the parent to seek work or attend school, etc]. Any conduct of a parent that does not affect the relationship with the child is not to be considered. Abandonment of the family home by a parent is not to be considered if the parent fled due to physical harm or threats of physical harm by the other spouse. [Kentucky Revised Statutes; Title XXXV, Chapter 403, Section .270].

CHILD SUPPORT: Either or both parents may be ordered to provide a reasonable amount of child support, without regard to any marital misconduct, and based on the official Child Support Guidelines which are contained in the statute. These guidelines are presumed to be correct, but may be adjusted based on the following considerations: (1) a child's extraordinary medical or dental needs; (2) a child's extraordinary educational, job training, or special needs; (3) either parent's extraordinary needs, such as medical expenses; (4) the independent financial resources of the child; (5) the combined parental income in excess of the Kentucky child support guidelines amounts; (6) an agreement between the parents on child support, provided that no public assistance is being provided; and (7) any other extraordinary circumstance. In addition, the court may order a parent to provide health care insurance coverage for the child. [Kentucky Revised Statutes; Title XXXV, Chapter 403, Section .210 to .212].

LOUISIANA

STATE WEBSITE: http://www.legis.state.la.us/

DOWNLOAD STATE FORMS: None

FORMS PROVIDED ON CD: PETITION FOR DIVORCE

FORMS AVAILABLE ONLINE: State-wide forms not available. Check county websites for forms. For example; http://www.familycourt.org/forms/Divorce%20form%202.pdf

RESIDENCY REQUIREMENTS AND WHERE TO FILE: The spouse filing for divorce must have been a resident of Louisiana for 12 months prior to filing for divorce. The divorce must be filed in the parish of the respondent/defendant, made in writing, signed by the party making it, and registered by the Recorder. [Louisiana Code of Civil Procedure; Article 42].

LEGAL GROUNDS FOR DIVORCE: No-Fault: That a spouse desires a divorce is a grounds for divorce in Louisiana. There are no requirements to show marital breakdown, fault, living separate and apart, or any other basis for a divorce. After the filing of the petition, the divorce will be granted after a period of 180 days has elapsed from the filing date and if the spouses have lived separate and apart since the filing of the divorce petition. Reconciliation is essentially the only defense to a divorce sought on these grounds. [Louisiana Civil Code Annotated; Title V, Article 102].
General: In the case of a covenant marriage: (1) That the spouses have been living separate and apart for a period of 2 years or more on the date of filing the petition; (2) that the other spouse has committed adultery; (3) that the other spouse has committed a felony and has been sentenced to death or imprisonment with hard labor; (4) physical or sexual abuse of a spouse or child; (5) abandonment for 1 year or more; and (6) living separate and apart for 1 year or more after a legal separation. [Louisiana Civil Code Annotated; Title V, Article 103 and Louisiana Revised Statutes; Section 9-308].

NAME OF COURT IN WHICH TO FILE FOR DIVORCE: District Court. "_____ Judicial District Court, Parish of _____, Louisiana." [Louisiana Code of Civil Procedure].

TITLE OF DIVORCE ACTION: Petition for Divorce.

NAME USED TO DESCRIBE SPOUSE FILING FOR DIVORCE: Petitioner/Plaintiff.

NAME USED TO DESCRIBE OTHER SPOUSE IN DIVORCE: Respondent/Defendant.

TITLE OF FINAL DIVORCE PAPERS: Final Judgment of Divorce.

LEGAL SEPARATION: The grounds for legal separation (separation from bed and board) in Louisiana are the same as those for divorce from a covenant marriage (with the addition of habitual drunkenness). However, a spouse may petition the court for spousal and/or child support and restitution of separate property during a marriage. This is intended to provide for those spouses who desire to live apart, but not divorce. [Louisiana Statutes Annotated; Article 9, Chapters 291 and 307].

SIMPLIFIED OR SPECIAL DIVORCE PROCEDURES: The new no-fault divorce grounds in Louisiana are very simplified. No answer need be made by a respondent to a Petition for Divorce filed in Louisiana. In order to obtain a final Judgment of Divorce, a motion entitled "Rule to Show Cause" must be filed with the court. However, each judicial district in Louisiana may have specific individual rules pertaining to divorce actions. Please refer to the Louisiana Rules of Court for the rules in a particular judicial district. [Louisiana Civil Code Annotated; Article 102, Louisiana Forms; Forms 370+, and Louisiana Code of Civil Procedure; Articles 3951 to 3956].

MEDIATION OR COUNSELING REQUIREMENTS: If child custody is an issue, the court may require that the parents submit to mediation. [Louisiana Civil Code Annotated; Article 131 and Louisiana Revised Statutes Annotated; Article 9, Section 351].

PROPERTY DISTRIBUTION: Louisiana is a "community property" state. A spouse's separate property, consisting of property acquired prior to the marriage and property acquired by gift or inheritance, is awarded to that spouse. The community property is divided equally between the spouses. Personal property necessary for the safety and well-being of the spouse filing for divorce and any children in his or her custody (including food, eating utensils, clothing, and any other items necessary for their safety and well-being) will be awarded to the spouse filing. Either spouse may ask the court for use and occupancy of the family residence pending the final division of the community property. The court bases the temporary award of the family residence on the following factors: (1) the value of each spouse's personal property; (2) the economic circumstances of each spouse at the time the division of property is to become effective; and (3) needs of the children. In addition, a spouse may be awarded a sum of money for his or her financial contributions made during a marriage to the education or training of a spouse that increased the other spouse's earning capacity. [Louisiana Civil Code Annotated; Article 121 and Louisiana Statutes Annotated; Article 9, Chapter 384].

ALIMONY/MAINTENANCE/SPOUSAL SUPPORT: During the divorce proceeding, either spouse may be ordered to pay temporary alimony. Permanent periodic alimony may be granted to the spouse who is without fault. Such alimony shall not exceed one-third of the other spouse's income. The factors considered are: (1) the effect of child custody on the spouse's earning capacity; (2) the time necessary to acquire sufficient education and training to enable the spouse to find appropriate employment; (3) the income, means, and assets of the spouses and the liquidity of the assets; (4) the comparative financial obligations of the spouses; (5) the age and health of the spouses; (6) the needs of the parties; (7) the earning capacity of the parties; (8) the duration of the marriage; (9) the tax consequences of the parties; and (10) any other relevant circumstances. Permanent alimony may be revoked upon remarriage or cohabitation. [Louisiana Civil Code Annotated; Articles 111 and 112].

SPOUSE'S NAME: There is no statutory provision in Louisiana for restoration of a spouse's name upon divorce. Case law notes the allowance of resumption of a wife's maiden name. In addition, a person may generally petition the court for change of name. [Louisiana Statutes Annotated; Article 13-4751 and Louisiana Case Law].

CHILD CUSTODY: Joint or sole custody is awarded based on the best interests of the child. The following order of preference is established: (1) to both parents; (2) to either parent [without regard to race or sex of the parents]; (3) to the person or persons with whom the child has been living; or (4) to any other person that the court feels suitable and able to provide an adequate and stable environment for the child. Unless shown otherwise or unless the parents agree otherwise, joint custody is presumed to be in the best interests of the child and will be awarded based on the following factors: (1) physical, emotional, mental, religious, and social needs of the child; (2) capability and desire of each parent to meet the child's needs; (3) preference of the child, if the child is of sufficient age and capacity; (4) the love and affection existing between the child and each parent; (5) the length of time the child has lived in a stable, satisfactory environment and the desirability of maintaining continuity; (6) the desire and ability of each parent to allow an open and loving frequent relationship between the child and the other parent; (7) the wishes of the parents; (8) the child's adjustment to his or her home, school, and community; (9) the mental and physical health of all individuals involved; (10) the permanence as a family unit of the existing or proposed custodial home; (11) the distance between the potential residences; (12) the moral fitness of the parents; and (13) any other relevant factor. The conduct of the proposed guardian is to be considered only as it bears on his or her relationship with the child. The parents must submit a plan for joint custody which designates: (1) the child's residence; (2) the rights of access and communication between the parents and child; and (3) child support amounts. A parent not granted custody is entitled to visitation rights unless that parent has subjected the child to physical or sexual abuse. The court may order the parents to attend a court-approved parenting seminar. [Louisiana Civil Code Annotated; Articles 131- 134, Louisiana Statutes Annotated; Article 9, Section 306, and Louisiana Case Law].

CHILD SUPPORT: Both parents are obligated to support any children of a marriage. The factors for consideration listed in the statute are: (1) the needs of the child and (2) the actual resources of each parent. In addition, Louisiana has adopted detailed Child Support Guideline provisions which are contained in the statute. These guidelines are presumed to be correct, unless 1 of the following factors make the guidelines unjust or not in the best interests of the child: (1) extraordinary medical expenses of the child or parent responsible for support payments; (2) the permanent or temporary total disability of the parent responsible for support; (3) the need for immediate or temporary support; (4) an extraordinary community debt of the parents; (5) that the combined income of the parents is less than that in the guideline charts; and (6) any other relevant consideration. [Louisiana Revised Statutes Annotated; Article 9, Sections 302+].

MAINE

STATE WEBSITE: http://janus.state.me.us/legis/

DOWNLOAD STATE FORMS: http://www.courts.state.me.us/rules_forms_fees/pub_forms.html#forms

FORMS PROVIDED ON CD: Complaint for Divorce with Children, Complaint for Divorce with no Children

FORMS AVAILABLE ONLINE: Complaint for Divorce with Children, Complaint for Divorce with no Children,

RESIDENCY REQUIREMENTS AND WHERE TO FILE: Either spouse must be a resident of Maine, or the marriage or the grounds for divorce must have occurred in Maine. Otherwise, a person filing for divorce must be a resident of Maine for 6 months immediately prior to filing. The divorce may be filed for in the District Court in the county where either spouse resides. However, the defendant spouse has the right to have the proceeding moved to Superior Court. [Maine Revised Statutes Annotated; Title 4, Chapter 5, Section 155 and Title 19-A, Chapter 29, Section 901].

LEGAL GROUNDS FOR DIVORCE: No-Fault: Irreconcilable marital differences. [Maine Revised Statutes Annotated; Title 19-A, Chapter 29, Section 902].

General: (1) Impotence; (2) adultery; (3) alcoholism and/or drug addiction; (4) confinement for incurable insanity for 7 consecutive years; (5) desertion for 3 years; (6) cruelty or abuse; and (7) nonsupport whereby a spouse is able to provide support but grossly, wantonly, or cruelly neglects to provide suitable maintenance for the complaining spouse. [Maine Revised Statutes Annotated; Title 19-A, Chapter 29, Section 902].

NAME OF COURT IN WHICH TO FILE FOR DIVORCE: District Court or Superior Court. "State of Maine, _____ Court, _____ County." [Maine Revised Statutes Annotated; Title 19-A, Chapter 29, Section 902].

TITLE OF DIVORCE ACTION: Complaint for Divorce.

NAME USED TO DESCRIBE SPOUSE FILING FOR DIVORCE: Plaintiff.

NAME USED TO DESCRIBE OTHER SPOUSE IN DIVORCE: Defendant.

TITLE OF FINAL DIVORCE PAPERS: Judgment of Divorce.

LEGAL SEPARATION: Legal separation will be granted if the spouses are or desire to be living apart with just cause for more than 60 days. If there are minor children, mediation between the spouses is required. [Maine Revised Statutes Annotated; Title 19-A, Chapter 27, Section 851].

SIMPLIFIED OR SPECIAL DIVORCE PROCEDURES: If the divorce is not contested, testimony of a corroborating witness is not necessary. [Maine Revised Statutes Annotated; Title 19-A, Chapter 29, Section 901].

MEDIATION OR COUNSELING REQUIREMENTS: Mediation is mandatory in Maine if 1 of the spouses denies that there are irreconcilable differences or it is a contested divorce and children are involved. In addition, at any time a court may order mediation. [Maine Revised Statutes Annotated; Title 19-A, Chapter 29, Section 902 and Chapter 3, Section 251].

PROPERTY DISTRIBUTION: Maine is an "equitable distribution" state. Each spouse retains his or her individual property, including: (1) any gifts or inheritances; (2) any property acquired prior to marriage; and (3) any increase in the value of or property acquired in exchange for property listed in (1) or (2). The marital property is divided between the spouses after considering the following factors: (1) the contribution of each spouse to the acquisition of the marital property, including the contribution of each spouse as homemaker; (2) the value of each spouse's property; and (3) the economic circumstances of each spouse at the time the division of property is to become effective, including the desirability of awarding the family home or the right to live in the home for a reasonable period of time to the spouse having custody of any children. Marital fault is not a factor. [Maine Revised Statutes Annotated; Title 19-A, Chapter 29, Section 953].

ALIMONY/MAINTENANCE/SPOUSAL SUPPORT: Either spouse may be ordered to pay a reasonable amount of alimony. The court may also order that a spouse's real estate be awarded to the other spouse for life or that a lump sum amount be awarded as alimony. Marital fault is not a factor. There is a presumption that no general alimony or support be awarded if the marriage was for less than 10 years and, for marriages lasting from 10 to 20 years, the alimony not last over one-half the length of the marriage. In addition, the court may award "transitional" support for a spouse's short-term needs and/or for assistance on reentry into the workforce. The factors for consideration set out in the statute are: (1) the duration of the marriage; (2) the age of the spouses; (3) the standard of living established during the marriage; (4) the ability of each spouse to pay; (5) the employment history and employment potential of each spouse; (6) the income history and income potential of each spouse; (7) the education and training of each spouse; (8) the provisions for retirement and health insurance benefits for each spouse; (9) the tax consequences of the division of marital property, including the tax consequences of the sale of the marital home; (10) the health and disabilities of each spouse; (11) the tax consequences of an alimony award; (12) the contributions of either spouse as homemaker; (13) the contributions of either spouse to the education or earning potential to the other spouse; (14) economic misconduct of either spouse resulting in the diminution of marital property or income; (15) the ability of the party seeking support to become self-supporting within a reasonable length of time; (16) the effect of income from marital or non-marital property or child support payments on either spouse's need for or ability to pay spousal support; and (17) any other factors the court considers appropriate. [Maine Revised Statutes Annotated; Title 19-A, Chapter 27, Section 851 and Chapter 29, Section 951-A].

SPOUSE'S NAME: During or after a divorce or annulment, and upon request, a spouse may have their name changed. [Maine Revised Statutes Annotated; Title 19-A, Chapter 29, Section 1051].

CHILD CUSTODY: Based on the best interests of the child, 3 types of custody may be awarded: (1) responsibilities for the child's welfare are divided, either exclusively or proportionately. The responsibilities to be divided are: primary physical residence, parent-child contact, support, education, medical and dental care, religious upbringing, travel boundaries and expenses, and any other aspects. A parent awarded responsibility for any aspect may be required to inform the other parent of any major changes; (2) parental responsibilities are shared [most or all of the responsibilities are made on the basis of joint decisions and the parents retain equal parental rights and responsibilities; or (3) one parent is granted full and exclusive rights and responsibility for the child's welfare, except for the responsibility of child support. The factors to be considered are: (1) the age of the child; (2) the motivation of the parents and their capacities to give the child love, affection, and guidance; (3) the preference of the child, if the child is of sufficient age and capacity; (4) the length of time the child has lived in a stable, satisfactory environment and the desirability of maintaining continuity; (5) the desire and ability of each parent to allow an open and loving frequent relationship between the child and the other parent; (6) the child's adjustment to his or her home, school, and community; (7) the relationship of the child with parents, siblings, and other significant family members; (8) the stability of the home environment likely to be offered by each parent; (9) a need to promote continuity and stability in the life of the child; (10) the parent's capacity and willingness to cooperate; (11) methods for dispute resolution; (12) the effect on the child of 1 parent having sole authority over his or her upbringing; (13) the existence of any domestic violence or child abuse; (14) any history of child abuse by a parent; (15) any misuse of "protection from abuse" orders to gain a tactical advantage in the case; (16) whether the child, if under age 1, is being breastfed; and (17) any other factors having a reasonable bearing on the child's upbringing. No preference is to be given because of a parent's sex or because of the child's age or sex. In any child custody case, the court may order an investigation of the parents and child by the Department of Human Services. [Maine Revised Statutes Annotated; Title 19-A, Chapter 51, Section 1501 and Chapter 55, Section 1653].

CHILD SUPPORT: Either or both parents may be ordered to pay child support, regardless of any marital fault. An order for support may require that a parent be responsible for an insurance policy covering the child's medical, hospital, and other health care expenses. There are official Child Support Guidelines and forms These guidelines are presumed to be correct. Deviation from the guidelines is allowed under the following circumstances: (1) the non-primary residential caretaker is providing residential care over 30% of the time; (2) the number of children requiring support is over 6; (3) child support, spousal support, and property division is being decided at the same time; (4) the financial resources of the child; (5) the financial resources and needs of each parent, including any nonrecurring income not included in the definition of gross income; (6) the standard of living the child would have had if the marriage had continued; (7) the physical and emotional condition of the child; (8) the educational needs of the child; (9) inflation in relation to the cost of living; (9) income and financial contributions of a spouse of each parent; (10) other dependents of the parent required to pay support; (11) the tax consequences of a support award; (12) any non-income-producing assets of over $10,000.00 owned by either parent; (13) whether any of the children are over 12 years old; and (14) the cost of transportation of any child. [Maine Revised Statutes Annotated; Title 19-A, Chapter 63, Sections 2001- 2009].

MARYLAND

STATE WEBSITE: http://www.michie.com/maryland/lpext.dll?f=templates&fn=main-h.htm&2.0

DOWNLOAD STATE FORMS: http://www.courts.state.md.us/family/forms/divorce.html

FORMS PROVIDED ON CD: Complaint for Absolute Divorce, Financial Statement

FORMS AVAILABLE ONLINE: Complaint for Absolute Divorce, Financial Statement

RESIDENCY REQUIREMENTS AND WHERE TO FILE: If the grounds for divorce occurred out-side of Maryland, 1 of the spouses must have lived in Maryland for at least 1 year prior to filing for divorce. Otherwise, either spouse may file for divorce in Maryland. If insanity is the grounds for divorce, the residency requirement is increased to 2 years. The divorce may be filed for in a county where either spouse resides. [Annotated Code of Maryland; Family Law, Section 7-101, 7-103 and Maryland Rules, Rule 9-201].

LEGAL GROUNDS FOR (ABSOLUTE) DIVORCE: No-Fault: (1) The spouses have voluntarily lived separate and apart for 1 year without interruption or cohabitation and there is no reasonable expectation of reconciliation or (2) the spouses have lived separate and apart without interruption for 2 years. [Annotated Code of Maryland; Family Law, Section 7-103].

General: (1) Adultery; (2) deliberate desertion for 12 months with no chance for reconciliation; (3) confinement for incurable insanity of at least 3 years; (4) conviction of a felony or a misdemeanor with at least a 3-year sentence and after 1 year having been served; (5) cruelty, with no chance for reconciliation; and (6) vicious conduct, with no chance for reconciliation. [Annotated Code of Maryland; Family Law, Section 7-103].

NAME OF COURT IN WHICH TO FILE FOR DIVORCE: Circuit Court. "In the Circuit Court for _____, Maryland."

TITLE OF DIVORCE ACTION: Bill for Divorce.

NAME USED TO DESCRIBE SPOUSE FILING FOR DIVORCE: Plaintiff.

NAME USED TO DESCRIBE OTHER SPOUSE IN DIVORCE: Defendant.

TITLE OF FINAL DIVORCE PAPERS: Decree of Divorce.

LEGAL SEPARATION: The grounds for a legal separation (limited divorce) are: (1) willful deser-tion; (2) cruel and inhuman treatment; and (3) voluntary separation and living separate and apart without cohabitation. The legal separation may be temporary or permanent. The spouses must make a good-faith effort to reconcile their differences. [Annotated Code of Maryland; Family Law, Section 7-102].

SIMPLIFIED OR SPECIAL DIVORCE PROCEDURES: Summary divorces are not permitted in Maryland. However, marital settlement agreements are specifically authorized by statute and may be used for full corroboration of a plaintiff's testimony that a separation was voluntary if: (1) the agreement states that the spouses voluntarily agreed to separate and (2) the agreement was signed under oath before the application for divorce was filed. In addition, each spouse must file a Financial Statement Affidavit and a Joint Statement of Marital and Non-Marital Property. If parties are not represented by an attorney, a phone number must appear on the Bill for Divorce. The financial statement form is contained in Maryland Rules, Rule 9-203. The form for the Joint Property Statement is contained in Maryland Rules, Rule 9-207. Finally, in a default situation, the divorce may be granted only upon actual testimony of the plaintiff spouse. [Annotated Code of Maryland; Courts and Judicial Procedure, Section 3-409 and Maryland Rules; Rules 9-202, 9-203, 9-206, and 9-207].

MEDIATION OR COUNSELING REQUIREMENTS: Maryland specifically declares that it is in the best interests of children that there be mediated resolutions of parental disputes regarding custody. A court may order an educational seminar if children are involved. In cases where the custody of a child is in dispute, the court may order the parents to attempt to mediate that issue, unless there is a history of physical or sexual abuse of the child. [Maryland Rules, Rule 9-205].

PROPERTY DISTRIBUTION: Maryland is an "equitable distribution" state. The spouses retain their separate property, including: (1) any gifts and inheritances; (2) property acquired prior to the marriage; and (3) property which is directly traceable to property listed in (1) or (2). Marital property, including retirement benefits and military pensions, is then divided on an equitable basis. The court may order a division of the property, a sale of the property and a division of the proceeds, or a money award as an adjustment of the values. The following factors are considered: (1) the monetary and non-monetary contributions of each spouse to the acquisition of the marital property, including the contribution of each spouse as homemaker; (2) the value of each spouse's property; (3) the economic circumstances of each spouse at the time the division of property is to become effective; (4) the length of the marriage; (5) whether the property award is instead of or in addition to alimony; (6) how and by whom the property was acquired, including any retirement, profit-sharing, or deferred compensation plans; (7) the circumstances that contributed to the estrangement of the spouses; (8) the age and physical and mental condition of the spouses; and (9) any other factor necessary to do equity and justice between the spouses. [Annotated Code of Maryland; Family Law, Sections 8-202, 8-203, and 8-205].

ALIMONY/MAINTENANCE/SPOUSAL SUPPORT: Either spouse may be awarded alimony based on the following factors: (1) the time necessary to acquire sufficient education and training to enable the spouse to find appropriate employment and that spouse's future earning capacity; (2) the standard of living established during the marriage; (3) the duration of the marriage; (3) the ability of the spouse from whom support is sought to meet his or her needs while meeting those of the spouse seeking support; (4) the financial resources of the spouse seeking alimony, including marital property apportioned to such spouse and such spouse's ability to meet his or her needs independently; (5) the comparative financial resources of the spouses, including their comparative earning abilities in the labor market; (6) the contribution of each spouse to the marriage, including services rendered in homemaking, childcare, education, and career-building of the other spouse; (7) the age of the spouses; (8) the physical and emotional conditions of the spouses; (9) any mutual agreement between the spouses concerning financial or service contributions by 1 spouse with the expectation of future reciprocation or compensation by the other; (10) the ability of the spouse seeking alimony to become self-supporting; (11) the circumstances which lead to the breakdown of the marriage; and (12) any other factor the court deems just and equitable. [Annotated Code of Maryland; Family Law, Section 11-106].

SPOUSE'S NAME: Either spouse's former or birth name may be restored if the purpose is not illegal, fraudulent, or immoral. [Annotated Code of Maryland; Family Law, Section 7-105].

CHILD CUSTODY: Joint or sole custody may be awarded to either or both parents, based on the best interests of the child. Custody may be denied if the child has been abused by the parent seeking custody. There are no other factors for consideration set out in the statute. The court shall attempt to allow the child to live in the environment and community that is familiar to the child and will generally allow the use and possession of the family home by the person with custody of the child(ren). [Annotated Code of Maryland; Family Law, Sections 5-203, 8-207, 8-208, and 9-101 and Maryland Case Law].

CHILD SUPPORT: Child support may be awarded. There are specific child support guidelines and charts supplied in the statute. There is a presumption that the amount shown for support in the guidelines is correct. However, the amount may be adjusted up or down if it is shown to be inappropriate or unjust under the circumstances of the case. In determining whether the amount would be unjust, the court may consider: (1) the terms of any marital settlement agreement between the parents, including any provisions for payments of marital debts, mortgages, college education expenses, the right to occupy the family home, and any other financial terms and (2) the presence in the household of either parent of other children that the parent has a duty to support. The family home may be awarded to the parent who has custody of a child to enable the child to continue to live in the environment and community that is familiar to the child. A grandparent may be financially responsible for their grandchild if the parent is an unemancipated minor. An official child support worksheet is in Rule 9-206.[Annotated Code of Mary-land; Family Law, Sections 8-206, 12-101, 12-201, 12-202, 12-203, and 12-204 and Maryland Rules; Rule 9-206 (Child Support Guidelines)].

MASSACHUSETTS

STATE WEBSITE: http://www.state.ma.us/legis/laws/mgl/index.htm

DOWNLOAD STATE FORMS: http://www.mass.gov/courts/selfhelp/index.html

FORMS PROVIDED ON CD: Complaint for Divorce, Joint Petition for Divorce, Financial Statement Short Form, Financial Statement Long Form

FORMS AVAILABLE ONLINE: Complaint for Divorce, Joint Petition for Divorce, Financial Statement Short Form, Financial Statement Long Form, Complaint for Custody-Support-Visitation

RESIDENCY REQUIREMENTS AND WHERE TO FILE: If the grounds for divorce occurred in Massachusetts, 1 spouse must be a resident. If the grounds occurred outside of the state, the spouse filing must have been a resident for 1 year. The divorce should be filed for in the county in which the spouses last lived together. If neither spouse currently lives in that county, then the divorce may be filed for in a county where either spouse currently resides. [Massachusetts General Laws Annotated; Chapter 208, Sections 4, 5, and 6].

LEGAL GROUNDS FOR DIVORCE: No-Fault: Irretrievable breakdown of the marriage (may be filed for either with or without a separation agreement. For no-fault divorce filed in conjunction with a separation agreement, see below under *Simplified Or Special Divorce Procedures*.) [Massachusetts General Laws Annotated; Chapter 208, Sections 1, 1A, and 1B].

General: (1) Impotence; (2) imprisonment for over 5 years; (3) adultery; (4) alcoholism and/or drug addiction; (5) desertion without support of spouse for 1 year before the filing for divorce; (6) cruel and inhuman treatment; and (7) nonsupport whereby a spouse is able to provide support but grossly, wantonly, or cruelly refuses or neglects to provide suitable maintenance for the complaining spouse. [Massachusetts General Laws Annotated; Chapter 208, Sections 1, 1A, 1B, and 2].

NAME OF COURT IN WHICH TO FILE FOR DIVORCE: Probate Court for the Commonwealth of Massachusetts. "Commonwealth of Massachusetts, The Trial Court, The Probate and Family Court Department, _____ Division." [Massachusetts General Laws Annotated; Chapter 208, Section 6B].

TITLE OF DIVORCE ACTION: For fault-based divorce: Complaint for Divorce. For no-fault divorce with or without a separation agreement: Petition for Divorce. See below under *Simplified Or Special Divorce Procedures*.

NAME USED TO DESCRIBE SPOUSE FILING FOR DIVORCE: For fault-based divorce: Plaintiff. For no-fault divorce without a separation agreement: Petitioner. For no-fault divorce with a separation agreement: Co-Petitioner.

NAME USED TO DESCRIBE OTHER SPOUSE IN DIVORCE: For fault-based divorce: Defendant. For no-fault divorce without a separation agreement: Respondent. For no-fault divorce with a separation agreement: Co-Petitioner.

TITLE OF FINAL DIVORCE PAPERS: Judgment of Divorce.

LEGAL SEPARATION: The grounds for legal separation are: (1) a spouse fails without cause to provide support; (2) desertion; or (3) gives the other spouse justifiable cause to live apart. The court may award support to the spouse and children living apart. If the grounds for legal separation occurred in Massachusetts, 1 spouse must be a resident. If the grounds occurred outside of the state, the spouse filing must have been a resident for 1 year. [Massachusetts General Laws Annotated; Chapter 208, Section 20].

SIMPLIFIED OR SPECIAL DIVORCE PROCEDURES: An action for divorce on the grounds of irretrievable breakdown of the marriage may be instituted by filing: (1) a petition signed by both spouses; (2) a sworn affidavit that an irretrievable breakdown of the marriage exists; and (3) a notarized separation agreement signed by both spouses. A marital settlement agreement is an acceptable substitute for a separation agreement. No summons will be required. Such petitions are to be given a speedy hearing. Marital fault is not to be considered in any decision of the court on property division or maintenance. In addition, there are sample divorce forms for use in divorces set out in the Massachusetts Rules of Court Appendix of Forms. A Financial Statement must be filed in all divorce cases. There is an official Child Support Guidelines Worksheet contained in the Appendix of Forms. Finally, in every action for divorce, a Public Health Statistical Report must be filed by each spouse. Copies of this form are available from the offices of the Registers of Probate. [Massachusetts General Laws Annotated; Chapter 208, Sections 1A and 6B and Massachusetts Rules of Court; Appendix of Forms].

MEDIATION OR COUNSELING REQUIREMENTS: In cases where "irreconcilable differences" are used as the grounds for divorce, the court may refer the spouses and children for marriage and family counseling. [Massachusetts General Laws Annotated; Chapter 208, Sections 1A and Massachusetts Rules of Court].

PROPERTY DISTRIBUTION: Massachusetts is an "equitable distribution" state. The court may divide all of the spouse's property, including any gifts and inheritances, based on the following factors: (1) the contribution of each spouse to the acquisition, preservation, or appreciation in value of the property, including the contribution of each spouse as homemaker; (2) the length of the marriage; (3) the age and health of the spouses; (4) the occupation of the spouses; (5) the amount and sources of income of the spouses; (6) the vocational skills of the spouses; (7) the employability of the spouses; (8) the liabilities and needs of each spouse and the opportunity of each for further acquisition of capital assets and income; (9) the conduct of the parties during the marriage [if the grounds for divorce are fault-based]; and (10) any health insurance coverage. Fault is not a factor if the grounds for the divorce are irretrievable breakdown of the marriage filed in conjunction with a separation/settlement agreement. [Massachusetts General Laws Annotated; Chapter 208, Sections 1A and 34].

ALIMONY/MAINTENANCE/SPOUSAL SUPPORT: Either spouse may be ordered to pay maintenance to the other. The factors to be considered are: (1) the contribution of each spouse to the acquisition, preservation, or appreciation in value of any property, including the contribution of each spouse as homemaker; (2) the length of the marriage; (3) the age and health of the spouses; (4) the occupation of the spouses; (5) the amount and sources of income of the spouses; (6) the vocational skills of the spouses; (7) the employability of the spouses; (8) the liabilities and needs of each spouse and the opportunity of each for further acquisition of capital assets and income; (9) the conduct of the parties during the marriage [if the grounds for divorce are fault-based]; (10) any health insurance coverage; and (11) the present and future needs of any children of the marriage. Fault is not a factor if the grounds for the divorce are irretrievable breakdown of the marriage filed in conjunction with a separation/settlement agreement. Health insurance coverage may be ordered to be provided as part of the maintenance award. [Massachusetts General Laws Annotated; Chapter 208, Sections 1A and 34].

SPOUSE'S NAME: The wife may be restored to the use of her former or maiden name. [Massachusetts General Laws Annotated; Chapter 208, Section 23].

CHILD CUSTODY: Custody may be awarded to either or both parents or to a third party. If there is no marital misconduct, the rights of each parent to custody shall be deemed to be equal. The happiness and welfare of the child shall be the factors that the court considers. In making this consideration, the court shall consider: (1) whether or not the child's present or past living conditions adversely affect his physical, mental, moral, or emotional health; (2) whether any family member abuses alcohol or other drugs; (3) whether either parent has deserted the child; (4) whether either parent has committed any acts of domestic violence; and (5) whether the parents have a history of being able and willing to cooperate in matters concerning the child. Joint custody may be awarded if both parents agree and unless the court finds that joint custody is not in the best interests of the child. If the issue of custody is contested and the parents desire some form of shared custody, a shared parenting plan must be submitted to the court. Provisions in a Marital Settlement Agreement relating to child custody will fulfill this requirement. [Massachusetts General Laws Annotated; Chapter 208, Sections 28 and 31].

CHILD SUPPORT: The court may order either parent to provide maintenance, support (including health insurance), and education for any minor child. There are official Child Support Guidelines. These guidelines are presumed to be correct unless there is a showing that the amount would be unjust or inappropriate under the particular circumstances in a case. Reasons for deviation from the Guidelines are: (1) the parent to pay support has other minor children and there are insufficient financial resources available; (2) the parent to pay support has extraordinary expenses [travel-related visitation expenses, uninsured medical expenses, etc.]; and (3) other unusual circumstances. There is an official Child Support Guidelines Worksheet contained in the Appendix of Forms. [Massachusetts General Laws Annotated; Chapter 208, Section 28 and Massachusetts Rules of Court; Appendix of Forms].

MICHIGAN

STATE WEBSITE: http://www.michiganlegislature.org/

DOWNLOAD STATE FORMS: No state forms available online.

FORMS PROVIDED ON CD: COMPLAINT FOR DIVORCE

FORMS AVAILABLE ONLINE: None

RESIDENCY REQUIREMENTS AND WHERE TO FILE: Immediately prior to filing for divorce, 1 of the spouses must have been a resident of Michigan for 180 days and a resident of the county for 10 days where the divorce is filed. However, a person may file for divorce in any county in the state without meeting the 10-day residency requirement if the defendant was born in or is a citizen of a foreign country and there are minor children in the marriage who are at risk of being taken out of the country by the defendant. [Michigan Compiled Laws Annotated; Section 552.9].

LEGAL GROUNDS FOR DIVORCE: No-Fault: A breakdown of the marriage relationship to the extent that the objects of matrimony have been destroyed and there remains no reasonable likelihood that the marriage can be preserved. [Michigan Compiled Laws Annotated; Section 552.6].
General: A breakdown of the marriage relationship to the extent that the objects of matrimony have been destroyed and there remains no reasonable likelihood that the marriage can be preserved are the only grounds for divorce in Michigan. [Michigan Compiled Laws Annotated; Section 552.6].

NAME OF COURT IN WHICH TO FILE FOR DIVORCE: Circuit Court. "State of Michigan, _____ Judicial Circuit, _____ County." [Michigan Compiled Laws Annotated; Section 552.6].

TITLE OF DIVORCE ACTION: Complaint for Divorce.

NAME USED TO DESCRIBE SPOUSE FILING FOR DIVORCE: Plaintiff.

NAME USED TO DESCRIBE OTHER SPOUSE IN DIVORCE: Defendant.

TITLE OF FINAL DIVORCE PAPERS: Judgment of Divorce.

LEGAL SEPARATION: The only grounds for legal separation (separate maintenance) in Michigan is a breakdown of the marriage relationship to the extent that the objects of matrimony have been destroyed and there remains no reasonable likelihood that the marriage can be preserved. There is no residency requirement specified in the statute. [Michigan Compiled Laws Annotated; Section 552.7].

SIMPLIFIED OR SPECIAL DIVORCE PROCEDURES: There are mandatory official approved and simplified (fill-in-the-blank) forms available for all phases of the divorce process. These forms are contained in the official Michigan Supreme Court Administrative Office Forms Book and should be available from the Clerk of the Circuit Court in any Michigan county. In addition, the Michigan Friend of the Court Bureau is to supply each party in a divorce case with a pamphlet discussing the court procedures, the rights and responsibilities of the parties, the availability of mediation, human services, and joint custody. [Michigan Court Rules 3.204 and Michigan Compiled Laws Annotated; Section 552.505].

MEDIATION OR COUNSELING REQUIREMENTS: Voluntary mediation services are available in all situations involving custody and visitation of children. [Michigan Compiled Laws Annotated; Section 552.513].

PROPERTY DISTRIBUTION: Michigan is an "equitable distribution" state. The court may divide the all of the spouse's property, including any gifts or inheritances, in a just and reasonable manner, if it appears that the spouse contributed to the acquisition, improvement, or accumulation of the property. The factors to be considered are: (1) the contribution of each spouse to the acquisition of the marital property, including the contribution of each spouse as homemaker; (2) the length of the marriage; (3) any retirement benefits, including social security, civil service, and military and railroad retirement benefits; (4) any prior marriage of each spouse; (5) the circumstances that contributed to the estrangement of the spouses; (6) the source of the property; (7) the cause of the divorce; and (8) each spouse's financial circumstances and rights to any insurance policies. [Michigan Compiled Laws Annotated; Sections 552.19, 552.101, and 552.401 and Michigan Case Law].

ALIMONY/MAINTENANCE/SPOUSAL SUPPORT: Either spouse may be ordered to pay alimony. The alimony may be awarded if the property awarded to a spouse is insufficient to allow that spouse suitable support and maintenance. Factors for consideration specified in the statute are: (1) the ability of either spouse to pay; (2) the character and situation of the spouses; and (3) all other circumstances of the case. All payments of spousal support shall be ordered to be made through the Michigan Friend of the Court Bureau. [Michigan Compiled Laws Annotated; Sections 552.13, 552.23, and 552.452].

SPOUSE'S NAME: At the wife's request, the court may restore the birth or former name, if there is no fraudulent intent. [Michigan Compiled Laws Annotated; Section 552.391].

CHILD CUSTODY: Sole or joint custody is awarded based on the best interests of the child and on the following factors: (1) moral character and prudence of the parents; (2) physical, emotional, mental, religious, and social needs of the child; (3) capability and desire of each parent to meet the child's emotional, educational, and other needs; (4) preference of the child, if the child is of sufficient age and capacity; (5) the love and affection and other emotional ties existing between the child and each parent; (6) the length of time the child has lived in a stable, satisfactory environment and the desirability of maintaining continuity; (7) the desire and ability of each parent to allow an open and loving frequent relationship between the child and the other parent; (8) the child's adjustment to his or her home, school, and community; (9) the mental and physical health of all individuals involved; (10) the permanence as a family unit of the proposed custodial home or homes; and (11) any other factors.

If joint custody is an issue, the court will consider all of the above factors and the following additional factors: (1) whether the parents will be able to cooperate and generally agree concerning important decisions affecting the welfare of the child and (2) if the parents agree on joint custody. [Michigan Compiled Laws Annotated; Sections 552.16, 722.23, and 722.26a].

CHILD SUPPORT: Either parent may be ordered to provide a just and proper amount of child support. There is a Child Support Formula to be used as a guideline and it is presumed to be correct unless shown to be unjust or inappropriate under the circumstances in a particular case. Their is a manual available from the Michigan Friend of the Court Bureau. The court may require the parent providing support to file a bond guaranteeing the support payments. Support may include health care, dental care, childcare, and education of the child. The Judgment of Divorce must include a provision that requires 1 or both of the parents to provide health care coverage, if such coverage is available at a reasonable cost as a benefit of employment. All payments of child support shall be ordered to be made through the Michigan Friend of the Court Bureau. Each parent will be required to keep the Michigan Friend of the Court Bureau informed of their address, sources of income, and health insurance coverage. [Michigan Compiled Laws Annotated; Sections 552.15, 552.16, 552.452, and 552.519].

MINNESOTA

STATE WEBSITE: http://www.leg.state.mn.us/leg/statutes.htm

DOWNLOAD STATE FORMS: http://www.mncourts.gov/default.aspx?page=513&category=55

FORMS PROVIDED ON CD: Petition for Dissolution with Children, Petition for Dissolution without Children, Joint Petition for Dissolution without Children

FORMS AVAILABLE ONLINE: Petition for Dissolution with Children, Petition for Dissolution without Children, Joint Petition for Dissolution without Children, Instructions, Child Support and Alimony Forms

RESIDENCY REQUIREMENTS AND WHERE TO FILE: One of the spouses must have been a resident of Minnesota for at least 180 days immediately before the petition for dissolution of marriage is filed. The dissolution of marriage may be filed for in a county where either spouse resides. [Minnesota Statutes Annotated; Chapters 518.07 and 518.09].

LEGAL GROUNDS FOR DISSOLUTION OF MARRIAGE: No-Fault: Irrevocable breakdown of the marriage shown by: (1) Living separate and apart for 180 days or (2) serious marital discord adversely affecting the attitude of 1 or both of the spouses toward the marriage. [Minnesota Statutes Annotated; Chapters 518.06 and 518.13]. General: Irrevocable breakdown of the marriage is the only grounds for dissolution of marriage in Minnesota. [Minnesota Statutes Annotated; Chapter 518.06].

NAME OF COURT IN WHICH TO FILE FOR DISSOLUTION OF MARRIAGE: County Court or District Court. "State of Minnesota, District Court, County of _____, _____ Judicial District."

TITLE OF DISSOLUTION OF MARRIAGE ACTION: Petition for Dissolution of Marriage. "In Re: The Marriage of _____ and _____."

NAME USED TO DESCRIBE SPOUSE FILING FOR DISSOLUTION OF MARRIAGE: Petitioner (or Co-Petitioner if the petition is filed jointly). See below under *Simplified Or Special Dissolution Of Marriage Procedures*.

NAME USED TO DESCRIBE OTHER SPOUSE IN DISSOLUTION OF MARRIAGE: Respondent (or Co-Petitioner if the petition is filed jointly). See below under *Simplified Or Special Dissolution Of Marriage Procedures*.

TITLE OF FINAL DISSOLUTION OF MARRIAGE PAPERS: Decree of Dissolution of Marriage.

LEGAL SEPARATION: The grounds for a legal separation in Minnesota are that it will be granted if the court finds that the spouses need a legal separation. One of the spouses must have been a resident of Minnesota for at least 6 months before the petition for legal separation is filed. [Minnesota Statutes Annotated; Chapters 518.06 and 518.07].

SIMPLIFIED OR SPECIAL DISSOLUTION OF MARRIAGE PROCEDURES: The petition may be brought by both spouses jointly as Co-Petitioners. This eliminates the need for service of process or the use of a summons. [Minnesota Statutes Annotated; Chapters 518.09 and 518.11].

MEDIATION OR COUNSELING REQUIREMENTS: Mediation may be ordered in cases in which the custody of children is contested, unless there is a history of spousal abuse or physical or sexual child abuse. [Minnesota Statutes Annotated; Chapter 518.619].

PROPERTY DISTRIBUTION: Minnesota is an "equitable distribution" state. Each spouse retains his or her non-marital (separate) property, consisting of: (1) property acquired prior to the marriage; (2) any gifts or inheritances; (3) property exchanged for such non-marital property; or (4) an increase in value of such non-marital property. All other marital property, including any pension and retirement plans, is divided, without regard to fault, after a consideration of the following factors: (1) the contribution of each spouse to the acquisition of the marital property, including the contribution of each spouse as homemaker; (2) the economic circumstances of each spouse at the time the division of property is to become effective; (3) the length of the marriage; (4) the age and health of the spouses; (5) the occupation of the spouses; (6) the amount and sources of income of the spouses; (7) the vocational skills of the spouses; (8) the employability of the spouses; (9) the liabilities and needs of each spouse and the opportunity of each for further acquisition of capital assets and income; (10) any prior marriage of each spouse; and (11) any other factor necessary to do equity and justice between the spouses. [Minnesota Statutes Annotated; Chapter 518.58].

ALIMONY/MAINTENANCE/SPOUSAL SUPPORT: Either spouse may be awarded maintenance, without regard to marital fault, if the spouse seeking maintenance: (1) lacks sufficient property to provide for reasonable needs considering the standard of living attained during the marriage; (2) is unable to provide adequate self-support, considering the standard of living attained during the marriage, through appropriate employment; or (3) is the custodian of a child whose condition or circumstances make it appropriate that the custodian not be required to seek employment outside the home. The award of maintenance is based on a consideration of the following factors: (1) the sacrifices the homemaker has made in terms of earnings, employment, experience, and opportunities; (2) the time necessary to acquire sufficient education and training to enable the spouse to find appropriate employment, that spouse's future earning capacity, and the probability of completing education and training and becoming fully or partially self-supporting; (3) the standard of living established during the marriage; (4) the duration of the marriage and, in the case of a homemaker, the length of absence from employment and the extent to which any education, skills, or experience have become outmoded and earning capacity has become permanently diminished; (5) the ability of the spouse from whom support is sought to meet his or her needs while meeting those of the spouse seeking support; (6) the financial resources of the spouse seeking maintenance, including marital property apportioned to such spouse and such spouse's ability to meet his or her needs independently; (7) the contribution of each spouse to the marriage, including services rendered in homemaking, childcare, education, and career-building of the other spouse; (8) the age of the spouses; (9) the physical and emotional conditions of the spouses; (10) any loss of earnings, seniority, retirement benefits, or other employment opportunities foregone by the spouse seeking maintenance; and (11) any other factor the court deems just and equitable. If the spouse receives public aid, the payments are to be made through the public aid agency. [Minnesota Statutes Annotated; Chapters 518A and 518.552].

SPOUSE'S NAME: Upon request, either spouse may change his or her name, unless there is intent to mislead or defraud. [Minnesota Statutes Annotated; Chapter 518.27].

CHILD CUSTODY: Joint or sole custody may be awarded. Sole custody will be awarded based on the best interests of the child and the following: (1) the child's cultural background; (2) physical and mental health of all parties; (3) capability and desire of each parent to give the child love, affection, and guidance and to continue raising the child in the child's culture and religion or creed, if any; (4)

preference of the child, if the child is of sufficient age and capacity; (5) the length of time the child has lived in a stable, satisfactory environment and the desirability of maintaining continuity; (6) the wishes of the parents; (7) the child's adjustment to his or her home, school, and community; (8) the mental and physical health of all individuals involved; (9) the relationship of the child with parents, siblings, and other significant family members; (10) the conduct of the proposed guardian only as it bears on his or her relationship with the child; (11) the stability of the home environment likely to be offered by each parent; (12) a need to promote continuity and stability in the life of the child; (13) the effect of any child or spouse abuse on the child; (14) the child's primary caretaker; and (15) any other factors. The primary caretaker factor is not a presumption in favor of the primary caretaker, but is only 1 factor in the decision.If both parents request joint custody, there is a presumption that such an arrangement will be in the best interests of the child, unless there has been any spousal abuse. If there has been any history of spousal abuse, there is a presumption that joint custody is not in the best interests of the child. Joint custody will be based on a consideration of the above factors and the following: (1) dispute resolution methods; (2) the effect of 1 parent having custody; and (3) the ability of the parents to cooperate and make decisions jointly. If both parents seek custody of a child who is too young to express a preference, the "primary caretaker" is to be awarded custody. [Minnesota Statutes Annotated; Chapter 518.17 and Minnesota Case Law].

CHILD SUPPORT: In determining child support, the following factors are considered: (1) the financial resources of the child; (2) the financial resources, earnings, income, and assets of the parents; (3) the standard of living the child would have enjoyed if the marriage had not been dissolved; (4) the physical and emotional conditions and educational needs of the child; (5) the amount of public aid received by the child or parent; (6) any income tax consequences of the payment of support; and (7) any debt of the parents. Misconduct of a parent in the marriage is not to be considered. If the parent to receive the support payments is receiving or has applied for public aid, the support payments must be made to the public agency responsible for child support enforcement in Minnesota. There are official child support guidelines contained in Minnesota Statutes Annotated; Chapter 518.551. [Minnesota Statutes Annotated; Chapters 518A].

MISSISSIPPI

STATE WEBSITE: http://www.sos.state.ms.us/ed_pubs/mscode/

DOWNLOAD STATE FORMS: No state forms available online.

FORMS PROVIDED ON CD: BILL OF COMPLAINT FOR DIVORCE

FORMS AVAILABLE ONLINE: None

RESIDENCY REQUIREMENTS AND WHERE TO FILE: One of the spouses must have been a resident for at least 6 months and not have secured residency for the purpose of obtaining a divorce. A member of the armed services and his or her spouse are considered residents if stationed in Mississippi. A divorce on the grounds of irreconcilable differences should be filed for in: (1) the county where either spouse resides, if both spouses are residents of Mississippi or (2) the county where 1 spouse resides if the other spouse is a non-resident of Mississippi. A divorce sought on fault-based grounds should be filed for in: (1) the county where the defendant resides if he or she is a resident of Mississippi; (2) the county where the plaintiff resides if the defendant is a non-resident of Mississippi; or (3) the county where the spouses last lived prior to separating, if the defendant is still a resident of Mississippi. [Mississippi Code Annotated; Section 93, Chapters 5-5 and 5-11].

LEGAL GROUNDS FOR DIVORCE: No-Fault: Irreconcilable differences. See also below under *Simplified or Special Divorce Procedures.* [Mississippi Code Annotated; Section 93, Chapters 5-1, 5-2, and 5-7].

General: (1) Impotence; (2) adultery; (3) imprisonment; (4) alcoholism and/or drug addiction; (5) confinement for incurable insanity for at least 3 years before the divorce is filed; (6) wife is pregnant by another at the time of marriage without husband's knowledge; (7) willful desertion for at least 1 year; (8) cruel and inhuman treatment; (9) spouse lacked mental capacity to consent [including temporary incapacity resulting from drug or alcohol use]; and (10) incest. In addition, an affidavit must be filed stating that there is no collusion between the spouses. [Mississippi Code Annotated; Section 93, Chapters 5-1 and 5-7].

NAME OF COURT IN WHICH TO FILE FOR DIVORCE: Chancery Court. "Chancery Court of ____ _____ County, State of Mississippi." [Mississippi Code Annotated; Section 93, Chapter 5-11].

TITLE OF DIVORCE ACTION: Bill of Complaint for Divorce.

NAME USED TO DESCRIBE SPOUSE FILING FOR DIVORCE: Complainant.

NAME USED TO DESCRIBE OTHER SPOUSE IN DIVORCE: Defendant.

TITLE OF FINAL DIVORCE PAPERS: Decree of Divorce.

LEGAL SEPARATION: There are no provisions in Mississippi for legal separation.

SIMPLIFIED OR SPECIAL DIVORCE PROCEDURES: A no-fault divorce on the grounds of irreconcilable differences will be granted if: (1) a joint bill of complaint for divorce is filed by both the husband and wife or (2) a bill of complaint has been filed and: (a) the defendant has entered an appearance by written waiver of process or (b) has been personally served with the divorce papers. In addition, if there is a written agreement between the spouses for the care and custody of any children and for the division of all property, the court may incorporate such an agreement into the divorce judgment. If the spouses cannot agree on the terms of an agreement, they must consent to the divorce in writing and consent to allow the court to decide all contested issues. There is a 60-day waiting period after filing before a hearing may be scheduled. A bill filed meeting these qualifications will be taken as proved and no testimony or proof will be required at the hearing. However, if the defendant denies that there are irreconcilable differences, the divorce may not be granted on these grounds. [Mississippi Code Annotated; Section 93, Chapter 5-2].

MEDIATION OR COUNSELING REQUIREMENTS: There is no legal provision in Mississippi for mediation.

PROPERTY DISTRIBUTION: Mississippi is a "title" state. Each spouse retains his or her property for which they have title. There are no statutory provisions in Mississippi for considerations regarding property division. However, Mississippi has judicially adopted the "equitable division" systems of property division. Recent court decisions have allowed for a wife's contributions to the acquisition of assets to provide the court with authority to divide any jointly accumulated assets on an "equitable" basis. A 1994 case (*Ferguson v. Ferguson*) spelled out a set of factors for the equitable division of marital property: (1) a spouse's substantial contribution to the accumulation of property; (2) the degree to which a spouse has previously expended or disposed of any marital property; (3) the market and emotional value of the property in question; (4) the value of any non-marital or separate property; (5) the tax consequences of the division of property; (6) the extent to which property division may eliminate the need for alimony or any other future friction between the parties; (7) the needs of the party, considering income, assets, and earning capacity; and (8) any other equitable factors. [Mississippi Case Law].

ALIMONY/MAINTENANCE/SPOUSAL SUPPORT: Either spouse may be awarded maintenance if it is equitable and just. There are no other factors for consideration specified in the statute. However, a 1996 case (*Parsons v. Parsons*) spelled out a set of factors for consideration: (1) the spouses' income and expenses; (2) the spouses' health and earnings; (3) the spouses' needs, obligations, and assets; (4) the presence of any children; (5) the spouses' ages; (6) the standard of living during the marriage; (7) any tax consequences; (8) any marital fault; (9) any wasteful dissipation of assets; and (10) any other just and equitable factors. [Mississippi Code Annotated; Section 93, Chapter 5-23 and Mississippi Case Law].

SPOUSE'S NAME: Either spouse may petition the court for a name change. [Mississippi Code Annotated; Section 93, Chapter 17-1].

CHILD CUSTODY: Joint or sole child custody is awarded based on the best interests of the child. There are no specific factors for consideration in the statute. It is presumed that a court will not award custody to a parent with a history of family violence. The court may award: (1) joint physical and legal custody to 1 or both parents; (2) physical custody to both parents and legal custody to 1 parent; (3) legal custody to both parents and physical custody to 1 parent; or (4) custody to a third party if the parents have abandoned the child or are unfit. If irreconcilable differences are the grounds for divorce, joint custody may be awarded if both parents apply for joint custody. If both parents apply for joint custody, there is a presumption that joint custody is in the best interests of the child. Otherwise, either parent may apply for joint custody. If both parents are fit and the child is 12 or older, the child may choose the parent he or she wishes to live with. If child abuse is alleged by either parent, the court shall order an investigation by the Mississippi Department of Public Welfare. [Mississippi Code Annotated; Section 93, Chapters 5-23, 5-24, and 11-65].

CHILD SUPPORT: Child support may be ordered as the court finds just and equitable. Where both parents have income or estates, each parent may be ordered to provide support in proportion to his or her relative financial ability. A parent may be required to provide health insurance coverage for the child, if such insurance coverage is available at a reasonable cost through an employer or organization. A bond or sureties may be required to guarantee payments. There are specific child support guidelines contained in the statute. [Mississippi Code Annotated; Section 93, Chapters 5-23 and 11-65].

MISSOURI

STATE WEBSITE: http://www.moga.state.mo.us/

DOWNLOAD STATE FORMS: http://www.courts.mo.gov/

FORMS PROVIDED ON CD: Petition for Dissolution of Marriage

FORMS AVAILABLE ONLINE: Petition for Dissolution of Marriage, Statement of Income and Expense, Parenting Plan, Child Support Forms

RESIDENCY REQUIREMENTS AND WHERE TO FILE: One of the spouses must be a resident of Missouri for 90 days before filing for dissolution of marriage. The dissolution of marriage should be filed in the county where the Petitioner resides. In addition, there is a 30-day waiting period after filing before a dissolution of marriage will be granted. [Annotated Missouri Statutes; Title 30, Chapter 452, Sections 300 and 305].

LEGAL GROUNDS FOR DISSOLUTION OF MARRIAGE: No-Fault: Irretrievable breakdown of the marriage and no reasonable likelihood that the marriage can be preserved. [Annotated Missouri Statutes; Title 30, Chapter 452, Section 305].

General: Irretrievable breakdown of the marriage with no reasonable likelihood that the marriage can be preserved is the only grounds for dissolution of marriage in Missouri. [Annotated Missouri Statutes; Title 30, Chapter 452, Section 305].

NAME OF COURT IN WHICH TO FILE FOR DISSOLUTION OF MARRIAGE: Circuit Court. "In the Circuit Court of _____ County, Missouri."

TITLE OF DISSOLUTION OF MARRIAGE ACTION: Petition for Dissolution of Marriage. "In Re the Marriage of _____ and _____." [Annotated Missouri Statutes; Title 30, Chapter 452, Section 300].

NAME USED TO DESCRIBE SPOUSE FILING FOR DISSOLUTION OF MARRIAGE: Petitioner (or Co-Petitioner if the petition is filed jointly). See below under *Simplified Or Special Dissolution Of Marriage Procedures*.

NAME USED TO DESCRIBE OTHER SPOUSE IN DISSOLUTION OF MARRIAGE: Respondent (or Co-Petitioner if the petition is filed jointly). See below under *Simplified Or Special Dissolution Of Marriage Procedures*.

TITLE OF FINAL DISSOLUTION OF MARRIAGE PAPERS: Decree of Dissolution of Marriage.

LEGAL SEPARATION: The grounds for legal separation in Missouri are an irretrievable breakdown of the marriage, which may include the following factors: (1) adultery; (2) abandonment for at least 6 months; (3) separation caused by misconduct in the 12 months before filing the petition; (4) spousal behavior that the other spouse cannot reasonably be expected to live with; and (5) living separate and apart continuously for 24 months. One of the spouses must be a resident of Missouri for 90 days before filing for legal separation. [Annotated Missouri Statutes; Title 30, Chapter 452, Sections 305 and 320].

SIMPLIFIED OR SPECIAL DISSOLUTION OF MARRIAGE PROCEDURES: Missouri allows for a joint petition by both spouses to be filed. In such cases, each spouse should be titled as a "Co-Petitioner." Settlement agreements are expressly authorized by statute in Missouri. In addition, some counties have approved pre-printed forms for filing for dissolution of marriage which are available upon request from the court clerk. [Annotated Missouri Statutes; Title 30, Chapter 452, Sections 320 and 325].

MEDIATION OR COUNSELING REQUIREMENTS: The court can delay a divorce proceeding for 30 to 180 days and suggest that the spouses seek counseling. [Annotated Missouri Statutes; Title 30, Chapter 452, Section 320].

PROPERTY DISTRIBUTION: Missouri is an "equitable distribution" state. Each spouse retains his or her separate property obtained prior to the marriage, including any gifts or inheritances. In addition, any property exchanged for separate property or interest obtained from holding separate property remains as separate. Commingled property does not become marital solely by virtue of the act of commingling. Marital property (all property acquired after the marriage whether held jointly or individually, except if: (1) gift or inheritance; (2) received in exchange for non-marital property; (3) an increase in non-marital property; or (4) property excluded by a written agreement between the spouses) is divided after a consideration of the following factors: (1) the contribution of each spouse to the acquisition of the marital property, including the contribution of each spouse as homemaker; (2) the value of each spouse's property; (3) the economic circumstances of each spouse at the time the division of property is to become effective; (4) the conduct of the spouses during the marriage generally and as it relates to the disposition of their property; (5) the desirability of awarding the family home to the spouse having custody of the children; and (6) any custodial arrangements for children. [Annotated Missouri Statutes; Title 30, Chapter 452, Section 330 and Missouri Case Law].

ALIMONY/MAINTENANCE/SPOUSAL SUPPORT: Either spouse may be awarded maintenance if that spouse can show: (1) an inability to support himself or herself and (2) a lack of sufficient property (including his or her share of any marital property) to provide for his or her own needs; or (3) that the spouse seeking support is the custodian of a child whose condition or circumstances make it appropriate for that spouse not to seek outside employment. The following factors are considered: (1) the time necessary to acquire sufficient education and training to enable the spouse to find appropriate employment and that spouse's future earning capacity; (2) the standard of living established during the marriage; (3) the duration of the marriage; (4) the ability of the spouse from whom support is sought to meet his or her needs while meeting those of the spouse seeking support; (5) the financial resources of the spouse seeking maintenance, including marital property apportioned to such spouse and such spouse's ability to meet his or her needs independently; (6) the age of the spouses; (7) the physical and emotional conditions of the spouses; (8) the obligations, assets, and separate property of the spouses; (9) the comparative earning capacities of each spouse; and (10) the conduct of the spouses during the marriage. The court may order the payments to be made through the circuit clerk. [Annotated Missouri Statutes; Title 30, Chapter 452, Sections 335 and 345].

SPOUSE'S NAME: A spouse may petition the court for a change of name. A public notice of any name change should be published in a local newspaper in the county where the person resides. [Annotated Missouri Statutes; Chapter 527, Sections 270 and 290].

CHILD CUSTODY: Joint or sole custody is awarded based on the best interests of the child and upon consideration of the following factors: (1) the preference of the child; (2) the wishes of the

304

parents and any proposed parenting plan submitted by both parents; (3) the child's adjustment to his or her home, school, and community; (4) the mental and physical health of all individuals involved; (5) any history of child or spouse abuse; (6) the child's need for a continuing relationship with both parents; (7) both parents' willingness and ability to perform parental obligations; (8) the intention of either parent to relocate his or her residence; (9) which parent is more likely to allow the child frequent and meaningful contact with the other parent; and (10) the relationship of the child with parents, siblings, and other significant family members. Domestic violence against a child is a bar to custody. No preference is to be given because of parent's sex, age, or financial status, or the child's age or sex. There is now a legislative encouragement of joint custody or arrangements which will encourage the parents to both share in the decision-making responsibility of caring for the child. An award of joint custody must include a joint custody plan. A parent not granted custody is entitled to reasonable visitation. [Annotated Missouri Statutes; Title 30, Chapter 452, Sections 375 and 400 and Missouri Case Law].

CHILD SUPPORT: Either or both parents may be ordered to provide child support. Marital misconduct is not to be considered as a factor. The following factors are considered: (1) the child's custody arrangements; (2) the financial resources and needs of the child; (3) the standard of living the child would have enjoyed if the marriage had not been dissolved; (4) the physical and emotional conditions and educational needs of the child; and (5) the financial resources, needs, and obligations of both the noncustodial and the custodial parent. A parent may be required to provide health insurance coverage for any children if such coverage is available at a reasonable cost from an employer, union, or other organization. There are official child support guidelines contained in the statute which are presumed to be correct unless shown to be unjust or inappropriate under the particular circumstances of the case. The court may order the payments to be made through the circuit clerk. [Annotated Missouri Statutes; Title 30, Chapter 452, Sections 340 and 345].

MONTANA

STATE WEBSITE: http://leg.state.mt.us/

DOWNLOAD STATE FORMS: http://www.montanacourts.org/library/topics/end_marriage.asp

FORMS PROVIDED ON CD: Petition for Dissolution with Children, Petition for Dissolution without Children, Joint Petition for Dissolution with Children, Joint Petition for Dissolution without Children, Declaration of Disclosure

FORMS AVAILABLE ONLINE: Petition for Dissolution with Children, Petition for Dissolution without Children, Joint Petition for Dissolution with Children, Joint Petition for Dissolution without Children, Parenting Plan, Declaration of Disclosure, Legal Separation Packet,

RESIDENCY REQUIREMENTS AND WHERE TO FILE: One of the spouses must be a resident of Montana for 90 days immediately prior to filing. The dissolution of marriage should be filed for in the county where the petitioner has been a resident for the previous 90 days. [Montana Code Annotated; Section 25, Title 2-118 and Section 40, Title 4-104].

LEGAL GROUNDS FOR DISSOLUTION OF MARRIAGE: No-Fault: Irretrievable breakdown of the marriage shown by: (1) serious marital discord which adversely affects the attitude of both spouses towards the marriage and no reasonable prospect of reconciliation or (2) living separate and apart for 180 days prior to filing. [Montana Code Annotated; Section 40, Title 4-104].

General: Irretrievable breakdown of the marriage and living separate and apart for 180 days prior to filing are the only grounds for dissolution of marriage in Montana. [Montana Code Annotated; Section 40, Title 4-104].

NAME OF COURT IN WHICH TO FILE FOR DISSOLUTION OF MARRIAGE: District Court. "District Court for the State of Montana and for the County of _____."

TITLE OF DISSOLUTION OF MARRIAGE ACTION: Petition for Dissolution of Marriage. "In Re the Marriage of _____ and _____." [Montana Code Annotated; Section 40, Titles 1-105 and 4-103].

NAME USED TO DESCRIBE SPOUSE FILING FOR DISSOLUTION OF MARRIAGE: Petitioner (or Co-Petitioner if the petition is filed jointly). See below under *Simplified Or Special Dissolution Of Marriage Procedures.*

NAME USED TO DESCRIBE OTHER SPOUSE IN DISSOLUTION OF MARRIAGE: Respondent (or Co-Petitioner if the petition is filed jointly). See below under *Simplified Or Special Dissolution Of Marriage Procedures.*

TITLE OF FINAL DISSOLUTION OF MARRIAGE PAPERS: Decree of Dissolution of Marriage.

LEGAL SEPARATION: Irretrievable breakdown of the marriage is the only grounds for legal separation in Montana. One of the spouses must be a resident of Montana for 90 days immediately prior to filing for legal separation. [Montana Code Annotated; Section 40, Title 4-104].

SIMPLIFIED OR SPECIAL DISSOLUTION OF MARRIAGE PROCEDURES: Joint petitions for dissolution of marriage are allowed. In such cases, both spouses should be titled as "Co-Petitioners" on the petition. In addition, separation or settlement agreements are specifically authorized by law. [Montana Code Annotated; Section 40, Title 4-107].

MEDIATION OR COUNSELING REQUIREMENTS: If there are: (1) minor children; (2) 1 spouse denies that the marriage is irretrievably broken; or (3) 1 or both spouses wish to attempt an amicable settlement of their differences, the court may delay the proceedings for 30 to 60 days and refer the spouses to 1 of the following: (1) a psychiatrist; (2) a physician; (3) an attorney; (4) a social worker; (5) a pastor or director of any religious denomination to which the spouses belong; or (6) any other person who is competent and qualified in personal counseling. [Montana Code Annotated; Section 40, Titles 3-121, 3-124, and 4-107].

PROPERTY DISTRIBUTION: Montana is an "equitable distribution" state. All of the spouse's property, including any held prior to the marriage and any gifts and inheritances, is divided by the court, without regard to marital misconduct, based on consideration of the following factors: (1) the contribution of each spouse to the acquisition of the marital property, including the contribution of each spouse as homemaker; (2) the length of the marriage; (3) the age and health of the spouses; (4) the occupation of the spouses; (5) the amount and sources of income of the spouses; (6) the vocational skills of the spouses; (7) the employability of the spouses; (8) the liabilities and needs of each spouse and the opportunity of each for further acquisition of capital assets and income; (9) the time necessary for a spouse to acquire sufficient education to enable the spouse to find appropriate employment; (10) any premarital agreement; (11) any prior marriage of each spouse; (12) whether the property award is instead of or in addition to maintenance; and (13) any custodial provisions for the children. [Montana Code Annotated; Section 40, Title 4-202].

ALIMONY/MAINTENANCE/SPOUSAL SUPPORT: Either spouse may be awarded maintenance if that spouse can show: (1) an inability to support himself or herself and (2) a lack of sufficient property (including his or her share of any marital property) to provide for his or her own needs; or (3) that the spouse seeking support is the custodian of a child whose condition or circumstances make it appropriate for that spouse not to seek outside employment. The award is made without regard to marital fault, based on the following factors: (1) the time necessary to acquire sufficient education and training to enable the spouse to find appropriate employment and that spouse's future earning capacity; (2) the standard of living established during the marriage; (3) the duration of the marriage; (4) the ability of the spouse from whom support is sought to meet his or her needs while meeting those of the spouse seeking support; (5) the financial resources of the spouse seeking maintenance, including marital property apportioned to such spouse and any child support and such spouse's ability to meet his or her needs independently; (6) the age of the spouses; and (7) the physical and emotional conditions of the spouses. [Montana Code Annotated; Section 40, Title 4-203].

SPOUSE'S NAME: Upon the wife's request, her former or maiden name will be restored. [Montana Code Annotated; Section 40, Title 4-108].

CHILD CUSTODY: "Parenting" is now the legal terminology in use in Montana to describe the concept of custody. "Parenting Plans" are now the Montana description of child custody arrangements. Sole or joint parenting is awarded based on the best interests of the child and upon a consideration of the following factors: (1) the preference of the child; (2) the wishes of the parents; (3) the child's adjustment to his or her home, school, and community; (4) the mental and physical health of all individuals involved; (5) any history of child or spouse abuse or threats of abuse; (6) any chemical dependency or abuse by a parent; (7) the relationship of the child with parents, siblings, and other significant family members; (8) the continuity and stability of the child's care; (9) the developmental needs of the child; (10) whether a parent has failed to pay any of the child's birth-related costs; (11) whether the child has frequent and continuing contact with both parents [a consideration of any spousal or child abuse by either parent or anyone residing in a parent's household is considered also]; (12) whether a parent has knowingly failed to support the child; and (13) any adverse effects on the child resulting from 1 parent's continuous and annoying efforts to amend parenting plans [annoying is meant to refer to efforts to: (a) amend a parenting plan within 6 months of a prior plan and (b) efforts to amend a final parenting plan without having made a good-faith effort to comply with the plan]. The parents must submit a parenting plan to the court; although they may choose to submit a temporary or "interim" parenting plan. A parent's sex is not to be considered. [Montana Code Annotated; Section 40, Titles 4-104, 4-108, and 4-212].

CHILD SUPPORT: Either or both parents may be ordered to pay child support, based on a consideration of the following factors: (1) the financial resources of the child; (2) the standard of living the child would have enjoyed if the marriage had not been dissolved; (3) the physical and emotional conditions and educational and medical needs of the child; (4) the financial resources, needs, and obligations of both the noncustodial and the custodial parent; (5) the age of the child; (6) the cost of any daycare; (7) the parenting plan for the child; (8) the needs of any other person that a parent is obligated to support; and (9) the provision of health and medical insurance for the child. A portion of the parents' property may be set aside in a trust fund for the support of the children. A parent may be ordered to provide health insurance coverage for a child if such coverage is available at a reasonable cost. There are uniform child support guidelines adopted by the Department of Public Health and Human Services that are to be considered by the court. Child support payments may be required to be made through the Department of Health and Human Services. [Montana Code Annotated; Section 40, Titles 4-204 and 5-209].

NEBRASKA

STATE WEBSITE: http://uniweb.legislature.ne.gov/QS/laws.html

DOWNLOAD STATE FORMS: http://www.supremecourt.ne.gov/self-help/simple-divorce.shtml

FORMS PROVIDED ON CD: Complaint for Divorce With Children, Complaint for Divorce Without Children, Financial Affidavit for Child Support

FORMS AVAILABLE ONLINE: Complaint for Divorce With Children, Complaint for Divorce Without Children, Financial Affidavit for Child Support, Parenting Plan

RESIDENCY REQUIREMENTS AND WHERE TO FILE: (1) One of the spouses must have been a resident of Ne-braska for at least 1 year or (2) the marriage was performed in Nebraska and 1 of the spouses has lived in Nebraska for the entire marriage. The dissolution of marriage may be filed for in a county where either spouse resides. There is a 60-day waiting period after service of the petition for dissolution of marriage on the respondent before the case can be decided in court. [Revised Statutes of Nebraska; Chapter 42, Sections 342 and 349].

LEGAL GROUNDS FOR DISSOLUTION OF MARRIAGE: No-Fault: Irretrievable breakdown of the marriage. [Revised Statutes of Nebraska; Chapter 42, Section 361].

General: Spouse lacked mental capacity to consent (including temporary incapacity resulting from drug or alcohol use). [Revised Statutes of Nebraska; Chapter 42, Section 362].

NAME OF COURT IN WHICH TO FILE FOR DISSOLUTION OF MARRIAGE: District Court. "In the District Court for _____ County, Nebraska." [Revised Statutes of Nebraska; Chapter 42, Section 353].

TITLE OF DISSOLUTION OF MARRIAGE ACTION: Complaint for Dissolution of Marriage.

NAME USED TO DESCRIBE SPOUSE FILING FOR DISSOLUTION OF MARRIAGE: Petitioner.

NAME USED TO DESCRIBE OTHER SPOUSE IN DISSOLUTION OF MARRIAGE: Respondent.

TITLE OF FINAL DISSOLUTION OF MARRIAGE PAPERS: Decree of Dissolution of Marriage.

LEGAL SEPARATION: Irretrievable breakdown of the marriage is the only grounds for a legal separation in Nebraska. There are no residency requirements specified in the statute. If the residency requirements for dissolution of marriage are met after the petition for legal separation has been filed, the spouse filing may change the proceeding to a proceeding for dissolution of marriage. [Revised Statutes of Nebraska; Chapter 42, Section 350].

SIMPLIFIED OR SPECIAL DISSOLUTION OF MARRIAGE PROCEDURES: Joint petitions for dissolution of marriage may be filed by both spouses. In such cases, the spouses should be referred to as "Co-Petitioners" on the court documents. In addition, marital settlement agreements are specifically authorized by law. [Revised Statutes of Nebraska; Chapter 42, Sections 361 and 366].

MEDIATION OR COUNSELING REQUIREMENTS: A dissolution of marriage will not be granted until every reasonable effort for a reconciliation has been made. If it appears to the court that there is some reasonable possibility of reconciliation, dissolution of marriage actions may be transferred to a conciliation court or the spouses may be referred to a qualified marriage counselor, family service agency, or other agency which provides conciliation services. Official conciliation counselors are available in counties of over 250,000 persons. [Revised Statutes of Nebraska; Chapter 42, Sections 360 and 808].

PROPERTY DISTRIBUTION: Nebraska is an "equitable distribution" jurisdiction. The spouses retain their separate property acquired prior to the marriage. All of the spouse's marital property, including any gifts and inheritances acquired during the marriage, may be divided, based on a consideration of the following factors: (1) the contribution of each spouse including the care and education of the children, to the acquisition of the marital property, including the contribution of each spouse as homemaker; (2) the economic circumstances of each spouse at the time the division of property is to become effective; (3) the length of the marriage; (4) any custodial provisions for the children; and (5) any interruption of career or education of the spouse. [Revised Statutes of Nebraska; Chapter 42, Section 365].

ALIMONY/MAINTENANCE/SPOUSAL SUPPORT: Either spouse may be ordered to pay reasonable spousal support, without regard to marital fault, based on a consideration of the following factors: (1) the circumstances of both spouses; (2) the duration of the marriage; (3) the contribution of each spouse to the marriage, including services rendered in homemaking, childcare, education, and career-building of the other spouse; (4) any interruption of personal careers or education; and (5) the ability of the supported spouse to engage in gainful employment without interfering with the interests of any minor children in his or her custody. Reasonable security for the payments may be required. [Revised Statutes of Nebraska; Chapter 42, Section 365].

SPOUSE'S NAME: Either spouse may include a request to restore his or her former name in the petition for dissolution of marriage. [Nebraska Case Law].

CHILD CUSTODY: Joint or sole custody of children is determined according to the best interests of the child and based on a consideration of the following factors: (1) the general health, welfare, and social behavior of the child; (2) the preference of the child, if the child is of sufficient age and capacity; (3) the child's relationship with each parent prior to the filing for dissolution of marriage; and (4) any credible evidence of child or spousal abuse. No preference is to be given because of parent's sex. Joint custody may be awarded if both parents agree. [Revised Statutes of Nebraska; Chapter 42, Section 364].

CHILD SUPPORT: The amount of child support is determined based on a consideration of the earning capacity of each parent. There are official Supreme Court child support guidelines and worksheets which should be available from the clerk of the court. [Revised Statutes of Nebraska; Chapter 42, Section 364].

NEVADA

STATE WEBSITE: http://www.leg.state.nv.us/law1.cfm

DOWNLOAD STATE FORMS: http://www.nvsupremecourt.us/documents/index.php?packetID=244

FORMS PROVIDED ON CD: Complaint for Divorce With Children, Complaint for Divorce Without Children, Financial Declaration

FORMS AVAILABLE ONLINE: Complaint for Divorce With Children, Complaint for Divorce Without Children, Financial Declaration

RESIDENCY REQUIREMENTS AND WHERE TO FILE: The divorce may be filed in the county: (1) where either spouse resides; (2) where the spouses last lived together; (3) where the cause of the divorce took place; or (4) where the plaintiff resided for 6 weeks immediately prior to filing for divorce. One of the spouses must have been a resident of Nevada for at least 6 weeks prior to filing for divorce, unless the cause for the divorce took place in the county in Nevada where the spouses actually lived at the time of the happening of the cause. [Nevada Revised Statutes; Chapter 125, Section 020].

LEGAL GROUNDS FOR DIVORCE: No-Fault: (1) Incompatibility or (2) living separate and apart without cohabitation for 1 year. [Nevada Revised Statutes; Chapter 125, Section 010].

General: Insanity which existed for at least 2 years before filing for the divorce. [Nevada Revised Statutes; Chapter 125, Section 010].

NAME OF COURT IN WHICH TO FILE FOR DIVORCE: District Court. "In the District Court for _____ County, Nevada." [Nevada Revised Statutes; Chapter 125, Section 020].

TITLE OF DIVORCE ACTION: Complaint for Divorce.

NAME USED TO DESCRIBE SPOUSE FILING FOR DIVORCE: Plaintiff.

NAME USED TO DESCRIBE OTHER SPOUSE IN DIVORCE: Defendant.

TITLE OF FINAL DIVORCE PAPERS: Decree of Divorce.

LEGAL SEPARATION: If a spouse has any of the grounds for divorce or if he or she has been deserted for over 90 days, a suit for separate maintenance of himself or herself and any children may be filed. In addition, the spouses may agree to an immediate separation and make appropriate provisions for spousal and child support. There is no residency requirement specified in the statute. [Nevada Revised Statutes; Chapter 125, Section 190].

SIMPLIFIED OR SPECIAL DIVORCE PROCEDURES: There are 2 provisions for summary divorce in Nevada. First, a summary divorce may be granted if the following conditions are met: (1) either spouse has been a resident of the state for at least 6 weeks; (2) the spouses are incompatible or have lived separate and apart without cohabitation for 1 year; (3) there are no minor children (born or adopted) and the wife is not pregnant, *or* the spouses have signed an agreement specifying the custody and support of the children; (4) there is no community or joint property, or the spouses have signed an agreement regarding the division of their property and the assumption of their liabilities, and have signed any deeds, titles, or other evidences of transfer of property; (5) both spouses waive their rights to spousal support [maintenance] or the spouses have signed an agreement specifying the amount of spousal support; (6) both spouses waive: [a] their rights to notice of entry of the final decree of divorce; [b] their rights to appeal the divorce; [c] their rights to request findings of fact and conclusions of law in the divorce proceeding; and [d] their rights to a new trial; and (7) both spouses want the court to enter the decree of divorce. A Summary Proceeding for Divorce is begun by filing a joint petition, signed under oath, together with an Affidavit of Corroboration of Residency by a witness. In addition, a spouse may apply for a divorce by default by affidavit. In such situations, oral testimony will not normally be required. If there is a marital settlement agreement, it should be identified in the affidavit and attached to it when filed. The affidavit should: (1) state that the residency requirements have been met; (2) state that all of the information in the petition is correct and true on the personal knowledge of the person signing the affidavit; (3) state that the affidavit contains only facts that would be admissible into evidence; (4) give factual support for each allegation in the application; and (5) establish that the person signing the affidavit is competent to testify. Each divorce filed must also contain a Civil Cover sheet, a Verification of Pleadings, a Request for Submission, and an Affidavit of Residency. Finally, there are specific provisions authorizing separation agreements and marital settlement agreements. [Nevada Revised Statutes; Chapter 123, Sections 020 and 090 and Chapter 125; Sections 181 to 184].

MEDIATION OR COUNSELING REQUIREMENTS: There are no legal provisions in Nevada for divorce mediation.

PROPERTY DISTRIBUTION: Nevada is a "community property" state. The spouses retain all of their separate property, acquired prior to the marriage or by gift or inheritance. The court will divide all of the spouse's community property and all of the property held jointly by the spouses, including any military retirement benefits. Marital fault is not mentioned as a factor. Either spouse's property is also then subject to distribution for alimony or child support. Separate property which 1 spouse contributed to purchase or improve community property may be returned to the contributing spouse. [Nevada Revised Statutes; Chapter 125, Section 150 and 210].

ALIMONY/MAINTENANCE/SPOUSAL SUPPORT: Unless there is a premarital agreement otherwise, either spouse may be awarded alimony, without regard to marital fault. The alimony may be a lump-sum or periodic payments. [Nevada Revised Statutes; Chapter 125, Section 150].

SPOUSE'S NAME: For a reasonable cause, the court will restore the wife's former name. [Nevada Revised Statutes; Chapter 125, Section 130].

CHILD CUSTODY: Joint or sole custody is awarded based on the best interests of the child and upon the following factors: (1) the preference of the child, if the child is of sufficient age and capacity; (2) the wishes of the parents [no preference is to be given because of parent's sex]; (3) whether either parent has committed domestic violence; and (4) other relevant factors. There is a presumption of joint custody if both parents have signed an agreement for joint custody or both agree to joint custody in open court. There is also a presumption that it is not in the best interests of a child to have custody awarded to a parent who has committed domestic violence. [Nevada Revised Statutes; Chapter 125, Sections 480 and 490].

CHILD SUPPORT: Temporary (during the divorce proceeding) and permanent child support may be granted. There are official Child Support percentages contained in Nevada Revised Statutes; Chapter 125B, Section 070. These guidelines are presumed to be correct unless there is a showing that the needs of the child would not be met under the particular circumstances in a case. Factors for deviation from the guideline percentages are: (1) the cost of health insurance; (2) the cost of childcare; (3) any special educational needs of the child; (4) the age of the child; (5) the responsibility of the parents for the support of others; (6) the value of services contributed by the parents; (7) any public aid paid to the child; (8) any pregnancy expenses; (9) any visitation travel expenses; (10) the amount of time the child spends with each parent; (11) the relative income of each parent; and (12) any other necessary expenses. [Nevada Revised Statutes; Chapter 125, Section 230 and Chapter 125B, Section 070, 080, and 090].

NEW HAMPSHIRE

STATE WEBSITE: http://www.state.nh.us/

DOWNLOAD STATE FORMS: http://www.courts.state.nh.us/superior/forms

FORMS PROVIDED ON CD: Petition for Divorce, Joint Petition for Divorce, Financial Affidavit

FORMS AVAILABLE ONLINE: Petition for Divorce, Joint Petition for Divorce, Financial Affidavit, Petition for Legal Separation, Joint Petition for Legal Separation, Parenting Plan, Petition to Establish Paternity and/ or Support

RESIDENCY REQUIREMENTS AND WHERE TO FILE: (1) Both spouses must be residents of the state when the divorce is filed for; (2) the spouse filing for divorce must have been a resident of New Hampshire for 1 year immediately prior to filing for divorce and the other spouse was personally served with process within the state; or (3) the cause of divorce must have arisen in New Hampshire and 1 of the spouses must be living in New Hampshire when the divorce is filed for. The divorce may be filed for in a county where either spouse resides. [New Hampshire Revised Statutes Annotated; Chapters 458:5, 458:6, and 458.9].

LEGAL GROUNDS FOR DIVORCE: No-Fault: Irreconcilable differences which have caused the irremediable breakdown of the marriage. When either party has seriously effected the health or endangered the reason of the other party. When either party joins a religious sect that believes marriage is unlawful. [New Hampshire Revised Statutes Annotated; Chapter 458:7-a].

General: (1) Impotence; (2) adultery; (3) abandonment and not being heard of for 2 years; (4) imprisonment with a sentence of more than 1 year served; (5) physical abuse or reasonable apprehension of physical abuse; (6) desertion without support of spouse by husband for 2 years; (7) extreme cruelty; (8) habitual intemperance (drunkenness) for 2 years; (9) living separate and apart without cohabitation for 2 years; and (10) mental abuse. [New Hampshire Revised Statutes Annotated; Chapters 458:7, 458:7a, and 458:26].

NAME OF COURT IN WHICH TO FILE FOR DIVORCE: Superior Court. "The State of New Hampshire, Superior Court in and for _____."

TITLE OF DIVORCE ACTION: Petition for Divorce.

NAME USED TO DESCRIBE SPOUSE FILING FOR DIVORCE: Petitioner.

NAME USED TO DESCRIBE OTHER SPOUSE IN DIVORCE: Respondent.

TITLE OF FINAL DIVORCE PAPERS: Decree of Divorce.

LEGAL SEPARATION: The grounds for legal separation (limited divorce) in New Hampshire are the same as for divorce: (1) the spouse filing for legal separation must have been a resident of New Hampshire for 1 year or (2) the cause of legal separation must have arisen in New Hampshire and 1 of the spouses must be living in New Hampshire when the action for legal separation is filed for. [New Hampshire Revised Statutes Annotated; Chapters 458:5, 458:6, 458:7, 458:7a, and 458:26].

SIMPLIFIED OR SPECIAL DIVORCE PROCEDURES: There are no legal provisions in New Hampshire for simplified divorce procedures.

MEDIATION OR COUNSELING REQUIREMENTS: At either spouse's request or if the court feels that there is a reasonable chance at reconciliation, it may delay the divorce proceedings and order the spouses to submit to marriage counseling. There are also provisions for voluntary marital mediation of issues involved in the divorce. [New Hampshire Revised Statutes Annotated; Chapters 458:6, 458:7B, and 458:15-c].

PROPERTY DISTRIBUTION: New Hampshire is an "equitable distribution" state. The court will divide all of the spouse's property, including: (1) gifts; (2) inheritances; (3) property acquired prior to the marriage; and (4) any retirement or pension benefits, as is equitable and just. An equal division is presumed to be equitable. The factors for consideration specified in the statute are: (1) the length of the marriage; (2) the age and health of the spouses; (3) the occupation of the spouses; (4) the vocational skills of the spouses; (5) the employability of the spouses; (6) the value of spouse's separate property; (7) the amount and sources of income of the spouses; (8) the liabilities and needs of each spouse; (9) the opportunity of each for further acquisition of capital assets and income; (10) the ability of the custodial parent to engage in gainful employment without interfering with the interests of any minor children in custody; (11) the need of the custodial parent to occupy or own the marital residence and any household furnishings; (12) the actions of either spouse during the marriage which contributed to the increase or decrease in value of any property; (13) any significant disparity between the spouses in relation to the contribution of each spouse to the acquisition of the marital property, including the contribution of each spouse to the care and education of the children and the care and management of the home; (14) the expectation of any retirement or pension benefits; (15) the federal income tax consequences of the court's division of the property; (16) any marital fault if such fault caused the breakdown of the marriage and caused pain and suffering or economic loss; (17) the value of any property acquired prior to marriage or exchanged for property acquired prior to marriage; (18) the value of any gifts or inheritances; (19) any direct or indirect contribution to the education or career development of the other spouse; (20) any interruption in education or career opportunities to benefit the other's career, the marriage, or any children; (21) the social and economic status of each spouse; and (22) any other relevant factor. [New Hampshire Revised Statutes Annotated; Chapter 458:16-a].

ALIMONY/MAINTENANCE/SPOUSAL SUPPORT: Either spouse may be ordered to pay support to the other if: (1) the spouse in need lacks sufficient income or property to provide for reasonable needs, taking into account the standard of living during the marriage; (2) the spouse to pay is able to meet his or her reasonable needs, taking into account the standard of living during the marriage; and (3) the spouse in need is unable to support himself or herself at a reasonable standard of living or is the custodian of a child whose condition or circumstances make it appropriate that the custodian not seek employment outside the home. The factors for consideration are: (1) the duration of the marriage; (2) the age of the spouses; (3) the physical and emotional conditions of the spouses; (4) the vocational skills and employability of the spouse seeking support; (5) the tax consequences to each spouse; (6) the amount and sources of income of the spouses; (7) the occupation of the spouses; (8) the value of each spouse's property; (9) the liabilities and needs of each spouse; (10) the opportunity of each for further acquisition of capital assets and income; (11) any marital fault if such fault caused the breakdown of the marriage and caused pain and suffering or economic loss; (12) the contribution of each spouse to the acquisition, preservation, or appreciation in value of the marital property, including any non-economic contributions of each spouse to the family unit; and (13) the social and economic status of each spouse. [New Hampshire Revised Statutes Annotated; Chapter 458:19].

The No-Fault Divorce Toolkit

SPOUSE'S NAME: A spouse's former name may be restored in a divorce. [New Hampshire Revised Statutes Annotated; Chapter 458:24].

CHILD CUSTODY: Joint legal custody (joint responsibility for all parental rights and decisions, except physical custody) is presumed to be in the best interests of the child unless there has been child abuse by 1 of the parents. Custody is awarded based on a consideration of the following factors: (1) preference of the child if child is of appropriate age; (2) overall welfare of the child; (3) any findings or recommendations of a neutral mediator; and (4) any other factors. No preference is given to either parent based on the parent's sex. Repeated and unwarranted interference by a parent with primary custody with the visitation rights of the other parent is a factor in modifying custody arrangements. Stepparents or grandparents may be granted visitation rights. [New Hampshire Revised Statutes Annotated; Chapter 461-A:6].

CHILD SUPPORT: The court may order reasonable provisions for the support and education of a child. There are specific child support guidelines set out in the statute. There is a presumption that the amount set forth in the guidelines is correct, unless it is shown that the amount is unjust or inappropriate under the particular circumstances of a case. The factors for consideration for adjusting the amount up or down which are specified in the statute are: (1) any extraordinary medical, dental, or educational expenses of the child; (2) a significantly higher or lower income of either parent; (3) the economic consequences of the presence of any stepparents, stepchildren, or natural or adopted children; (4) any reasonable costs associated with physical custody; (5) the economic consequences to either parent of the disposition of the marital home; (6) any state or federal tax consequences; (7) any split or shared custody arrangements; (8) the costs of providing college educations to any natural or adopted children; and (9) any other significant factor. The court may order health insurance coverage as a method of support. There are also provisions for wage assignments and wage withholding to secure the payment of any child support. [New Hampshire Revised Statutes Annotated; Chapters 461-A:6, 461-A:14, and 458-C:1-5].

NEW JERSEY

STATE WEBSITE: http://www.njleg.state.nj.us/

DOWNLOAD STATE FORMS: http://www.judiciary.state.nj.us/

FORMS PROVIDED ON CD: Complaint for Divorce

FORMS AVAILABLE ONLINE: Confidential Litigation Information Sheet, Mediation Forms, Support Orders

RESIDENCY REQUIREMENTS AND WHERE TO FILE: (1) One of the spouses must be a resident of New Jersey for at least 1 year prior to filing for divorce or (2) when the cause for divorce is adultery and took place in New Jersey, 1 of the spouses must have been a resident (no time limit). The divorce may be filed for in any county in New Jersey. [New Jersey Statutes Annotated; Title 2A, Chapters 34-8 and 34-10].

LEGAL GROUNDS FOR DIVORCE: No-Fault: Living separate and apart for 18 months and no reasonable prospect of reconciliation. [New Jersey Statutes Annotated; Title 2A, Chapter 34-2].

General: (1) Adultery; (2) imprisonment for 18 months; (3) unnatural sexual behavior before or after marriage; (4) alcoholism and/or drug addiction; (5) confinement for incurable insanity; (6) willful desertion for 1 year; (7) cruel and inhuman treatment; (8) separation for 2 years caused by confinement for mental illness; and (9) extreme cruelty. [New Jersey Statutes Annotated; Title 2A, Chapter 34-2].

NAME OF COURT IN WHICH TO FILE FOR DIVORCE: Superior Court. "Superior Court of New Jersey, Chancery Division, Family Part, _____ County."

TITLE OF DIVORCE ACTION: Complaint for Divorce.

NAME USED TO DESCRIBE SPOUSE FILING FOR DIVORCE: Plaintiff.

NAME USED TO DESCRIBE OTHER SPOUSE IN DIVORCE: Defendant.

TITLE OF FINAL DIVORCE PAPERS: Judgment of Divorce.

LEGAL SEPARATION: The grounds for legal separation (or a divorce from bed and board) are the same as for divorce. One of the spouses must be a resident of New Jersey for at least 1 year prior to filing for legal separation or when the cause for legal separation is adultery and took place in New Jersey, 1 of the spouses must have been a resident (no time limit). [New Jersey Statutes Annotated; Title 2A, Chapter 34-2].

SIMPLIFIED OR SPECIAL DIVORCE PROCEDURES: The filing of an acknowledgment of service of process or appearance is specifically authorized. Also, there is a required Case Information Statement which must be filed as shown in New Jersey Civil Practice Rules, Appendix V. [New Jersey Statutes Annotated; Title 2A, Chapter 34-11].

MEDIATION OR COUNSELING REQUIREMENTS: No legal provisions in New Jersey for divorce mediation.

PROPERTY DISTRIBUTION: New Jersey is an "equitable distribution" state. A spouse's separate property acquired before a marriage is retained by that spouse. All of the spouse's other property (except that acquired by gift and inheritance) is divided equitably, based on the following factors: (1) the value of each spouse's marital property; (2) the value of the separate property of the spouses; (3) the length of the marriage; (4) the age and health of the spouses; (5) the amount and sources of income of the spouses; (6) the liabilities and needs of each spouse and the opportunity of each for further acquisition of capital assets and income; (7) the standard of living established during the marriage; (8) how and by whom the property was acquired; (9) the tax consequences to each spouse; (10) the contribution of each spouse to the acquisition of the marital property, including the contribution of each spouse as homemaker; (11) the economic circumstances of each spouse at the time the division of property is to become effective; (12) any written agreement between the spouses; (13) the income and earning capacity of the spouses; (14) the educational background, training, and employment skills of the spouses; (15) any custodial responsibilities; (16) the length of absence from the job market; (17) the time and expense necessary to enable the spouse to acquire sufficient education or training to enable the spouse to become self-supporting at a standard of living reasonably comparable to that enjoyed during the marriage; (18) the need for the parent with custody of any children to own or occupy the marital residence; (19) the need to create a trust fund for the future medical or educational needs of a spouse or children; and (20) any other factor necessary to do equity and justice between the spouses. [New Jersey Statutes Annotated; Title 2A, Chapter 34-23.1].

ALIMONY/MAINTENANCE/SPOUSAL SUPPORT: Either spouse may be ordered to pay alimony, without regard to marital fault, based on the following factors: (1) the duration of the marriage; (2) the actual needs, obligations, and ability to pay of each spouse; (3) the standard of living established during the marriage and the likelihood that each spouse can maintain a comparable standard of living; (4) the time and expense necessary to acquire sufficient education and training to enable the spouse to find appropriate employment and that spouse's future earning capacity; (5) the age of the spouses; (6) the physical and emotional conditions of the spouses; (7) the earning capacities, educational levels, vocational skills, and employability of the spouses; (8) the length of absence from the job market; (9) any child custodial responsibilities of the spouse; (10) the availability of training and employment; (11) the opportunity for the future acquisition of capital and income; (12) the history or financial and non-financial contributions of each spouse to the marriage, including the contribution of each spouse to the care and education of children and interruption of personal careers or educational opportunities; (13) the equitable distribution of property and any payouts from this property, if a consideration of this income is fair and just [however, income from retirement benefits which are treated as an asset for purposes of equitable distribution are not to be considered]; (14) any investment income available to either spouse; (15) the tax consequences of any alimony; and (16) any other factor the court deems just and equitable. [New Jersey Statutes Annotated; Title 2A, Chapter 34-23].

SPOUSE'S NAME: The court may allow either spouse to use his or her former name. [New Jersey Statutes Annotated; Title 2A, Chapter 34-21].

CHILD CUSTODY: Sole or joint custody may be awarded based on the following factors: (1) the physical, emotional, mental, religious, and social needs of the child and (2) the preference of the child, if the child is of sufficient age and capacity. No preference is to be given because of parent's sex. A father may not forcibly take a minor child from a mother's actual physical custody. [New Jersey Statutes Annotated; Title 2A, Chapter 34-23 and New Jersey Case Law].

CHILD SUPPORT: The court may award child support for the care, maintenance, and education of a child. The factors for consideration specified in the statute are. (1) the needs and liability of the child; (2) the standard of living and economic circumstances of both parents; (3) the financial resources, needs, and obligations of both the non-custodial and the custodial parent; (4) the earning ability of each parent, including educational background, training, employment skills, work experience, custodial responsibility for the children, cost of childcare, and the length and cost of education and training to obtain employment; (5) the need and capacity of the child for education, including higher education; (6) the age and health of the child and the parents; (7) the income, assets, and earning ability of the child; (8) the responsibility of the parents for the support of others; and (9) any other relevant factors. There are specific New Jersey Supreme Court child support guidelines contained in New Jersey Civil Practice Rules, Appendix IX. [New Jersey Statutes Annotated; Title 2A, Chapter 34-23].

NEW MEXICO

STATE WEBSITE: http://www.conwaygreene.com/NewMexico.htm

DOWNLOAD STATE FORMS: http://www.supremecourt.nm.org./cgi-bin/download.cgi/supctforms/dom-rel

FORMS PROVIDED ON CD: Petition for Dissolution with Children, Petition for Dissolution without Children, Domestic Relations Cover Sheet

FORMS AVAILABLE ONLINE: Petition for Dissolution with Children, Petition for Dissolution without Children, Domestic Relations Cover Sheet,

RESIDENCY REQUIREMENTS AND WHERE TO FILE: One of the spouses must have been a resident of New Mexico for at least 6 months immediately preceding the filing for dissolution of marriage and have a home in New Mexico. The dissolution of marriage may be filed in any county where either spouse resides. [New Mexico Statutes Annotated; Chapter 40, Article 4, Section 40-4-5].

LEGAL GROUNDS FOR DISSOLUTION OF MARRIAGE: No-Fault: Incompatibility because of discord and conflicts of personalities such that the legitimate ends of the marriage relationship have been destroyed preventing any reasonable expectation of reconciliation. [New Mexico Statutes Annotated; Chapter 40, Article 4, Sections 40-4-1 and 40-4-2].

General: (1) Adultery; (2) abandonment; and (3) cruel and inhuman treatment. [New Mexico Statutes Annotated; Chapter 40, Article 4, Section 40-4-1].

NAME OF COURT IN WHICH TO FILE FOR DISSOLUTION OF MARRIAGE: District Court. "State of New Mexico, In the District Court, _____ County."

TITLE OF DISSOLUTION OF MARRIAGE ACTION: Petition for Dissolution of Marriage.

NAME USED TO DESCRIBE SPOUSE FILING FOR DISSOLUTION OF MARRIAGE: Petitioner.

NAME USED TO DESCRIBE OTHER SPOUSE IN DISSOLUTION OF MARRIAGE: Respondent.

TITLE OF FINAL DISSOLUTION OF MARRIAGE PAPERS: Decree of Dissolution of Marriage.

LEGAL SEPARATION: If the spouses have permanently separated and do not live together or cohabit, either spouse may begin proceedings for property division, child custody and support, and maintenance, without asking for a dissolution of marriage. One of the spouses must have been a resident of New Mexico for at least 6 months immediately preceding the filing for legal separation and have a home in New Mexico. [New Mexico Statutes Annotated; Chapter 40, Article 4, Section 40-4-3].

SIMPLIFIED OR SPECIAL DISSOLUTION OF MARRIAGE PROCEDURES: Marital settlement agreements and contracts for separation are specifically authorized by law and must be in writing. Any marital settlement agreements should be recorded in the county where the spouses reside. [New Mexico Statutes Annotated; Chapter 40, Article 4, Sections 40-2-4 and 40-2-5].

MEDIATION OR COUNSELING REQUIREMENTS: There are provisions in New Mexico for the establishment of domestic relations mediation programs. If such programs have been established in the county where the dissolution of marriage is filed for, parents may request the use of such programs, or the court may order the parents to enter the program. [New Mexico Statutes Annotated; Chapter 40, Article 4, Section 40-12-5].

PROPERTY DISTRIBUTION: New Mexico is a "community property" state. Each spouse retains his or her separate property acquired prior to the marriage, designated as separate property by a written agreement, and any gifts or inheritances. New Mexico uses a "quasi-community" property definition: All property, except separate property, that a spouse acquires outside of New Mexico which would have been community property if they had acquired it in New Mexico. "Quasi-community" property is treated like standard community property. The spouse's community property is to be divided equally between the spouses. Marital fault is not considered. There are no factors for consideration set out in the statute. [New Mexico Statutes Annotated; Chapter 40, Article 4, Sections 40-3-8 and 40-4-7].

ALIMONY/MAINTENANCE/SPOUSAL SUPPORT: Either spouse may be awarded a just and proper amount of maintenance, without regard to marital fault. The factors that the court will consider are: (1) the duration of the marriage; (2) the spouse's current and future earning capacities; (3) the good faith efforts of the spouses to maintain employment or become self-supporting; (4) the needs and obligations of each spouse; (5) the age, health, and means of the spouses; (6) the amount of property that each spouse owns; (7) the spouses' standard of living during the marriage; (8) the maintenance of medical and life insurance during the marriage; (9) the assets and property of the spouses, including any income-producing property [however, requiring a spouse to sell assets shall not be considered unless there are exceptional circumstances]; (10) each spouse's liabilities; and (11) any marital separation or settlement agreements. [New Mexico Statutes Annotated; Chapter 40, Article 4, Section 40-4-7 and New Mexico Case Law].

SPOUSE'S NAME: The court may order the restoration of a spouse's former name. [New Mexico Statutes Annotated; Chapter 40, Article 4, Section 40-8-1].

CHILD CUSTODY: Joint or sole child custody is to be determined according to the best interests of the child. There is a presumption that joint custody is in the best interests of the child, unless shown otherwise. The factors for consideration in all custody situations are: (1) the wishes of the child; (2) the wishes of the parents; (3) the relationship of the child with parents, siblings, and other significant family members; (4) the child's adjustment to his or her home, school, and community; and (5) the mental and physical health of all individuals involved. If a minor is 14 years old or older, the court may consider the wishes of the minor.

In addition, the factors that are considered in determining joint custody are as follows: (1) the ability of the parents to cooperate and make decisions jointly; (2) the physical proximity of the parents to each other as this relates to the practical considerations of where the child will reside; (3) whether an award of joint custody will promote more frequent or continuing contact between the child and each of the parents; (4) the love, affection, and other emotional ties existing between the parents and the child; (5) the capacity and disposition of the parents to provide the child with food, clothing, medical care, and other material needs; (6) whether each parent is willing to accept all the responsibilities of parenting, including a willingness to accept or relinquish care at specified times; (7) whether each parent is able to allow the other to provide care without intrusion; (8) the suitability of a parenting plan for the implementation of joint custody; and (9) whether any domestic abuse has occurred. [New Mexico Statutes Annotated; Chapter 40, Article 4, Sections 40-4-9 and 40-4-9.1].

CHILD SUPPORT: Either parent may be ordered to provide child support, based on a consideration of the financial resources of that parent. Any welfare benefits are not considered. Specific child support guidelines and worksheets are provided. Separate worksheets are provided for determining child support amounts for parents with visitation and for parents with shared responsibility. Shared responsibility or joint custody is defined as each parent having the child in their home at least 35% of the time during a year. Chid Support Guidelines are contained in New Mexico Statutes Annotated; Article 4, Section 40-4-11.1. These guidelines are presumed to be correct unless there is a showing that the amount of support would be unjust or inappropriate under the particular circumstances of a case, specifically: (1) any extraordinary uninsured medical, dental, or counseling expenses for the child of over $100.00 per year; (2) any extraordinary educational expenses for the child; and (3) any transportation and communication expenses for long-distance visitation or time-sharing. A substantial hardship for either parent or the child may also justify an adjustment of the amount of the child support payment. The assignment and withholding of wages to secure the payment of child support payments may be ordered. [New Mexico Statutes Annotated; Chapter 27 Article 2, Sections 27-2-27 and Chapter 40, Article 4, Sections 40-4-7, 40-4-11, and 40-4-11.1].

NEW YORK

STATE WEBSITE: http://www.assembly.state.ny.us

DOWNLOAD STATE FORMS: http://www.courts.state.ny.us/forms/index.shtml

FORMS PROVIDED ON CD: Verified Complaint with Children Under 21, Verified Complaint without Children Under 21, Net Worth Statement

FORMS AVAILABLE ONLINE: Verified Complaint with Children Under 21, Verified Complaint without Children Under 21, Net Worth Statement, Instructions, Parenting Plan

RESIDENCY REQUIREMENTS AND WHERE TO FILE: If only 1 spouse resides in New York at the time of filing the divorce, the residency requirement is 2 years. However, the requirement is reduced to 1 year if: (1) the spouses were married in New York and either spouse is still a resident; (2) they once resided in New York and either spouse is still a resident; or (3) the grounds for divorce arose in New York. In addition, there is no residency time limit requirement if both of the spouses were residents of New York at the time of filing the divorce and the grounds for divorce arose in New York. The divorce may be filed for in a county where either spouse resides. [Consolidated Laws of New York Annotated; Domestic Relations Law, Article 13, Sections 230 - 231 and New York Civil Practice Laws and Rules; Rule 503].

LEGAL GROUNDS FOR DIVORCE: No-Fault: (1) Living separate and apart for 1 year under the terms of a separation agreement which is in writing and signed and notarized [proof of compliance with the terms of the settlement agreement must be submitted when the divorce is filed. In addition, a copy of the agreement or a brief memorandum of the agreement must be filed in the office of the clerk of the county] or (2) living separate and apart for 1 year under the terms of a judicial separation decree. [Consolidated Laws of New York Annotated; Domestic Relations Law, Article 10, Section 170 and Article 13, Section 230].

General: (1) Adultery; (2) abandonment for 1 year; (3) imprisonment for 3 or more consecutive years; and (4) cruel and inhuman treatment. [Consolidated Laws of New York Annotated; Domestic Relations Law, Article 10, Section 170].

NAME OF COURT IN WHICH TO FILE FOR DIVORCE: Supreme Court. "Supreme Court of the State of New York, _____ County."

TITLE OF DIVORCE ACTION: Complaint for Divorce.

NAME USED TO DESCRIBE SPOUSE FILING FOR DIVORCE: Plaintiff.

NAME USED TO DESCRIBE OTHER SPOUSE IN DIVORCE: Defendant.

TITLE OF FINAL DIVORCE PAPERS: Judgment of Divorce.

LEGAL SEPARATION: The grounds for legal separation (separation from bed and board) in New York are: (1) adultery; (2) abandonment; (3) imprisonment for 3 or more consecutive years; (4) neglect of and failure to provide support for a wife; and (5) cruel and inhuman treatment. If only 1 spouse resides in New York at the time of filing the legal separation, the residency requirement is

2 years. However, the requirement is reduced to 1 year if: (1) the spouses were married in New York and either spouse is still a resident; (2) they once resided in New York and either spouse is still a resident; or (3) the grounds for legal separation arose in New York. In addition, there is no residency time limit requirement if both of the spouses were residents of New York at the time of filing the legal separation and the grounds for legal separation arose in New York. [Consolidated Laws of New York Annotated; Domestic Relations Law, Article 11, Section 200 and Article 13, Sections 230 - 231].

SIMPLIFIED OR SPECIAL DIVORCE PROCEDURES: A summary divorce may be granted in New York if: (1) the spouses lived apart for 1 year according to the terms of a separation decree or a separation agreement and (2) satisfactory proof is submitted to the court that the spouse seeking the divorce has substantially performed all the terms and conditions of the separation decree or separation agreement. There are sample divorce forms contained in the statute (Forms 1 and 12 for no-fault grounds), including the language necessary to state specific grounds and residency requirements. In addition, New York requires a financial disclosure to be filed in every divorce action. [Consolidated Laws of New York Annotated; Domestic Relations Law, Article 10, Section 170 and Article 13, Section 236].

MEDIATION OR COUNSELING REQUIREMENTS: There are no legal provisions in New York for divorce mediation.

PROPERTY DISTRIBUTION: New York is an "equitable distribution" state. Separate property, including property acquired before a marriage and any gifts or inheritances whenever acquired, is to remain with the spouse who owns it. Separate property also includes any increase in value or property acquired in exchange for separate property. Marital property acquired during the marriage will be equitably divided between the spouses, based on the following factors: (1) the contribution of each spouse to the acquisition of the marital property, including the contribution of each spouse as homemaker; (2) the income and value of each spouse's property at the time of the marriage and at the time of filing for divorce; (3) the probable future economic circumstances of each spouse; (4) the length of the marriage; (5) the age and health of the spouses; (6) the amount and sources of income of the spouses; (7) the probable future financial circumstances of each spouse; (8) the potential loss of inheritance or pension rights upon dissolution of the marriage; (9) whether the property award is instead of or in addition to maintenance; (10) custodial provisions for the children and the need for a custodial parent to occupy the marital home; (11) the type of marital property in question [whether it is liquid or non-liquid]; (12) the impossibility or difficulty of evaluating an interest in an asset such as a business, profession, or corporation and the desirability of keeping such an asset intact and free from interference by the other spouse; (13) the tax consequences to each party; (14) the wasteful dissipation of assets; (15) any transfer of property made in anticipation of divorce; (16) any equitable claim that a spouse has in marital property, including joint efforts and expenditures, and contribution and services as a spouse, parent, wage earner, and homemaker, and to the career and career potential of the other spouse; and (17) any other factor necessary to do equity and justice between the spouses. Marital fault may be considered. Financial disclosure of assets and income are mandatory. [Consolidated Laws of New York Annotated; Domestic Relations Law, Article 13, Section 236, Part B].

ALIMONY/MAINTENANCE/SPOUSAL SUPPORT: Either spouse may be awarded maintenance, without regard to marital fault, based on a consideration of the following factors: (1) the income and property of the spouses, including any marital property divided as a result of the dissolution of marriage; (2) any transfer of property made in anticipation of divorce; (3) the duration of the marriage;

(4) the wasteful dissipation of marital property; (5) the contribution of each spouse to the marriage and the career of the other spouse, including services rendered in homemaking, childcare, education, and career-building of the other spouse; (6) the tax consequences to each spouse; (7) any custodial and child support responsibilities; (8) the ability of the spouse seeking support to become self-supporting and the time and training necessary; (9) any reduced lifetime earning capacity as the result of having foregone or delayed education, training, employment, or career opportunities during the marriage; (10) whether the spouse from whom maintenance is sought has sufficient property and income to provide maintenance for the other spouse; (11) the age and health of both spouses; (12) the present and future earning capacities of both spouses; and (13) any other factor the court deems just and equitable. [Consolidated Laws of New York Annotated; Domestic Relations Law, Article 13, Section 236, Part B].

SPOUSE'S NAME: At the wife's request, upon divorce the court may restore her maiden or other former name. [Consolidated Laws of New York Annotated; Domestic Relations Law, Article 13, Section 240a].

CHILD CUSTODY: Joint or sole child custody is to be determined according to the best interests of the child. Neither parent is entitled to a preference. There are no factors specified in the statute. [Consolidated Laws of New York Annotated; Domestic Relations Law, Article 13, Section 240 and New York Case Law].

CHILD SUPPORT: Health insurance coverage may be ordered to be provided. Marital misconduct of either parent is not to be considered. There are specific Child Support Guidelines in the statute and which are presumed to be correct, unless there is a showing that the amount of support would be unjust or inappropriate. The factors to be considered are: (1) the financial resources of the child and the parents; (2) the standard of living the child would have enjoyed if the marriage had not been dissolved; (3) the physical and emotional health of the child and any special needs or aptitudes of the child; (4) the financial resources, needs, and obligations of both the noncustodial and the custodial parent; (5) the tax consequences to each parent; (6) the non-monetary contributions that the parents will make towards the care and well-being of the child; (7) the educational needs of either parent; (8) whether 1 parent's income is substantially less than the other parent's; (8) the needs of other children of the non-custodial parent; (9) if the child does not receive public aid, any extraordinary expenses required for the non-custodial parent to exercise visitation rights; and (10) any other relevant factors. Security may be required for the payments. [Consolidated Laws of New York Annotated; Domestic Relations Law, Article 13, Sections 236-Part B, 240, and 243 and New York Case Law].

NORTH CAROLINA

STATE WEBSITE: http://www.ncga.state.nc.us/Statutes/Statutes.aspl

DOWNLOAD STATE FORMS: http://www.rosen.com/ppf/ID/1/index.asp

FORMS PROVIDED ON CD: Complaint with Children, Complaint without Children, Domestic Civil Action Cover Sheet, Financial Affidavit for Cabarrus County, Financial Affidavit for Mecklenburg County

FORMS AVAILABLE ONLINE: Complaint with Children, Complaint without Children, Domestic Civil Action Cover Sheet, Financial Affidavit for Cabarrus County, Financial Affidavit for Mecklenburg County, Court Complaint for Custody, Support, Alimony, and Property Division

RESIDENCY REQUIREMENTS AND WHERE TO FILE: Either spouse must have been a resident of North Carolina for at least 6 months prior to filing for divorce. Divorce may be filed for in the county of residence of either spouse. [General Statutes of North Carolina; Chapter 50, Section 50-8].

LEGAL GROUNDS FOR DIVORCE: No-Fault: Living separate and apart without cohabitation for 1 year. [General Statutes of North Carolina; Chapter 50, Section 50-6].
General: (1) Confinement for incurable insanity for 3 years or (2) incurable mental illness based on examinations for 3 years. [General Statutes of North Carolina; Chapter 50, Sections 50-5.1].

NAME OF COURT IN WHICH TO FILE FOR DIVORCE: Superior Court or District Court. "In the General Court of Justice, _____ Division, North Carolina, _____ County."

TITLE OF DIVORCE ACTION: Complaint for Divorce.

NAME USED TO DESCRIBE SPOUSE FILING FOR DIVORCE: Plaintiff.

NAME USED TO DESCRIBE OTHER SPOUSE IN DIVORCE: Defendant.

TITLE OF FINAL DIVORCE PAPERS: Decree of Divorce.

LEGAL SEPARATION: The grounds for legal separation (divorce from bed and board) are as follows: (1) abandonment; (2) adultery; (3) alcoholism and/or drug addiction; (4) cruel and inhuman treatment endangering the life of the spouse; (5) personal indignities rendering life burdensome and intolerable; and (6) turning a spouse out-of-doors. Either spouse must have been a resident of North Carolina for at least 6 months prior to filing for divorce from bed and board. [General Statutes of North Carolina; Chapter 50, Sections 50-7 and 50-8].

SIMPLIFIED OR SPECIAL DIVORCE PROCEDURES: There are no legal provisions in North Carolina for simplified divorce procedures. However, premarital and marital property settlement agreements are specifically recognized as valid. The payment or non-payment of alimony may be the subject of a marital settlement agreement. [General Statutes of North Carolina; Chapter 50, Sections 50-16.6(6) and 50-20(d)].

MEDIATION OR COUNSELING REQUIREMENTS: If child custody is a contested issue, the court may order the parents to submit to mandatory mediation of that issue. [General Statutes of North Carolina; Chapter 50, Section 50-13.1].

PROPERTY DISTRIBUTION: North Carolina is an "equitable distribution" state. Separate property, including: (1) any property acquired before the marriage; (2) any gifts and inheritances acquired during the marriage; (3) any property acquired in exchange for separate property; and (4) any increase in the value of separate property, will be retained by the spouse who owns it. Marital property (property acquired by either or both spouses during the marriage and before the separation, including any pension or retirement fund benefits) will be divided equally unless the court finds that an equal division is not fair. The division is based on the following factors: (1) any direct or indirect contributions to the career or education of the other spouse; (2) any depletion or waste of property; (3) the net value of the property; (4) the liquid or non-liquid character of the property; (5) the contribution of each spouse to the acquisition of the marital property, including the contribution of each spouse as homemaker; (6) the economic circumstances of each spouse at the time the division of property is to become effective; (7) any increase or decrease in the value of the separate property of the spouse during the marriage or the depletion of the separate property for marital purposes; (8) the length of the marriage; (9) the age and health of the spouses; (10) the federal income tax consequences of the court's division of the property; (11) liabilities of the spouses; (12) any retirement benefits, including social security, civil service, military and railroad retirement benefits; (13) any prior alimony or child support obligations of each spouse; (14) the desirability of the spouse with custody of any children occupying the marital residence; and (15) any other factor necessary to do equity and justice between the spouses. [General Statutes of North Carolina; Chapter 50, Section 50-20].

ALIMONY/MAINTENANCE/SPOUSAL SUPPORT: Either spouse may be awarded alimony. The factors for consideration are: (1) the standard of living established during the marriage; (2) the comparative financial resources of the spouses, including their comparative earning abilities in the labor market and their incomes; (3) the mental, physical, and emotional conditions of the spouses; (4) the marital misconduct of the spouses; (5) the ages of the spouses; (6) the contribution of 1 spouse to the education, training, or earning power of the other spouse; (7) the effect of a spouse having primary custody of a child; (8) the relative education of the spouses and the time necessary for a spouse to acquire sufficient education or training to become self-sufficient; (9) the contribution of a spouse as a homemaker; (10) the tax consequences; and (11) any other factor the court deems just and equitable. The court may require bond for security for the alimony payments. Alimony may not be paid to the spouse committing adultery. [General Statutes of North Carolina; Chapter 50, Sections 50-16.3a and 50-16.6(b)].

SPOUSE'S NAME: Upon request, the court may allow a woman to resume the use of her former or maiden name. A woman may also make application to the clerk of the court for resumption of the use of her maiden or former name. [General Statutes of North Carolina; Chapter 50, Section 50-12].

CHILD CUSTODY: Joint or sole child custody is determined according to the interests and welfare of the child. There is no presumption that either parent is better suited to have custody. No other factors for consideration are specified in the statute. [General Statutes of North Carolina; Chapter 50, Section 50-13.2].

CHILD SUPPORT: Both parents are primarily responsible for the support of a minor child and either parent may be ordered to pay child support. The factors to be considered are: (1) the needs of the child; (2) the relative ability of the parents to provide support; (3) the childcare and homemaker contributions of each parent; (4) the assets of the child; and (5) any other relevant factors. A grandparent may be liable for child support if the parent is an unemancipated minor. There are official child support guidelines which are presumed to be correct, unless there is a showing that the amount of support would be unjust or inappropriate. Child support worksheets are also provided. Child support payments may be required to be paid through the clerk of the court. Income withholding may be used if child support payments become delinquent. Child support obligations may be required to be secured by a bond or mortgage. The court may require a parent to provide health insurance coverage for a child. [General Statutes of North Carolina; Chapter 50, Section 50-13.4. Child Support Guidelines and Worksheets are contained in the Annotated Rules of North Carolina].

NORTH DAKOTA

STATE WEBSITE: http://www.legis.nd.gov/

DOWNLOAD STATE FORMS: http://www.ndcourts.com/court/forms

FORMS PROVIDED ON CD: Divorce Complaint

FORMS AVAILABLE ONLINE: Divorce Complaint, Instructions, Property and Debt Listing

RESIDENCY REQUIREMENTS AND WHERE TO FILE: The spouse filing for divorce must be a resident of North Dakota for at least 6 months prior to the entry of the final divorce. If the defendant is a resident of North Dakota, the divorce must be filed in the county where the defendant resides. If the defendant is not a resident, the divorce may be filed for in any county that the plaintiff designates in the complaint. [North Dakota Century Code; Volume 3A, Chapters 14-05-17 and 28-04-05].

LEGAL GROUNDS FOR DIVORCE: No-Fault: Irreconcilable differences. [North Dakota Century Code; Volume 3A, Chapter 14-05-03].

General: (1) Adultery; (2) conviction of a felony; (4) willful desertion; (5) cruel and inhuman treatment; (6) willful neglect; and (7) Alcohol and/or drug abuse. [North Dakota Century Code; Volume 3A, Chapter 14-05-03].

NAME OF COURT IN WHICH TO FILE FOR DIVORCE: District Court. "State of North Dakota, County of _____, In the District Court, _____ Judicial District."

TITLE OF DIVORCE ACTION: Complaint for Divorce.

NAME USED TO DESCRIBE SPOUSE FILING FOR DIVORCE: Plaintiff.

NAME USED TO DESCRIBE OTHER SPOUSE IN DIVORCE: Defendant.

TITLE OF FINAL DIVORCE PAPERS: Decree of Divorce.

LEGAL SEPARATION: The grounds for legal separation (separation from bed and board) in North Dakota are: (1) irreconcilable differences; (2) adultery; (3) conviction of a felony; (4) willful desertion; (5) cruel and inhuman treatment; (6) willful neglect; and (7) drug and/or alcohol abuse. The spouse filing for legal separation must be a resident of North Dakota for at least 6 months prior to the entry of the legal separation. [North Dakota Century Code; Volume 3A, Chapters 14-05-03.1, 14-05-17, 14-06-01, 14-06-06].

SIMPLIFIED OR SPECIAL DIVORCE PROCEDURES: Separation agreements are specifically authorized by statute. [North Dakota Century Code; Volume 3A, Chapter 14-07-07].

MEDIATION OR COUNSELING REQUIREMENTS: In an action for divorce or legal separation where child support or child custody is an issue, the court may order the parents to submit to mediation, unless there has been physical or sexual abuse of a spouse or child. [North Dakota Century Code; Volume 3A, Chapter 14-09.1-02].

PROPERTY DISTRIBUTION: North Dakota is an "equitable distribution" state. All of the spouse's property, including gifts, inheritances, and any acquired prior to the marriage, will be equitably distributed as the court feels is just and proper. There are no factors for consideration specified in the statute. [North Dakota Century Code; Volume 3A, Chapter 14-05-24].

ALIMONY/MAINTENANCE/SPOUSAL SUPPORT: Either spouse may be required to make allowances for the support of the other spouse for his or her entire life or a shorter period. All of the circumstances of the situation, including any marital fault, may be considered. There are no other specific factors for consideration set out in the statute. [North Dakota Century Code; Volume 3A, Chapter 14-05-24.1].

SPOUSE'S NAME: Upon request, a wife's former or maiden name may be restored. [North Dakota Case Law].

CHILD CUSTODY: Child custody is awarded according to the best interests and welfare of the child, and based on the following factors: (1) moral fitness of the parents; (2) capability and desire of each parent to meet the child's needs including food, clothing, medical care, and other material needs; (3) preference of the child, if the child is of sufficient age and capacity; (4) the love and affection existing between the child and each parent; (5) the length of time the child has lived in a stable, satisfactory environment and the desirability of maintaining continuity; (6) the child's adjustment to his or her home, school, and community; (7) the mental and physical health of all individuals involved; (8) the stability of the home environment likely to be offered by each parent; (9) the child's interaction with anyone who resides with a parent, including such person's history of violence of any type; (10) any spouse or child abuse, sexual abuse, or history of domestic violence or violence of any type; (11) the capacity and disposition of the parents to give the child love, affection, guidance, and continue the child's education; (12) the permanence, as a family unit, of the proposed or existing custodial home; (13) the making of any false accusations by 1 parent against the other; and (14) any other factors. Any evidence of child or spouse abuse or domestic violence creates a presumption that custody or visitation with that parent would not be in the best interests of the child. If there is any evidence of sexual abuse of a child, the court is required to prohibit any visitation or contact with that parent unless the parent has completed counseling and the court determines that supervised visitation is in the best interests of the child. Both parents are considered to be equally entitled to custody of a child. [North Dakota Century Code; Volume 3A, Chapters 14-05-22, 14-09-06, 14-09-06.1, and 14-09-06.2].

CHILD SUPPORT: Either parent may be ordered to pay child support. The amount awarded will be based on a consideration of the following factors: (1) the net income of the parents; (2) the other resources available to the parents; and (3) any circumstances that might be considered in reducing the amount of support on the basis of hardship. There are specific child support guidelines that the court will consider which have been prepared by the North Dakota Department of Human Services. Child support payments are required to be paid through the state disbursement office. All child support orders will be reviewed every 3 years, unless neither parent requests such a review. [North Dakota Century Code; Volume 3A, Chapters 14-09-08, 14-09-08.1, 14-09-08.4, and 14-09-09.7].

OHIO

STATE WEBSITE: http://codes.ohio.gov/

DOWNLOAD STATE FORMS: None

FORMS PROVIDED ON CD: None

FORMS AVAILABLE ONLINE: State-wide forms not available. Check county websites for forms. For example; http://www.domesticcourt.org/default.asp?Section=5

RESIDENCY REQUIREMENTS AND WHERE TO FILE: The spouse filing for divorce or dissolution of marriage must have been a resident of Ohio for at least 6 months and a resident of the county for at least 90 days immediately prior to filing. [Ohio Revised Code Annotated; Title XXXI, Section 3105.03 and Ohio Rules of Civil Procedure; Rule 3].

LEGAL GROUNDS FOR DIVORCE/DISSOLUTION OF MARRIAGE: No-Fault (used for Dissolution of Marriage): (1) Incompatibility, unless denied by the other spouse or (2) living separate and apart without cohabitation and without interruption for 1 year. [Ohio Revised Code Annotated; Title XXXI, Section 3105.01]. General (used for Divorce): (1) Adultery; (2) imprisonment; (3) willful desertion for 1 year; (4) cruel and inhuman treatment; (5) bigamy; (6) habitual intemperance (drunkenness); (7) when a final divorce decree has been obtained outside of the state of Ohio that does not release the other spouse from the obligations of the marriage inside the state of Ohio; (8) fraud; and (9) neglect. [Ohio Revised Code Annotated; Title XXXI, Section 3105.01].

NAME OF COURT IN WHICH TO FILE FOR DIVORCE/DISSOLUTION OF MARRIAGE: Court of Common Pleas. "In the Court of Common Pleas of _____ County, Ohio."

TITLE OF DIVORCE/DISSOLUTION OF MARRIAGE ACTION: Petition for Dissolution of Marriage or Complaint for Divorce. See below under *Simplified Or Special Divorce/Dissolution Of Marriage Procedures.*

NAME USED TO DESCRIBE SPOUSE FILING FOR DIVORCE/DISSOLUTION OF MARRIAGE: Petitioner, if in Petition for Dissolution of Marriage or Plaintiff, if in Complaint for Divorce. See below under *Simplified Or Special Divorce/Dissolution Of Marriage Procedures.*

NAME USED TO DESCRIBE OTHER SPOUSE IN DIVORCE/DISSOLUTION OF MARRIAGE: Co-Petitioner, if in Petition for Dissolution of Marriage or Defendant, in Complaint for Divorce. See below under *Simplified Or Special Divorce/Dissolution Of Marriage Procedures.*

TITLE OF FINAL DIVORCE/DISSOLUTION OF MARRIAGE PAPERS: Decree of Dissolution of Marriage or Decree of Divorce. See below under *Simplified Or Special Divorce/Dissolution Of Marriage Procedures.*

LEGAL SEPARATION: Legal separation may be sought for the following grounds: (1) adultery; (2) imprisonment; (3) willful desertion for 1 year; (4) cruel and inhuman treatment; (5) bigamy; (6) habitual intemperance (drunkenness); (7) when a final divorce decree has been obtained outside of the state of Ohio that does not release the other spouse from the obligations of the marriage inside the state of Ohio; (8) fraud; (9) neglect; (10) incompatibility; or (11) living separate and apart without cohabitation and without interruption for 1 year. [Ohio Revised Code Annotated; Title XXXI, Sections 3105.01 and 3105.17].

SIMPLIFIED OR SPECIAL DIVORCE/DISSOLUTION OF MARRIAGE PROCEDURES: Both spouses may jointly file a petition for dissolution of marriage. The petition must: (1) be signed by both spouses and (2) have attached to it a separation agreement which provides for: [a] division of property; [b] spousal support (including, if the spouses desire, the authorization of the court to modify any spousal support terms); and [c] custody, visitation, and child support, if there are any minor children. The spouses may include a parenting plan in the agreement. Between 30 and 90 days after filing such a petition, both spouses must appear in court and state under oath that he or she: (1) voluntarily signed the agreement; (2) is satisfied with the agreement; and (3) seeks dissolution of the marriage. In addition, settlement agreements are also authorized by statute and may be used in a divorce proceeding. A sample divorce complaint form is contained in Ohio Rules of Civil Procedure, Appendix of Forms, Form #20. In addition, separation agreements are specifically authorized. Finally, there may be local court rules which apply to divorce proceedings in Ohio. [Ohio Revised Code Annotated; Title XXXI, Sections 3105.03, 3105.10, and 3105.61-65 and Ohio Rules of Civil Procedure; Appendix of Forms].

MEDIATION OR COUNSELING REQUIREMENTS: At the request of either spouse or on the court's own initiative, the court may order the spouses to undergo conciliation procedures for up to 90 days. The court will set forth the procedures and name the conciliator. In addition, the court may order that parents attend mediation sessions on issues of child custody and visitation matters. [Ohio Revised Code Annotated; Title XXXI, Sections 3105.091 and 3117.01+].

PROPERTY DISTRIBUTION: Ohio is an "equitable division" state. Each spouse retains her or his separate property, including gifts, inheritances, property acquired prior to the marriage, income, or appreciation of separate property, and individual personal injury awards. An equitable division of all of the spouse's marital property acquired during the marriage, is allowed based on the following factors: (1) the desirability of awarding the family home, or right to reside in it, to the spouse with custody of the children; (2) the liquidity of the property to be distributed; (3) the financial resources of both spouses; (4) the needs and obligations of each spouse; (5) the economic desirability of retaining an asset intact; (6) the tax consequences of the division; (7) the duration of the marriage; (8 the costs of any sale of an asset, if a sale is necessary for division purposes; (9) any property division under a valid separation agreement; and (10) any other relevant factor. The division of the marital property will be equal, unless such a division would be inequitable. Marital fault is not a consideration. The amount of any spousal support award is not to be considered in the division of property. [Ohio Revised Code Annotated; Title XXXI, Section 3105.171].

ALIMONY/MAINTENANCE/SPOUSAL SUPPORT: Either spouse may be awarded reasonable spousal support, in lump sum or in periodic payments, based on a consideration of the following factors: (1) whether the spouse seeking support is the custodian of a child whose condition or circumstances make it appropriate for that spouse not to seek outside employment; (2) the earning ability of both spouses; (3) the income of both spouses, including marital property apportioned to each spouse and each spouse's ability to meet his or her needs independently; (4) the contribution of each spouse to the education, earning ability, and career-building of the other spouse, including the spouse's contribution to the earning of a professional degree by the other spouse; (5) the age of the spouses; (6) the physical, mental, and emotional conditions of the spouses; (7) the relative assets and liabilities of the spouses, including any court-ordered payments; (8) the educational level of each spouse at the time of the marriage and at the time the action for support is commenced; (9) the standard of living during the marriage; (10) any pension or retirement benefits of either spouse; (11) the duration of the marriage; (12) the tax consequences of the award; (13) the time and expense necessary for the spouse seeking support to acquire education, training, or job experience to obtain appropriate employment; (14) the lost income-producing capacity of either spouse resulting from marital responsibilities; and (15) any other relevant factor. Marital fault is not a consideration. The court may require a spouse to provide health insurance coverage for the other spouse. [Ohio Revised Code Annotated; Title XXXI, Sections 3105.18, 3105.71, and 3105.171].

SPOUSE'S NAME: Upon request, the court will restore a person's former or maiden name. [Ohio Revised Code Annotated; Title XXXI, Sections 3105.16 and 3105.34].

CHILD CUSTODY: Shared parenting or sole child custody may be awarded according to the best interests of the child. Factors to be considered are: (1) the preference of the child, if the child is of sufficient age and capacity; (2) the child's adjustment to his or her home, school, and community; (3) the mental and physical health of all individuals involved; (4) the relationship of the child with parents, siblings, and other significant family members; (5) whether 1 parent has willfully denied visitation to the other parent; (6) whether either parent has failed to make child support payments to any child; (7) whether either parent lives or intends to live outside of Ohio; (8) the ability of the parents to cooperate and make joint decisions; (9) the ability of each parent to encourage the sharing of love, affection, and contact between the child and the other parent; (10) any history of child abuse, spouse abuse, or domestic violence by a parent or anyone who is or will be a member of the household where the child will reside, or parental kidnapping; (11) the geographic proximity of the parents to each other as it relates to shared parenting; (12) the child's and parent's available time; (13) the recommendation of any *guardian ad litem* (court-appointed guardian) of the child; and (14) any other relevant factors. Both parents are considered to have equal rights to custody. In addition, for shared parenting to be awarded, both parents must request it and submit a plan for shared parenting. The financial status of a parent is not to be considered for allocating any parental rights and responsibilities. The court may require an investigation of the parents and any evidence of neglect or child or spousal abuse will be considered against the granting of shared parenting or such parent being granted the status as residential parent. [Ohio Revised Code Annotated; Title XXXI, Sections 3105.21, 3109.03, 3109.04, and 3109.051].

CHILD SUPPORT: Either or both parents may be ordered to pay child support. Marital misconduct is not to be considered in this award. Health care insurance may be ordered to be provided for the child. Child support payments may be ordered to be paid through the state child support agency. There are official child support guidelines that are presumed to be correct unless there is a showing that the amount of the support award would be unjust or inappropriate under the particular circumstances of a case. Factors which may be considered in adjusting a child support amount are: (1) special or unusual needs of a child; (2) obligations for other minor or handicapped children; (3) other court-ordered payments; (4) extended visitation or extraordinary costs for visitation; (5) mandatory wage deductions [including union dues]; (6) disparity in income between the parents' households; (7) benefits that either parent receives from remarriage or sharing living expenses with others; (8) the amount of taxes paid by a parent; (9) significant contributions from a parent [including lessons, sports equipment, or clothing]; (10) the financial resources and earning capacity of the child; (11) the standard of living and circumstances of each parent and the standard of living the child would have enjoyed if the marriage had not been dissolved; (12) the physical and emotional conditions and needs of the child; (13) the medical and educational needs of the child; (14) the relative financial resources, other assets and resources, needs, and obligations of both the noncustodial and the custodial parent; (15) the need and capacity of the child for an education and the educational opportunities of the child; (16) the age of the child; (17) the earning ability of each parent; (18) the responsibility of each parent for the support of others; (19) the value of services contributed by the custodial parent; and (20) any other relevant factor. A child support computation worksheet is also contained in the statute. [Ohio Revised Code Annotated; Title XXXI, Sections 3105, 3105.71 and 3119.01 to 3119.76].

OKLAHOMA

STATE WEBSITE: http://www.lsb.state.ok.us/

DOWNLOAD STATE FORMS: http://www.oscn.net/static/forms/start.asp

FORMS PROVIDED ON CD: Domestic Relations Cover Sheet, Financial Affidavit

FORMS AVAILABLE ONLINE: Domestic Relations Cover Sheet, Financial Affidavit

RESIDENCY REQUIREMENTS AND WHERE TO FILE: Either spouse must have been a resident of Oklahoma for 6 months immediately prior to filing for divorce. The divorce may be filed for in the county in which the plaintiff has been a resident for 30 days or in the county where the defendant resides. [Oklahoma Statutes Annotated; Title 43, Sections 102 and 103].

LEGAL GROUNDS FOR DIVORCE: No-Fault: Incompatibility. [Oklahoma Statutes Annotated; Title 43, Section 101].

General: (1) Impotence; (2) adultery; (3) abandonment for 1 year; (4) imprisonment; (5) confinement for incurable insanity for 5 years; (6) cruel and inhuman treatment; (7) fraud; (8) habitual intemperance (drunkenness); (9) the wife pregnant by another at the time of the marriage; (10) gross neglect; and (11) a foreign divorce which is not valid in Oklahoma. [Oklahoma Statutes Annotated; Title 43, Section 101].

NAME OF COURT IN WHICH TO FILE FOR DIVORCE: District Court. "State of Oklahoma, In the District Court, _____ County."

TITLE OF DIVORCE ACTION: Petition for Divorce.

NAME USED TO DESCRIBE SPOUSE FILING FOR DIVORCE: Petitioner.

NAME USED TO DESCRIBE OTHER SPOUSE IN DIVORCE: Respondent.

TITLE OF FINAL DIVORCE PAPERS: Decree of Divorce.

LEGAL SEPARATION: A spouse may sue the other spouse for separate maintenance without filing for divorce. The action may be brought in any county where either spouse resides. The grounds for requesting non-divorce-based alimony are: (1) impotence; (2) adultery; (3) abandonment for 1 year; (4) imprisonment; (5) confinement for incurable insanity for 5 years; (6) cruel and inhuman treatment; (7) fraud; (8) habitual intemperance (drunkenness); (9) the wife pregnant by another at the time of the marriage; (10) gross neglect; and (11) incompatibility. [Oklahoma Statutes Annotated; Title 43, Sections 101, 103 and 129].

SIMPLIFIED OR SPECIAL DIVORCE PROCEDURES: Separation agreements are specifically authorized by statute. [Oklahoma Statutes Annotated; Title 43, Section 205].

MEDIATION OR COUNSELING REQUIREMENTS: The court may appoint an arbitrator for joint custody disputes which take place after a divorce. [Oklahoma Statutes Annotated; Title 43, Section 109].

PROPERTY DISTRIBUTION: Oklahoma is an "equitable distribution" state. Each spouse is entitled to keep: (1) the property owned by him or her before the marriage and (2) any gifts or inheritances acquired during the marriage. All property held or acquired jointly during the marriage will be divided between the spouses in a just and reasonable manner. A portion of the jointly-held property may be set aside to 1 spouse for the support of any children who may live with that spouse. The only factors for consideration set out in the statute are: (1) the way in which the property in question was held and (2) the time and manner of the acquisition of the property. An automatic injunction against disposing or damaging of property or altering any insurance policy goes into effect at the time of the first court hearing. Marital fault is not a factor. [Oklahoma Statutes Annotated; Title 43, Sections 110 and 121].

ALIMONY/MAINTENANCE/SPOUSAL SUPPORT: Alimony may be awarded to either spouse. The award may be in money or property, in lump sum or installments, having regard for the value of the property at the time of the award. Marital fault is not a consideration. There are no other factors for consideration set out in the statute. Alimony payments may be required to be paid through the clerk of the court. [Oklahoma Statutes Annotated; Title 43, Sections 121 and 136].

SPOUSE'S NAME: Upon request, a wife may have her former or maiden name restored upon divorce. [Oklahoma Statutes Annotated; Title 43, Section 121].

CHILD CUSTODY: Joint or sole child custody may be awarded based on the best interests of the child and upon a consideration of the preference of the child, if the child is of sufficient age to form an intelligent preference. When it is in the best interests of the child, the court shall assure that children have frequent and continuing contact with both parents and encourage the parents to share the rights and responsibilities of child-rearing. However, there is neither a preference for or against joint or sole custody. In determining custody, the court shall consider which parent is likely to allow frequent contact with the other parent. There is no preference either for or against private, public, or home schooling of children. The sex of the parent is not to be taken into consideration. Failure to allow visitation may be considered against the best interests of the child. The court may require that the parents submit a joint custody plan to the court if joint custody is desired. [Oklahoma Statutes Annotated; Title 43, Sections 109 and 112].

CHILD SUPPORT: The parent awarded custody of the child must provide for the education and support of the child to the best of his or her ability. If such support is inadequate, the non-custodial parent must assist in the support to the best of his or her ability. A portion of the non-custodial parent's property may be set aside for the custodial parent's use in supporting the child. The only factors for consideration set out in the statute are: (1) the income and means of the parents and (2) the property and assets of the parents. There are official child support guidelines and compilation forms in the statute and forms are provided by the Oklahoma Department of Human Services and are available from any court clerk. The amount of support as shown by the guidelines is presumed to be correct unless it is shown to be unjust, unreasonable, inappropriate, or inequitable under the particular circumstances of a case. Child support computation forms are available from the clerk of the court. Child support payments may be required to be paid through the clerk of the court. Security or bond may be required for the payments and income withholding may be used to guarantee the payments. [Oklahoma Statutes Annotated; Title 43, Sections 110, 112, 118, 119, 121, and 136 and Title 56, Sections 235+].

OREGON

STATE WEBSITE: http://www.leg.state.or.us/billsset.htm

DOWNLOAD STATE FORMS: http://www.ojd.state.or.us/osca/cpsd/courtimprovement/familylaw/index.htm

FORMS PROVIDED ON CD: Petition for Summary Dissolution, Petition for Dissolution with Children, Petition for Dissolution without Children

FORMS AVAILABLE ONLINE: Petition for Summary Dissolution, Petition for Dissolution with Children, Petition for Dissolution without Children, Instructions, Certificate re: Pending Child Support Proceedings and/or Existing Child Support Orders/ Judgments

RESIDENCY REQUIREMENTS AND WHERE TO FILE: If the marriage was not performed in Oregon, 1 of the spouses must have been a resident of Oregon for 6 months immediately prior to filing. If the marriage was performed in Oregon and either of the spouses is a resident at the time of filing, there is no durational residency requirement. The dissolution of marriage may be filed in a county where either spouse resides. There is a 90-day waiting period before a hearing will be scheduled which begins after the respondent has been served with papers or the publication of the summons. An affidavit signed by both parties will wave the waiting period. [Oregon Revised Statutes; Volume 3, Sections 107.065, and 107.075].

LEGAL GROUNDS FOR DISSOLUTION OF MARRIAGE: No-Fault: Irreconcilable differences between the spouses which have caused the irremediable breakdown of the marriage. Misconduct of the spouses will only be considered when child custody is an issue or if necessary to prove irreconcilable differences. [Oregon Revised Statutes; Volume 3, Sections 107.025 and 107.036].

General: (1) Consent to marriage was obtained by fraud, duress, or force; (2) minor married without lawful consent; and (3) spouse lacked mental capacity to consent [including temporary incapacity resulting from drug or alcohol use]. Misconduct of the spouses will only be considered when child custody is an issue. [Oregon Revised Statutes; Volume 3, Section 107.015].

NAME OF COURT IN WHICH TO FILE FOR DIVORCE: Circuit Court. "In the Circuit Court for the State of Oregon for the County of _____."

TITLE OF DIVORCE ACTION: Petition for Dissolution of Marriage. "In the Matter of the Marriage of _____ and _____."

NAME USED TO DESCRIBE SPOUSE FILING FOR DISSOLUTION OF MARRIAGE: Petitioner (or Co-Petitioner if the petition is filed jointly). See below under *Simplified Or Special Dissolution Of Marriage Procedures.*

NAME USED TO DESCRIBE OTHER SPOUSE IN DISSOLUTION OF MARRIAGE: Respondent (or Co-Petitioner if the petition is filed jointly). See below under *Simplified Or Special Dissolution Of Marriage Procedures.*

TITLE OF FINAL DISSOLUTION OF MARRIAGE PAPERS: Decree of Dissolution of Marriage.

The No-Fault Divorce Toolkit

LEGAL SEPARATION: The grounds for legal separation (separation from bed and board) in Oregon are irreconcilable differences between the spouses which have caused the irretrievable breakdown of the marriage. The spouses may enter a separation agreement to live apart for at least 1 year. At least 1 of the spouses must be a resident of Oregon when the action for legal separation is filed. The legal separation may be filed for in a county where either spouse lives. [Oregon Revised Statutes; Volume 3, Sections 107.025, 107.075, 107.455, and 107.475].

SIMPLIFIED OR SPECIAL DISSOLUTION OF MARRIAGE PROCEDURES: The spouses may qualify for a summary dissolution of marriage procedure if the following qualifications are met: (1) the residency requirements are fulfilled; (2) There are no minor children, born or adopted, and the wife is not pregnant; (3) the marriage is not over 10 years in length; (4) neither spouse owns any real estate; (5) there are no unpaid debts in excess of $15,000 incurred by either or both spouses during the marriage; (6) the total value of all of the spouse's personal property is less than $30,000, excluding any unpaid balances on loans; (7) the petitioner waives the right to spousal support [alimony]; and (8) the petitioner waives the right to any *pendente lite* (preliminary) orders, except for the prevention of spouse abuse [temporary court orders pending the final divorce]. There are specific mandatory forms for filing for summary dissolution of marriage that are available from the clerk of the court in each circuit. Separation agreements are also expressly authorized. In addition, in all other cases, the spouses can jointly file for a dissolution of marriage. [Oregon Revised Statutes; Volume 3, Sections 107.055, 107.065, 107.085, 107.105, and 107.485+].

MEDIATION OR COUNSELING REQUIREMENTS: Either spouse or the court may delay the dissolution of marriage proceedings for 45 days while a reconciliation or settlement is attempted. In addition, if child custody or child support issues are contested, the court will refer the parents to mediation for up to 90 days. [Oregon Revised Statutes; Volume 3, Sections 107.179, 107.540, and 107.550].

PROPERTY DISTRIBUTION: Oregon is an "equitable distribution" state. All of the spouses' property is subject to division by the court, including any gifts, inheritances, and property acquired prior to the marriage. Regardless of whether the property is held jointly or individually, there is a presumption that the spouses contributed equally to the acquisition of any property, unless shown otherwise. All property will be divided, without regard to any fault of the spouses, based on the following factors: (1) the cost of any sale of assets; (2) the amount of taxes and liens on the property; (3) the contribution of each spouse to the acquisition of the marital property, including the contribution of each spouse as homemaker; (4) any retirement benefits, including social security, civil service, military and railroad retirement benefits; (5) any life insurance coverage; and (6) whether the property award is instead of or in addition to spousal support. [Oregon Revised Statutes; Volume 3, Sections 107.036 and 107.105].

ALIMONY/MAINTENANCE/SPOUSAL SUPPORT: Either spouse may be ordered to pay spousal support to the other spouse, without regard to marital fault. Oregon recognizes three separate types of spousal support: (1) transitional support: as needed for a spouse to gain the education or training to reenter the job market or advance his or her job skills; (2) compensatory support: as needed to compensate a spouse who has provided significant financial or other support to the education, career, or earning capacity of the other spouse; and (3) standard support: the amount needed for one spouse to support the other for a specific or continuing period of time. Each type of support has different factors that are to be considered. The factors for consideration are: (1) transitional support factors: (a) the duration of the marriage; (b) a spouse's training and employment skills; (c) a spouse's work experience; (d) the financial needs and resources of each spouse; (e) the tax consequences to each spouse; and (f) any other factors the court feels are just and equitable. The factors for (2) compensatory support are: (a) the duration of the marriage; (b) the amount, duration, and nature of the spouse's contribution, (c) the relative earning capacities of the spouses; (d) the extent to which the marriage assets have benefitted from the contribution; (e) the tax consequences to each spouse; and (f) any other factors the court feels are just and equitable. For (3) standard support, the factors are: (a) the duration of the marriage; (b) the age of the spouses; (c) the health of the spouses, including their physical, mental, and emotional condition; (d) the standard of living established during the marriage: (e) the relative income and earning capacity of the spouses, recognizing the wage earner's income may be a basis for support apart from the income that the supported spouse may receive from the marital property distribution (f) a spouse's training and employment skills; (g) a spouse's work experience; (h) the financial needs and resources of each spouse; (i) the tax consequences to each spouse; (j) a spouse's child custody and support responsibilities; and (k) any other factors the court feels are just and equitable. The court may order the spouse to pay the support to carry life insurance with the other spouse as beneficiary. In addition, a spouse may have a right to continued health insurance coverage under the other spouse's policy. [Oregon Revised Statutes; Volume 3, Sections 107.036, 107.105, 107.412, and Volume 16, 743.600].

SPOUSE'S NAME: The spouses may resume the use of their prior names after a dissolution of marriage. [Oregon Revised Statutes; Volume 3, Section 107.105].

CHILD CUSTODY: Joint custody, joint responsibility for the child, and extensive contact between the child and both parents is encouraged. Parents must provide a parenting plan. Joint or sole custody is determined based on the best interests of the child and the following factors: (1) the love and affection existing between the child and other family members; (2) the attitude of the child; (3) the desirability of maintaining continuity; (4) any spouse abuse; (5) the relationship of the child with parents, siblings, and other significant family members; and (6) the parent's interests and attitudes towards the child. The conduct, income, social environment, and lifestyle of the proposed guardian is to be considered only if it is shown to cause emotional or physical damage to the child. No preference is to be given because of parent's sex. Final judgement must include insurance health benefits and mandatory statement. The court will not order joint custody unless both parents agree to the terms of the custody. [Oregon Revised Statutes; Volume 3, Sections 107.102, 107.105, 107.106, 107.137, and 107.169.]

CHILD SUPPORT: Either parent may be ordered to pay child support, based on the following factors: (1) the ability of each parent to borrow; (2) the parent's earnings history; (3) the reasonable necessities of each parent; (4) the physical, emotional, and educational needs of the child; (5) the relative financial means of the parents, including their income, resources, and property; (6) the potential earnings of the parents; (7) the needs of any other dependents of a parent; (8) any social security or veteran's benefits paid to the child; and (9) any other relevant factors. There are official child support scales and formulas available. The child support payments may be required to be paid through the clerk of the court. There may be court orders issued to withhold wages to pay for the child support. Every child support award must also contain provisions for the payment of any uninsured medical care for the child and the payment of health insurance for the child. The court may also order the parent required to pay support to maintain life insurance coverage with the child as beneficiary. [Oregon Revised Statutes; Volume 1, Sections 25.275 and Volume 3, 107.105, 107.106, and 107.820].

PENNSYLVANIA

STATE WEBSITE: http://members.aol.com/StatutesPA/Index.html

DOWNLOAD STATE FORMS: None

FORMS PROVIDED ON CD: None

FORMS AVAILABLE ONLINE: State-wide forms not available. Check county websites for forms. For example; http://www.alleghenycourts.us/family/adult/court_manual.asp.

RESIDENCY REQUIREMENTS AND WHERE TO FILE: Either spouse must have been a resident of Pennsylvania for at least 6 months before filing. The divorce may be filed for in a county where: (1) the defendant resides; (2) the plaintiff resides, if the defendant does not live in Pennsylvania; (3) the marriage home was, if the plaintiff continuously resided in the same county; (4) prior to 6 months after separation, and if the defendant agrees, the plaintiff resides; (5) prior to 6 months after separation, and if neither spouse lives in the county of the marriage home, either spouse lives; and (6) after 6 months after separation, either spouse lives. [Pennsylvania Consolidated Statutes Annotated; Title 23, Section 3104].

LEGAL GROUNDS FOR DIVORCE: No-Fault: (1) Irretrievable breakdown of the marriage with the spouses living separate and apart without cohabitation for 2 years or (2) irretrievable breakdown of the marriage and the spouses have both filed affidavits that they consent to the divorce. In the case of no-fault ground (1) the court may delay the case for 90 to 120 days if it appears that there is a reasonable chance for reconciliation. In the case of no-fault ground (2), 90 days must elapse after the filing for divorce before the court will grant a divorce. [Pennsylvania Consolidated Statutes Annotated; Title 23, Section 3301].

General: (1) Adultery; (2) bigamy; (3) imprisonment for 2 or more years; (4) confinement for incurable insanity for 18 months; (5) willful desertion for 1 year; (6) cruel and inhuman treatment endangering the life of the spouse; and (7) personal indignities. [Pennsylvania Consolidated Statutes Annotated; Title 23, Section 3301 and Pennsylvania Case Law].

NAME OF COURT IN WHICH TO FILE FOR DIVORCE: Court of Common Pleas. "Court of Common Pleas, _____ County, Pennsylvania."

TITLE OF DIVORCE ACTION: Complaint for Divorce.

NAME USED TO DESCRIBE SPOUSE FILING FOR DIVORCE: Plaintiff.

NAME USED TO DESCRIBE OTHER SPOUSE IN DIVORCE: Defendant.

TITLE OF FINAL DIVORCE PAPERS: Decree of Divorce.

LEGAL SEPARATION: The spouses may enter into a binding separation agreement if it is made on reasonable terms. There is no residency requirement specified by statute. [Pennsylvania Consolidated Statutes Annotated; Title 23, Section 3301].

SIMPLIFIED OR SPECIAL DIVORCE PROCEDURES: The spouses may file for divorce on the grounds of irretrievable breakdown of the marriage and if both spouses consent to the divorce, it will be handled in an expedited manner. There are official sample forms for filing a complaint for divorce on the grounds of irretrievable breakdown of the marriage. There are also official forms available for filing the required affidavit of consent. There are also other sample divorce proceeding forms available in Pennsylvania Rules of Civil Procedure, Actions of Divorce of Annulment Section, Rule 1920.1+. In addition, separation agreements are expressly authorized. [Pennsylvania Consolidated Statutes Annotated; Title 23, Section 3301 and Pennsylvania Rules of Civil Procedure; Rules 1920.1+].

MEDIATION OR COUNSELING REQUIREMENTS: If the court determines that there is a reasonable prospect for reconciliation, it may order the spouses to seek counseling for a period of between 90 and 120 days. Upon the request of 1 of the spouses, 3 counseling sessions may be required. If no reconciliation is reached and 1 of the spouses states that the marriage is irretrievably broken, a divorce may be granted. Counseling sessions may also be ordered by the court in conjunction with child custody and are mandatory if a parent has been convicted of a violent or abusive crime. [Pennsylvania Consolidated Statutes Annotated; Title 23, Sections 3302 and 5303].

PROPERTY DISTRIBUTION: Pennsylvania is an "equitable distribution" state. Separate property that is: (1) acquired prior to the marriage; (2) acquired in exchange for any separate property; (3) any gifts and inheritances; and (4) any property designated as separate in a valid agreement between the spouses, will be retained by the spouse owning it. All other marital property will be divided equitably, without regard to any marital misconduct, based on the following factors: (1) the contribution or dissipation of each spouse to the acquisition, preservation, depreciation, or appreciation of the marital property, including the contribution of each spouse as homemaker; (2) the age and health of the spouses; (3) the vocational skills of the spouses; (4) the value of each spouse's property; (5) the economic circumstances of each spouse at the time the division of property is to become effective; (6) the length of the marriage; (7) the tax consequences to each spouse; (8) the occupation of the spouses; (9) the amount and sources of income of the spouses, including retirement and any other benefits; (10) the vocational skills of the spouses; (11) the employability of the spouses; (12) the liabilities and needs of each spouse and the opportunity of each for further acquisition of capital assets and income; (13) the standard of living established during the marriage; (14) whether a spouse will have custody of any minor children; (15) any contributions toward the education, training, or increased earning power of the other spouse; (16) any prior marital obligations; and (17) any other factor necessary to do equity and justice between the spouses. The court may require a spouse to purchase or maintain life insurance and name the other spouse as beneficiary. Both spouses will be required to submit an inventory and appraisal of their property. [Pennsylvania Consolidated Statutes Annotated; Title 23, Sections 3501, 3502, and 3505].

ALIMONY/MAINTENANCE/SPOUSAL SUPPORT: Alimony may be awarded to either spouse if necessary. In determining the alimony award, the following factors are considered: (1) whether the spouse seeking alimony lacks sufficient property to provide for his or her own needs; (2) whether the spouse is unable to be self-supporting through appropriate employment; (3) whether the spouse seeking alimony is the custodian of a child; (4) the time necessary to acquire sufficient education and training to enable the spouse to find appropriate employment and that spouse's future earning capacity; (5) any tax consequences; (6) the standard of living established during the marriage; (7) the duration of the marriage; (8) the financial resources of the spouse seeking alimony, including marital property apportioned to such spouse and such spouse's separate property; (9) the comparative financial resources of the spouses; (10) the needs and obligations of each spouse; (11) the contribution of each spouse to the marriage, including services rendered in homemaking; (12) the age of the spouses; (13) the physical, mental, and emotional conditions of the spouses; (14) the probable duration of the need of the spouse seeking support and alimony; (15) the educational level of each spouse at the time of the marriage and the time necessary for the spouse to acquire sufficient education to find appropriate employment; (16) the contribution by 1 spouse to the education, training, or increased earning power of the other; (17) the spouse's sources of income, including medical, insurance, retirement benefits, inheritances, assets, and liabilities, and any property brought into the marriage by either spouse; (18) any marital misconduct; and (19) any other factor the court deems just and equitable. There are official spousal support guidelines now in use in Pennsylvania and these are presumed to be correct unless there is a showing that the amount would be unjust or inappropriate under the particular circumstances of a case. Alimony payments may be ordered to be paid through the Domestic Relations Section of the court. [Pennsylvania Consolidated Statutes Annotated; Title 23, Sections 3701, 3702, 3704, and 3706].

SPOUSE'S NAME: Any person may resume the use of his or her former or maiden name upon divorce. A written notice to that effect must be filed in the office of the clerk of the court where the divorce was entered. [Pennsylvania Consolidated Statutes Annotated; Title 54, Section 704].

CHILD CUSTODY: Joint (shared) or sole custody may be awarded based on the best interests of the child and upon a consideration of the following factors: (1) which parent is more likely to encourage, permit, and allow frequent and continuing contact, including physical access between the other parent and the child; (2) whether either parent has engaged in any violent, criminally sexual, abusive, or harassing behavior; (3) the preference of the child; and (4) any factor that affects the child's physical, intellectual, or emotional well-being. Both parents may be required to attend counseling sessions regarding child custody. The recommendations of the counselor may be used in determining child custody. In shared custody situations, the court may also require the parents to submit a written plan for child custody to the court. [Pennsylvania Consolidated Statutes Annotated, Title 23, Sections 5302, 5303, 5304, and 5305].

CHILD SUPPORT: Either or both parents may be ordered to provide child support according to their ability to pay. The factors for consideration set out by statute are: (1) the net income of the parents; (2) the earning capacity of the parents; (3) the assets of the parents; (4) any unusual needs of the child or the parents; and (5) any extraordinary expenses. Child support payments may be ordered to be paid through the Domestic Relations Section of the court. There are official child support guidelines available and these are presumed to be correct unless there is a showing that the amount would be unjust or inappropriate under the particular circumstances of a case. The court may require that health insurance coverage be provided for any child if it is available at a reasonable cost. Child support payments may be ordered to be paid through the Domestic Relations Section of the court. [Pennsylvania Consolidated Statutes Annotated; Title 23, Section 4322 and Pennsylvania Case Law].

RHODE ISLAND

STATE WEBSITE: http://www.rilin.state.ri.us/Statutes/Statutes.html

DOWNLOAD STATE FORMS: http://www.courts.state.ri.us/family/forms.htm

FORMS PROVIDED ON CD: Complaint for Divorce

FORMS AVAILABLE ONLINE: Mediation Eligibility, Confidential Mediation Statement

RESIDENCY REQUIREMENTS AND WHERE TO FILE: Either spouse must have been a resident of Rhode Island for 1 year prior to filing for divorce. The divorce may be filed for in the county of residence of the plaintiff, unless the 1-year residency requirement has been satisfied by the defendant's residence. In such case, the divorce must be filed for in the county of the defendant's residence. [General Laws of Rhode Island; Title 15, Chapter 15-5-12].

LEGAL GROUNDS FOR DIVORCE: No-Fault: (1) Irreconcilable differences which have caused the irremediable breakdown of the marriage or (2) living separate and apart without cohabitation for 3 years. [General Laws of Rhode Island; Title 15, Chapters 15-5-3, 15-5-3.1, and 15-5-5].

General: (1) Impotence; (2) adultery; (3) abandonment and presumed dead; (4) alcoholism and/or drug addiction; (5) willful desertion for 5 years [or less within the discretion of the court]; (6) cruel and inhuman treatment; (7) bigamy; and (8) gross neglect. [General Laws of Rhode Island; Title 15, Chapter 15-5-2].

NAME OF COURT IN WHICH TO FILE FOR DIVORCE: Family Court. "State of Rhode Island, Family Court, _____ Division."

TITLE OF DIVORCE ACTION: Complaint for Divorce. [Rhode Island Rules of Procedure for Domestic Relations; Rule 7].

NAME USED TO DESCRIBE SPOUSE FILING FOR DIVORCE: Plaintiff.

NAME USED TO DESCRIBE OTHER SPOUSE IN DIVORCE: Defendant.

TITLE OF FINAL DIVORCE PAPERS: Final Judgment of Divorce.

LEGAL SEPARATION: Legal separation (or divorce from bed and board) may be granted for the same grounds as that required for a divorce. The spouse seeking legal separation must have been a resident for a period of time that the court deems proper. [General Laws of Rhode Island; Title 15, Chapters 15-5-1, 15-5-2, 15-5-3, 15-5-5, and 15-5-9 and Rhode Island Case Law].

SIMPLIFIED OR SPECIAL DIVORCE PROCEDURES: A court hearing will be required in all divorce cases. An official Financial Statement must be filed in all divorce cases. In addition, an official Child Support Guidelines form must be filed in all cases involving minor children. Official sample forms are available for use in preparing the Complaint for Divorce and other documents are found in Rhode Island Rules of Procedure for Domestic Relations, Appendix of Forms. [Rhode Island Rules of Procedure for Domestic Relations; Appendix of Forms].

MEDIATION OR COUNSELING REQUIREMENTS: In cases which involve child custody or visitation, the court may direct the parents to participate in mediation in an effort to resolve any differences. There is an official Family Court counseling form which must be filed with the Complaint for Divorce. [General Laws of Rhode Island; Title 15, Chapter 15-5-29].

PROPERTY DISTRIBUTION: Rhode Island is an "equitable distribution" state. Separate property which a spouse owned prior to the marriage and any property which a spouse receives by gift or inherits (either before or during a marriage) is not subject to division. Any other property (including any income from separate property that was earned during the marriage) may be divided by the court. The following factors are considered: (1) the contribution of each spouse to the acquisition, preservation, or appreciation in value of the marital property, including the contribution of each spouse as homemaker; (2) the length of the marriage; (3) the conduct of the spouses during the marriage; (4) the health and ages of the spouses; (5) the amount and sources of income of the spouses; (6) the occupation and employability of each of the spouses; (7) the contribution by 1 spouse to the education, training, licensure, business, or increased earning power of the other; (8) the need of a custodial parent to occupy or own the marital residence and to use or own the household effects according to the best interests of any children; (9) either spouse's wasteful dissipation or unfair transfer of any assets in contemplation of divorce; (10) the opportunity of each spouse for acquisition of assets and income; and (11) any other factor which is just and proper. [General Laws of Rhode Island; Title 15, Chapter 15-5-16.1].

ALIMONY/MAINTENANCE/SPOUSAL SUPPORT: Either spouse may be awarded alimony after a divorce or legal separation. In determining the amount of alimony, the following factors are to be considered: (1) the extent to which either spouse is unable to support himself or herself adequately because of his or her position as primary caretaker of a child whose age, condition, or circumstances make it appropriate that the parent not seek employment outside of the home; (2) the extent to which either party is unable to support himself or herself; (3) the extent to which a spouse was absent from employment while fulfilling homemaking responsibilities; (4) the extent to which a spouse's education may have become outmoded and his or her earning capacity diminished; (5) the time and expense required for a supported spouse to acquire the appropriate education and training to develop marketable skills and become employed; (6) the probability, given the spouse's age and skills, of completing education and training and becoming self-supporting; (7) the standard of living during the marriage; (8) the opportunity for either spouse for the future acquisition of capital assets and income; (9) the ability of the supporting spouse to pay, taking into consideration the supporting spouse's earning capacity, earned and unearned income, assets, debts, and standard of living; (10) the length of the marriage; (11) the conduct of the spouses during the marriage; (12) the health, age, station, occupation, amount and sources of income, vocational skills, and employability of the spouses; (13) the liability and needs of the spouses; and (14) any other factors which are just and proper. [General Laws of Rhode Island; Title 15, Chapters 15-5-16 and 15-5-16.1].

SPOUSE'S NAME: Any woman may request that her name be changed. [General Laws of Rhode Island; Title 15, Chapter 15-5-17].

CHILD CUSTODY: Child custody is determined according to the best interests of the child. Reasonable visitation should be granted to the non-custodial parent, unless it would be harmful to the child. There are no factors for consideration set out by statute. There is no specific provision for joint custody in Rhode Island. [General Laws of Rhode Island; Title 15, Chapter 15-5-16].

CHILD SUPPORT: Either parent may be ordered to provide child support, after a consideration of the following factors: (1) the financial resources of the child; (2) the standard of living the child would have enjoyed if the marriage had not been dissolved; (3) the physical and emotional conditions and educational needs of the child; (4) the needs of the noncustodial parent; (5) the financial resources of both the noncustodial and the custodial parent; and (6) any other factors. Family Court child support guidelines have been adopted. In order to guarantee child support payments, the court may require: (1) income or property assignments; (2) posting of bond; or (3) wage withholding. There is an official Child Support Guidelines Form which must be filed in cases involving minor children. [General Laws of Rhode Island; Title 15, Chapters 15-5-16.1, 15-5-16.2, 15-5-16.6, 15-5-22, and 15-9-1 and Rhode Island Rules of Procedure for Domestic Relations; Appendix of Forms].

SOUTH CAROLINA

STATE WEBSITE: http://www.scstatehouse.net/code/statmast.htm

DOWNLOAD STATE FORMS: http://www.judicial.state.sc.us/forms/searchFormTitle.cfm

FORMS PROVIDED ON CD: Financial Declaration, Family Court Cover Sheet

FORMS AVAILABLE ONLINE: Directions for Payment of Child Support or Alimony, Financial Declaration, Family Court Cover Sheet, ADR Rule 4 Order Appointing Mediator

RESIDENCY REQUIREMENTS AND WHERE TO FILE: The spouse filing for divorce must have been a resident of South Carolina for at least 1 year, unless both spouses are residents, in which case the spouse filing must only have been a resident for 3 months. There is a required 90-day delay from the time of filing to the time of the final decree of divorce. The divorce may be filed for in: (1) the county where the defendant resides; (2) the county where the plaintiff resides if the defendant does not live in South Carolina or cannot be found; or (3) the county where the spouses last lived together if both still live in South Carolina. [Code of Laws of South Carolina; Chapter 3, Sections 20-3-30, 20-3-60, and 20-3-80].

LEGAL GROUNDS FOR DIVORCE: No-Fault: Living separate and apart without cohabitation for 1 year. [Code of Laws of South Carolina; Chapter 3, Section 20-3-10]. General: (1) Adultery; (2) alcoholism and/or drug addiction; (3) physical cruelty; and (4) willful desertion for 1 year. [Code of Laws of South Carolina; Chapter 3, Section 20-3-10].

NAME OF COURT IN WHICH TO FILE FOR DIVORCE: Family Court. "State of South Carolina, The Family Court of the _____ Judicial Circuit." [Code of Laws of South Carolina; Chapter 3, Section 20-7-420].

TITLE OF DIVORCE ACTION: Complaint for Divorce.

NAME USED TO DESCRIBE SPOUSE FILING FOR DIVORCE: Plaintiff.

NAME USED TO DESCRIBE OTHER SPOUSE IN DIVORCE: Defendant.

TITLE OF FINAL DIVORCE PAPERS: Decree of Divorce.

LEGAL SEPARATION: South Carolina authorizes legal separation (separate maintenance). [Code of Laws of South Carolina; Chapter 3, Section 20-3-140].

SIMPLIFIED OR SPECIAL DIVORCE PROCEDURES: The court is authorized to develop and make available sample or mandatory forms for use in divorce matters. These may be available locally from the clerk of the court. [South Carolina Rules of Family Court; Rule 3].

MEDIATION OR COUNSELING REQUIREMENTS: The court may refer the spouses to a referee, who must make an honest effort to bring about a reconciliation between the spouses. In such cases, no divorce may be granted unless certified by the judge or the referee that the reconciliation efforts were unsuccessful. No final decree will be granted until 3 months after the initial filing of the complaint. [Code of Laws of South Carolina; Chapter 3, Sections 20-3-80, 20-3-90, and 20-7-850].

PROPERTY DISTRIBUTION: South Carolina is an "equitable distribution" state. Each spouse is entitled to keep his or her non-marital property, consisting of property: (1) which was acquired prior to the marriage; (2) acquired by gift or inheritance; (3) acquired in exchange for non-marital property; or (4) was acquired due to an increase in the value of any non-marital property. All other property acquired during the marriage is subject to division, based on a consideration of the following factors: (1) the duration of the marriage; (2) the age of the spouses; (3) any marital misconduct; (4) any economic misconduct; (5) the value of the marital property; (6) the contribution of each spouse to the acquisition of the marital property, including the contribution of each spouse as homemaker; (7) the income of each spouse; (8) the earning potential of each spouse and the opportunity for the future acquisition of capital assets; (9) the physical and emotional health of each spouse; (10) the needs of each spouse for additional training or education in order to achieve his or her earning potential; (11) the non-marital property of each spouse; (12) any retirement benefits; (13) whether alimony has been awarded; (14) the desirability of awarding the family home to the spouse having custody of any children; (15) the tax consequences; (16) any other support obligations of either spouse; (17) any marital debts of the spouses; (18) any child custody arrangements; and (19) any other relevant factors. [Code of Laws of South Carolina; Chapter 3, Sections 20-7-472 and 20-7-473].

ALIMONY/MAINTENANCE/SPOUSAL SUPPORT: Either spouse may be awarded alimony. The factors for consideration are: (1) the duration of the marriage and the ages of the spouses when married and when divorced; (2) the physical and emotional conditions of the spouses; (3) the educational background of each spouse and the need of additional training or education to reach the spouse's income potential; (4) the employment history and earning capacity of each spouse; (5) the standard of living during the marriage; (6) the current and expected earnings of each spouse; (7) the marital and separate property of each spouse; (8) the custody of any children and its effect on the ability of the custodial spouse to work full-time; (9) any marital misconduct; (10) any tax consequences; (11) any prior support obligations; (12) the current and expected expenses and needs of both spouses; and (13) any other relevant factors. The court may require the posting of bond as security for the payment of alimony and may require a spouse to carry life insurance and name the other spouse as beneficiary. [Code of Laws of South Carolina, Chapter 3, Sections 20-3-120, 20-3-130, 20-3-140 and South Carolina Case Law].

SPOUSE'S NAME: Upon request, the court may allow a spouse to resume the use of his or her former name. [Code of Laws of South Carolina; Chapter 3, Section 20-3-180].

CHILD CUSTODY: In awarding child custody, the factors for consideration are as follows: (1) the circumstances of the spouses; (2) the nature of the case; (3) the religious faith of the parents and child; (4) the welfare of the child; and (5) the best spiritual and other interests of the child. The parents both have equal rights regarding any award of custody of children. [Code of Laws of South Carolina; Chapter 3, Sections 20-3-160, 20-7-100, and 20-7-1520].

CHILD SUPPORT: Both parents have joint responsibility for child support. The court may require income withholding for the guarantee of child support payments. There are official child support guidelines which are presumed to be correct unless 1 of the following factors requires a deviation from the amount: (1) educational expenses for the child or a spouse; (2) the equitable distribution of property; (3) any consumer debts; (4) if the family has more than 6 children; (5) unreimbursed extraordinary medical or dental expenses of either parent; (6) mandatory retirement deductions of either parent; (7) support obligations for other dependents; (8) unreimbursed extraordinary medical or dental expenses of the child; (9) other court-ordered payments; (10) any available income of the child; (11) a substantial disparity in the income of the parents which makes it impractical for the non-custodial parent to pay the guideline amount; (12) the effect of alimony on the circumstances; and (13) any agreements between the spouses, if in the best interests of the child. [Code of Laws of South Carolina; Chapter 3, Sections 20-3-160, 20-7-40, 20-7-100, 20-7-852, 20-7-1315, and 43-5-580 and South Carolina Case Law].

SOUTH DAKOTA

STATE WEBSITE: http://legis.state.sd.us/statutes/index.aspx

DOWNLOAD STATE FORMS: http://www.sdjudicial.com/

FORMS PROVIDED ON CD: Complaint for Divorce Without Children, Complaint for Divorce With Children, Financial Affidavit

FORMS AVAILABLE ONLINE: Complaint for Divorce Without Children, Complaint for Divorce With Children, Financial Affidavit

RESIDENCY REQUIREMENTS AND WHERE TO FILE: The spouse filing for divorce must be a resident of South Dakota or a member of the Armed Forces stationed in South Dakota at the time of the filing and must remain a resident until the divorce is final. There is no durational residency requirement. The divorce may be filed for in the county where either spouse resides, but the defendant has the right to have it transferred to his or her county of residence if desired. In addition, there is a 60-day waiting period after filing before a hearing will be held or the divorce will be granted. [South Dakota Codified Laws; Volume 9A, Title 25, Chapters 25-4-30, 25-4-30.1, and 25-4-34].

LEGAL GROUNDS FOR DIVORCE: No-Fault: Irreconcilable differences which have caused the irretrievable breakdown of the marriage. [South Dakota Codified Laws; Title 25, Chapters 25-4-2, 25-4-17.2, and 25-4-18]. General: (1) Adultery; (2) conviction of a felony; (3) willful desertion; (4) cruel and inhuman treatment; (5) willful neglect; and (6) habitual intemperance [drunkenness]. [South Dakota Codified Laws; Title 25, Chapters 25-4-2 and 25-4-18].

NAME OF COURT IN WHICH TO FILE FOR DIVORCE: Circuit Court. "State of South Dakota, County of _____, In the Circuit Court, _____ Judicial District."

TITLE OF DIVORCE ACTION: Complaint for Divorce.

NAME USED TO DESCRIBE SPOUSE FILING FOR DIVORCE: Plaintiff.

NAME USED TO DESCRIBE OTHER SPOUSE IN DIVORCE: Defendant.

TITLE OF FINAL DIVORCE PAPERS: Decree of Divorce.

LEGAL SEPARATION: The grounds for legal separation (separate maintenance) in South Dakota are the same as for divorce. The spouse filing for legal separation must be a resident of South Dakota or a member of the Armed Forces stationed in South Dakota at the time of the filing and must remain a resident until the legal separation is final. [South Dakota Codified Laws; Title 25, Chapters 25-4-17.2 and 25-4-40].

SIMPLIFIED OR SPECIAL DIVORCE PROCEDURES: If both spouses consent to the use of "irreconcilable differences" as the grounds for divorce, the court may grant the divorce based entirely on affidavits of the spouses which establish the required residency and grounds for the divorce. In such cases, a personal appearance in court by either of the spouses will not generally be required. [South Dakota Codified Laws; Title 25, Chapter 25-4-17.3].

MEDIATION OR COUNSELING REQUIREMENTS: If the court determines that there is a reasonable possibility for reconciliation between the spouses, the divorce proceedings can be delayed for up to 30 days while the spouses seek counseling. [South Dakota Codified Laws; Title 25, Chapter 25-4-17.2].

PROPERTY DISTRIBUTION: South Dakota is an "equitable distribution" state. All of the spouse's property is equitably divided by the court. Marital fault is not to be considered unless it is relevant to the acquisition of property during the marriage. The only factor specified in the statute is a consideration of the equity and circumstances of the spouses. South Dakota courts have interpreted this to include the following factors for consideration: (1) the contribution of each spouse to the acquisition of the marital property, including the contribution of each spouse as homemaker; (2) the value of each spouse's property; (3) the length of the marriage; (4) the age and health of the spouses; (5) the present and potential earning capability of each spouse; (6) the value of the property; and (7) the income-producing capacity of the spouse's assets. [South Dakota Codified Laws; Title 25, Chapters 25-4-44 and 25-4-45.1 and South Dakota Case Law].

ALIMONY/MAINTENANCE/SPOUSAL SUPPORT: Either spouse may be awarded maintenance for life or a shorter period. The only factor specified in the statute is a consideration of the circumstances of the spouses. South Dakota courts have interpreted this to include the following factors for consideration: (1) the duration of the marriage; (2) the ability of the spouse from whom support is sought to meet his or her needs while meeting those of the spouse seeking support; (3) the financial resources of the spouse seeking maintenance, including marital property apportioned to such spouse and such spouse's ability to meet his or her needs independently; (4) the comparative financial resources of the spouses, including their comparative earning abilities in the labor market; (5) the age of the spouses; (6) the physical and emotional conditions of the spouses; (7) the fault of the spouses during the marriage. Reasonable security may be required to guarantee the payment of maintenance. [South Dakota Codified Laws; Title 25, Chapters 25-4-42, 25-4-44, 25-4-45.1, 25-7A-20 and South Dakota Case Law].

SPOUSE'S NAME: Upon request or on the court's own initiative, a wife's former or maiden name may be restored. [South Dakota Codified Laws; Title 25, Chapter 25-4-47].

CHILD CUSTODY: Sole or joint child custody is to be awarded based on the discretion of the court and the best interests of the child. Fault is not to be considered unless it is relevant to the fitness of a parent to have custody. Neither parent is considered the preferred parent based on the parent's sex. The preference of the child may be considered. In joint custody decisions, the court may consider the expressed desires of the parents and the best interests of the child. No other specific factors are specified. There are specific Child Visitation Guidelines established by the South Dakota Supreme Court which shall be used to establish visitation schedules, unless the parents provide a signed agreement providing otherwise. [South Dakota Codified Laws; Title 25, Chapters 25-3-11, 25-4-25, 25-4-45.1, 25-4A-12, and 25-5-7.1 to 25-5-7.3 and South Dakota Case Law].

CHILD SUPPORT: Either or both parents may be ordered to provide child support. There is an official child support obligation schedule set forth in the statute. Deviation from the official schedule may be based on a consideration of the following factors: (1) the financial condition of either parent that would make application of the schedule inequitable; (2) income tax consequences; (3) any special needs of the child; (4) income from other persons; (5) the effect of custody and visitation provisions; (6) childcare expenses necessary to obtain employment, education, or training; (7) agreements between the parents which provide other forms of support for the direct benefit of the child; (8) a voluntary reduction in the income of either parent; and (9) any other support obligations of a parent. The support payments may be ordered to be paid through the court clerk. Wage withholding orders may also be ordered. [South Dakota Codified Laws; Title 25, Chapters 25-3-11, 25-4-38, 25-4-45 and 25-7-6.2 to 25-7-6.12.].

TENNESSEE

STATE WEBSITE: http://www.michie.com/tennessee/lpext.dll?f=templates&fn=main-h.htm&cp=tncode

DOWNLOAD STATE FORMS: http://www.tsc.state.tn.us/geninfo/programs/Parenting/Parenting.htm

FORMS PROVIDED ON CD: PETITION FOR DIVORCE

FORMS AVAILABLE ONLINE: Parenting Plan

RESIDENCY REQUIREMENTS AND WHERE TO FILE: The spouse seeking divorce must have been a resident of Tennessee when the grounds for divorce arose. If the grounds for divorce arose outside of Tennessee and the petitioner resided outside of Tennessee, either spouse must have been a resident for 6 months prior to filing. The divorce may be filed for in any of the following counties: (1) the county in which both spouses lived at the time of their separation; (2) the county in which the respondent lives if he or she is a resident of Tennessee; or (3) the county in which the petitioner lives if the respondent is a non-resident of Tennessee. [Tennessee Code Annotated; Volume 6A, Title 36, Sections 36-4-104 and 36-4-105].

LEGAL GROUNDS FOR DIVORCE: No-Fault: (1) Irreconcilable differences if: [a] there has been no denial of this ground; [b] the spouses submit a properly signed marital dissolution agreement (see below under *Simplified or Special Divorce Procedures*); or [c] this grounds for divorce is combined with a general fault-based grounds or (2) living separate and apart without cohabitation for 2 years when there are no minor children. [Tennessee Code Annotated; Volume 6A, Title 36, Sections 36-4-101 and 36-4-103].
General: (1) Impotence; (2) adultery; (3) conviction of a felony and imprisonment; (4) alcoholism and/or drug addiction; (5) wife is pregnant by another at the time of marriage without husband's knowledge; (6) willful desertion for 1 year; (7) bigamy; (8) endangering the life of the spouse; (9) conviction of an infamous crime; (10) refusing to move to Tennessee with a spouse and willfully absenting oneself from a new residence for 2 years; (11) cruel and inhuman treatment or unsafe and improper marital conduct; (12) indignities that make the spouse's life intolerable; and (13) abandonment, neglect, or banning the spouse from the home. [Tennessee Code Annotated; Volume 6A, Title 36, Section 36-4-101].

NAME OF COURT IN WHICH TO FILE FOR DIVORCE: Circuit Court or Chancery Court. "In the _____ Court of _____ County, Tennessee."

TITLE OF DIVORCE ACTION: Petition for Divorce.

NAME USED TO DESCRIBE SPOUSE FILING FOR DIVORCE: Petitioner.

NAME USED TO DESCRIBE OTHER SPOUSE IN DIVORCE: Respondent.

TITLE OF FINAL DIVORCE PAPERS: Final Decree of Divorce.

LEGAL SEPARATION: The grounds for legal separation (divorce from bed and board) are the same as for a divorce. If the legal separation has been in effect for 2 years and the spouses have not reconciled, either spouse may request that the separation be converted to an absolute divorce. [Tennessee Code Annotated; Volume 6A, Title 36, Sections 36-4-102 and 36-4-119].

SIMPLIFIED OR SPECIAL DIVORCE PROCEDURES: If the divorce is based on irreconcilable differences, the spouses may enter into a notarized marital settlement agreement. The agreement must. (1) make specific reference to a pending divorce by the name of the court and the docket number or (2) state that the respondent is aware that a divorce will be filed for in the state of Tennessee; and (3) state that the respondent waives service of process and waives filing an answer. The waiver of service will be valid for 180 days after the respondent signs the agreement and will constitute a general appearance by the respondent and give the court personal jurisdiction over the respondent and will constitute a default judgment. The petition for divorce must have been on file for over 60 days before a hearing will be held if the spouses have no minor children and 90 days if they have any minor children. The spouses must make adequate and sufficient provisions in their marital settlement agreement for the care and custody of any minor children and for an adequate settlement of their property. The spouses may also make provisions in their settlement for alimony. A final decree may be entered without any corroborating proof or testimony by the petitioner or respondent. If the respondent contests or denies that there are irreconcilable differences, a divorce may not be granted on those grounds, unless there is a valid marital settlement agreement. Some counties may require the respondent to sign any appearance and waiver form before the court clerk for it to be valid. In addition, in any petition for divorce, the wife's maiden name must be stated and the race and color of each spouse must be stated. Financial affidavits may also be required. [Tennessee Code Annotated; Volume 6A, Title 36, Sections 36-4-103, 36-4-106, and 36-4-116 and Tennessee Rules of Court].

MEDIATION OR COUNSELING REQUIREMENTS: Upon request, the court may delay a divorce proceeding to allow an attempt at reconciliation. In addition, in those cases which involve child custody considerations, the court may order either or both parents to an educational seminar concerning the effects of divorce on children. [Tennessee Code Annotated; Volume 6A, Title 36, Sections 36-4-126, 36-4-130, and 36-6-101].

PROPERTY DISTRIBUTION: Tennessee is an "equitable distribution" state. The separate property of each spouse is retained by that spouse. Separate property is property that was: (1) acquired prior to marriage; (2) by gift or inheritance; (3) in exchange for any separate property, or (4) obtained from income or appreciation of separate property, if the other spouse did not contribute to the preservation and appreciation. The court may prefer to award the marital home and goods to the spouse with physical custody. The marital property, including: (1) any property acquired during the marriage by either spouse; (2) any increase in value of any property to which the spouses contributed to the upkeep and appreciation; and (3) any retirement benefits, is divided by the court, without regard to any marital fault, and after a consideration of the following factors: (1) the contribution of each spouse to the acquisition, preservation, appreciation, or dissipation of the marital property, including the contribution of each spouse as homemaker, wage-earner, or parent; (2) the value of each spouse's property at the time of the marriage and at present; (3) the economic circumstances of each spouse at the time the division of property is to become effective; (4) the length of the marriage; (5) the age and health of the spouses; (6) the vocational skills of the spouses; (7) the liabilities and needs of each spouse and the opportunity of each for further acquisition of capital assets and income; (8) the federal income tax consequences of the court's division of the property; (9) the present and potential earning capability of each spouse; (10) the tangible and intangible contributions made by 1 spouse to the education, training, or increased earning power of the other spouse; (11) the relative ability of each party for the future acquisition of capital and income; (12) the employability and earning capacity of the spouses; (13) any social security benefits; and (14) any other factors necessary to do equity and justice between the spouses. [Tennessee Code Annotated; Volume 6A, Title 36, Section 36-4-121].

ALIMONY/MAINTENANCE/SPOUSAL SUPPORT: Spousal support may take the form of lump sum, periodic, or rehabilitative support. Tennessee favors rehabilitative support; however, if this is not feasible, the court may grant long-term alimony until the death or remarriage of the supported spouse.

Spousal support may be awarded to either spouse, based on a consideration of the following: (1) the value of any separate property and the value of the spouse's share of any marital property; (2) whether the spouse seeking alimony is the custodian of a child whose circumstances make it appropriate for that spouse not to seek outside employment; (3) the need for sufficient education and training to enable the spouse to find appropriate employment; (4) the standard of living during the marriage; (5) the duration of the marriage; (6) the comparative financial resources of the spouses, including their comparative earning abilities in the labor market and any retirement, pension, or profit-sharing benefits; (7) the needs and obligations of each spouse; (8) the tangible and intangible contributions of each spouse to the marriage, including services rendered in homemaking, childcare, and contributions to the education, earning capacity, and career-building of the other spouse; (9) the relative education and training of the spouses and the opportunity of each party to secure education and training; (10) the age of the spouses; (11) the physical and mental condition of the spouse; (12) the tax consequences to each spouse; (13) the vocational skills and employability of the spouse seeking alimony; (14) the conduct of the spouses during the marriage; and (15) any other factor the court deems just and equitable. The court may require that spousal support payments be made through the clerk of the court. Spousal support payments may include expenses of job training and education. [Tennessee Code Annotated; Volume 6A, Title 36, Section 36-5-101].

SPOUSE'S NAME: There is no statutory provision in Tennessee for the restoration of a wife's name upon divorce. However, case law provides that a wife may resume the use of her former or maiden name [Tennessee Case Law].

CHILD CUSTODY: Joint or sole custody is awarded according to the best interests of the child and considering the child's preference. There is a presumption that joint custody is in the best interests of the child when the parents have an agreement to that effect or agree in open court to joint custody. There is no presumption that either parent is more suited to obtain custody. Custody will be granted based on the best interests of the child and a consideration of the following: (1) the love, affection, and emotional ties between the parents and child; (2) the importance of continuity and the length of time the child has lived in a stable and satisfactory environment unless parent disrupted continuity by fleeing domestic violence; (3) whether there has been any domestic violence or physical or mental abuse to the child, spouse, or any other person and whether a parent has had to relocate to avoid such violence; (4) the stability of the family unit; (5) the mental and physical health of the parents; (6) the home, school, and community record of the child; (7) the reasonable preference of a child over 12 years of age; (8) the character and behavior of any person who lives in or visits the parent's home and such person's interactions with the child; and (9) each parent's past and potential performance of parenting duties, including a willingness and ability to facilitate and encourage a close and continuing parent-child relationship with the other parent. [Tennessee Code Annotated; Volume 6A, Title 36, Sections 36-6-101 and 36-6-106].

CHILD SUPPORT: Either or both of the parents may be ordered to provide child support. The court may require that health insurance coverage be provided for the child or that the spouse to who is to pay the support maintain a life insurance policy for the benefit of the child. The court can require that the child support payments be paid through the clerk of the court. The posting of bond, wage assignments, and wage withholding may also be ordered. There are official child support guidelines in the Rules of Tennessee Dept. of Human Services, Child Support Division, Chapter 1240-2-4 which are presumed to be correct unless there is a showing that the amount would be unjust or inappropriate under the particular circumstances of the case. Standardized forms for determining child support are also available. [Tennessee Code Annotated; Volume 6A, Title 36, Sections 36-5-101 and 36-5-501 and Tennessee Court Rules Annotated, Supreme Court Rules; Tennessee Uniform Administrative Rules Act, Title 4, Chapter 5; Rules of Tennessee Dept. of Human Services, Child Support Division, Chapter 1240-2-4].

TEXAS

STATE WEBSITE: http://www.capitol.state.tx.us/

DOWNLOAD STATE FORMS: http://www.texaslawhelp.org/documents/clusters/TX/194/English/index.shtml

FORMS PROVIDED ON CD: Petition for Divorce with Children, Petition for Divorce without Children,

FORMS AVAILABLE ONLINE: Petition for Divorce with Children, Petition for Divorce without Children, Order to Withhold Earnings for Child Support

RESIDENCY REQUIREMENTS AND WHERE TO FILE: One of the spouses must have resided in Texas for 6 months prior to filing and 90 days prior to filing in the county where the divorce is filed. In addition, there is a 60-day waiting period after filing before a divorce will be granted. [Texas Codes Annotated; Family Code, Chapter 6.301].

LEGAL GROUNDS FOR DIVORCE: No-Fault: (1) The marriage has become insupportable because of discord or conflict of personalities that has destroyed the legitimate ends of the marriage relationship and prevents any reasonable expectation of reconciliation or (2) living separate and apart without cohabitation for 3 years. [Texas Codes Annotated; Family Code, Chapters 6.001 and 6.006].

General: (1) Adultery; (2) abandonment; (3) confinement for incurable insanity for 3 years; (4) conviction of a felony and imprisonment for over 1 year; and (5) cruel and inhuman treatment. [Texas Codes Annotated; Family Code, Chapters 6.001 to 6.007].

NAME OF COURT IN WHICH TO FILE FOR DIVORCE: District Court. "In the District Court of _____ County, Texas, _____ Judicial District."

TITLE OF DIVORCE ACTION: Petition for Divorce. "In the Matter of the Marriage of _____ and _____." [Texas Codes Annotated; Family Code, Chapter 6.401].

NAME USED TO DESCRIBE SPOUSE FILING FOR DIVORCE: Petitioner.

NAME USED TO DESCRIBE OTHER SPOUSE IN DIVORCE: Respondent.

TITLE OF FINAL DIVORCE PAPERS: Decree of Divorce.

LEGAL SEPARATION: Separation agreements are expressly authorized by statute. [Texas Codes Annotated; Family Code, Chapter 7.006].

SIMPLIFIED OR SPECIAL DIVORCE PROCEDURES: Separation agreements and property settlements are expressly authorized, including agreements regarding conservatorship and child support provisions. [Texas Codes Annotated; Family Code, Chapter 7.006].

MEDIATION OR COUNSELING REQUIREMENTS: It is the official policy of the state of Texas to promote amicable and non-judicial settlements of issues regarding children and families. Upon written agreement of the spouses or the court's own decision, the court may refer the divorce proceeding to mediation. The mediated settlement of the case is binding if it is signed by the spouses, any attorneys of the spouses, and provides that the agreement is not subject to revocation. In addition, upon request, the court can order both spouses to consult a marriage counselor. If the counselor's report indicates a reasonable expectation of reconciliation, the court can order further counseling for up to 60 additional days. Upon every filing for divorce, the court clerk is required to furnish a statement to the person filing regarding the availability of marital counseling services. In addition, if there has been a history of conflict and difficulties in resolving questions of access to any children, the court may order either parent to participate in counseling. [Texas Codes Annotated; Family Code, Chapters 102.001, 153.010, 6.505, and 6.602].

PROPERTY DISTRIBUTION: Texas is a "community property" state. The spouse's separate property, consisting of: (1) any property owned prior to the marriage; (2) any property acquired during the marriage by gift or inheritance; and (3) any recovery for personal injuries which occurred during the marriage, will be retained by the spouse who owns it. The "community" property, consisting of any other property acquired by either spouse during the marriage, will be divided equally, unless the court finds that equal division would be unjust. In addition, the court may divide property acquired by either spouse while residing outside of Texas which would have been community property if they had acquired it while residing in Texas. The only factors for consideration specified in the statute are a due regard for the rights of each party and any children. Any property possessed by either spouse during the marriage is presumed to be community property unless it can be shown that the property is actually separate property. A court can determine the rights of the spouses in any pension or retirement plan or their rights under any insurance policy. [Texas Codes Annotated; Family Code, Chapters 7.001 to 7.006].

ALIMONY/MAINTENANCE/SPOUSAL SUPPORT: The court may award maintenance for a spouse only if: (1) the spouse from whom maintenance is requested has been convicted of family violence within 2 years before the suit for dissolution or (2) the duration of the marriage was 10 years or longer and the spouse seeking maintenance: [a] lacks sufficient property to provide for his or her reasonable minimum needs; [b] is unable to support himself or herself through employment because of an incapacitating physical or mental disability; [c] is the custodian of a child who requires substantial care and supervision because of a physical or mental disability which makes it necessary that the spouse not be employed outside the home; or [d] clearly lacks earning ability in the labor market adequate to provide for the spouse's minimum reasonable needs. If the court determines that a spouse is eligible for maintenance, the following factors are then considered in the award: (1) the financial resources of the spouse seeking maintenance, including both separate and community property and liabilities; (2) the spouse's ability to meet his or her needs independently; (3) the education and employment skills of the spouses; (4) the time necessary for the supported spouse to acquire sufficient training or education to enable him or her to find employment; (5) the availability and feasibility of that training; (6) the duration of the marriage; (7) the age, employment history, earning ability, and physical and emotional condition of the spouse seeking maintenance; (8) the ability of the supporting spouse to meet their own needs and make any child support payments; (9) excessive or abnormal expenditures, concealment, or destruction of any property by either spouse; (10) the comparative financial resources of the spouses, including medical, retirement, insurance, or other benefits, and any separate property; (11) the contribution of 1 spouse to the education, training, or increased earning power of the other spouse; (12) the contribution of either spouse as homemaker; (13) any marital misconduct of the spouse seeking maintenance; (14) the efforts of the spouse seeking maintenance to seek employment counseling; and (15) any property brought to the marriage. The amount of monthly maintenance can be no more than the lower of $2,500.00 or 20% of the paying spouse's monthly gross income. [Texas Codes Annotated; Family Code, Chapters 8.001 to 8.055].

SPOUSE'S NAME: Upon request, the name of either spouse may be changed. [Texas Codes Annotated; Family Code, Chapters 45.105 and 45.106].

CHILD CUSTODY: Joint or sole managing conservatorship (custody) is determined according to the best interests of the child. The sex of the parents is not a factor for consideration. The wishes of the child may be considered. The factors to be considered in determining the terms and conditions for possession of a child by the possessory conservator (parent with visitation) are as follows: (1) the age, circumstances, needs, and best interests of the child; (2) the circumstances of the parents; (3) evidence of any spouse or child abuse; and (4) any other relevant factor. The factors specified in the statute for consideration in decisions regarding joint managing conservatorship are: (1) whether the physical, psychological, or emotional needs and development of the child will benefit; (2) the ability of the parents to give first priority to the welfare of the child and reach shared decisions in the child's best interests; (3) whether each parent can encourage and accept a positive relationship between the child and the other parent; (4) whether both parents participated in child rearing before the filing of the suit; (5) the geographical proximity of the homes of the parents; (6) if the child is 12 years old or older, the preference of the child; and (7) any other relevant factor. The court may not award joint managing conservatorship if there is any credible evidence of spousal or child abuse or neglect. Parents may file a written agreement with the court regarding joint managing conservatorship. The court will award joint managing conservatorship based on an agreement between the parents if the agreement: (1) establishes the county of residence of the child; (2) states the rights and duties of each parent regarding the child's present and future care, support, and education; (3) includes provisions to minimize disruption of the child's schooling, daily routine, and association with friends; (4) was entered into voluntarily and knowingly; and (5) is in the best interests of the child. In addition, there are standard terms for a court's order on a child's conservatorship set out in the statute that are presumed to be the minimum allowable time that the parent who is not awarded the primary physical residence of the child is to have the child. [Texas Codes Annotated; Family Code, Chapters 153.004 to 153.434].

CHILD SUPPORT: Either or both parents may be ordered to make periodic, lump-sum, or both types of child support payments. There are official child support guidelines set out in the statute and these are presumed to be reasonable and in the best interests of the child. The factors for consideration are: (1) the age and needs of the child; (2) the ability of the parents to contribute to the support of the child; (3) any financial resources available for the support of the child; (4) the amount of possession and access to the child; (5) the net resources of the parent to pay support, including the earning potential of the parent to pay support if the actual income of that parent is significantly less than what that parent could earn, if intentionally unemployed or underemployed; (6) any childcare expenses necessary for the employment of either parent; (7) whether a parent has custody of another child and any child support expenses being paid or received for the care of another child; (8) the amount of alimony being currently paid or received; (9) provisions for health care; (10) any educational or health care needs of the child, including college expenses; (11) any benefits a parent receives from an employer; (12) any debts or obligations of a parent; (13) any wage or salary deductions of the parents; (14) the cost of traveling to visit the child; (15) any positive or negative cash flow from any assets, including a business or investments; (16) any provisions for health care or insurance; (17) any special or extraordinary educational, health care, or other expenses of the parents or the child; (18) whether either parent has a car or housing furnished by an employer or other person or business; and (19) any other relevant factor. The court may order health insurance coverage to be provided for the child. In addition, the court may order income withholding to secure the payment of child support. [Texas Codes Annotated; Family Code, Chapters 154.001 to 154.309].

UTAH

STATE WEBSITE: http://www.le.state.ut.us/

DOWNLOAD STATE FORMS: http://www.utcourts.gov/resources/forms/

FORMS PROVIDED ON CD: PETITION FOR DIVORCE

FORMS AVAILABLE ONLINE: Child Support and Welfare Forms, Divorce Mediation

RESIDENCY REQUIREMENTS AND WHERE TO FILE: The spouse filing for divorce must have been a resident of Utah (or a member of the Armed Forces stationed in Utah) and a resident for more than 3 months immediately prior to filing of the county where the divorce is filed. In addition, there is a 90-day waiting period after filing before a divorce will be granted. [Utah Code Annotated; Sections 30-3-1 and 30-3-18].

LEGAL GROUNDS FOR DIVORCE: No-Fault: (1) Irreconcilable differences of the marriage or (2) living separate and apart without cohabitation for 3 years under a judicial decree of separation. [Utah Code Annotated; Section 30-3-1].

General: (1) Impotence; (2) adultery; (3) conviction of a felony; (4) willful desertion for 1 year; (5) cruel and inhuman treatment; (6) willful neglect; (7) incurable insanity; and (8) habitual intemperance (drunkenness). [Utah Code Annotated; Section 30-3-1].

NAME OF COURT IN WHICH TO FILE FOR DIVORCE: District Court (may be Family Court Division of District Court). "In the District Court of the _____ Judicial District, in and for _____ County, State of Utah."

TITLE OF DIVORCE ACTION: Petition for Divorce.

NAME USED TO DESCRIBE SPOUSE FILING FOR DIVORCE: Petitioner.

NAME USED TO DESCRIBE OTHER SPOUSE IN DIVORCE: Respondent.

TITLE OF FINAL DIVORCE PAPERS: Decree of Divorce.

LEGAL SEPARATION: The grounds for legal separation are: (1) willful desertion; (2) living separate and apart without cohabitation; and (3) gross neglect. The deserting spouse must be a resident of Utah, or own property in the state in which the deserted spouse lives. [Utah Code Annotated; Section 30-4-1].

SIMPLIFIED OR SPECIAL DIVORCE PROCEDURES: Uncontested divorce hearings may be held before a court commissioner. However, a divorce cannot be granted upon default, and legal evidence and testimony must be taken in every divorce case. However, in a default case, the evidence may be contained in an affidavit of the petitioner. In addition, a sample Petition for Divorce is contained in Utah Rules of Civil Procedure, Appendix of Forms, Form #18. Finally, a financial verification form is also required in child support cases. [Utah Code Annotated; Sections 30-3-4, 78A-5-107 and 78B-12-203, Utah Rules of Civil Procedure, Appendix of Forms, and the Utah Rules of the Judicial Council].

MEDIATION OR COUNSELING REQUIREMENTS: There is a 90-day waiting period after filing for divorce before any hearing may be held. Upon the request of either or both of the spouses (shown by filing a Petition for Conciliation with the court), the court may refer both of the spouses to a domestic relations counselor. If child custody is involved, both parents must attend a course in the effects of divorce on children. This requirement may be waived if the court determines that it is unnecessary. [Utah Code Annotated; Sections 30-3-4, 30-3-11.3, 30-3-16.2, and 30-3-18].

PROPERTY DISTRIBUTION: Utah is an "equitable distribution" state. All of the spouse's property, including gifts, inheritances, and any property acquired prior to or during the marriage, will be divided equitably by the court. There are no factors for consideration specified in the statute. [Utah Code Annotated; Sections 30-3-5 and 30-3-12].

ALIMONY/MAINTENANCE/SPOUSAL SUPPORT: Either spouse may be ordered to pay an equitable amount of alimony to the other. The following factors are to be considered: (1) the financial condition and needs of the recipient spouse; (2) the recipient's earning capacity and ability to produce income; (3) the ability of the paying spouse to provide support; (4) the length of the marriage; (5) the standard of living at the time of separation; (6) any marital fault of the spouses; (7) if the marriage has been of long duration and the marriage dissolves on the threshold of a major change in the income of 1 of the spouses; (8) if 1 spouse's earning capacity or education has been greatly enhanced by the other's efforts; and (9) whether spouse has custody of any children; (10) whether spouse worked in a business operated and/or owned by the other spouse; and (11) any other relevant factors. In general, the court will not award alimony for a period longer than the marriage existed. Alimony terminates upon remarriage or cohabitation with another person. [Utah Code Annotated; Sections 30-3-3 and 30-3-5].

SPOUSE'S NAME: There is no statutory provision in Utah for restoration of a wife's maiden name upon divorce. However, there is a general statutory provision for changing a name upon petition to the court. [Utah Code Annotated; Section 42-1-1].

CHILD CUSTODY: Joint or sole child custody is determined according to the best interests of the child and after a consideration of the following factors: (1) the past conduct and moral standards of the parents; (2) the welfare of the child; (3) the child's preference; (4) which parent is likely to act in the best interests of the child; and (5) which parent is likely to allow frequent and continuing contact with the other parent. If there is an allegation of child abuse by either spouse, the court must order an investigation by the Division of Family Services or the Utah Department of Human Services. Joint custody may be ordered if: (1) it will be in the best interests of the child and (2) both parents agree to joint custody; or (3) both parents filed a parenting plan for joint custody; and it is based upon a consideration of the following factors: (1) whether the physical, psychological, or emotional needs and development of the child will benefit; (2) the ability of the parents to give first priority to the welfare of the child and reach shared decisions in the child's best interests; (3) whether each parent can encourage and accept a positive relationship between the child and the other parent; (4) whether both parents participated in child-rearing before the filing of the divorce; (5) the geographical proximity of the homes of the parents; (6) if the child is of sufficient age and maturity, the preference of the child; (7) the maturity of the parents and their willingness and ability to protect the child from conflict that may arise between the parents; (8) spousal or child abuse; (9) ability to cooperate; and (10) any other factor that the court finds relevant. The court may not discriminate against a parent with a disability when considering custody issues. The court may order that dispute resolution be attempted prior to any enforcement or modification of custody terms. There are also advisory visitation guidelines in the statutes. [Utah Code Annotated; Sections 30-2-10, 30-3-5, 30-3-5.2, 30-3-10, 30-3-10.1, 30-3-10.2, 30-3-10.3, and 30-3-33].

CHILD SUPPORT: Either or both parents may be ordered to provide child support, including medical and dental expenses and health insurance. The court may also order the non-custodial parent to provide daycare and childcare expenses while the custodial parent is at work or undergoing training. Income withholding may be ordered by a court to guarantee any child support payments. There are official Child Support Guidelines. These guidelines are presumed to be correct unless there is a showing that the amount would be unjust or inappropriate under the particular circumstances in a case. Factors for consideration in awarding support amounts outside the guidelines are: (1) the standard of living and situation of the parties; (2) the relative wealth and income of the parties; (3) the earning abilities of the parents; (4) the needs of the parents and the child; (5) the ages of the parents and the child; and (6) the responsibilities of the parents for the support of others. A child support worksheet is contained in the statute. In addition, a financial verification form is also required. [Utah Code Annotated; Sections 30-3-5, 30-3-5.1, and 78B-12-202 and 78B-12-203].

VERMONT

STATE WEBSITE: http://www.vermont.gov/

DOWNLOAD STATE FORMS: http://www.vermontjudiciary.org/Library/allforms.aspx

FORMS PROVIDED ON CD: Complaint for Divorce, Affidavit of Income and Assets Packet, Cover Sheet

FORMS AVAILABLE ONLINE: Complaint for Divorce, Affidavit of Income and Assets Packet, Cover Sheet, Child Support Order, Complaint for Support, and Complaint for Legal Separation.

RESIDENCY REQUIREMENTS AND WHERE TO FILE: Either spouse must have been a resident of Vermont for at least 6 months before the divorce is filed. Additionally, either spouse must have been a resident for 1 year before the divorce is made final. In cases involving child custody, there is a 6-month waiting period after the defendant has been served with the divorce papers before a hearing will be held. The divorce may be filed for in any county where either or both of the spouses reside. [Vermont Statutes Annotated; Title 15, Chapter 11, Subchapter 3, Sections 592 and 593 and Vermont Rules for Family Proceedings; Rule 4].

LEGAL GROUNDS FOR DIVORCE: No-Fault: Living separate and apart without cohabitation for 6 consecutive months and the resumption of marital relations is not reasonably probable. [Vermont Statutes Annotated; Title 15, Chapter 11, Subchapter 2, Sections 551 and 555].

General: (1) Adultery; (2) imprisonment for 3 years or more or for life; (3) willful desertion for 7 years; (4) cruel and inhuman treatment of intolerable severity; (5) incurable mental illness; and (6) gross neglect. [Vermont Statutes Annotated; Title 15, Chapter 11, Subchapter 2, Section 551].

NAME OF COURT IN WHICH TO FILE FOR DIVORCE: Family Court. "State of Vermont, Family Court, _____ County."

TITLE OF DIVORCE ACTION: Complaint for Divorce.

NAME USED TO DESCRIBE SPOUSE FILING FOR DIVORCE: Plaintiff.

NAME USED TO DESCRIBE OTHER SPOUSE IN DIVORCE: Defendant.

TITLE OF FINAL DIVORCE PAPERS: Decree of Divorce.

LEGAL SEPARATION: The grounds for legal separation (divorce from bed and board) are: (1) living separate and apart without cohabitation for 6 months; (2) adultery; (3) imprisonment for 3 years or more or for life; (4) willful desertion for 7 years; (5) cruel and inhuman treatment of intolerable severity; (6) incurable mental illness; and (7) gross neglect. Either spouse must be a resident of Vermont for 6 months before filing for legal separation. [Vermont Statutes Annotated; Title 15, Chapter 11, Subchapter 2, Sections 551, 555, Chapter 11, Subchapter 3, Section 592].

SIMPLIFIED OR SPECIAL DIVORCE PROCEDURES: Standard forms for filing of the complaint or petition are available. There are no legal provisions in Vermont for simplified divorce procedures. In all divorce cases in Vermont, a hearing is required and oral testimony of witnesses is required.

However, in cases involving children, the court may, without a hearing, accept the written agreement of the parents regarding the children. An official statistical data sheet must also be filed with the Complaint and a statement of income and assets must be filed. [Vermont Statutes Annotated; Title 15, Chapter 11, Subchapter 3A, Section 662 and Vermont Rules for Family Proceedings; Rule 4].

MEDIATION OR COUNSELING REQUIREMENTS: If 1 of the spouses denies under oath that they have lived apart for the required period, the court may delay the proceedings for 30 to 60 days and suggest that the spouses seek counseling. [Vermont Statutes Annotated; Title 15, Chapter 11, Subchapter 2, Section 552].

PROPERTY DISTRIBUTION: Vermont is an "equitable distribution" state. All of the spouses' property is subject to being divided on an equitable basis, regardless of when it was acquired or how the title is held, including any gifts and inheritances. The factors to be considered are: (1) the contribution of each spouse to the acquisition of the property, including the contribution of each spouse as homemaker; (2) the value of each spouse's property; (3) the length of the marriage; (4) the age and health of the spouses; (5) the occupation of the spouses; (6) the amount and sources of income of the spouses; (7) the vocational skills of the spouses; (8) the employability of the spouses; (9) the liabilities and needs of each spouse and the opportunity of each for further acquisition of capital assets and income; (10) whether the property award is instead of or in addition to maintenance; (11) how and by whom the property was acquired; (12) the merits of each spouse; (13) the burdens imposed upon either spouse for the benefit of the children; (14) any custodial provisions for the children, including the desirability of awarding the family home to the parent with custody of any children; (15) the conduct of the spouses during the marriage; and (16) the contribution by 1 spouse to the education, training, or increased earning power of the other. [Vermont Statutes Annotated; Title 15, Chapter 11, Subchapter 6, Section 751].

ALIMONY/MAINTENANCE/SPOUSAL SUPPORT: Either spouse may be ordered to pay maintenance to the other, without regard to marital fault. The maintenance may be rehabilitative (temporary) or permanent and will be awarded if the court finds that the spouse seeking maintenance: (1) lacks sufficient income or property to provide for his or her reasonable needs and (2) is unable to support himself or herself through appropriate employment at the standard of living established during the marriage and is the custodian of any children. The factors to be considered are: (1) the time necessary to acquire sufficient education and training to enable the spouse to find appropriate employment and that spouse's future earning capacity; (2) the standard of living established during the marriage; (3) the duration of the marriage; (4) the ability of the spouse from whom support is sought to meet his or her needs while meeting those of the spouse seeking support; (5) the financial resources of the spouse seeking maintenance, including property apportioned to such spouse and such spouse's ability to meet his or her needs independently; (6) the age of the spouses; (7) the physical and emotional conditions of the spouses; and (8) the effects of inflation on the cost of living. The court may require security for any maintenance payments. [Vermont Statutes Annotated; Title 15, Chapter 11, Subchapter 6, Sections 752 and 757].

SPOUSE'S NAME: A wife may resume the use of her former or maiden name upon divorce, unless a good cause is shown why she should not. [Vermont Statutes Annotated; Title 15, Chapter 11, Subchapter 2, Section 558].

CHILD CUSTODY: Joint or sole child custody may be awarded based on the best interests of the child and upon a consideration of all relevant factors, including the following: (1) the wishes of the parents; (2) the child's adjustment to his or her home, school, and community; (3) the relationship of the child with parents, siblings, and other significant family members; (4) the ability and disposition of each parent to provide love, affection, and guidance; (5) the ability of each parent to provide food, clothing, medical care, other material needs, and a safe environment; (6) the ability of each parent to meet the child's present and future developmental needs; (7) the ability and disposition of each parent to foster a positive relationship and frequent and continuing contact with the other parent, including physical contact unless it will result in harm to the child or parent; (8) the quality of the child's relationship with the primary care provider, given the child's age and development; and (9) the ability and disposition of the parents to communicate, cooperate with each other, and make joint decisions concerning the children where parental rights and responsibilities are to be shared. Neither parent is assumed to have a superior right to have custody. No preference to be given because of parent's sex. [Vermont Statutes Annotated; Title 15, Chapter 11, Subchapter 3A, Section 664].

CHILD SUPPORT: Either or both of the parents may be required to pay child support, based on a consideration of the following factors: (1) the financial resources of the child; (2) the standard of living the child would have enjoyed if the marriage had not been dissolved; (3) the physical and emotional conditions and educational needs of the child; (4) the financial resources, needs, and obligations of both the non-custodial and the custodial parent; (5) inflation with relation to the cost of living; (6) the costs of any educational needs of either parent; (7) any travel expenses related to parent-child contact; and (8) any other relevant factors. Health insurance coverage for the child may be ordered to be provided. The court may require security or wage withholding. Every order of child support must be made subject to a wage assignment in the event of delinquency and require the payments to be made to the registry in the Office of Child Support, unless the situation falls under an exception to the rules shown in Vermont Statutes Annotated; Title 33, Section 4103. There are official child support guidelines available from the Vermont Department of Human Services which are presumed to be correct, unless they are shown to be unfair under the circumstances. There is an official child support computation worksheet available. [Vermont Statutes Annotated; Title 15, Chapter 11, Subchapter 3A, Sections 653 to 669, Chapter 11, Subchapter 3A, Section 757, and Chapter 11, Subchapter 7, Sections 781 to 783, Title 33, Part 3, Chapter 41, Section 4103, and Vermont Rules for Family Proceedings; Rule 4].

VIRGINIA

STATE WEBSITE: http://leg1.state.va.us/lis.htm

DOWNLOAD STATE FORMS: http://www.courts.state.va.us/forms/district/jdr.html

FORMS PROVIDED ON CD: Complaint for Divorce

FORMS AVAILABLE ONLINE: State-wide forms not available. Check county websites for forms. For example; http://www.co.hanover.va.us/

RESIDENCY REQUIREMENTS AND WHERE TO FILE: One of the spouses must have been a resident of Virginia for at least 6 months prior to filing for divorce. The divorce may be filed for in: (1) the county or city in which the spouses last lived together or (2) at the option of the plaintiff: [a] the county or city where the defendant resides, if the defendant is a resident of Virginia or [b] if the defendant is a non-resident of Virginia, the county or city where the plaintiff resides. [Code of Virginia; Title 8.01, Chapter 5, Section 261 and Title 20, Chapter 6, Sections 96 and 97].

LEGAL GROUNDS FOR DIVORCE: No-Fault: (1) Living separate and apart without cohabitation for 1 year or (2) living separate and apart without cohabitation for 6 months if there are no minor children and the spouses have entered into a separation agreement. [Code of Virginia; Title 20, Chapter 6, Section 91].

General: (1) Adultery (including homosexual acts); (2) abandonment; (3) conviction of a felony and imprisonment for 1 year; (4) cruelty; and (5) willful desertion. [Code of Virginia; Title 20, Chapter 6, Section 91].

NAME OF COURT IN WHICH TO FILE FOR DIVORCE: Circuit Court, Juvenile and Domestic Relations Court, or Family Court. "Virginia: In the _____ Court of _____."

TITLE OF DIVORCE ACTION: Complaint for Divorce.

NAME USED TO DESCRIBE SPOUSE FILING FOR DIVORCE: Plaintiff.

NAME USED TO DESCRIBE OTHER SPOUSE IN DIVORCE: Defendant.

TITLE OF FINAL DIVORCE PAPERS: Decree of Divorce.

LEGAL SEPARATION: The grounds for legal separation are: (1) cruelty; (2) willful desertion; (3) abandonment; and (4) reasonable apprehension of bodily injury. One of the spouses must have been a resident of Virginia for at least 6 months prior to filing for legal separation. [Code of Virginia; Title 20, Chapter 6, Sections 95 and 97].

SIMPLIFIED OR SPECIAL DIVORCE PROCEDURES: Separation agreements are specifically authorized by statute and will reduce the time required for living apart by 6 months. In addition, a spouse may waive service of process, but the waiver of service of process form must be signed in front of the clerk of the court. The testimony of either spouse must also, generally, be corroborated by a witness. [Code of Virginia; Title 20, Chapter 6, Sections 99, 99.1:1, 107.3, and 109.1].

MEDIATION OR COUNSELING REQUIREMENTS: There are no legal provisions in Virginia for divorce mediation.

PROPERTY DISTRIBUTION: Virginia is an "equitable distribution" state. The separate property of each spouse, consisting of: (1) property acquired prior to the marriage; (2) any gifts and inheritances; (3) any increase in the value of separate property, unless marital property or significant personal efforts contributed to such increases; and (4) any property acquired in exchange for separate property; will be retained by the spouse who owns it. The marital property, consisting of: (1) all property acquired during the marriage that is not separate property; (2) all property titled in the names of both spouses, whether as joint tenants or tenants-by-the entireties; (3) income from or increase in value of separate property during the marriage if the income or increase arose from significant personal efforts; (4) any separate property which is commingled with marital property and cannot be clearly traced; will be divided equitably by the court. The court may also order a payment from 1 spouse's retirement benefits, profit-sharing benefits, personal injury award, or worker's compensation award, to the other spouse. The factors for consideration are: (1) the contribution of each spouse to the acquisition, care, and maintenance of the marital property; (2) the liquid or non-liquid character of the property; (3) the length of the marriage; (4) the age and health of the spouses; (5) the tax consequences; (6) any debts and liabilities of the spouses, the basis for such debts and liabilities, and the property which serves as security for such debts and liabilities; (7) how and by whom the property was acquired; (8) the circumstances that contributed to the divorce; (9) the contributions, monetary and non-monetary, of each spouse to the well-being of the family; and (10) any other factor necessary to do equity and justice between the spouses. [Code of Virginia; Title 20, Chapter 6, Section 107.3].

ALIMONY/MAINTENANCE/SPOUSAL SUPPORT: Either spouse may be awarded maintenance, to be paid in either a lump sum, periodic payments, or both. The factors for consideration are: (1) the opportunity, ability and time necessary to acquire sufficient education and training to enable the spouse to find appropriate employment, and that spouse's future earning capacity; (2) the standard of living established during the marriage; (3) the duration of the marriage; (4) the financial resources of the spouses, including marital property apportioned to such spouse; (5) the contribution of each spouse to the marriage, including services rendered in homemaking, childcare, education, and career-building of the other spouse; (6) the tax consequences to each spouse; (7) the age of the spouses; (8) the physical and emotional conditions of the spouses; (9) the educational level of each spouse at the time of the marriage and at the time the action for support is commenced; (10) the property of the spouses; (11) the circumstances which contributed to the divorce; (12) the extent to which the age, condition, or circumstances of any child of the spouses makes it appropriate that the custodial spouse not seek outside employment; (13) any income from pension, profit-sharing, or retirement plans; (14) any contributions by either spouse to the well-being of the family; (15) the earning capacity of the spouses, including the skills, education, and training of the spouses and their employment opportunities; (16) any decisions made during the marriage regarding employment, career, education, and parenting that affected a spouse's earning potential, including the length of time absent from the job market; and (17) any other factor the court deems just and equitable. However, permanent maintenance will not be awarded to a spouse who was at fault in a divorce granted on the grounds of adultery, unless such a denial of support would be unjust. [Code of Virginia; Title 20, Chapter 6, Sections 95, 107.1 and 108.1].

SPOUSE'S NAME: Upon request, a spouse may have his or her former name restored. [Code of Virginia; Title 20, Chapter 6, Section 121.4].

CHILD CUSTODY: Joint or sole child custody will be awarded based on the welfare of the child, and upon a consideration of the following factors: (1) the age of the child; (2) the child's preference;

(3) the needs of the child; (4) the love and affection existing between the child and each parent; (5) the mental and physical health of all individuals involved; (6) the material needs of the child; (7) the role each parent has played in the care of the child; and (8) any other factors necessary for the best interests of the child. No preference is to be given to either parent. [Code of Virginia; Title 20, Chapter 6, Section 107.2].

CHILD SUPPORT: Official child support guidelines are provided in the statute, which are presumed to be correct unless there is a showing that the amount would be unjust or inappropriate under the particular circumstances of the case based on the factors below. Child support may be ordered to be paid by either parent, and is based on a consideration of the following factors: (1) the financial resources of the child; (2) the standard of living the child would have enjoyed if the marriage had not been dissolved; (3) the physical and emotional conditions and educational needs of the child; (4) the earning capacity of each parent; (5) the age and health of the child; (6) the division of marital property; (7) the monetary or non-monetary contributions of the parents to the family's well-being; (8) the education of the parents; (9) the ability of the parents to secure education and training; (10) the income tax consequences of child support; (11) any special medical, dental, or childcare expenses; (12) the obligations, needs, and financial resources of the parents; and (13) any other relevant factors. And the following additional factors: (1) support provided for other children or family members; (2) custody arrangements; (3) voluntary unemployment or under-employment, unless it is the custodial parent and the child is not in school, childcare services are not available, and the cost of childcare services are not included in the computations for child support; (4) debts incurred during the marriage for the benefit of the child; (5) debts incurred for the purpose of producing income; (6) direct court-ordered payments for health insurance or educational expenses of the child; and (7) any extraordinary capital gains, such as gains from the sale of the marital home. [Code of Virginia; Title 20, Chapter 6, Sections 107.2, 108.1, and 108.2].

WASHINGTON

STATE WEBSITE: http://www1.leg.wa.gov/WorkingWithLeg/

DOWNLOAD STATE FORMS: http://www.courts.wa.gov/forms/

FORMS PROVIDED ON CD: Petition for Dissolution of Marriage, Financial Declaration

FORMS AVAILABLE ONLINE: Petition for Dissolution of Marriage, Financial Declaration, Confidential Information Form, Order of Child Support, Parenting Plan

RESIDENCY REQUIREMENTS AND WHERE TO FILE: The spouse filing for dissolution of marriage must be a resident of Washington or a member of the Armed Forces stationed in Washington. The dissolution of marriage may be filed for in any county where either the petitioner or respondent resides. In addition, the court will not act on the petition until 90 days has elapsed from the filing and the service of summons on the respondent. [Revised Code of Washington Annotated; Title 26, Chapters 26.09.010 and 26.09.030].

LEGAL GROUNDS FOR DISSOLUTION OF MARRIAGE: No-Fault: Irretrievable breakdown of the marriage. [Revised Code of Washington Annotated; Title 26, Chapter 26.09.030].

General: Irretrievable breakdown of the marriage is the only grounds for dissolution of marriage in Washington. [Revised Code of Washington Annotated; Title 26, Chapter 26.09.030].

NAME OF COURT IN WHICH TO FILE FOR DISSOLUTION OF MARRIAGE: Superior Court, or Family Court (on request). "In the _____ Court of the State of Washington, in and for the County of _____."

TITLE OF DISSOLUTION OF MARRIAGE ACTION: Petition for Dissolution of Marriage. "In Re the Marriage of _____ and _____."

NAME USED TO DESCRIBE SPOUSE FILING FOR DISSOLUTION OF MARRIAGE: Petitioner.

NAME USED TO DESCRIBE OTHER SPOUSE IN DISSOLUTION OF MARRIAGE: Respondent.

TITLE OF FINAL DISSOLUTION OF MARRIAGE PAPERS: Decree of Dissolution of Marriage.

LEGAL SEPARATION: The only grounds for legal separation in Washington is the irretrievable breakdown of the marriage. The spouse filing for legal separation must be a resident of Washington or a member of the Armed Forces stationed in Washington. The court will not act on the petition until 90 days has elapsed from the filing and the service of summons on the respondent. [Revised Code of Washington Annotated; Title 26, Chapter 26.09.030].

SIMPLIFIED OR SPECIAL DISSOLUTION OF MARRIAGE PROCEDURES: All divorce cases must be filed on official Washington forms. The forms are available in printed version from the Washington Office of the Administrator for the Courts. Separation agreements are specifically authorized by law and, if fair, all portions of the agreements are binding on the court, except those relating to parental rights and responsibilities. The spouses must file a Washington Department of Health Certificate with the petition. There are also certain local court rules which apply to dissolutions of marriage. These are found in Washington Local Court Rules, Rule 94.04. [Revised Code of Washington Annotated; Title 26, Chapters 26.09.020, 26.09.070, and 26.09.080].

MEDIATION OR COUNSELING REQUIREMENTS: Upon the request of either of the spouses, or on the court's own initiative, the spouses may be referred to a counseling service of their choice. A report must be requested from the counseling service within 60 days of the referral. Contested issues relating to custody or visitation will be referred to mediation. There may also be mandatory settlement conferences if there are contested issues. [Revised Code of Washington Annotated; Title 26, Chapters 26.09.015, 26.09.030, and 26.09.181].

PROPERTY DISTRIBUTION: Washington is a "community property" state. Each spouse retains his or her separate property, consisting of: (1) all property acquired prior to marriage; (2) any gifts or inheritances; and (3) any increase in value of the separate property. "Quasi-community" property is property that is acquired while a spouse resides outside of Washington, but that would have been considered community property if acquired while they were living in Washington. "Quasi-community" property is divided as if it were community property. The court will divide the community property of the spouses, consisting of all other property acquired during the marriage, equally or equitably, after a consideration of the following: (1) the nature and extent of each spouse's separate property; (2) the economic circumstances of each spouse at the time the division of property is to become effective; (3) the length of the marriage; (4) the nature and extent of community property; and (5) the desirability of awarding the family home and the right of occupancy for reasonable periods to the custodial parent if there are minor children. Marital misconduct is not to be considered. [Revised Code of Washington Annotated; Title 26, Chapters 26.09.080, 26.16.010, 26.16.020, 26.16.030, and 26.16.220].

ALIMONY/MAINTENANCE/SPOUSAL SUPPORT: Either spouse may be ordered to pay maintenance to the other spouse. Marital misconduct is not to be considered. The factors for consideration are: (1) the time necessary to acquire sufficient education and training to enable the spouse to find appropriate employment and that spouse's future earning capacity; (2) the standard of living established during the marriage; (3) the duration of the marriage; (4) the ability of the spouse from whom support is sought to meet his or her needs while meeting those of the spouse seeking support; (5) the financial resources of the spouse seeking maintenance, including separate or community property apportioned to such spouse and such spouse's ability to meet his or her needs independently; (6) the needs and obligations of each spouse; (7) the age of the spouses; (8) the physical and emotional conditions of the spouses; and (9) any child support responsibilities for a child living with the parent. Maintenance payments may be required to be paid through the clerk of the court or through the Washington State Support Registry if there are also child support payments being made. [Revised Code of Washington Annotated; Title 26, Chapters 26.09.050, 26.09.090, and 26.09.120].

SPOUSE'S NAME: Upon request and for a just and reasonable cause, the wife's former or maiden name may be restored. [Revised Code of Washington Annotated; Title 26, Chapter 26.09.150].

CHILD CUSTODY: Joint or sole child custody will be determined according to the best interests of the child. Every petition for dissolution of marriage in which a minor child is involved must include a proposed parenting plan. The parents may make an agreement regarding a parenting plan. The parenting plan should contain provisions for: (1) dispute resolution; (2) a residential schedule for the child; and (3) allocation of decision-making authority relating to the child. The factors which are considered in determining decision-making authority are: (1) if both parents agree to mutual decision-making; (2) the existence of any physical or sexual child or spouse abuse, neglect, or abandonment; (3) the history of participation of each parent in the decision-making process; (4) whether the parents have demonstrated an ability and desire to cooperate in the decision-making process; and (5) the parents' geographical proximity to each other, to the extent that it would affect their ability to make timely mutual decisions. The factors which are considered in determining residential provisions for the child are: (1) the strength, nature, and stability of the child's relationship with each parent, including the parent's performance of daily parental functions; (2) any spouse or child abuse, neglect, or substance abuse; (3) the history of participation of each parent in child-rearing; (4) the wishes of the parents; (5) the wishes of the child, if of sufficient age and maturity to express an opinion; (6) the child's relationship with siblings and other significant family members; and (7) any agreement between the parties. Factor (1) is to be given the most weight. Equal-time alternating residential provisions will only be ordered if: (1) there is no child or spouse abuse, neglect, abandonment, or substance abuse; (2) the parents have agreed to such provisions; (3) there is a history of shared parenting and cooperation; (4) the parents are available to each other, especially in terms of geographic location; and (5) the provisions are in the best interests of the child. The court may order an investigation concerning parenting arrangements for the child. [Revised Code of Washington Annotated; Title 26, Chapters 26.09.181 to 26.09.220].

CHILD SUPPORT: Either parent may be ordered to pay child support. Marital misconduct is not a factor to be considered. All relevant factors may be considered. Official child support guidelines and worksheets are available from the Washington Department of Social and Health Services and from the clerk of the court. The official guidelines are presumed to be correct, unless there is a showing that the amount is unjust or inappropriate under the particular circumstances of a case. Mandatory wage assignments may be required if the child support payments are over 15 days past due. Child support payments may be required to be paid through the Washington State Support Registry or directly to the parent, if an approved payment plan is accepted by the court. The court may require either parent to provide health insurance coverage for the child. [Revised Code of Washington Annotated; Title 26, Chapters 26.09.040, 26.09.050, 26.09.100, 26.09.120, 26.18.070, 26.23.050, and 26-19 Appendix].

The No-Fault Divorce Toolkit

WEST VIRGINIA

STATE WEBSITE: http://www.legis.state.wv.us/

DOWNLOAD STATE FORMS: http://www.state.wv.us/wvsca/rules/FamilyCourt/index.htm

FORMS PROVIDED ON CD: Petition for Divorce, Financial Statement

FORMS AVAILABLE ONLINE: Petition for Divorce, Financial Statement, Instructions, Proposed Parenting Plan, Petition for Support / Allocation of Custodial Responsibility

RESIDENCY REQUIREMENTS AND WHERE TO FILE: One of the spouses must have been a resident of West Virginia for at least 1 year immediately prior to filing. However, if the marriage was performed in West Virginia and 1 spouse is a resident when filing, there is no durational time limit. The divorce should be filed for in the county: (1) in which the spouses last lived together; (2) where the defendant lives if a resident; or (3) where the plaintiff lives, if the defendant is a non-resident. [West Virginia Code; Sections 48-5-103, 48-5-105, and 48-5-106].

LEGAL GROUNDS FOR DIVORCE: No-Fault: (1) Irreconcilable differences have arisen between the spouses or (2) living separate and apart without cohabitation and without interruption for 1 year. [West Virginia Code; Section 48-5-201 and 48-5-202].

General: (1) Adultery; (2) abandonment for 6 months; (3) alcoholism and/or drug addiction; (4) confinement for incurable insanity for 3 years; (5) physical abuse or reasonable apprehension of physical abuse of a spouse or of a child; (6) conviction of a felony; (7) cruel and inhuman treatment, including false accusations of adultery or homosexuality; (8) willful neglect of a spouse or a child; and (9) habitual intemperance (drunkenness). [West Virginia Code; Sections 48-5-203 to 48-5-209].

NAME OF COURT IN WHICH TO FILE FOR DIVORCE: Circuit Court. "Circuit Court of _____ County, West Virginia."

TITLE OF DIVORCE ACTION: Petition for Divorce.

NAME USED TO DESCRIBE SPOUSE FILING FOR DIVORCE: Petitioner.

NAME USED TO DESCRIBE OTHER SPOUSE IN DIVORCE: Respondent.

TITLE OF FINAL DIVORCE PAPERS: Decree of Divorce.

LEGAL SEPARATION: The grounds for legal separation (separate maintenance) are the same as for divorce. One of the spouses must have been a resident of West Virginia for at least 1 year prior to filing for legal separation. [West Virginia Code; Section 48-5-501].

SIMPLIFIED OR SPECIAL DIVORCE PROCEDURES: If 1 spouse files a verified complaint for divorce on the grounds of "irreconcilable differences," the other spouse may file a verified "answer" admitting the "irreconcilable differences" and a divorce will be granted. Circuit clerks are required to have supplies of an official "petition" and an "answer" form on hand, free of charge. No witnesses will be necessary for any proof for a divorce on the grounds of "irreconcilable differences." In other cases, witnesses will be required. The court may approve or reject a marital settlement agreement of the spouses. Standard financial disclosure forms are required to be filed. [West Virginia Code; Sections 48-5-402, 48-5-403, 48-6-201, 48-7-201, and 48-7-203 and West Virginia Rules of Civil Procedure; Rule 80].

MEDIATION OR COUNSELING REQUIREMENTS: If the divorce involves a minor child, the court will order the parents to attend a parent education class to educate parents about the effects of divorce and custody disputes on children and teach parents methods to help children minimize their trauma. [West Virginia Code; Section 48-9-104].

PROPERTY DISTRIBUTION: West Virginia is an "equitable distribution" state. Each spouse may retain his or her separate property: (1) acquired prior to the marriage; (2) acquired by gift or inheritance during the marriage; (3) any increase in value of the separate property; and (4) any property acquired in exchange for any separate property. Marital property, consisting of all other property acquired during the marriage, is to be divided equally and without regard to any marital misconduct. However, this equal division may be altered based on consideration of the following factors: (1) the contribution of each spouse to the acquisition, preservation, maintenance, or increase in value of the marital property, including the contribution of each spouse as homemaker and in childcare; (2) the value of each spouse's separate property; (3) the conduct of the spouses during the marriage only as it relates to the disposition of their property; (4) the value of the labor performed in a family business, in the actual maintenance or improvement of tangible or intangible marital property; (5) the contribution of 1 spouse towards the education or training of the other that has increased the income-earning ability of the other spouse; (6) the foregoing by either spouse of employment or other income-earning activity through an understanding of the spouses or at the insistence of the other spouse; and (7) any other factor necessary to do equity and justice between the spouses. The court may, if necessary, award a spouse's separate property to the other spouse. [West Virginia Code; Sections 48-5-604 to 48-5-612 and 48-7-101 to 48-7-112].

ALIMONY/MAINTENANCE/SPOUSAL SUPPORT: Either spouse may be ordered to provide the other spouse with alimony. Factors to be considered are: (1) whether the spouse seeking alimony is the custodian of a child whose condition or circumstances make it appropriate for that spouse not to seek outside employment; (2) time and expense necessary to acquire sufficient education and training to enable the spouse to find appropriate employment and that spouse's future earning capacity; (3) duration of the marriage; (4) comparative financial resources of the spouses, including their comparative earning abilities in the labor market; (5) amount of time the spouses actually lived together as wife and husband; (6) tax consequences to each spouse; (7) age of the spouses; (8) physical and emotional conditions of the spouses; (9) vocational skills and employability of the spouse seeking alimony; (10) any custodial and child support responsibilities; (11) educational level of each spouse at the time of marriage and at the time the action for divorce is commenced; (12) cost of education of minor children and of health care for each spouse and the minor children; (13) distribution of marital property; (14) any legal obligations of the spouses to support themselves or others; (15) present employment or other income of each spouse; (16) whether either spouse has fore-gone or postponed economic, education, or career opportunities during the marriage; (17) standard of living during the marriage; (18) any financial or other contribution from 1 spouse to aid the education, training, vocational skills, career, or earning capacity of the other spouse; (19) financial needs of each spouse; and (20) any other factor the court deems just and equitable. Marital misconduct of the spouses will be considered and compared. The court may require health and/or hospitalization insurance coverage as alimony. [West Virginia Code; Sections 48-6-301 and 48-8-104 and West Virginia Case Law].

SPOUSE'S NAME: Upon request, either spouse may resume the use of his or her former name. [West Virginia Code; Section 48-5-613].

CHILD CUSTODY: Either parent may be awarded custody and all considerations are to be in the best interest of the child. There is a presumption in favor of the parent who has been the primary caretaker of the child. The factors for consideration are: (1) the stability of the child; (2) any parenting plans or other written agreement regarding child custody; (3) the continuity of existing parent-child relationships; (4) meaningful contact between the child and both parents; (5) maintaining care by parents who love the child, know how to provide for the child's needs, and place a high priority on doing so; (6) security from exposure to physical or emotional harm; (7) predictable decision-making and avoidance of prolonged uncertainty regarding the child's care and control; and (8) fairness between the parents [as a secondary factor]; and (9) any domestic violence. In addition, West Virginia provides specific guidelines for preparing Parenting Plans in the statute. [West Virginia Code; Sections 48-9-102, 48-9-201, and 48-11-201].

CHILD SUPPORT: Either parent may be required to provide periodic child support payments, including health insurance coverage. Child support guidelines are available from the West Virginia Child Advocate Office and are in the statute. The following factors that may be possible reasons for deviation from the official child support guidelines: (1) special needs of the child or parent, including but not limited to, the special needs of a minor or adult child who is physically or mentally disabled; (2) educational expenses for the child or the parent; (3) families with more than 6 children; (4) long-distance visitation costs; (5) if the child resides with another person; (6) needs of another child or children to whom the parent owes a duty of support; (7) the extent to which the parent's income depends on nonrecurring or nonguaranteed income; or (8) whether the total of spousal support, child support, and childcare costs subtracted from a parent's income reduces that income to less than the federal poverty level. One of the parents may also be granted exclusive use of the family home and all the goods and furniture necessary to help in the rearing of the children. The court may require health and hospitalization insurance coverage as child support. Provisions for income withholding shall be included in every divorce decree to guarantee the support payments. [West Virginia Code; Sections 48-13-301 and 48-13-702].

WISCONSIN

STATE WEBSITE: http://www.legis.state.wi.us/

DOWNLOAD STATE FORMS: http://wicourts.gov/forms1/circuit.htm#civil

FORMS PROVIDED ON CD: Divorce Petition with Minor Children, Divorce Petition without Minor Children, (Simplified) Joint Petition for Divorce or Legal Separation with Minor Children, and (Simplified) Joint Petition for Divorce or Legal Separation without Minor Children, Financial Disclosure Statement, Income and Asset Statement.

FORMS AVAILABLE ONLINE: Divorce Petition with Minor Children, Divorce Petition without Minor Children, (Simplified) Joint Petition for Divorce or Legal Separation with Minor Children, (Simplified) Joint Petition for Divorce or Legal Separation without Minor Children, Financial Disclosure Statement, Income and Asset Statement, Request for Court Ordered Mediation, Proposed Parenting Plan, Instruction Sheets.

RESIDENCY REQUIREMENTS AND WHERE TO FILE: One of the spouses must have been a resident of Wisconsin for 6 months and of the county for 30 days immediately prior to filing where the divorce is filed. No hearing on the divorce will be scheduled until 120 days after the defendant is served the summons or after the filing of a joint petition. [Wisconsin Statutes Annotated; Sections 767.301 and 767.335].

LEGAL GROUNDS FOR DIVORCE: No-Fault: Irretrievable breakdown of the marriage. The irretrievable breakdown of the marriage may be shown by: (1) a joint petition by both spouses requesting a divorce on these grounds; (2) living separate and apart for 12 months immediately prior to filing; or (3) if the court finds an irretrievable breakdown of the marriage with no possible chance at reconciliation. [Wisconsin Statutes Annotated; Section 767.315].

General: Irretrievable breakdown of the marriage is the only grounds for divorce in Wisconsin. [Wisconsin Statutes Annotated; Section 767.315].

NAME OF COURT IN WHICH TO FILE FOR DIVORCE: Circuit Court/Family Court. "State of Wisconsin: Circuit Court, _____ County."

TITLE OF DIVORCE ACTION: Petition for Divorce. "In Re the Marriage of _____ and _____."

NAME USED TO DESCRIBE SPOUSE FILING FOR DIVORCE: Petitioner (or Co-Petitioner if the petition is filed jointly). See below under *Simplified Or Special Divorce Procedures*.

NAME USED TO DESCRIBE OTHER SPOUSE IN DIVORCE: Respondent (or Co-Petitioner if the petition is filed jointly). See below under *Simplified Or Special Divorce Procedures*.

TITLE OF FINAL DIVORCE PAPERS: Decree of Divorce.

LEGAL SEPARATION: Irretrievable breakdown of the marriage is the only grounds for legal separation in Wisconsin. The residency requirements are the same as for divorce. [Wisconsin Statutes Annotated; Sections 767.301 and 767.315].

The No-Fault Divorce Toolkit

SIMPLIFIED OR SPECIAL DIVORCE PROCEDURES: The spouses may file a joint petition for divorce in which they both consent to personal jurisdiction of the court and waive service of process. A copy of a guide to Wisconsin Court procedures for obtaining a divorce is to be provided to the spouses upon filing for divorce. In all cases, a financial disclosure form must be filed. Also, if children are involved, an official child support form (which is available from the court clerk) must be filed with the petition. In addition, separation agreements are specifically authorized by law. Finally, in cases in which both spouses agree that the marriage is broken and have agreed on all material issues, the case may be held before a family court commissioner. [Wisconsin Statutes Annotated; Sections 766.58, 767.105, 767.117, 767.34 and 767.127].

MEDIATION OR COUNSELING REQUIREMENTS: The court must inform the spouses of the availability of counseling services. Upon request or on the court's own initiative, the court may order counseling and delay the divorce proceedings for up to 90 days. If custody of a child is a contested issue, mediation is required. If joint custody is requested, mediation may be required. In addition, the court may order parents in any child custody situation to attend an educational program on the effects of divorce on children. [Wisconsin Statutes Annotated; Sections 767.105, 767.082, 767.335, 767.405 and 767.401].

PROPERTY DISTRIBUTION: Wisconsin is now a "community property" state. There is a presumption that all marital property should be divided equally. Marital property is all of the spouse's property except separate property consisting of: (1) property inherited by either spouse; (2) property received as a gift by either spouse; or (3) property paid for by funds acquired by inheritance or gift. The equal distribution may be altered by the court, without regard to marital misconduct, based on the following factors: (1) the contribution of each spouse to the acquisition of the marital property, including the contribution of each spouse as homemaker; (2) the value of each spouse's separate property; (3) the length of the marriage; (4) the age and health of the spouses; (5) the occupation of the spouses; (6) the amount and sources of income of the spouses; (7) the vocational skills of the spouses; (8) the employability and earning capacity of the spouses; (9) the federal income tax consequences of the court's division of the property; (10) the standard of living established during the marriage; (11) the time necessary for a spouse to acquire sufficient education to enable the spouse to find appropriate employment; (12) any premarital or marital settlement agreements; (13) any retirement benefits; (14) whether the property award is instead of or in addition to maintenance; (15) any custodial provisions for the children; and (16) any other relevant factor. The court may also divide any of the spouse's separate property in order to prevent a hardship on a spouse or on the children of the marriage. [Wisconsin Statutes Annotated; Sections 766.01 to 766.97 and 767.61].

ALIMONY/MAINTENANCE/SPOUSAL SUPPORT: Either spouse may be ordered to pay maintenance to the other spouse, without regard to marital misconduct. The factors for consideration are as follows: (1) the time necessary to acquire sufficient education and training to enable the spouse to find appropriate employment and that spouse's future earning capacity; (2) the duration of the marriage; (3) the financial resources of the spouse seeking maintenance, including marital property apportioned to such spouse and such spouse's ability to meet his or her needs independently; (4) the comparative financial resources of the spouses, including their comparative earning abilities; (5) the contribution of each spouse to the marriage, including services rendered in homemaking, childcare, education, and career-building of the other spouse; (6) the tax consequences to each spouse; (7) the age of the spouses; (8) the physical and emotional conditions of the spouses; (9) the vocational skills and employability of the spouse seeking maintenance; (10) the length of absence from the job market of the spouse seeking maintenance; (11) the probable duration of the need of the spouse seeking maintenance; (12) any custodial and child support responsibilities; (13) the educational level of each spouse at the time of the marriage and at the time the divorce is filed for;

(14) any mutual agreement between the spouses; and (15) any other relevant factor. The court may combine maintenance and child support payments into a single "family support" payment. The maintenance payments may be required to be paid through the clerk of the court. [Wisconsin Statutes Annotated; Sections 767.56, 767.531, and 767.241].

SPOUSE'S NAME: Upon request, either spouse's former name may be restored. [Wisconsin Statutes Annotated; Section 767.395].

CHILD CUSTODY: Joint or sole child custody, "legal custody and physical placement," may be awarded based on the best interests of the child and the following: (1) the preference of the child; (2) the wishes of the parents; (3) the child's adjustment to his or her home, school, religion, and community; (4) the mental and physical health of all individuals involved; (5) the relationship of the child with parents, siblings, and other significant family members; (6) any findings or recommendations of a neutral mediator; (7) the availability of childcare; (8) any spouse or child abuse; (9) any significant drug or alcohol abuse; (10) whether 1 parent is likely to unreasonably interfere with the child's relationship with the other parent; (11) any parenting plan or other written agreement between the spouses regarding the child; (12) the amount of quality time that each parent has spent with the child in the past; (13) any changes that a parent proposes in order to spend more time with the child in the future; (14) the age of the child and the child's developmental and educational needs; (15) the cooperation and communication between the parents and whether either parent unreasonably refuses to cooperate with the other; (16) the need for regularly-occurring and meaningful periods of physical placement in order to provide predictability and stability for the child; and (17) any other factors [except the sex and race of the parent]. [Wisconsin Statutes Annotated; Section 767.41].

CHILD SUPPORT: Either or both parents may be ordered to pay child support and health care expenses. The factors to be considered are: (1) the financial resources of the child; (2) the standard of living the child would have enjoyed if the marriage had not been dissolved; (3) the physical and emotional conditions and educational needs of the child; (4) the financial resources, earning capacity, needs, and obligations of the parents; (5) the age and health of the child, including the need for health insurance; (6) the desirability of the parent having custody remaining in the home as a full-time parent; (7) the cost of daycare to the parent having custody if that parent works outside the home or the value of the childcare services performed by that parent; (8) the tax consequences to each parent; (9) the award of substantial periods of physical placement to both parents [joint custody]; (10) any extraordinary travel expenses incurred in exercising the right to periods of physical placement; (11) the best interests of the child; (12) maintenance received by either party; and (13) any other relevant factors. There are official guidelines and percentage standards for child support are available from the Wisconsin Department of Workforce Development Bureau of Child Support. The court may require that child support payments be guaranteed by an assignment of income, that the payments be made through the clerk of the court, or that health insurance be provided for the children. The court may also order a parent to seek employment. The court may order spousal maintenance and child support payments be combined into a "family support" payment. [Wisconsin Statutes Annotated; Sections 767.531, 767.75, 767.127, 767.57, 767.34, 767.511, and 767.513].

WYOMING

STATE WEBSITE: http://legisweb.state.wy.us/

DOWNLOAD STATE FORMS: http://courts.state.wy.us/

FORMS PROVIDED ON CD: Divorce Forms for Plaintiff without Children, Divorce Forms for Defendant without Children, Divorce Forms for Plaintiff with Children, Divorce Forms for Defendant with Children, and Simplified Divorce Complaint.

FORMS AVAILABLE ONLINE: Divorce Forms for Plaintiff without Children, Divorce Forms for Defendant without Children, Divorce Forms for Plaintiff with Children, Divorce Forms for Defendant with Children, Simplified Divorce Complaint, Child Support and Modification, and Child Custody and Modification.

RESIDENCY REQUIREMENTS AND WHERE TO FILE: (1) The spouse filing for divorce must have been a resident of Wyoming for 60 days immediately prior to filing or (2) the marriage must have been performed in Wyoming and the spouse filing must have resided in Wyoming from the time of the marriage until the time of the filing. The divorce may be filed for in the county where either spouse lives. There is a waiting period of 20 days after filing before a divorce will be granted. [Wyoming Statutes Annotated; Title 20, Chapters 20-2-104, 20-2-107, and 20-2-108].

LEGAL GROUNDS FOR DIVORCE: No-Fault: Irreconcilable differences. [Wyoming Statutes Annotated; Title 20, Chapter 20-2-104]. General: Confinement for incurable insanity for 2 years. [Wyoming Statutes Annotated; Title 20, Chapter 20-2-105].

NAME OF COURT IN WHICH TO FILE FOR DIVORCE: District Court. "In the District Court in and for _____ County, Wyoming."

TITLE OF DIVORCE ACTION: Complaint for Divorce.

NAME USED TO DESCRIBE SPOUSE FILING FOR DIVORCE: Plaintiff.

NAME USED TO DESCRIBE OTHER SPOUSE IN DIVORCE: Defendant.

TITLE OF FINAL DIVORCE PAPERS: Decree of Divorce.

LEGAL SEPARATION: The grounds for legal separation are the same as for divorce. The spouse filing for legal separation must have been a resident of Wyoming for 60 days immediately prior to filing or the marriage must have been performed in Wyoming and the spouse filing must have resided in Wyoming from the time of the marriage until the time of the filing. The legal separation may be filed for in the county where either spouse lives. [Wyoming Statutes Annotated; Title 20, Chapters 20-2-102, 20-2-104, 20-2-106, and 20-2-107].

SIMPLIFIED OR SPECIAL DIVORCE PROCEDURES: A sample Complaint for Divorce form is contained in Wyoming Court Rules Annotated, Appendix of Forms, Form #15. Financial Affidavits are required to be filed by both parents if child support is an issue in the case. [Wyoming Court Rules Annotated; Appendix of Forms, Form #15 and Wyoming Statutes Annotated; Chapter 20-2-308].

MEDIATION OR COUNSELING REQUIREMENTS: If child custody is involved, court may require parenting classes and/or mediation.

PROPERTY DISTRIBUTION: Wyoming is an "equitable distribution" state. All of the spouse's property will be divided in an equitable manner, including property acquired prior to the marriage, gifts, and inheritances, based on a consideration of the following factors: (1) the economic circumstances of each spouse at the time the division of property is to become effective; (2) how and by whom the property was acquired; (3) the merits of each spouse; (4) the burdens imposed upon either spouse for the benefit of the children or the spouses; and (5) any other factor necessary to do equity and justice between the spouses. [Wyoming Statutes Annotated; Title 20, Chapter 20-2-114].

ALIMONY/MAINTENANCE/SPOUSAL SUPPORT: Either spouse may be awarded alimony in the form of a specific sum or property after consideration of the other's ability to pay. Real estate or profits from real estate may be ordered transferred to the other spouse for alimony for life. Marital fault is not a factor. No other factors are specified in the statute. [Wyoming Statutes Annotated; Title 20, Chapter 20-2-114].

SPOUSE'S NAME: There is no statutory provision in Wyoming for the restoration of a wife's name upon divorce. However, there is a general statutory provision for name change upon petitioning the court. [Wyoming Statutes Annotated; Title 1, Chapter 1-25-101].

CHILD CUSTODY: Child custody may include joint, sole, or shared custody, as long as it is in the best interests of the child. Child custody will be awarded according to what appears to be most expedient and beneficial for the well-being of the child. The sex of the parent is not to be considered. Other factors to be considered are: (1) the quality of the relationship of the child with each parent; (2) the ability of each parent to provide adequate care for each child and to relinquish care to the other parent as specified; (3) how the child and each parent can best maintain and strengthen their relationships; (4) how the child and each parent interact and communicate and how such may be improved; (5) the ability and willingness of each parent to allow the other to provide care without intrusion; (6) the geographic distances between the parents' homes; (7) the current physical and mental ability of each parent to care for the child; (8) relative competency and fitness of each parent; (9) each parent's willingness to accept all responsibilities including abiding by all custody provisions; (10) any evidence of spousal or child abuse; and (11) any other necessary or relevant factors. If both parents are considered fit, the court may order any custody arrangement that encourages the parents to share in the rights and responsibilities of child-rearing. [Wyoming Statutes Annotated; Title 20, Chapter 20-2-201].

CHILD SUPPORT: Either parent may be ordered to pay child support. A trustee may be appointed to invest the support payments and apply the income to the support of the children. Child support payments shall be ordered to be paid through the clerk of the district court. A court may order income withholding to guarantee any child support payments. There are official Child Support Guidelines. These guidelines are presumed to be correct unless there is a showing that the amount would be unjust or inappropriate under the particular circumstances in a case. Deviation from the guidelines will be allowed after a consideration of the following factors: (1) the age of the child; (2) the cost of necessary childcare; (3) any special health care or educational needs of the child; (4) the responsibility of either parent for the support of others; (5) the value of services contributed by either parent; (6) any pregnancy expenses; (7) visitation transportation costs; (8) the ability of parents to provide health insurance through employment benefits; (9) the amount of time the child spends with each parent; (10) other necessary expenses for the child's benefit; (11) the relative net income and financial condition of each parent; (12) whether a parent has violated any terms of the divorce decree; (13) whether either parent is voluntarily unemployed or underemployed; and (14) any other relevant factors. [Wyoming Statutes Annotated; Title 20, Chapters 20-2-303 to 20-2-308].

Glossary

Agreement: A verbal or written resolution of disputed issues.

Alimony: A payment of support for one spouse provided by the other spouse. May be paid in periodic payments, one lump-sum payment, or a combination of both. May be paid temporarily or on a permanent basis. (Same as *spousal support* or *maintenance*.)

Annulment: A legal action that has the result of treating a marriage as if it had never occurred.

Child support: A legal, moral, and ethical obligation to provide full care and support for minor children.

Community property: Generally, all income and property that is acquired by either or both spouses during the course of a marriage, except property acquired by individual gift or inheritance. Community property does not include property that was acquired prior to a marriage. In most community property states, both spouses are considered to own an equal share of all of the community property. (See *separate property*.)

Contested divorce: A divorce where at least one issue has not been settled prior to court. A court must decide any issues that have not been agreed upon in a contested case.

Custodial parent: The parent with whom a child normally lives.

Divorce: A legal judgment that severs the marriage of two people and restores them to the status of single persons. (Same as *dissolution of marriage*.)

Dissolution of marriage: See *divorce*.

Equitable division: A method of property division in a divorce (or dissolution of marriage) that is generally based on a variety of factors in an attempt to allocate a fair and just amount of property to each spouse.

Fault-based divorce: A type of divorce that may only be granted on a showing that one of the spouses was guilty of some form of marital misconduct.

Guardian ad litem: Court-appointed legal guardian of a child's legal rights.

General grounds: Fault-based divorce grounds retained by some states.

Grounds: The legal basis for the divorce (or dissolution of marriage). The grounds may be no-fault or fault-based.

Hold-harmless: A phrase used to describe an agreement by which one person agrees to assume full liability for an obligation and to protect another person from any loss or expense based on that obligation.

Joint legal custody: A form of custody of minor children in which the parents share the responsibilities and major decision-making relating to the child. Generally, one parent is awarded actual physical custody of the child and the other parent is awarded liberal visitation rights. (See *joint physical custody*, *sole custody*, and *split custody*.)

Joint physical custody: A form of custody of minor children in which the parents share the actual physical custody of the child. Generally, an alternating method of custody is used. (See *joint legal custody*, *sole custody*, and *split custody*.)

Joint property: Property that is held or titled in the name of more than one person. (See *joint tenancy*, *community property*, and *marital property*.)

Joint tenancy: A form of joint ownership of property by which each joint owner has an equal share in the property. Generally, a joint tenancy is used in connection with a right of survivorship. (See *right of survivorship*.)

Jurisdiction: The power or authority of a court to rule in a particular case. A court must have jurisdiction over both the subject matter of the case and the people involved in the dispute in order to have the authority to hear a case and make binding decisions.

Legal court-ordered separation: A court order that specifies a couple is separated. Not provided for in all states.

Legal custody: The right to make all of the major decisions relating to the upbringing of the child.

Legal separation: A legal lawsuit for support while the spouses are living separate and apart. A legal separation may deal with the same issues as in a divorce, but does not end the marriage. (See *separate maintenance*.)

Lump-sum alimony: Spousal support made in a single payment or fixed amount, but paid in specific installments.

Maintenance: See *alimony* or *spousal support*.

Managing conservator: Another name for the parent with custody.

Marital property: Term used to describe the property that is subject to division by a court upon divorce or dissolution. Generally, all property that was acquired during a marriage by either or both spouses, except individual gifts and inheritances. Does not generally include property that was acquired by either spouse prior to the marriage. (See *community property*, *joint property*, *separate property*, and *non-marital property*.)

Marital Settlement Agreement: A written agreement entered into by divorcing spouses that spells out their rights and agreements regarding property, support, and children. (Same as *separation agreement*.)

Mediator: Professional trained in conflict resolution and methods of coaching disagreeing spouses.

No-fault divorce: A type of divorce that may be granted without the necessity of showing that either spouse was guilty of some form of marital misconduct.

Non-marital property: Term used to describe separate property in some states that provide for the equitable distribution of property. Generally, non-marital property consists of property acquired prior to a marriage and property acquired by individual gift or inheritance either before or during a marriage. (See *marital property*, *community property*, and *separate property*.)

Physical custody: The right to have the child live with the custodial parent.

Primary caretaker: The parent who provides the majority of the day-to-day care for a minor child.

Primary parental responsibility: Another name for *child custody*.

Quasi-community property: Property the spouses may have acquired before they moved to a particular state that would have been "community" property if they had lived in that state when they acquired it.

Residence: The place where a person lives. (Generally, same as *domicile*.)

Right of survivorship: The right of joint owners of a piece of property to automatically be given the other's share of the property upon the death of the other owner. Generally, this right must be specifically stated on any documents of title for it to apply. For example: a joint tenancy with the right of survivorship.

Separate maintenance: A lawsuit for support in a situation where the spouses live separate and apart but are not presently pursuing a divorce or dissolution. (Same as *legal separation*.)

Separate property: Property considered to be owned individually by one spouse and not subject to division upon divorce in most states. Separate property generally consists of property acquired prior to a marriage and property acquired by individual gift or inheritance either before or during a marriage. (See *marital property*, *community property*, and *non-marital property*.)

Separation agreement: See *Marital Settlement Agreement*.

Settlement agreement: The written version of a settlement that resolves certain issues. It is generally a valid contract.

Sole custody: A form of child custody in which one parent is given both physical custody of the child and the right to make all of the major decisions regarding the child's upbringing. Generally, the other parent is awarded reasonable visitation rights.

Split custody: A form of child custody in which the actual time of physical custody is split between the parents, with both retaining the rights to participate in decisions regarding the child. Also called "divided" or "alternating" custody. Sometimes referred to as *joint physical custody*. (See *joint custody* and *sole custody*.)
Spousal support: See *alimony* or *maintenance*.

Tenancy-by-the-entireties: A form of joint ownership in which two married persons hold title to a piece of property in equal shares and each has an automatic right to the other's share upon death.
Tenancy-in-common: A form of joint ownership in which two or more persons own particular shares of a piece of property. The shares need not be equal and the persons have no legal right to any shares of another upon death.

Uncontested Divorce: A divorce proceeding in which there is no dispute as to any of the legal issues involved. The lack of dispute may be because the other spouse is missing, refuses to participate in the proceeding, or agrees with the other spouse on all issues.

Visitation: The right of a parent who does not have physical custody to visit a child or have a child visit him or her.

Waiver: A written document that relinquishes a person's rights.

Index

Nova Publishing Company
Small Business and Consumer Legal Books and Software

Legal Toolkit Series

Estate Planning Toolkit	ISBN 13: 978-1-892949-44-8	Book w/CD	$39.95
Business Start-Up Toolkit	ISBN 13: 978-1-892949-43-1	Book w/CD	$39.95
No-Fautl Divorce Toolkit	ISBN 13: 978-1-892949-35-6	Book w/CD	$39.95
Legal Forms Toolkit (available May 2009)	ISBN 13: 978-1-892949-48-6	Book w/CD	$39.95
Personal Bankruptcy Toolkit	ISBN 13: 978-1-892949-42-4	Book w/CD	$29.95
Will and Living Will Toolkit	ISBN 13: 978-1-892949-47-9	Book w/CD	$29.95

Law Made Simple Series

Advance Health Care Directives Simplified	ISBN 13: 978-1-892949-23-3	Book w/CD	$24.95
Estate Planning Simplified	ISBN 1-892949-10-5	Book w/CD	$34.95
Living Trusts Simplified	ISBN 0-935755-51-9	Book w/CD	$28.95
Personal Legal Forms Simplified (3rd Edition)	ISBN 0-935755-97-7	Book w/CD	$28.95
Powers of Attorney Simplified	ISBN 13: 978-1-892949-40-0	Book w/CD	$24.95

Small Business Made Simple Series

Corporation: Small Business Start-up Kit (2nd Edition)	ISBN 1-892949-06-7	Book w/CD	$29.95
Employer Legal Forms	ISBN 13: 978-1-892949-26-4	Book w/CD	$24.95
Landlord Legal Forms	ISBN 13: 978-1-892949-24-0	Book w/CD	$24.95
Limited Liability Company: Start-up Kit (3rd Edition)	ISBN 13: 978-1-892949-37-0	Book w/CD	$29.95
Partnership: Start-up Kit (2nd Edition)	ISBN 1-892949-07-5	Book w/CD	$29.95
Real Estate Forms Simplified	ISBN 0-935755-09-1	Book w/CD	$29.95
S-Corporation: Small Business Start-up Kit (3rd Edition)	ISBN 13: 978-1-892949-36-3	Book w/CD	$29.95
Small Business Accounting Simplified (4th Edition)	ISBN 1-892949-17-2	Book only	$24.95
Small Business Bookkeeping System Simplified	ISBN 0-935755-74-8	Book only	$14.95
Small Business Legal Forms Simplified (4th Edition)	ISBN 0-935755-98-5	Book w/CD	$29.95
Small Business Payroll System Simplified	ISBN 0-935755-55-1	Book only	$14.95
Sole Proprietorship: Start-up Kit (2nd Edition)	ISBN 1-892949-08-3	Book w/CD	$29.95

Legal Self-Help Series

Divorce Yourself: The National Divorce Kit (6th Edition)	ISBN 1-892949-12-1	Book w/CD	$39.95
Prepare Your Own Will: The National Will Kit (6th Edition)	ISBN 1-892949-15-6	Book w/CD	$29.95

National Legal Kits

Simplified Divorce Kit (3 rd Edition)	ISBN 13: 978- 1-892949-39-4	Book w/CD	$24.95
Simplified Family Legal Forms Kit (2nd Edition)	ISBN 13: 978-1-892949-41-7	Book w/CD	$19.95
Simplified Incorporation Kit	ISBN 1-892949-33-4	Book w/CD	$19.95
Simplified Limited Liability Company Kit	ISBN 1-892949-32-6	Book w/CD	$19.95
Simplified Living Will Kit (2nd Edition)	ISBN 13: 978-1-892949-45-5	Book w/CD	$19.95
Simplified S-Corporation Kit	ISBN 1-892949-31-8	Book w/CD	$19.95
Simplified Will Kit (3rd Edition)	ISBN 1-892949-38-5	Book w/CD	$19.95

Ordering Information

Distributed by:
National Book Network
4501 Forbes Blvd. Suite 200
Lanham MD 20706

Shipping: $4.50 for first & $.75 for additionall
Phone orders with Visa/MC: (800) 462-6420
Fax orders with Visa/MC: (800) 338-4550
Internet: www.novapublishing.com
Free shipping on all internet orders (within in the U.S.)